EASY ON, EASY OFF

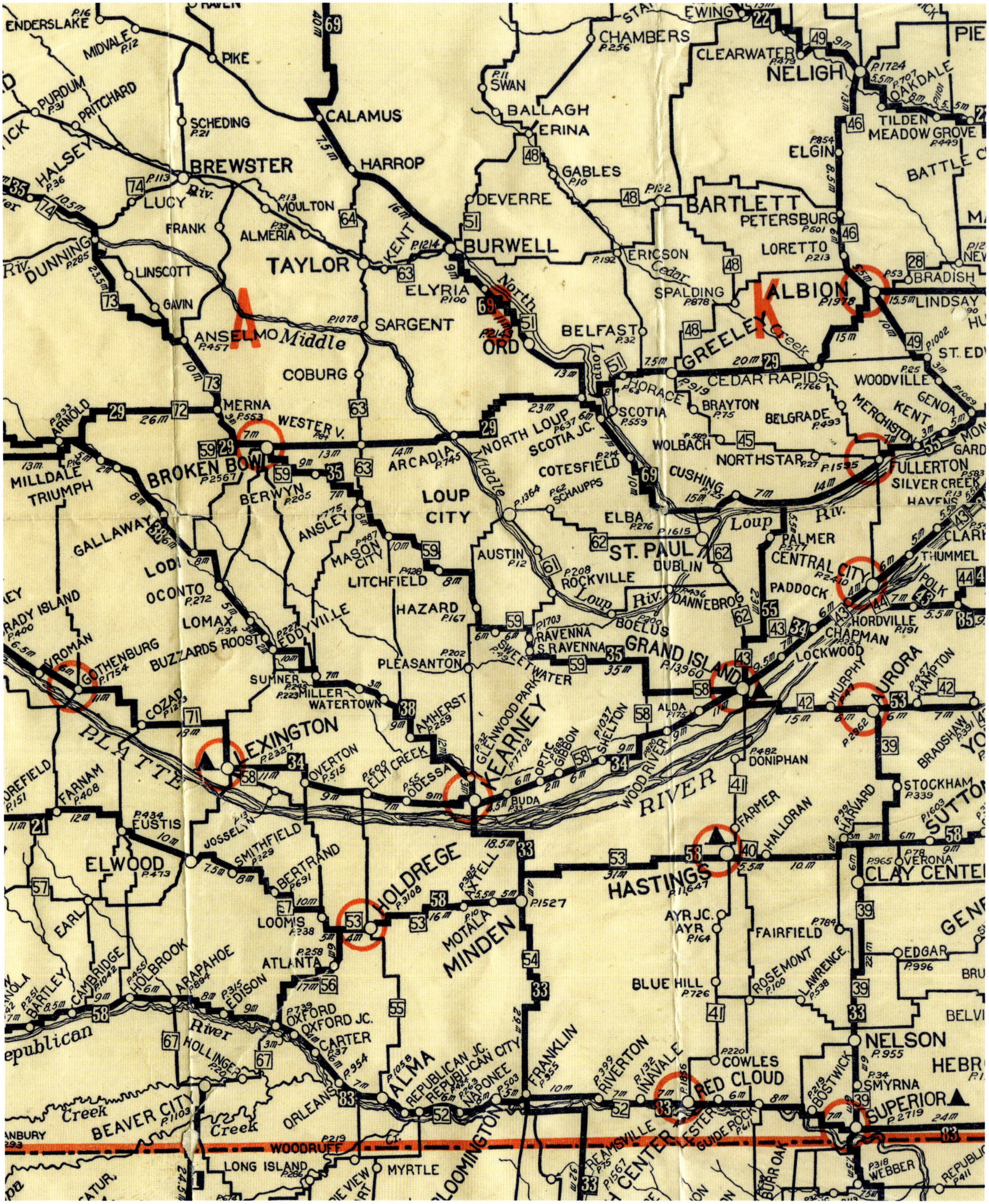

ENDERSLAKE
MIDVALE
PIKE
PURDUM
PRITCHARD
SCHEDING
CALAMUS
HALSEY
BREWSTER
HARROP
LUCY
MOULTON
FRANK
ALMERIA
DUNNING
TAYLOR
KENT
BURWELL
LINSCOTT
ELYRIA
GAVIN
SARGENT
ANSELMO
Middle
ORD
COBURG
MERNA
WESTER V.
ARNOLD
NORTH LOUP
SCOTIA JC.
MILLDALE
TRIUMPH
BROKEN BOW
ARCADIA
BERWYN
LOUP CITY
ANSLEY
GALLAWAY
MASON CITY
AUSTIN
LITCHFIELD
LODI
OCONTO
HAZARD
LOMAX
BUZZARDS ROOST
EDDYVILLE
GOTHENBURG
SUMNER
MILLER
WATERTOWN
PLEASANTON
AMHERST
COZAD
LEXINGTON
PLATTE
OVERTON
ELM CREEK
ODESSA
KEARNEY
FARNAM
FUSTIS
ELWOOD
JOSSELYN
SMITHFIELD
BERTRAND
LOOMIS
HOLDREGE
ATLANTA
EARL
CAMBRIDGE
HOLBROOK
ARAPAHOE
EDISON
BARTLEY
OXFORD
OXFORD JC.
CARTER
HOLLINGER
Republican
River
BEAVER CITY
Creek
ORLEANS
ALMA
REPUBLICAN JC.
REPUBLICAN CITY
NAPONEE
BLOOMINGTON
FRANKLIN
MOTALA
MINDEN
AXTELL
WOODRUFF
LONG ISLAND
MYRTLE
CHAMBERS
SWAN
BALLAGH
ERINA
GABLES
DEVERRE
EWING
CLEARWATER
NELIGH
OAKDALE
TILDEN
MEADOW GROVE
ELGIN
BATTLE CREEK
BARTLETT
PETERSBURG
LORETTO
ERICSON
Cedar
SPALDING
BRADISH
ALBION
LINDSAY
BELFAST
GREELEY
Creek
ST. EDWARD
CEDAR RAPIDS
WOODVILLE
GENOA
HORACE
BRAYTON
SCOTIA
BELGRADE
KENT
MERCHISTON
WOLBACH
NORTHSTAR
FULLERTON
COTESFIELD
SCHAUPPS
CUSHING
SILVER CREEK
ELBA
Loup
PALMER
ST. PAUL
DUBLIN
CENTRAL CITY
ROCKVILLE
THUMMEL
Loup Riv.
DANNEBROG
PADDOCK
POLK
BOELUS
CHAPMAN
RAVENNA
S. RAVENNA
SWEETWATER
GRAND ISLAND
LOCKWOOD
MURPHY
AURORA
HAMPTON
ALDA
GLENWOOD PARK
GIBBON
SHELTON
WOOD RIVER
DONIPHAN
BRADSHAW
OPTIC
BUDA
RIVER
STOCKHAM
FARMER
HALLORAN
HARVARD
SUTTON
HASTINGS
VERONA
CLAY CENTER
AYR JC.
AYR
FAIRFIELD
EDGAR
BLUE HILL
ROSEMONT
LAWRENCE
NELSON
COWLES
SMYRNA
RIVERTON
INAVALE
RED CLOUD
BOSTWICK
SUPERIOR
GUIDE ROCK
WEBBER

EASY ON, EASY OFF

The Urban Pathology of America's Small Towns

JACK WILLIAMS

UNIVERSITY OF VIRGINIA PRESS · *Charlottesville & London*

University of Virginia Press

Printed in the United States of America on acid-free paper
First published 2016

9 8 7 6 5 4 3 2 1

Library of Congress Cataloging-in-Publication Data
Names: Willliams, Jack, 1941– author.
Title: Easy On, easy off: the urban pathology of America's small towns / Jack Williams.
Description: Charlottesville: University of Virginia Press, 2016. | Includes bibliographical references and index.
Identifiers: LCCN 2016004605 | ISBN 9780813938851 (cloth: alk. paper) | ISBN 9780813938868 (pbk: alk. paper)
Subjects: LCSH: Small cities—United States. | Shrinking cities—United States. | Cultural landscapes—United States. | Automobiles—Social aspects—United States.
Classification: LCC HT123 .W483 2016 | DDC 307.76/20973—dc23
LC record available at http://lccn.loc.gov/2016004605

Furthermore:
a program of the J. M. Kaplan Fund

Publication of this volume was assisted by a grant from
Furthermore: a program of the J. M. Kaplan Fund.

To Clara
Who became a United States citizen during my years of writing this book and for

Fiona | Geneva | Mathilda | Gus | Grace
Who became citizens of the world

I look forward to an America which will not be afraid of grace and beauty—which will protect the beauty of our natural environment, which will preserve the great old American houses and squares and parks of our national past, and which will build handsome and balanced cities for our future.

— *John F. Kennedy, Remarks at Amherst College upon Receiving an Honorary Degree, 26 October 1963 (John F. Kennedy Presidential Library and Museum)*

CONTENTS

ACKNOWLEDGMENTS

During the years I researched this book, I traveled widely across the United States. Many people told me stories about their towns or directed me to old photographs or newspaper articles. It would be impossible to acknowledge everyone without writing another book on the small acts of kindness and generosity of Americans: the woman who filled my coffee thermos for free every day for two weeks at the drive-in at Exit 353, I-80 in Nebraska; the sheriff who took me up inside the dome of the Moultrie, Georgia, courthouse on a sweltering summer's afternoon; or the man in the tiny hotdog restaurant in Hawkinsville, Georgia, who remembered me visiting from years previously. I write about all their towns, and I thank them for sharing with me.

I have tried to faithfully credit the sources of each historic photograph and map, but it should be remembered that each discovery required the help of a person, someone who allowed me to sift through boxes of old prints or spend a day searching forgotten records for a requested image. I owe much to these dedicated historians in so many libraries and archives across the country.

The staff at the Library of Congress Map and Photographic Collections provided me with images and prints of exceptional quality. The professionalism and assistance of the Library of Congress as custodians of such wonderful, extensive, and accessible resources never ceases to astound me.

Jim Reisdoff, editor of the *South Platte Press* and author of several books about Nebraska, graciously spent time with me, sharing his perspective on the history of Nebraska's railroads. Sharon Fong, with the Isleton Museum, gave me a day-long tour of the town of Isleton, California, and explained its history of Chinese immigrants.

On my first visit to Arizona's eastern mountains, I spent a wonderful and very productive dinner and evening at Apache Junction with dear friends, Doug and Ethel-Marie Le Vasseur. Ethel-Marie's two brothers, Patrick and Stephen

D'Luzansky, quizzed me unmercifully, trying to find holes in my book's hypotheses as well as giving me invaluable advice on my travels to Globe and Clifton. I thank them for their advice and will always treasure the memory of their enthusiasm for adventure.

When I began *Easy On, Easy Off,* I was a professor at the School of Architecture, Auburn University, with the advantage of graduate research assistants who helped with explorations of different regions. Graduate students from Portugal, Sara Farracho and Filipa Santos, worked with me on the maps and drawings of Georgia and Nebraska. Two exchange students from Beijing Forestry University in China, Cao Xi and Tongfei Zhou, developed the figure-ground studies of Nebraska and of New England mill towns. The work of these four students included far more places and towns than could be included in this book.

During the writing of *Easy On, Easy Off,* I received two extraordinary fellowships. While neither grant related directly to *Easy On, Easy Off,* both provided me with opportunities to study comparable towns and regions in other countries. These grants were crucial to my understanding of urban form, and I want to comment briefly about each.

In 2005 the Asian Cultural Council awarded me a grant to study small villages in China. With the help of my colleague and old friend Li Xiong, affectionately known as Bear, we explored towns in Anhui, Zheliang, and Shanxi Provinces. We were joined by faculty and graduate students from the School of Landscape Architecture, Beijing Forestry University, as we explored beautiful villages in remote rural areas of China as sort of a traveling seminar on urban form and cultural preservation. Our many discussions gave me confidence as I formulated my own theses about America. I owe much to these friends and their insights and comparisons about a rich culture far older than ours. I will always remember one of Bear's comments, as it has stayed with me all these years. I asked him at the end of a hot humid day of exploring villages near Hongcun, "Bear, what is the most beautiful village you have seen?" He answered, "The next one." That sense of anticipation about small towns, that the next one would be the most beautiful gem of urbanism, always came to my mind as I entered a new town. I hope this book will remind Bear of that thrill of anticipation. China's issues with its small villages and urbanization are similar to ours with one important difference. The Chinese government actively promotes the change from rural towns to concentrated, dense urban living, even to the point of moving people and destroying old villages. It is an experiment fraught with momentous consequences.

In 2007 I was awarded the Fulbright Distinguished Chair in Landscape Architecture and Urban Design. I spent my time abroad in Portugal, studying the white villages of the Alentejo and teaching at Universidades Lusíada de Lisboa. My research explored the many layers of Portuguese towns through field studies, photographs, and sketches, so I was able to develop many of the methodologies that I use in *Easy On, Easy Off.* I was helped in my explorations by António Poças and three of his wonderful colleagues. I affectionately refer to them as the gang of four, from our many discussions under a tree in a courtyard of Lusíada over morning coffee. These architects are all dear friends whose suggestions and perceptions about urbanism lie scattered among the pages that follow in many hidden places. I hope they enjoy this book and will open it under the same tree, enjoying coffee, smiling at our shared memories.

Michael Robinson, professor in the Master of Landscape Architecture Program at Auburn University, debated ideas of urbanism with me on student reviews. I miss these animated discussions, for I learned much from them. I owe the idea of boustrophedon in the first portion of chapter 5, "Winds of the Pleistocene," to Michael.

My good friend and colleague Professor Scott Finn, as director of the Auburn University Rome Program, shared both his hospitality and professional insight during several extended trips exploring the small, lesser-known villages of Tuscany and Umbria. These villages should be the subject of a similar study to *Easy On, Easy Off.*

A young architect and my racquetball partner in San Francisco, Matt Stanton, developed the digital graphics used throughout this book, from location maps to spliced Sanborn maps. I would give him a rough sketch, and he would translate it digitally into one of the many beautiful drawings throughout *Easy On, Easy Off.* I owe much to his own considerable graphic design skills.

Ben Farmer, my former student and now a valued colleague, rescued me from my Luddism by coordinating and converting many of the digital files into formats requested by the University of Virginia Press. I owe my digital sanity to his timely and comprehensive expertise.

The Alabama State Council on the Arts awarded me a fellowship that enabled me to continue my research of southern courthouse squares begun in *East 40 Degrees* and carried over into the courthouse squares of Southern Georgia that became "Vanquished Forests" and "One Standard of Justice" in chapter 4.

I am indebted to the Graham Foundation for the Fine Arts for an Individual Fellowship.

The Foundation for the Studies of Landscape Architecture awarded the manuscript of *Easy On, Easy Off* the David Coffin Publication Grant in 2010 and 2014.

I gratefully acknowledge a grant from Furthermore, a program of the J. M. Kaplan Fund, which assisted publication of this volume.

Boyd Zenner, acquisitions editor of the University of Virginia Press, continually encouraged me as I missed one promised deadline after another. Without her guidance and patience, I would never have completed either my first book, *East 40 Degrees,* or this, my second work. We can now embark upon the third volume that will complete this trilogy on America's small towns.

My daughter Tamsen encouraged me to persevere over many delightful lunches in New Haven after discussions about art in the Yale Art Gallery. My daughter Megan edited the entire manuscript, rescuing it from my spelling and grammar mistakes. Her efforts have made it a far better book.

The subtitle, "Urban Pathology," was given to me by my wife, Clara, who suggested it from her perspective as a veterinary ophthalmologist with an interest in histo-ocular pathology. I find the use of the word "pathology" most telling about these towns, for this book is about their slow disintegration. Clara's patience and encouragement over the many years of my writing have made my journey most satisfying.

Finally, my thanks to my ever-earnest Labrador, Bruno. On those dreary days filled with uncertainty and half-written yellow-lined pads, he would lie patiently on my studio rug, until, tolerant no longer, his wet nose pressed my hand, his gesture for me to put down my pen. Out into the bitter bite of a grey New England winter, old man, black dog, white snow.

EASY ON, EASY OFF

Portrait of Orleans by Edward Hopper (1882–1967); oil on canvas, 26 × 40 in.

INTRODUCTION

EDWARD HOPPER'S evocative painting *Portrait of Orleans* hangs in a first-floor gallery of the de Young Museum in San Francisco. Its subject, the town of Orleans, is one of Massachusetts' fashionable mid-Cape communities. Hopper's home and studio were in nearby South Truro. During summers on Cape Cod, Hopper painted many images of its landscapes and towns. Completed in 1950, *Portrait of Orleans* presents an archetypal American small town, as such towns may have been before our automobile usage exploded in the optimistic years of the late 1940s and early 1950s. Hopper must have been aware of this cultural context as the painting's foreground contains two prominent symbols of the burgeoning automobile industry, a stack of tires and a gasoline sign. While the intersection, the street, and several of the buildings still exist, the painting, like all of Hopper's work, was never intended as an accurate rendering of a real place. Rather, *Portrait of Orleans* is a fragment of Hopper's own inner reality: an image captured not just in time but as a whisper of a story only partly apprehended. The painting's title *Portrait* implies a scene that stands still, a quiescent moment that is unresolved, but it is a moment relentlessly devoid of identifying details.

The Esso sign on its base of five stacked tires frames the right side of the composition, hanging presidium-like over a view that recedes in a one-point perspective to the intense blue of the distant bay. A wide expanse of pavement, void of cars, forms the foreground; the empty asphalt occupies fully a third of the canvas's area. Two automobiles are parked in the distance while a third approaches from a perpendicular street, about to turn into the town's tiny center. The three cars are rendered the same, an anonymous, almost ominous black with no details that suggest make or manufacturer. They are generic cars seemingly without occupants. A lone woman in a dress and white-brimmed hat walks along the otherwise totally empty sidewalk. Bent slightly forward, she appears tentative and lost. Her singularity within the town's space only reinforces the emptiness of the entire composition. Alone and without purpose, the woman has a presence that unsettles the viewer, as do the figures in many of Hopper's paintings. Her appearance in the center of the picture gives *Portrait of Orleans* a ghost-like quality, as though the people that once inhabited the street's sidewalks have left before the viewer arrived.

The general impression of the entire composition is that of a small commercial center with storefronts and offices, yet lacking any clues about possible inhabitants or building usage. Blue shadows cast by tall trees on the left of the frame encroach into the street space. The trees are in full leaf and the woman's dress is sleeveless so it is obviously summer. The exact hour on the clock is one of the few pieces of actual information in the painting, yet even that is ambiguous. The hands of the clock indicate seven, but from the oblique light, it is impossible to tell if the time of day is early morning or early evening. An indistinct sign hanging on a white handrail gives no clue as to the building's use. The seven second-story windows in the white and tan structures have all their interior shades drawn down to the exact same height.

A lone streetlight projects from the single telephone pole. The glass insulators on the pole's cross piece carry no wires, nor are there other poles continuing down the street to carry the implied wires. Hopper deliberately withheld a lot of information: the invisible wires, the illegible signs, the lack of people and cars; all reinforce the sense of emptiness in the town's center. The buildings together, however, do make a tiny urban composition explicitly implied by their connection to each other and by the consistent way they all address the sidewalk. Such urban compositions were familiar in rural towns across all regions of the United States in the mid-twentieth century. From the single-porticoed gas station placed diagonally at a cross roads in Georgia to the tight groupings of commercial structures that front main streets in every midwestern community, the connection of building to building and to the public space of the street suggests the importance of their uses to each other. This convergence of functions, buildings, and people is the very essence of small-town America. Hopper captured the main street space that exists in thousands of places across this country, yet his space seems to illustrate an irretrievable moment in the past. Because it contains so few suggestions tied to a specific place, *Portrait of Orleans* becomes ordinary and general, standing for any small town. Through Hopper's process of distillation, the mood of his painting is, however, profoundly disturbing, for the street is empty, the stores vacant of any commercial prompts like sale posters or signs. No merchandise spills onto the sidewalk, and no one, save the lone woman, peruses the store front windows. It is as though something has happened, something cataclysmic, and all the inhabitants have disappeared.

Something cataclysmic is happening, and the painting offers two obvious hints as to what that might be: the stack of tires and the Esso sign. The momentous change will not be a single event, but rather very gradual shifts over a half century. In the sixty-plus years since Hopper painted *Portrait of Orleans* our infatuation with automobiles, as symbolized by the two familiar components, gasoline and tires, has decimated Orleans and every other similar small town in America. In 1950, America was just beginning its love affair with big cars, tail fins, and "muscle" horsepower. Oil and rubber tire companies were the two most influential industries lobbying for more roads so that we would buy more cars, purchase more gas, and use more tires. In 1956, construction started on the interstate highway system, and our fascination with automobiles, gas, roads, and tires reached extremes. In his painting, Hopper has presciently given us both the symbols, the Esso sign and the stack of tires, and in the somber mood of the painting's space, the resultant consequences of our obsession.

The sense of general alienation is found in all of Hopper's work, whether in cities, rural locations, or interior spaces. It is possible to interpolate from his paintings a critique of modernity, a sense of a shift in America's perception of the past and of community. The automobile is a key symbol of modernity in his images. Even the implied absence of an automobile in his painting *Gas* emphasizes the loneliness of the attendant. Alienation, emptiness, fragments of realty all permeate his scenes. American society was to experience this shift in the next decade as the halcyon optimism of the 1950s was replaced by the darker currents of the 1960s, after Vietnam and the civil rights struggle. This cultural shift perhaps had its most poignant expression in the vacancy of our small towns as Hopper so beautifully and evocatively captured in *Portrait of Orleans*. This painting represents thousands of places across America, thousands of towns whose commercial centers mirror the emptiness of the Orleans main street. In my research for this book, I visited several hundred small towns all across America. In many, I found main streets lined with boarded-up storefronts, few people, and one or two cars, streets where time was arrested, streets whose desolate silence sought a narrative. So I filled in the towns' stories, their histories that have a beginning and a present but, like Hopper's painting, have no end, no resolution. In that sense, *Easy On, Easy Off* provides the narratives that explain the emptiness of *Portrait of Orleans*.

I begin each of the five narratives that follow with the natural histories of different representative American landscapes. I have chosen glaciated landscapes of southern New England, political demarcations of Georgia's coastal plains, farmlands of Nebraska's Great Plains, an arid, mountainous area of Arizona's Sonora Desert, and, lastly, a drained fluvial delta in California's agriculturally rich Central Valley. I use these specific landscapes and their histories to explain fundamental shifts in our rural settlement patterns from regionally distinctive small towns to auto-dependent extruded commercial centers. These new places are accepted and familiar transformations to our daily lives, yet we usually derogatorily refer to them as sprawl, strips, or malls. Congestion or worse—the opposite, empty parking lots—and vacant stores have become symbolic of contemporary American culture. They are so deeply embedded in our collective consciousness that a simple golden-arched logo can suggest a common experience shared by "100 billion served." Malls and strips are totally dependent on automobile access as cars give us the choice to travel long distances in search of cheaper prices beyond our local communities. With these overwhelming choices, we condemn our traditional communities to obsolescence, and they sadly become accurate reflections of Hopper's *Portrait of Orleans,* forgotten, empty spaces.

My explorations of our pragmatic embrace of places accessible only by automobile began by chance ten years ago. The beautiful courthouse squares of America's South fascinated me, so I started a systematic compilation of their unique typology. In my frequent travels across the rural parts of Mississippi, Alabama, and Georgia, my only choices for overnight accommodations were located at highway intersections. Several times I returned to the same familiar Best Western or Holiday Inn at an interstate exit. It became obvious to me that another settlement pattern overlay the region of my original study, that a broader narrative existed besides that evidenced in the historical town centers. These ubiquitous accommodations at highway exits are part of a newer narrative begun in 1956 with the construction of the Interstate Highway System. I sensed this same newer narrative existed along our long-distance highways in areas beyond the Deep South, so I decided to journey north and then west across the United States, exploring my assumptions about the linkage between our modern limited-access highways and our older regional landscapes. The title of this book comes directly from my extensive travels. *Easy On, Easy Off* is a play on the familiar phrase "easy off, easy on," found on highway signs that advertise fast food. Usually the sign reads "such and such food, next exit, quick easy off, easy on." As this choice of title suggests, I began my investigations at the interstate exits where these two narratives intersect, that of the present high-speed highway and that of a perpendicular and slower-speed regional road. As the next chapter discusses, the title *Easy On, Easy Off* is, as well, an ironic commentary on the disjunction between modernity and the past.

America's regional landscapes and rural towns have been used and discarded in a profligate process of resource exploitation. We appear unable to realize the rich continuity of the disparate cultures that comprise America, and that collective amnesia makes us powerless to protect the past. Consequently, we lose the correspondence between our contemporary built world and our heritage, and the process of history becomes one of excavation and rediscovery. As we reattach histories to places, we both reconnect and reinterpret meaning, yet the passage of time and our interpretive biases can easily distort these connections. Landscapes can be especially tenacious repositories of meaning because their evolution requires generations of care and investment. The spatial organization of the regional places about which I write resulted from years, if not decades, of toil. Generally cultures hold dear what takes greatest effort to gain, so I anticipated that the beautiful towns in the five regions that I explored would be preserved. I found, however, that this was seldom the case, and that the past was quickly erased.

Our interstate highways were built quickly, and their exit ramp developments, such as strip malls and service plazas, grew even faster. It is difficult to understand the meaning of these contemporary highway landscapes, for their very ordinariness camouflages hidden assumptions. Retracing the past to pick up the threads of forgotten narratives of the American open road allowed me to regain perspective about America's infatuation with the car and to understand how automobile travel changed this country. The common and often beautiful gasoline company road maps once given free to American motorists provide a glimpse into the early days of highway travel decades before the construction of interstates. Illustrations and explanations of these maps begin each of my discussions of different landscapes across America.

I write about small towns because they are beautiful, and beauty of urban form is not a resource to be squandered lightly. I argue chapter by chapter, town by town, for an aesthetic of urban form. Great cities are truly great works of art splashed across wide canvases. Towns are smaller but no less works of art than cities. Small towns are little *bozzetto,* tiny models or sketches of urbanism and community. *Easy On, Easy Off* asks the reader to see these towns, not as derelict and empty, but as compositions of buildings and spaces that have similar merit to any work of art such as a painting or sculpture. Because towns are visually rich as well as repositories of meaning, we should advocate their preservation, yet we do not. The unanswered question this book asks about ourselves is, why do we let the past slip away so easily?

Urban form is an elusive concept and an idea even more difficult to represent graphically. Essentially all parts of a town—the building masses, the public spaces of streets, the town's topographic setting—together constitute its form. In the chapters ahead, I often use a graphic convention borrowed from architectural studies, the figure-ground, to distill out the salient formal aspects of a community. These diagrams show the buildings of a town as black solids, or figures, without any of the usual contextual clues such as topography or roads. These contextual aspects would be considered the ground, but in a figure-ground study, the ground is the white of the paper. Even though it is rendered blank, the ground is implied space. While a figure-ground is a reification, figure-ground studies allow one to isolate the two dimensional aspects of urban form without the confusion of other layers of information. A figure-ground is like a radiograph, a picture produced upon a sensitive surface such as photographic film. Solids such as buildings are black; voids or spaces in between are the white of the underlying surface. A figure-ground, like a radiograph, measures density: the density of buildings or mass or, by interpolation, the density of retail or civic activities, and the corresponding density of human activity. Using figure-grounds, I search for patterns of clusters or coalescence, or of openness or space. Even though they are two dimensional, figure-ground studies aid greatly in understanding three-dimensional urban form.

I use figure-grounds to illustrate the concise forms of courthouse-square towns in Georgia, to show the radiating form of the mill town of Webster, Massachusetts, and as another way to document the racial segregation of Isleton, California. Each figure-ground study of a contemporary off-ramp town should be compared with figure-grounds of these historical town centers.

Along with different primary and secondary texts, my scholarship relies mainly on the interpretation of images such as maps, drawings, photographs, and, especially, the reality on the ground. I write from direct experience and observation as translated through my sketchbooks. The "Note on Research, Writing, and Resources" at the end of this book explains in detail my methods of gathering and synthesizing information. Alternatively, the reader may prefer to read this "Note" first to better understand my unconventional research progression and its influence on several of my conclusions.

History, along with art and literature, was one of Jorge Luis Borges's three fantasies. By fantasy he meant that the study of history was not absolute but filled with choices of time, narrator, and place. My historical fantasies, then, my choices of narrators and places, are the stories of urban forms we call towns and their agriculture, industry, or infrastructure. These urban forms arise from our response to topography, geology, and geography. I concentrate on the specific coupling of our settlements with the natural processes that have shaped our earth. As a landscape architect, I firmly believe that the inescapable correspondence between culture and the natural world tells much about ourselves, our histories, and our values.

Because my writing compares contemporary settlement patterns with examples from the past, I must admit my own bias and its influence on the central themes of this book. The passage of time is an integral and important aspect of my fantasy of history. Time allows us to adjust, calibrate, and recalibrate our cultures to the changes we inevitability make to our world. Time also affords the opportunity to experiment and adapt to the natural processes that shape our earth. Our collective memory of these mistakes and successes shapes our perception of our landscapes. In the chapters ahead, I trace narratives of towns over different periods of time for evidence of corrections or readjustments that attempted to reverse apparently inevitable declines.

Cities, towns, and landscapes have histories that may include single significant events, multiple similar occurrences, or a multitude of individual anonymous actions. We assign values to these histories: they become tragic, heroic, common, or ordinary. As these histories accumulate over time, our physical environments, towns, buildings, streets, squares, agricultural and industrial landscapes become repositories of these cultural values. When architecture, urban form, or landscapes embody our values, communities attribute meaning to them and designate them important places. Americans value the landscape of the Gettysburg battlefield because it embodies the dark struggle and heroic triumph of our Civil War. We agree that the Mall in Washington between the Capitol and the Lincoln Memorial is one of the most important and meaningful spaces in America because of its multiple markers of our many histories. Of course, there are less dramatic, far more modest places than Gettysburg or this nation's capital. In the pages that follow, I identify and describe examples of valued places found in America's ordinary, vernacular rural towns and landscapes.

My bias for the enriching capacity of history has a corollary. The more entangled and intricate the past, the greater the opportunity for a perfect amalgamation of form and meaning. The accumulation of many sedimented layers of history renders our urban and landscape compositions not only more meaningful but also more beautiful. Let me give a detailed example that is illustrated twice in this book, the classical facades found on small-town banks; one in Globe, Arizona, one in Kenesaw, Nebraska. Classical elements were originally weight-bearing structural elements; now they are decorative only. The classical orders were chosen for banks because they represent stability and permanence. The rich and complicated history of classicism stretches back through 2,500 years of continual reinterpretation. The Romans canonized the orders; the Renaissance rediscovered them; and nineteenth-century neoclassicism codified them, to mention but a few obvious manifestations of classicism in western architecture. The smallest anonymous bank partakes of this same long tradition. Their classical facades served dual public and private functions: both as a grandiose building entrance while simultaneously anchoring well-proportioned public spaces. This complex use of a continuous architectural tradition embeds a bank's elevation deeper into its urban and cultural context. Because these complexities are manifest in physical form, we recognize the symbolic meaning of the bank as an institution of trust once respected in thousands of small towns. Even isolated and detached from their original purpose, these tiny banks still retain a quiet and dignified beauty.

In the chapters ahead, I search region by region for cultural threads that connect us to the past similar to the histories of these banks' elevations. I expand my explorations beyond individual buildings to include explanations and meanings contained in landscapes and towns. These investigations have not been easy, for many strands of histories have been severed from our consciousness by our constant quest for faster and more convenient transportation. Even the two banks I illustrate are empty now, unable to survive without offering their customers the ease of drive-through tellers. This obsession with convenience and the compression of distance through speed of travel has dramatically changed our world. As our turbulent present reshapes and supplants our past, I find the transformation from small towns to malls and big box retailers unfortunate and ultimately disheartening. This transformation is especially tragic when one realizes that I only write about regions and small towns that exist in the rural expanses between the far greater rings of sprawl that engulf our major cities. The only consolation is that these contemporary changes may be transitory—that the passage of time will work its alchemy, as it sometime does, and we will again discover the beauty of a present that arises from a continuity with the past.

1

EASY ON, EASY OFF

"EXIT 18, TWELVE MILES AHEAD," reads the large billboard: "McDonald's Easy off, Easy on." Colorful logos on blue backgrounds announce the services at the next exit. Slowing slightly we steer onto the interstate off-ramp. Small directional signs along the exit ramp give specific distances to the available restaurants, gas stations, and accommodations. We make our choices instantly without decreasing our exiting speed of thirty-five miles per hour. A right turn onto a two-lane road, and we arrive at McDonald's with plenty of parking, or, if we prefer to remain in our car, a drive-through. Across the street a brilliant yellow and orange sign reassures us of readily available self-service fuel. We order our meal through a speaker box and then drive over to slot a credit card into a gasoline pump. Within ten minutes, gassed up and fed, we rejoin the interstate at our set speed of sixty-five miles per hour. We have no sense of where we stopped other than exit 18.

"Easy off, Easy on" tells us that we can exit from any limited-access highway, grab a fast meal, fill our gas tank, and return to our travels with no inconvenience or traffic delays. The American motorist knows exactly what to expect: simplicity of access and standardization of services. The small signs with directional arrows on exit ramps give distances in tenths of a mile to further emphasize the convenience of these services—food, fuel, and accommodations. Whether it is a McDonald's, Waffle House, or Cracker Barrel, or any of the many other national eateries, each chain's menu will be the same regardless of its location across the United States. The interior design and decorations of each franchise will not vary from north to south, east to west. We expect standardization, convenient distances, abundant well-lit parking, and easy traffic flows.

"Easy off, Easy on" is such a euphonious phrase, and its concept is so embedded in our contemporary culture that we forget the assumptions beneath its obvious repetitive emphasis. We require convenience and familiarity when we exit from limited-access highways. Fueling opportunities should be frequent and quick. We no longer consider "full service," for it takes too much time to deal with an attendant. We access the pump, pay with a credit card, and are on our way without ever speaking to another person. A telling comparison can be made between the message conveyed on the cover of a 1930s California-Nevada highway map and today's experience. On the map's front cover a smiling attendant stands between two "Flying A" gasoline pumps with the quote *"Let's get ASSOCIATED."* The back cover promotes both petroleum products and "smiling, cheerful service." Today's Citgo or Shell fuel pump sits between two metal pylons with three hoses, a credit card punch-keyboard, advertisements for acquiring more credit cards, and increasingly, a closed-circuit TV. All interactions are with machines—impersonal, convenient, and standardized.

The consumption of food should be equally "fast." The eateries along our highways are not places to linger over a meal, but rather places of consumption and movement. One enters directly from a parking lot into a restaurant. Additionally the eateries have drive-through lanes making it possible to obtain food with the initial human interaction through a speaker box. "Easy off, Easy on" means immunity from the most basic interpersonal communication such as asking for twenty dollars of gas or a Big Mac.

These familiar brand franchises guarantee a level of consistency across their regions and the entire country. Waffle House waffles will be the same in Colorado or North Carolina. One has to travel far from the highway to find a restaurant that serves meals prepared in a traditional way with fresh ingredients cooked to order. Such a detour from "Easy off, Easy on" would involve exploration, risks, and time commitments alien to our highway culture.

Food marts are hybrid establishments found at highway rest stops. They combine gas with food in a single complex, thus adding another level of convenience. Plastic wrapped packaged food is shelved alongside other travel necessities or served through a smaller version of a restaurant chain with minimal seating grafted onto the gas station. Frequently food marts are labeled "service stations" because they offer multiple services: gas, food, and shopping. A service station used to be an automotive garage that offered specific facilities such as lubrication, fan belt replacement, or tire changes. Our modern cars require less maintenance than those of fifty years ago, so the descriptive name remains, but the inventory of services has changed.

Cover of a Texaco road map of California and Nevada, 1935

Self-service gas stations with their associated food marts or eateries and motels belong to our interstate highways. As motorists crisscross our country, they can be secure in the similarity and spacing of their primary needs for food, fuel, and rest. Detachment from anything local or regionally specific is the price we pay, however, for this convenience. These off-ramp sites are separated from their regional context and connect instead only to the highway. Recognizable lollipop-like signs rise above the surrounding landscape and are visible only from the highway. The signs and logos comprise a graphic language commonly understood and completely integrated into our culture and captured wonderfully in facile shorthand phrases such as "1 Block on Right."

Because these groupings of eating, fueling, and sleeping establishments are normally found at highway exits, their interval and availability corresponds with the spacing of highway interchanges. A Waffle House franchise map found on any Waffle House counter illustrates how tightly this restaurant chain is tied to interstate interchanges. Locations are keyed first to interstate numbers, then to exit numbers. These two numbers—I-75, exit 24—are enough information. No other locational clues are needed.

Easy On, Easy Off concentrates on highway intersections found in rural landscapes located outside of major metropolitan areas. Because interstates were engineered around small settlements rather than through them, these rural exits generate groupings of commercial establishments along the roads that connect the interstate to existing towns. A figure-ground diagram of a small southern town illustrates this spatial shift in urban form. The historic center and older buildings are black; the newer structures red. The older historic center with its courthouse and square surrounded by retail stores is in the middle of a small grid of residential streets. The commercial strip associated with the off-ramp extrudes down to the highway that passes diagonally in the lower right. The big-box franchises and motels group closest to the highway. These newer businesses have extracted the economic vitality from the older commercial core, destroying the balance between the small town and its surrounding markets. The development sequence is depressingly familiar. A highway interchange is constructed first in an essentially blank landscape; then the highway traffic generates the market for the necessary services. A gas station or food mart opens first, followed by other food establishments such as a Waffle House, Burger King, or McDonald's. Motel-type accommodations generally are built after several eateries and gas stations provide a slightly larger demand for additional services. These small groupings of buildings with substantial parking and access roads aggregate into what, for simplicity, these writings refer to as off-ramp towns. To call these places "towns" is perhaps a misnomer, for they lack the requisite civic, institutional, or dwelling functions that give towns their richness. Many do, however, grow to enormous size and area without civic buildings or permanent housing, becoming strip malls or strip developments that connect a nearby town or city to a highway interchange.

The word "interchange" implies a change or switch in the direction and speed of travel. As one decelerates from the highway and exits onto a local road, one also exchanges histories, for these rural or back roads have their own narratives that predate the imposition of the interstate. When the interstates were first engineered in the 1950s, decisions were made about the importance of local roads—which to intersect and which to pass over or under. Limited access to highways also means limited access

Figure-ground study of Washington, Georgia

from them to these regional places, for interstate travel locks one into a tube of space and visual experience that can only be escaped through the off-ramps. Our interstates hold us prisoners to our consistent speed in a sealed automobile capsule completely detached from anything local or even regional.

Even though the Interstate Highway System spans great distances across completely different landscapes, its off-ramp towns are similar from one coast to the other. Not only are the programmatic components the same, but the brands, franchises, logos, and spatial organizations are also uniform. The standardization of off-ramp facilities is one of the most recognizable examples of the homogenization of contemporary American culture and contrasts markedly with this country's historical patterns of recognizable regional differences.

Easy On, Easy Off locates five interstate highway exits within five different ecological and cultural regions of the United States. These five distinctive regional places bracket the country and are representative of the many landscapes of North America: an industrial region of the Northeast, mill towns on the watersheds of the Blackstone and French Rivers; a political landscape, the courthouse-square towns in southern Georgia; a typical midwestern agricultural landscape, farm communities of central Nebraska; mining towns of Arizona on the edge of the Colorado Plateau; and, lastly, in the promised land of the far West, a region of extreme ecological stress, forgotten camps in the Delta of California's Central Valley.

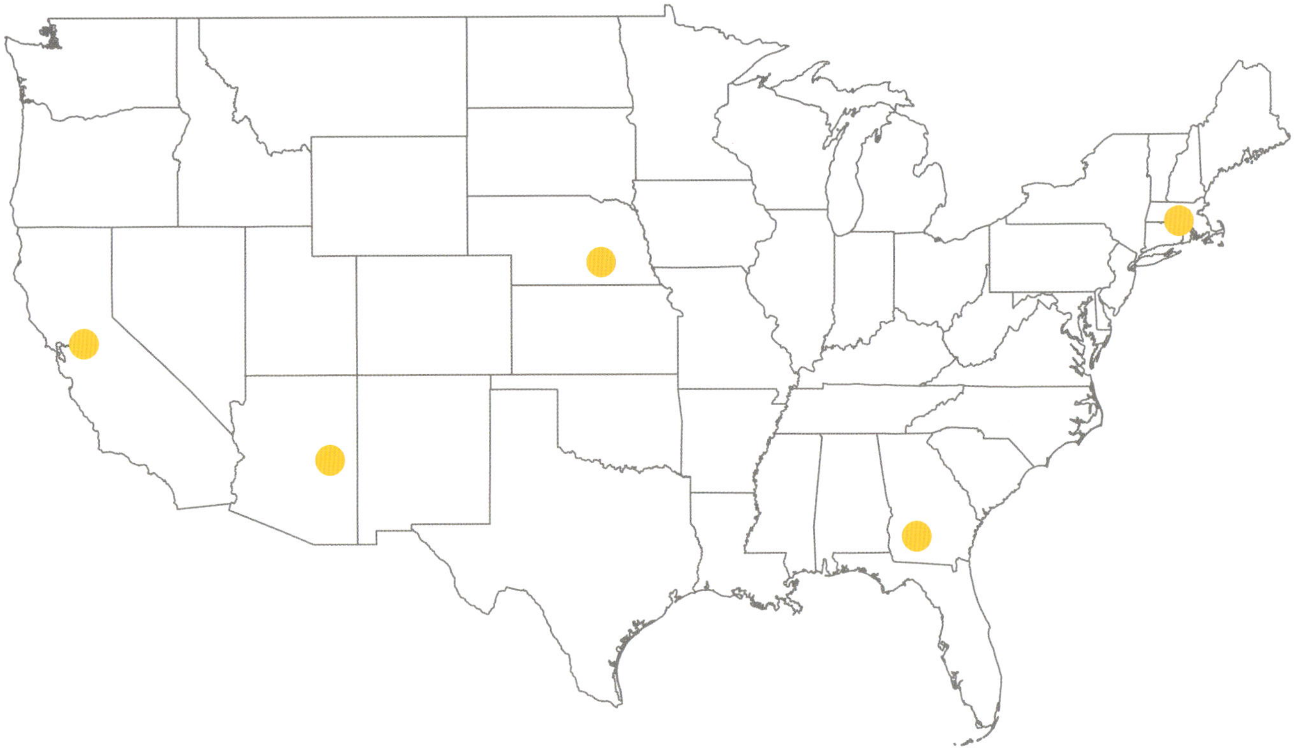

Location of the five highway exits discussed in this book

The book's organization is simple. The natural history of each region is described first to establish the connections between its natural and human histories. Each region's cultural history is then entered, figuratively and literally, from an interstate off-ramp. From the off-ramp, the writings trace the back roads—back in time—to understand the complexity of the landscapes through which the interstate passes. Each of the five regions in which the five off-ramp towns exist is distinctive and could be studied separately. All five together present a powerful and comprehensive exploration of eighteenth-, nineteenth-, and early-twentieth-century American cultural geography.

The investigation of mill towns begins with a natural ordering system—the watershed. But it is not just the watershed that is important—it is also the energy provided through differences in gradient that create a water power "head." Rapids along the fall line between the Piedmont and the coastal plains of Massachusetts, Connecticut, and Rhode Island provided this head needed to drive mill wheels in every mill, large or small. The settlement of mill towns followed the watershed upward away from the coast. The towns align like beads along the string of the fall line—actual geological faults where the waters from the mountains and hills of southern New England tumbled over exposed rocks to provide hydrological power. Mills arose at these falls, surrounded by towns whose buildings and infrastructures of rivers, canals, flumes, and dams shaped an entire region.

The exquisitely beautiful courthouse-square towns of southern Georgia provide the second study. Georgia contains the highest number of counties of any state except Texas. A day's ride for a circuit judge spaced these towns evenly on the Georgia coastal plain in a web of county roads connecting similar urban spaces. On a larger scale, these settlements resemble a neural network across an entire region that facilitated exchanges of political and judicial synapses.

Nebraska's agricultural lands offer a contrasting system of inhabitation and form the third investigation. In the central farmlands of the state, a cultural grid spreads uniformly and rigidly across the Great Plains. The grid is a cultural abstraction that regulates all apparent connections between ourselves and the underlying natural systems of the Great Plains. In the nineteenth century, Americans needed a framework that allowed the transition of this featureless landscape into private ownership; the earlier developed federal grid provided this armature. Mandated as a way of regulating land sales, the range and township lines still determine settlement patterns within the flatness of the Great Plains.

The starkly beautiful but somnambulant mining communities east of Phoenix, Arizona, comprise the fourth study. This mountainous region straddles the juncture between the Sonoran Desert and the Colorado Plateau. First silver and then copper mining brought these towns into existence. The collapse of copper prices worldwide left an artificially contoured and scoured landscape of vast open-pit mines.

The last landscape is the delta of the Sacramento and San Joaquin Rivers in California's Central Valley. The melting snows of the Sierra Nevada range flood every spring into mysterious marshes behind the constricting Carquinez Straits before pouring into San Francisco Bay. This fresh meltwater supplies the agriculture of the Central Valley and the distant cities of Los Angeles and San Diego. In the late nineteenth and early twentieth centuries, Chinese immigrants, newly experienced from their work on the Union Pacific Railroad, constructed levees and dikes around these marshes. A severely degraded and contested landscape, the mysterious California Delta offers a cautionary tale of human rapacity and resilience.

The central thesis of this book is that these regional differences are important and valuable and that the homogenizing effects of contemporary American culture put these unique histories at risk. Difference and diversity in any community matter, whether they be cultural or social constructs or ecological systems, for diversity provides greater opportunities for change and adaptation to unanticipated circumstances. The success of life on this planet is due to its ability to change, evolve, and adapt with new forms. As Charles Darwin records in the final page of *Origin of Species,* since the beginning of life's history, our earth has witnessed "endless forms most beautiful and most wonderful."[1]

The same is true for human culture. The surface of the earth holds countless varieties of human settlements, from sleepy towns on flat plains to precipitous villages fastened to steep mountains, from stoic encampments hidden in barren deserts to stilted houses in damp forests. Heroic examples exist of our abilities to inhabit almost any environment, except perhaps the frozen Antarctic. Even in the face of harsh climates, dangerous floods, or desert wastes, we persevere. Not only do we endure, but we have thrived and often constructed towns and cities of lasting beauty. Our persistence in seeking out new opportunities on the very edge of possibilities has been part of human culture since the first syllables of our recorded histories.

Sometimes over the millennia of our existence, we have occupied these places with gentle impacts. More often than not, however, we have destroyed the existing natural conditions. This book explores five different accommodations and adaptions between ourselves, our settlements, and the earth. It emphasizes our inhabitation of the earth, not as individuals or with single structures, or even with complete towns or cities. Instead, it searches for ways that entire settlement groupings over broad areas—large cultural constructs—couple with the environment and attach themselves to specific ecologies.

Change in the natural world can be slow tectonic movements of continents, sudden cataclysmic volcanic upheavals, or tiny imperceptible shifts in climatic conditions. The greatest change and challenge for all life forms now comes from the unrelenting human exploitation of resources. Daily, we are made aware of our unsustainable use of the earth's bounty, from fossil fuels to rain forests. The atmospheric changes caused by global warming threaten us all. As we destroy the biological diversity of flora and fauna in all corners of the globe, we also foreclose forever countless unknown opportunities for change, adaptation, and survival. Our zoos, botanical gardens, and natural history museums no longer serve as examples of earth's diversity, but as poignant repositories of vanishing species such as the Bengal tiger or the white rhinoceros.

Diversity of human cultures offers the same promise of infinite adaptability, not only in our physical artifacts but also in the richness of our ideas expressed through art, literature, and music or any of the multitude of our other achievements. Each of us has our favorite examples of special regional places whose uniqueness adds to our understanding of ourselves:

1. Darwin, *Origin of Species,* 490.

Mississippi Delta Blues recall an oppressive racial landscape where the only outlet for hope was music. Today, as evidenced by such legends as B.B. King or Muddy Waters, Blues is part of America's enduring musical legacy. The Spartan beauty of a Shaker table is a vestige of a marginalized religious sect whose passion for design influenced generations. Full-bodied Napa Valley wines, lilting soft-consonant Down East accents, sinfully sweet southern pecan pies, and golden yellow sweet corn from Nebraska all conjure up unique and different places.

The many single-crop agricultural methods that are necessary to feed our expanding populations severely limit earth's ecological diversity. These agricultural monocultures risk failure from a single disease, blight, or insect. Chapter 4 of *Easy On, Easy Off* discusses the destruction of the great longleaf pine ecosystem of America's coastal plain. The replacement monoculture of cotton was quickly and dramatically decimated by a tiny insect, the boll weevil. We are constructing social monocultures that are equally susceptible to single catastrophic failure. One of this book's subtheses is that the interstate highway is the most obvious manifestation of our increasing reliance on monocultures as we become more and more dependent upon a single resource, oil.

With human cultures, transportation shifts radically affect regional economies. Major modes of transportation can be quickly replaced by another more reliable, flexible, or faster form. America's coasts have decaying port cities whose empty harbors no longer contain forests of tall masts because steam power replaced wind power. The discovery of oil caused the replacement of steam locomotives by diesel engines—and the collapse of Appalachia's coal mining industry. Automobile and truck transportation supplanted trains, yet our highways, with all their associated services such as the automotive industry itself, malls, big-box retailers—and off-ramp towns—face an uncertain future. Off-ramp services along our highways depend upon a predictable flow of traffic, and because such services are spaced regularly, this traffic must be consistent. Reduce the number of cars, and every one of the off-ramp towns will close.

Cultural landscapes take many generations to emerge. Since this emergent quality is central to my argument, I turn now to an exploration of both words—"emergence" and "landscape." More than fifty years ago, Loren Eiseley connected life and emergence in *The Immense Journey,* his classic collection of beautiful and profound essays: "We are one of the many appearances of the thing called Life; we are not its perfect image, for it has no image except Life, and life is multitudinous and emergent in the stream of time."[2] Eiseley refers to all life since the beginning of its history on earth, and he emphasizes that emergence is one of its salient qualities.

2. Eiseley, *Immense Journey,* "The Snout," 59.

For Eiseley, the emergence of life has no discernible purpose yet is not random. Evolution is not a top-down, directed force moving forward, nor is the human species evolution's only or highest intent. As Eiseley said, we remain part of the same existence caught in one of the many tributaries of that same stream, and we leave our wonderful artifacts of human endeavor, our cities, our infrastructures, our landscapes as evidence. I have narrowed his observation to one specific and recent manifestation of life, human settlements. I suggest in the chapters on mill towns, courthouse-square towns, and farm communities that the ordered proliferation of similar town forms across a region is also an illustration of the idea of emergence. The courthouse-square towns of Georgia in chapter 4, for example, are all equidistant from one another, and all have similar urban forms. They came into existence—or emerged—simultaneously without any statewide or top-down direction. This discussion of emergence is an important part of this book, because the building of the Interstate Highway System was just the opposite, a mandate from the federal government, top-down, purposeful, and executed across a continent with no variation.

A familiar image from the natural world offers a simple visualization of the idea of emergence. In the sunlit shallows of a small pond, tiny minnows swim among rocks in search of food. A shadow passes across the water's surface, and instantaneously the fish form a single group for flight into deeper cover. No dominant leader controls these movements, yet all fish gather in a common mass to effect a singular escape. A school of fish emerges as a greater attribute than a collection of random minnows. A pattern arises from myriad decisions by many similar individuals that contains properties and qualities not found in any constituent parts.

The schooling of fish is a self-organizing bottom-up type of behavior. There is no leader, no head fish, no hierarchy. This is not to say that these are blindly instinctive reactions to danger signals. The individuals within the group share information and adapt to changing conditions with a similarly limited number of options: all minnows, for example, seek deeper currents for safety. There are many instances in nature of this kind of emergent behavior, from tiny slime molds in forest litter to vast areas of reforestation that occur after fires devastate entire ecosystems.

I borrow the concept of emergence from the *Immense Journey* to explain the seemingly random yet organized arrangements we use to populate regions with our many different landscape patterns and varieties of urban form. With their connecting transportation infrastructure, towns and cities arise from seemingly disconnected pragmatic responses to the natural environment without benefit of an over-all or top-down design, yet they are related in an organic whole across a region that remains distinct from larger, more dominant cultures. The basic concept of emergence and, by analogy, regionalism is that random or unrelated individual decisions can form a whole with an order beyond that intrinsic to its parts. To use a familiar analogy: the rich taste of a cake is more than the consistency of flour, the coagulation of egg whites, or the color of sugar. In human settlements, these "wholes" come into existence not only through an ordering of the parts but also through similar encounters with the physical world—topography, soil, water, or climate. In human societies, moreover, the parts can be religious norms, the need for wealth, or even protection from outsiders. The whole can be safety or political and cultural dominance. In the example of the towns and counties of southern Georgia in chapter 4, the whole that emerged was political power.

Geography and climate are but two of the most obvious influences, but our cultural responses to other natural processes also shape our places through space and time. Regions can assume many landscapes as they, like their underlying ecologies, emerge, shift, disappear, and reappear in different ways. Of course, other human complexities such as language, religion, or economic capital influence the formation of cultural systems. We generally privilege economic necessity in our explanations of these forces, yet similarity of physical and technological innovations driven by market opportunities can only partially explain regional coherence. As this book illustrates, influences other than economic forces shape a region with long and complex histories.

Over time a cultural matrix unfolds through a multitude of individual decisions, but the process can just as easily reverse, and a cultural or regional identity can vanish. Our landscapes are littered with forgotten remnants of earlier settlements, for we profligately abandon whole cities and entire cultures. All five regions that I discuss contain examples of derelict urban centers. In fact, it is difficult to find any region of the United States that does not contain similar evidence of the disintegration of its small towns. Emergence has a dark side: evolution and growth discard parts as well as incorporate them. The landscape is a palimpsest, written upon but also erased.

Viable regional systems and settlement configurations combine the flexibility of change with the stability of an ordering structure. They depend upon a constant flow of energy (water, sunlight), goods (cloth), produce (corn, cotton), or people (adjudications, elections), and they transform materials and ideas. This recycling is a key principle of human ecology that allows change, adaptability, and longevity. When this process stops, as in the mill towns of southern New England discussed in chapter 3 or the mining towns of Arizona in chapter 6, the entire system shuts down—as with a natural ecosystem, it collapses. The populations of mill and mining towns dramatically declined early in the twentieth century, leaving behind landscapes littered with vacant buildings and shattered lives.

Political and social interactions reflect the instrumentality of humans. We learn from our actions and change—hopefully for the better. These feedback loops are an essential characteristic of a highly complex and interrelated system or network. A social or political network is a nonlinear pattern of organization.[3] Like any network, there are areas of concentration or nodes, places where exchanges take place. Main streets in Nebraska farm communities act as nodes of commerce within a gridded network. The governmental and political organization of southern Georgia's counties and courthouse squares is a perfect example of another kind of network connected by weblike redundant roads. These systems, be they political, educational, economic, or any of the infinite interrelationships we are capable of, persist over time, and their histories build upon one another, not just in flat sequential layers but also in fragmented, tattered, or even fictitious layers.

Several of the regions studied in these writings have invented myths of an apocryphal reality. While southern Georgia was never a cotton-producing region prior to the Civil War, many local people living in Georgia still subscribe to the predominant notion of a South of columned plantations fantasized in *Gone with the Wind*. In fact, only after the Civil War and the destruction of the longleaf pine forests did cotton become an important crop in southern Georgia, and then as mostly segregated sharecrop holdings that were soon replaced by large mechanized farms. Many regions of the United States have similar founding myths that elaborate on the truth. These myths perpetuate an image that is vastly larger than any of their constituent histories. Ironically, we shape a region; then we select those partly fictitious histories that define it—and through such mythmaking we redefine ourselves. Our highways once generated similar myths. In *On the Road* Jack Kerouac defines the Beat Generation through his writings about his experiences across America. John Steinbeck narrates his discoveries of people and places in *Travels with Charlie*. These books and many others, however, tell of an America before interstates when highways gave direct access to towns and cities, as often the highway was the town's main street.

In a constantly emerging world, all of our political and social constructs partake of the same principles of emergence. Our communities are greater than individual inhabitants or individual buildings, and their histories are greater than isolated events. We have familiar names for our emergent conceptual totalities, words that conjure up abstract wholes such as culture, regions, or societies. These words all acknowledge the importance

3. Capra, *Hidden Connections*, 82.

of a larger construct composed of smaller units, yet we have difficulty expressing the process of emergence because of the extended passage of time. A culture must be able, therefore, to record its becoming so that it may resist time's corrosion. Collective memory is formalized with important buildings, or groups of buildings, such as courthouses, mill towers, churches, or entire communities—or even an entire landscape. Along with the written text of *Easy On, Easy Off,* drawings and especially photographs help explain these cultural markers and fit them into a spatial and historical context. The color photographs that illustrate the places discussed in this book remind us of these transitory connections through forgotten textures and isolated details, including images of a vanished, slower automobile culture that existed before the interstate highways. The most complex markers of a culture's transmitted values are its visible landscapes and the design and form of its towns and cities, thus my images privilege built form. While this book acknowledges the importance of all the myriad parts of our pasts, it emphasizes the totality of the spatial aspects of our landscapes. We see these spatial qualities; they give form to our world and should give beauty to our lives.

"Landscape" is a compound word with a complex etymology that means far more than a picturesque scene. In the first chapter of *Discovering the Vernacular Landscape,* J. B. Jackson seeks to define the "Word Itself."[4] By tracing its etymology, he arrives at several definitions. First he describes landscape as a "concrete, three-dimensional shared reality."[5] With this definition he eliminates any suggestion of private landscapes. The courthouse squares of southern Georgia admirably fit his definition of a public reality, although I question whose "public." Later he parses the meaning of "scape" to include organizations or systems.[6] Lastly he accepts an even broader definition: "a composition of man-made or man-modified spaces to serve as infrastructure or background for our collective existence; and if *background* seems inappropriately modest we should remember that in our modern use of the word it means that which underscores not only our identity and presence, but also our history."[7] Jackson argues for an totally inclusive definition of landscape. He only excludes the natural world untouched by humans.

The chapters in this book attempt to explore more fully the illusive concept of landscape. Throughout my writings, the word "landscape" is used in its fullest meaning: to include both cultural and natural worlds and their respective histories coupled together in a meaningful whole. For example, when I write in chapter 5 about the landscapes of Nebraska, I include the natural history of the Great Plains and the cultural histories of Native Americans and European settlers.

4. Jackson, *Vernacular Landscape,* 3–8.
5. Ibid., 5.
6. Ibid., 7.
7. Ibid., 8.

Our towns with their connecting infrastructure, our open agricultural fields, our neglected cities—even land left fallow—all hold meaning. As Fritjof Capra, in his insightful book *The Hidden Connections,* cautions us, "To understand the meaning of anything we need to relate it to other things in its environment, in its past, in its future. Nothing is meaningful in itself."[8] Landscapes tell us about ourselves, our values, and our relationships with the earth. They can be constructs of great beauty that tell of our ability to imagine thoughtful ways of dwelling on this earth, or they can degenerate into ugly and exploitative places of detachment.

The choice of meaning, however, should never be a single decision. As this book hypothesizes, wise choices are always many tiny incremental decisions over time that together make a larger whole. The elusive entities we call "regions" have distinctively different patterns of settlement that result from vastly different choices. It is instructive to trace these decisions so that we may grasp the possibilities of futures we can only dimly imagine. Our future on this planet depends upon this understanding of the consequences of our actions.

In America our world is being changed by a new spatial order that our interstate highways disperse uniformly from coast to coast. It is a transformation fascinating in its regularity and inevitability, yet deeply troubling because of its dependence upon fossil fuels, its usurpation of traditional cultural connectivity, and its ultimate unsustainability. *Easy On, Easy Off* examines regionalism and its tenuous preservation against the homogenizing effects of this newer and more dominant culture of off-ramp towns and strip malls. By arguing that off-ramp towns sever the distinctive past from our homogenized present, *Easy On, Easy Off* concludes that regional specificity and differences cannot be preserved. We are detaching ourselves from our environments, from our histories, and, ultimately, from each other. As we homogenize our culture, we disconnect it from the world in ways that render our once rich and distinctive landscapes meaningless. Our contemporary culture applies easily onto—and is just as easily torn off of—its underlying context. All too often today, we are visitors in haunted landscapes of abandoned towns and destroyed ecosystems, uninvolved, untouched, and unscathed. We have become "Easy on, Easy off."

8. Capra, *Hidden Connections,* 84.

Abandoned gasoline pump, rural Georgia

2

THE NEXT EXIT

ON JUNE 29, 1956, President Dwight Eisenhower signed the Federal Aid Highway Act and authorized twenty-five million dollars for the construction of the National System of Interstate and Defense Highways, so called to reflect the pragmatic military justification for its construction. The newly created Highway Trust Fund was to pay for these roads supported by a one-cent increase in the federal tax on gasoline and diesel fuels. The federal government paid 90 percent of all interstate highway construction costs. The act guaranteed that the interstate system would be built to the highest standards and pledged completion by 1972. Thus began what was and remains one of the largest public works projects ever undertaken. The interstate highways eventually cost far more than the originally allocated twenty-five million dollars and took considerably longer in some urban areas than the projected sixteen years. In 1956, however, Congress endorsed a truly grand vision of a national highway system connecting the entire country across vast distances.

The most effective aspect of the 1956 act was its dedicated funding account. As individual states had done since the early years of highway construction, the federal government taxed gasoline and other automotive supplies such as rubber and lubricants. These funds were held by the Federal Highway Trust to be used solely for the construction of more highways. More cars meant more gas and more gas tax revenues, creating a self-perpetuating loop of ever-expanding highways. Because each state received 90 percent funding from the federal government and could use this money for its own contracts, every road project created jobs and economic development for each participating state. No state could refuse such a bargain. The federal largess spread across the entire country, for each of

The interstate highways superimposed on the topography of the United States

the coterminous forty-eight states has at least two interstates. New York, for example, has twenty-nine, California twenty-five. With a couple of exceptions, every state capital is connected to an interstate. Two major routes, I-95 and I-90, traverse sixteen and thirteen states, respectively. Even Hawaii has interstates. By 1990, over 20 percent of all automobile travel and nearly 50 percent of all truck travel in the United States took place on the interstates.[1] The total interstate mileage in 1990 was 45,530, and by the beginning of the twenty-first century it approached 50,000.

The dream of a national transportation infrastructure began with the formation of the United States. Article 1, Section 8 of the United States Constitution gives Congress the power "to regulate commerce with foreign Nations, and among the several States" and "To establish Post Offices and post Roads." Early presidents such as Jefferson and Adams interpreted this clause to allow the federal government to build roads, canals, and other infrastructure that facilitated the movement of goods and trade among states. For example, Jefferson proposed a continuous chain of lighthouses along the Atlantic and Gulf Coasts as aids to navigation and sea trade. He built the Federal Road from Washington to New Orleans diagonally across the Southeast to facilitate communications between the capital and the major city of the newly acquired Louisiana Purchase. In the early years of nationhood, not all states agreed with this exercise of federal power, and several dissenting lawsuits were brought to the U.S. Supreme Court. Some

1. Rose, *Interstate*, 115.

individual states were not interested in having the federal government incur additional debt on their behalf, but the Supreme Court decided in favor of the federal government. The precedent was established for the federal government to construct transportation infrastructure in the interest of promoting trade and the movement of goods between states. For the first seventy-five years of its existence, the federal government was totally dependent on custom duties for its funding and stood to benefit greatly from increased trade. Trade and economic growth equated in the national consciousness with the success and health of the new country.

America's infatuation with roads began in earnest with the development of the internal combustion engine. The elegance of fancy horse-drawn carriages transferred easily to cars and their accouterments. An automotive calendar cover of 1906 designed by the American poster artist Edward Penfield positions a well-dressed woman in hat and "duster" before an elegant blue automobile. This early image equates status and luxury with automobile ownership, and this facile association of beautiful women and fast cars continues today. The mass production of automobiles, however, soon emphasized the practical inexpensive universal Ford over the extravagant touring car.

By 1914, there were five hundred thousand cars in America, and by 1922, there were ten million.[2] This remarkable growth in vehicles demanded hard-surfaced roads to facilitate travel. The task of building long-distance roads was beyond the ability of any single state, so in 1914 a federal-state partnership began that enabled the shared engineering and construction of all interstate federal highways, including the Interstate Highway System authorized in midcentury. This partnership, announced under the name of the American Association of State Highway Officials (AASHO), solved the fundamental issues of local control and federal funding. Under this agreement, the state highway departments determined the routes of federal roads and implemented their construction. Initially, the federal government provided 50 percent matching funds and set the standards for signage, design, and construction quality. By 1919, most states had a highway department, and within ten years, each state had instituted a gas tax to pay for its share of construction and maintenance costs.

America's roads contain four tiers of construction and maintenance responsibility: federal roads that cross state lines funded by the federal government and constructed and maintained by each state through which they pass; state highways that are designed, constructed, and maintained by individual states; county roads, often unpaved in rural states, that are the responsibility of counties; and, lastly, municipal streets within the incorporated boundaries of cities and towns. As envisioned in the 1956

2. Rae, *American Automobile,* 66–67.

Automobile Calendar cover, 1906

Interstate Highway System Act, the U.S. government constructed the first tier of the federal system at a scale and standard beyond anything imagined.

Interest in transregional highways grew with the increase in the manufacturing of more automobiles after the First World War. Early routes were given fanciful names such as the "Spanish Trail" that meandered across the South, or the "Dixie Short Route" from Detroit to Florida. These named routes often offered several alternative itineraries that made them confusing. Local merchants even provided their own route markers to detour traffic into their towns. Popular guidebooks advertised accommodations and restaurants to touring motorists. It was a leisurely and serendipitous way to travel that allowed stops in towns and along lively Main Streets.

The Lincoln Highway from Times Square in New York City to the Legion of Honor in San Francisco was one of the first transcontinental highways, but it was many roads aggregated together rather than a single direct route. A detail from a rare Rand McNally Pennsylvania road map of 1926 shows a segment of the Lincoln Highway traveling from Chambersburg, Pennsylvania, west toward Pittsburgh. The Lincoln Highway is labeled and also marked by the number "one" in a circle indicating it was a state highway. Contemporary Route 30 now follows the same path. I-70/76 parallels both roads. Unlike today's interstate, the Lincoln Highway went from town center to town center with no bypasses. During the 1920s, the federal government initiated a consistent numbering system in an attempt to organize disparate routes. Several of these early federal routes have become embedded in American folklore, such as Route 1 along the East Coast, Route 50 across the continent, and, most famously, Route 66, which cuts diagonally from the Midwest to California. None of these early efforts connected the country in a national network. It took the peace, prosperity, and cheap gas of the 1950s to create the political climate necessary to summon up the Interstate Highway System.

The numbering system used for the interstate highways reflects the earlier federal highway ordering. Odd-numbered routes orient north–south, and even-numbered routes run east–west. The interstates, however, reverse the distribution of the federal highway numbers to avoid two routes with the same number occurring next to each other in the same state. The interstates begin with low numbers in the West so that I-5 in California parallels the West Coast along with Federal Highway 101. I-95 in the East parallels the Atlantic coast and Federal Route 1 from Florida to Maine. At 1,927 miles, I-95 is the longest and most heavily traveled north–south interstate. The east–west routes begin their numbering in the south so that I-10 travels the Gulf Coast and Mexican border, while I-90 runs across the northern tier of states near the Canadian border. I-90 runs from Boston to Seattle for 3,120 miles, making it the longest single route in the entire system. City bypasses and spurs have their own three-digit numbering sequence consisting of a single digit prefixed to the two-digit number of a connecting primary interstate highway. Dead-end spurs begin with an odd number; circumferential routes start with an even number. The overall route selection was essentially determined in 1947 and delineated

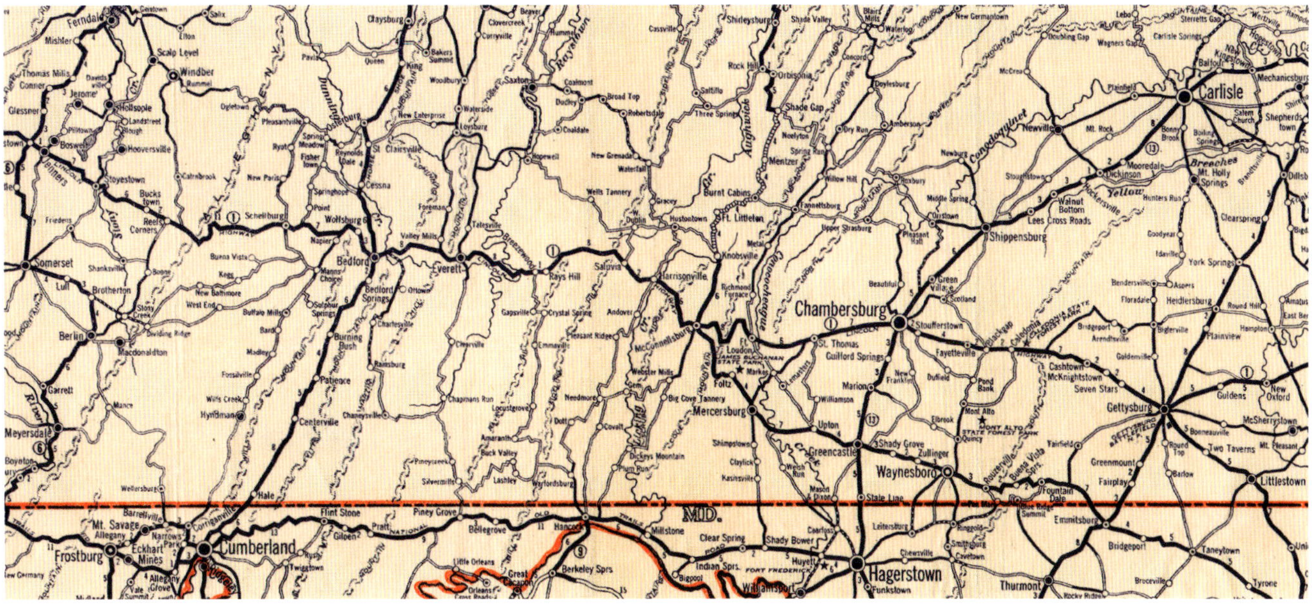

in the document *General Location of National System of Interstate Highways*, known as the *Yellow Book*.

Rand McNally road map, 1926, south-central Pennsylvania

The brightly colored *Yellow Book* is a thin pamphlet containing one hundred pages of maps printed on inexpensive government paper with a yellow cardboard cover. Its modest binding, however, belies the influence and impact its simple maps had on planning in American cities. A full-page map of the entire system in 1947 forms the frontispiece of this seemingly innocuous pamphlet. Each page thereafter diagrams the way an interstate highway was to intersect, cross, or enter into a major metropolitan area. The maps appear to be abstractions of metropolitan areas with the intended interstate drawn as a thick black line.

Close inspection reveals these maps to have been based on detailed and remarkably complete information. The definitive neighborhood boundaries were obviously drawn from accurate base materials. Quickly people realized the disruption, destruction, and segregation of complete neighborhoods represented by these black lines. In the 1960s and 1970s, public hearings and reviews exposed the damage that these proposed routes would do to disadvantaged neighborhoods. Bitterness and rancor blocked the construction of several interstates through cities and changed the public perception of the interstates from idealistic support to hostility and disappointment. Sadly, most American cities had already been devastated by the interstates' wholesale destruction of historic neighborhoods. The permanent scars of these highways disfigure most American cities, separating downtowns from river edges and ethnic neighborhoods from historic cores. Even now the federal government spends billions of dollars to undo one of the most egregious examples: the damage done by the elevated Central Artery to Boston, Massachusetts. The Central Artery separated Boston's historic core from its waterfront and its wonderful Italian neighborhood known as the North End. After spending billions of dollars, the federal government depressed the Central Artery below ground and reconnected the city. The *Yellow Book* is a remarkable document because of its specificity, its top-down implementation, and its initial lack of any public review. It was a blueprint for the destruction of urban America.

The ruin of so many American cities resulted from a fundamental conceptual flaw in the design and placement of the interstate highways. Essentially, no one considered how to end an interstate. A roadway that gathers trucks from thousands of miles and automobiles from closely neighboring suburbs and dumps them all within a few hours into a historic, dense urban core is disastrous. Anyone who has sat in morning rush-hour traffic can attest to this conceptual failure. A tube of space, hundreds of miles long, built for speed and convenience is difficult to terminate. Airplanes have terminals outside cities from which people and freight disperse. Railroads have freight terminals beyond city limits, and commuter rail lines have grand stations in city centers that daily allow thousands of pedestrians access to city streets. The terminal for a car, however, has to be a thousand single private parking spaces convenient to one's final destination.

The interstates, as built, were not interregional but intercity. Some cities, such as Atlanta, Nashville, and Denver, serve as nodes with several radiating routes. Others, such as Boise, Bismarck, or Amarillo, are simply way stations beside a major cross-country route. No interstate terminates anywhere except in a city or at another interstate. Early concepts for the interstate system proposed a continent-wide network that did not connect cities. Rather, it postulated transportation nodes outside metropolitan areas that functioned as automobile terminals much like airports where thousands of vehicles parked. Unfortunately, the connection from these mega-terminals to the inner city was never developed. We do have prototypes today in the enormous parking garages outside cities at the extensions of commuter rail systems. This forgotten idea of an "interregional" highway network highlights the problem of the interstates: they are a hermetically sealed transportation system imposed on an urban—or rural—landscape without regard for the realities of exiting, or entering, the flow of traffic.

A cursory examination of the complete Interstate Highway System map reveals an obvious truth about the United States: the greatest density of settlement lies east of the Mississippi River. Cities are closer together and have as many as six interstates passing through their centers. One travels through one city to arrive at another. West of the Mississippi, the interstates spread out in linear strands over great distances with immense areas not accessible from an interstate. The largest spaces occur in the West as the highways skirt the Great Basin Desert. Only one interstate crosses this vast and uninhabited expanse: Interstate 80 follows the overland route of the pioneering California Trail from Nebraska to California. A sweeping high-speed highway traces the same path that pioneers slowly walked one hundred years earlier. I-80 crosses the Great Basin of Utah and Nevada, hugging the Humboldt River that the earlier settlers desperately needed to water their animals. Today our cars carry their own sealed coolant systems across this same desert landscape as we retrace a forgotten history.

As interstate construction began in the 1950s, all state highway departments were required to follow the same standards such as widths of rights-of-way and pavements, curve radii, and slope gradients. The most important standard was controlled or limited access. All interstates, even those with many entrance or exit opportunities within dense metropolitan centers, limit access. On the longest continuous route, I-90, from Boston to Seattle, one can drive 3,020 miles without a stoplight or stop sign. At an average speed of sixty miles per hour, that means traveling across the continent in fifty hours. The only reasons for a long-distant traveler leaving the interstate are fuel, food, or rest. Long-haul trucks with their sleeping cabs traverse the continent nonstop, coast to coast, border to border.

Limited access was not a new concept that began with the interstates. The Pennsylvania Turnpike limited access by necessity in order to collect tolls. Early parkways such as the Merritt Parkway in Connecticut also controlled access and egress to maintain traffic flow, even though they were free. These parkways, turnpikes, and freeways were all built in the dense eastern United States. The interstates, however, carried this standard across the country into regions where exits were sometimes twenty-five or thirty miles apart. The interstates became long tubes of space that, once entered, tightly control the driver's options. A constant speed can be maintained for hours, so time becomes a measurement of distance rather than linear dimensions laid out on a surface. We say Atlanta is five hours from Nashville, or Chicago is nine hours from Memphis, with a degree of certainty not possible when travel could be interrupted by local traffic.

Road atlases now have time maps: maps that give distances between cities in hours and minutes rather than miles. The precision of these travel times—Atlanta to Nashville via Chattanooga 3.59 hours, or Salt Lake City to Denver 10.14 hours—evidences the confidence we have in consistent uninterrupted travel and the assumption that travel takes place only on an interstate. The average driving speed that underlies these times across the country works out to 62 miles per hour. Time maps take on an interesting diagrammatic quality, for they are made up of straight lines connecting point to point, as though there was no intervening topography, no deviation for mountain ranges or wide rivers. The interstates allow this detachment from the earth's surface because of limited access, so conceptually our travel hovers above the ground free from any constraints. A constant speed of one mile per minute becomes our measurement of distance.

The funding of the interstates through a tax on gas was a wonderful confluence of self-interests. The federal government dispensed tax revenues for individual states to use to create jobs in road construction. Senators and representatives reaped credit for public works in their districts and states. More roads meant more opportunities for more Americans to travel. Automobile manufacturers and all their material suppliers made more cars and more money to increase the wealth of stockholders. More cars meant more miles driven and more gas consumption and more tax revenues. The cycle spiraled ever upward to everyone's apparent advantage—so long as gas remained cheap. Gas remained so inexpensive into the golden automotive years of the 1950s that we could afford to add taxes to its price to fund the grand sweep of the interstates.

The United States was once oil rich. The western states such as Texas, Oklahoma, and California had huge underground oil reservoirs that were

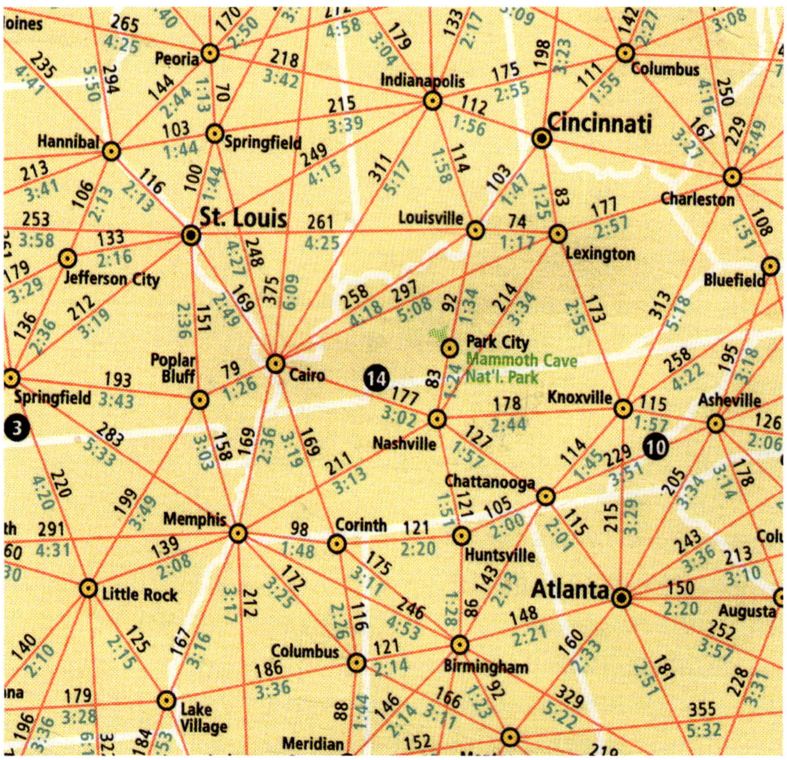

Detail from a Milage and Driving Time Map, Rand McNally Road Atlas, 2009

accessible to drilling and near the sources of refining and consumption. Fortunes were made—and lost—as hundreds of small regional oil companies competed with the few large conglomerates for the driving public's attention and patronage. These small oil companies generated local brand recognition and loyalty, allowing the many delivery systems of gas or service stations with pumps, modern architecture, and graphics to enter into American folklore as icons of the open road.

Companies such as Tydol, Parco, and Dixie Gas, with its logo, "the power to pass, that's Dixie Gas," are mostly forgotten except by collectors of the wonderful world of petroliana. The word "petroliana" refers to all the paraphernalia associated with vintage oil and gas distribution: motor oil cans, gas pumps with globe tops, and other advertising graphics. The red Pegasus, the flying horse of Mobile, implied limitless fantasy. The Texas company Texaco took its logos from the red star of the state flag: "Always trust your car to the man who wears the star." Although an example of the disjuncture between a symbol and its referent, the familiar Shell sign is one of the oldest gasoline station graphics. Royal Dutch Shell, one of today's giant international oil companies, was originally a supplier of mother-of-pearl harvested from sea shells gathered in the Far East.

Oil companies competed for customers through brand recognition using familiar and clear logos. Standard Oil, the financial engine that fueled the Rockefeller fortune, states the obvious in its name: it is both the standard for quality and offers the standard, the familiar. Standardized and recognizable service stations built by oil companies garnered brand loyalty. Drive-through porticos sheltered access to pumps in inclement weather. The building became the sign, and oil companies would repeat the exact same design regionally and eventually nationally. The American consumer readily accepted the parallel standardization of automobiles and automotive products, from fan belts to gasoline. Standardization was a welcome improvement in the decade before the Second World War from the haphazard and diverse gasoline stations scattered across rural America, where the quality of gas varied from station to station, and even the octane content was suspect. Photographs of old stations show a wonderful individuality and picturesque aspect appreciated today, but in actual experience, such stations made automobile travel uncertain and unreliable.

Service stations gave away excellent travel maps that advertised the parent oil company and all its motoring products. These free maps helped solidify brand loyalty. They were usually state road maps so that long-distance travelers could collect several contiguous states as a journey progressed. The cover graphics of these folded maps tell a great deal about car travel in America in its early decades. It was a friendly and familiar place with

Cover of a road map of Idaho, Standard Oil Company of California, 1939

Early gas station, with cross-roads store and bar "jook joint," Melrose, Natchitoches Parish, Louisiana, 1940

well-dressed happy drivers in big cars passing through unspoiled vistas. Travel was leisurely, travelers went from town to town on roads that passed down Main Streets; they stopped for lunch in family-run diners and spent nights in AAA-rated motor courts or hotels. Even the cars themselves were beautiful—long sleek machines with bold curves and shiny chrome grilles. The romance of the highway is tangible with idealized couples in open cars cruising through idyllic landscapes.

One of the most well-known road maps among collectors is a beautiful Shell 1933 California-Nevada three-panel spread. Composed fan-like around the ubiquitous shell logo are the colorful license plates of states and provinces. A lovely young woman with red lips sits in an open roadster with leather upholstery. Her gloved left hand rests easily on the steering wheel; her other hand steadies her terrier. Her white fur cloak drapes provocatively from her green dress as she looks intently at the viewer and casually beckons us to share limitless possibilities. The entire composition is a wonderful illustration of America's early romance with the car and the freedom and accessibility of the open road. This fantasy fueled our culture for the first half of the twentieth century. Travel on the great interstate highways became the apotheosis of this fantasy. Fast cars and wide roads promised easy access to all those places of the shiny license plates in a fancy convertible driven by a golden siren.

The covers of two maps published after the construction of the interstates tell a different story. Something happened; something was lost. The Pure Oil cover of 1968 shows ribbons of concrete seemingly detached from an abstracted landscape. A Wisconsin 1970 highway map cover presents an aerial photograph of a typical intersection. Both covers contain barren spaces without scale or reference. They could be anywhere. Gone is the romance, the innocence, the boosterism of earlier maps, replaced by the anonymity and vacuity of dual lanes of pavement stretching into an unknown and uncertain distance.

Before automobile travel, most towns, even small ones, had one or two small hotels with restaurants, because rail travel concentrated institutions and businesses within a short walk from stations. With the advent of auto touring, travelers at first used these same hotels and restaurants conveniently situated in a town center. The cost, difficulty of parking, and negotiation of the more elaborate services of a hotel, however, soon brought an alternative kind of accommodation into existence—the auto or motor court. Located at the periphery of a downtown, motor courts were small clusters of cabins with a separated central office. Parking was next to one's unit to afford easy unloading. For economy of construction, the cabins were often joined together in one long single structure.

California-Nevada highway map cover, Union Oil Company, 1939

Shell Oil Company map cover, 1933

1968 Minneapolis–St. Paul map cover, Pure Oil Division of the Union Oil Company of California, and 1970 Wisconsin highway map cover, Division of Highways

From such beginnings, the American motel came into existence. The word "motel" was first used for Arthur Heineman's "Milestone Mo-tel," opened in San Luis Obispo, California, in 1925.[3] Convenient, fast, and inexpensive, motels served only the motorists because of their location on the outskirts of towns beyond the access of pedestrians.

Motels were phenomenally lucrative commercial ventures in the United States after the Second World War. So successful that the prewar "mom and pop" establishments could not compete with the growing interests of big investors. The number of motels grew from twenty thousand in 1946 to fifty-six thousand in 1957.[4] The popularity of motels was based on their economy, their convenience, and, especially, their anonymity. They had no lobbies or public spaces where one's appearance was scrutinized by other guests after a long day of driving. There was no need for bellhops, doormen, or tipping. One could check in and out with minimum interaction.

The dramatic growth and business potential of motels soon attracted the attention of large hospitality chains like Best Western. Founded in Long Beach, California, in 1946 with the logo "the Nation's Friendliest Motel," Best Western today operates worldwide.[5] Other corporate chains such as Travelodge, Quality Court, and Howard Johnson's entered the market with several different franchise models. Essentially, the parent corporation provides business oversight and quality control along with marketing and advertising services. For the traveler, the brand name guarantees consistent and predictable services. With the construction of the limited-access

Early motel (Lilly's Auto Camp), Monterey Highway, Gilroy, California, 1933

3. Jakle and Sculle, *Gas Station in America*, 18.
4. Ibid., 20.
5. Ibid., 142.

Interstate Highway System, specific sites became more desirable and costly, so the larger chains competed with each other for exit locations. Price ranges stratified into several clearly identifiable brands such as budget, suites for businessmen with more expansive conference facilities, and expensive almost hotel-like multistory complexes. A given corporation or management company might own several market segments at the same exit. Today, competition limits the hospitality field to a few highly recognizable brands that assure the traveler predictable prices and services.

In-town hotels had restaurants: most motels did not. With the separation of these two functions, the motorist could either drive into town to eat or patronize roadside eateries such as diners. In the 1930s the silver train-like diner quickly proliferated along America's highways, offering parking and quick food. Other types of eating places soon competed with diners for the motorist's business. Several eateries, such as McDonald's, Burger King, and KFC, have become so embedded in American society as to be representative icons of contemporary culture.

Roadside services evolved in the latter half of the twentieth century into three distinct specialized facilities: gas stations, restaurants, and accommodations. First gas stations and then eateries and motels reoriented their architecture and site design to accommodate the requirements of cross-country automobile and truck traffic. Parking and access became the main determinants of architectural form with drive-ins and generous street frontage parking lots. Gas stations provided covered ports to protect self-service pump access. By positioning the actual structures to the rear or sides of lots, all three services promoted large parking spaces in front. Thus a new urban paradigm came into being, one that emphasized

Early restaurant (Jack Walton's Hot Barbecue), Fort Worth–Dallas highway, Texas, 1942

the primacy of space rather than form. Building facades no longer defined the public space of the street as in older towns—the parking lots did. The need for parking in front of buildings meant that these businesses were built on sites away from historic commercial cores. These mutually compatible automobile-accessible places positioned themselves across the country along heavily trafficked highways in perceived areas of high volume such as intersections and approaches to towns. On toll roads, with their limited access, food and fuel were grouped in "rest stops" accessible only from the highway. By the early 1950s, the elements and concepts of highway services were well established and accepted across the country.

Before delving into the five regional sections of this book, it is worth pausing for a moment to look again at a map of the United States to realize the extent and sweep of the interstate highways. These are great distances of thousands of miles across an enormous continent. Interstates cut through mountains, cross wide rivers, and navigate limitless prairies. They connect states, cities, and different landscapes and topographies; the immensity of their scope is mind-boggling. The sheer grandeur of the concept of transcontinental automobile travel dwarfs the scale of the five regions discussed in this book. The very boldness of imagining such great distances makes anything less seem insignificant. That is the promise of the open road: excitement and the future lie beyond the next horizon; by driving on, we can detach ourselves from our past. But as we shall see in the chapters ahead, history tells a different story.

Map of the Interstate Highway System. The yellow circles are the five study areas of this book.

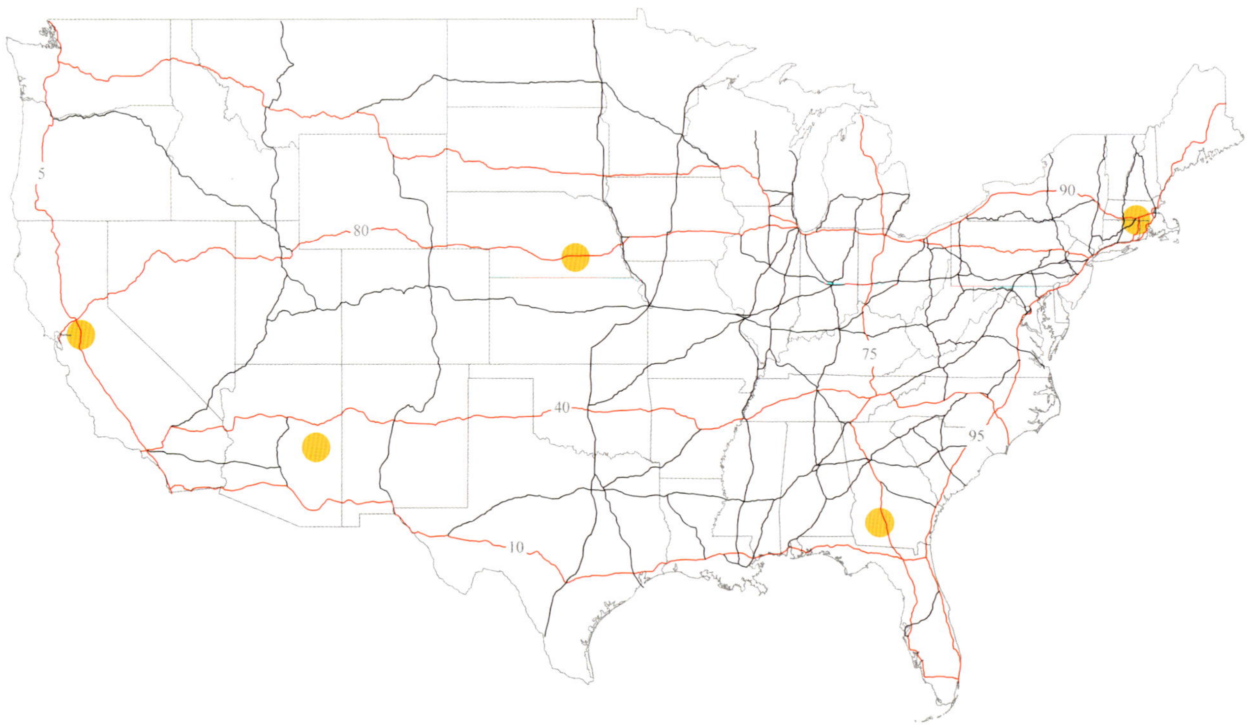

3

LANDSCAPES AND MILL TOWNS OF SOUTHERN NEW ENGLAND

THE UNIQUE GEOLOGICAL and topographical landscapes of New England provided the settings for hundreds of small gristmills and lumber mills. In the nineteenth century, the number of these sites grew to a remarkable density across an entire region, giving character and repute to the New England textile industry. Towns located around these complex and highly engineered sites that were positioned on the abundant and picturesque rivers and streams of Massachusetts, Connecticut, and Rhode Island. The rapid economic collapse of this substantial industry in the early twentieth century left behind a distinctive cultural landscape that has only further declined as the modern Interstate Highway System, with its expanding off-ramp towns and burgeoning strip malls, bypasses these mostly forgotten towns. After describing the geological and glacial history that shaped the New England landscape to the advantage of waterpower, this chapter explores the beautiful and still intact mill town of Webster, Massachusetts. Using old maps, historic drawings, photographs, and extensive field research, other neighboring mill seats in Connecticut and Rhode Island are reconstructed along with their associated repetitive worker housing. This finely textured landscape of small villages and narrow radiating roads has been overlaid and displaced by the wide highways that connect New England's major cities and sprawling suburbs with the vast interstate network across the United States.

Aqua currit

Density of settlements generates correspondingly dense networks of communication, especially roads, and the Interstate Highway System operates no differently. Any road map of the entire United States shows a concentrated network of interstates in the populated East versus widely spaced interstates in the West. Two important long-distant interstates, east–west I-90 and north–south I-95, converge in New England on the regional hub of Boston. Traffic approaching and leaving Boston's metropolitan area is so heavy that several additional circumferential interstates such as I-495 and Route 128 connect I-90 and I-95 like cross threads in a great spider web. One of these cross strands, I-395, connects Worcester, Massachusetts, with Norwich, Connecticut, and offers an alternative route between Boston and New York City that bypasses Providence, Rhode Island. On its way south, I-395 parallels an older Route 12 and the Thames River. Between Worcester and Norwich, Route 12, along with the now defunct New York and New England Rail Road, once connected a river corridor with some of the largest and most powerful mills in America.

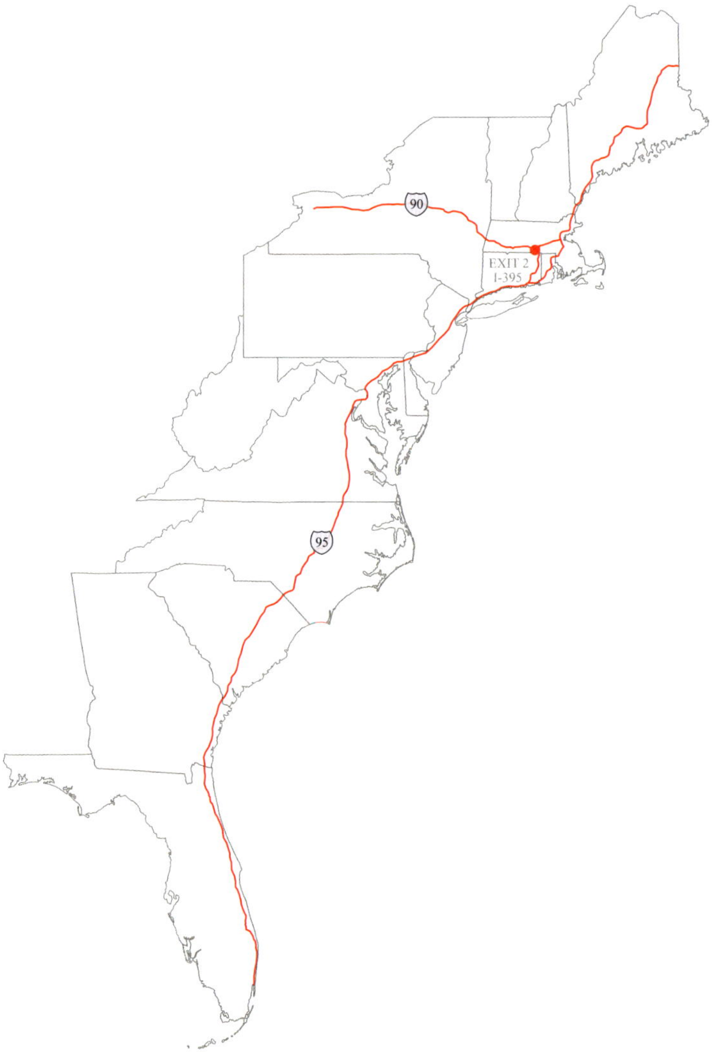

Location of Exit 2, I-295, Massachusetts

Norwich, Connecticut, is the Thames River's seaport even though it is at the head of a deep estuary sixteen miles from the open bay of Long Island Sound. The Thames estuary gathers the Quinebaug, Shetucket, and French Rivers as they and their many small tributaries flow south out of Connecticut and Massachusetts. In the early nineteenth century, the Thames River watershed, together with the nearby Pawtuxet and Blackstone Rivers, harnessed more waterpower than any other river systems in the world.

A detail from a 1935 Texaco road map of southern New England shows this region twenty years before the construction of the interstates or the improvements of the many other state and federal highways. The map centers on the intersection of Connecticut, Rhode Island, and Massachusetts. The dotted black lines added to the map indicate the later additions of the interstates. This region was settled early in the seventeenth century and consequently has a closely spaced network of towns and their connecting roads. Towns on this map form centers of multiple radiating short routes that promoted constant and frequent communications. As major ports in colonial America, both Norwich, Connecticut, and Providence, Rhode Island, were the centers of many converging roads, and this convergence was still obvious in 1935. We should not misinterpret the scale of these roads because of our experience with multilane highways. Red roads such as Route 6, 44, or 1 are two paved lanes only; blue roads are paved; all others are "improved" or rough gravel surfaces. This early road map illustrates several distinctive regional settlement characteristics. Many towns came into existence first as gristmill sites, and mills required frequent access from the surrounding farms, so each tiny town functioned as a small hub in a transportation web. Distances between towns, designated by small red numbers, are short, for the entire area of this portion of a larger map is less than forty miles across. While our present-day interstate travel dwarfs the small distances between towns such as Uxbridge and Whitinsville, Massachusetts, or between Putnam and Danielson, Connecticut, distance was not always measured in hundreds of miles. Even five miles in the seventeenth and eighteen centuries could take hours along rutted and muddy roads. The right-of-way of I-395 disrupts the finer underlying texture of evenly connected villages and towns, rendering the older settlement pattern invisible to the interstate traveler. I-395 essentially bypasses the towns. The detachment between the scale of the interstate and the older road network is so complete that most of the places discussed in this chapter are less than a mile from I-395, yet remain hidden from the interstate.

I-395 traverses the distance from I-90 to I-95 in less than an hour as it curves gently around the soft hills of southern Massachusetts before crossing quickly into northeastern Connecticut. Driving south on an October

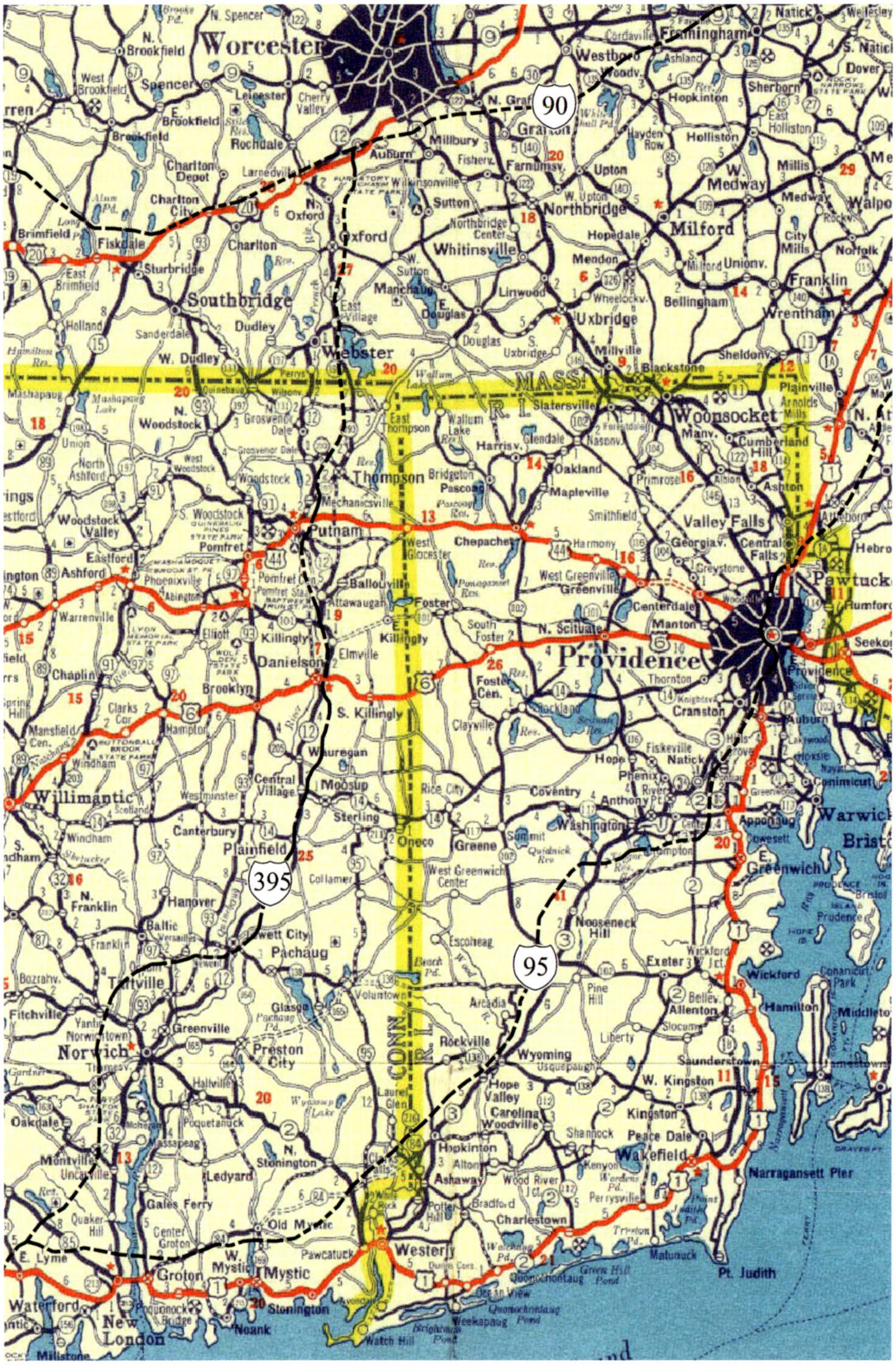

1935 Texaco New England road map. The black dotted lines represent the routes of interstate highways.

afternoon, one is enclosed in a continuous leafy tunnel of hardwoods lit by the vivid fall palette of orange maples and yellow beeches. The brilliant colors mask any glimpse of the settlements beyond the right-of-way and wide median. The only clues are the occasional tall brick chimneys rising smokeless above the tree canopy.

Just before the Connecticut state line, Exit 2 leaves I-395 and joins with Route 16, which connects Webster eastward to Boston through a landscape of tiny mill towns such as Uxbridge, Hopedale, and Milford. By turning west at Exit 2, I-395, and following signs to Webster's center, Route 16 immediately enters an unending commercial strip of fast-food chains (McDonald's, Burger King, KFC), service stations (Getty, Sunoco, Hi-Lo Gas), and, unexpectedly, three chain pharmacies—Rite-Aid, CVS, and Walgreens. Other food choices include Friendly's, Dunkin Donuts, Taco Bell, two Mexican restaurants, and one Chinese restaurant. There are two auto supply stores, a supermarket, an AT&T mobile phone store, and Hank's liquor store. An abandoned gas station ominously hints of recent economic decline. The eateries and gas stations along this commercial strip are announced by standard highway signs on I-395 that obviously serve the interstate travelers. Other establishments, such as the supermarket, the AT&T store, and BlockBuster Video serve the local community. The services for interstate travelers have gathered these other local establishments that siphon off economic opportunities from Webster's historic core. All stores sit back from the street behind parking lots in the all-too-familiar pattern of isolated buildings joined by undifferentiated open space. After less than a quarter of a mile, two opposing steeples of the Baptist and Catholic churches abruptly punctuate the open parking lots and setback buildings of the retail mini-malls and announce the entry into the stolidly beautiful Main Street of Webster, Massachusetts.

As the first example in this study, Exit 2, I-395, provides a clear diagram of the typical spatial organization of an off-ramp town and its relationship to an older downtown. The chain restaurants and gas stations could be anywhere; they group immediately at the exit ramp and provide no clear contextual relationships, except to the interstate. This short commercial strip is like a gasket that seals the interstate from Webster's history and makes the disjuncture between the two total and unequivocal.

Route 16 follows Webster's Main Street as it curves along a low flat ridge above three partly abandoned mills once powered by the French River. Webster's residential streets fan across the gentle slope away from the mills in row after row of multi-unit housing, "triple-deckers" and duplexes. There are few of that obvious expression of individual wealth, the single-family home. Webster's population has always been working

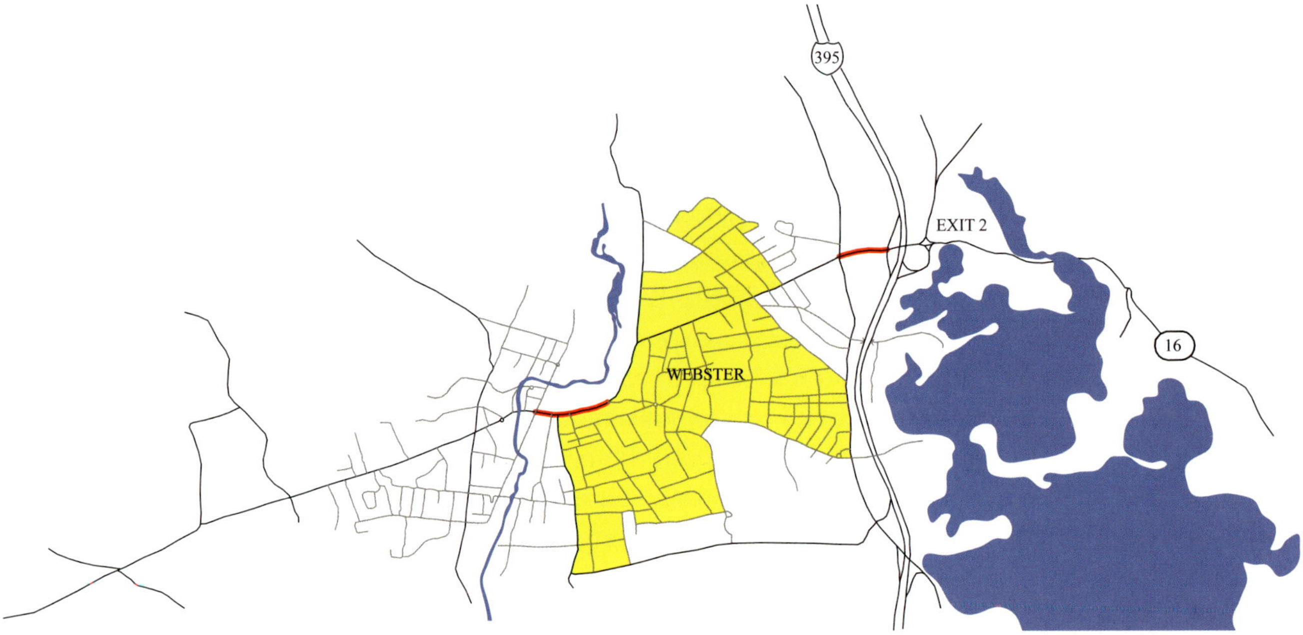

Map of the Town of Webster, Massachusetts, and its relationship to the interstate. The yellow is the town, and the two red strips are the historic center of the town and the commercial strip or off-ramp town at highway Exit 2.

people drawn together by their labor. A figure-ground study shows two of the mill complexes, the dense urban core of Main Street's commercial structures and the major residential streets radiating eastward. It is a classic diagram of concise urbanism centered on the community's source of wealth, the mills, with civic institutions, services, and dwellings all within walking distance.

On a late October weekday in Webster, brown leaves scatter sadly across the cracked sidewalks, a soft covering that offers no protection against the passage of time. The towers of St. Joseph's Roman Catholic Church hover above the neighborhoods like a hen gathering her flock; the expansive bronze doors depicting scenes from the life of Christ are closed reassuringly against the tribulations of the world. St Joseph's bells toll unexpectedly in the empty afternoon, reminding all that these bronze doors will soon swing wide and mercifully embrace the few remaining faithful of Webster's inhabitants.

Webster's history began in 1811 when Samuel Slater purchased land and water privileges, a woolen mill, and several existing small grain- and sawmills in what was then part of Dudley and Oxford. He quickly increased his holdings with a second and third mill and consolidated his business interests in southern New England. Because of disagreements with the citizens of Dudley and Oxford, Slater, with his two sons George and John, petitioned the Massachusetts General Court in 1831 to incorporate Webster as a separate municipality by taking land from both Oxford and Dudley. A year later, the state granted his petition, and Webster came into

Figure-ground study of Webster. The blue is the French River; the large black rectangles are the mills. The town's residential neighborhoods radiate out fanlike from Main Street.

existence as a company town made up of three villages: East, North, and South. Each village was dominated by a Slater Company mill. The total population in 1832 was less than two thousand. Within the next eighty years, however, Webster grew to eleven thousand as the mills prospered.[1]

A bird's-eye perspective of Webster drawn in 1892 serves as a guide to understanding this fascinating small city. Under his sons' management, the three Slater mills have grown into substantial complexes. The Slater Mills have been joined by others: the Stevens Linen Works, John Chase and Sons Fancy Gassimeres and Worsteds, A.J. Bates Shoe Factory, and Corbin and Sons Mill. Eight large mills supported a town of ten to eleven thousand people. In the bird's-eye perspective, the mills have smoking chimneys, indicating that by the late nineteenth century they used steam as well as water power. The Worcester and Providence Railroad trains pass through Webster with smoke pouring from the engine's stack as well. The six-storied Stevens Linen Mill in the lower right corner of the drawing derived its water power from a dammed mill pond on the Little River, a tributary of the French River. Although empty, the Stevens Mill still exists, an elegant structure of beautifully cut stone. In the perspective drawing, Webster has eight churches scattered throughout its neighborhoods representing six different denominations. The vignettes of the mills and the civic, commercial, and religious buildings illustrated above and below the map evidence the town's obvious prosperity. The grand houses of the mill owners are displayed in the lower left insets. An idealized bucolic agricultural landscape surrounds the entire town.

The northernmost Slater factory was a cotton mill with the full sequence of manufacturing, from carding to spinning to weaving. It had two boilers in the main complex and one in an old saw- and gristmill on the river. Most of the main operation's power came from waterwheels driven by an elaborate series of canals from a millpond upstream on the French River. In the perspective, the mill sits tucked into a bend in the river isolated by the tracks of the New York, New Haven and Hartford Railroad. The aptly named Mill Street leads to a row of stone tenements for mill workers. The French River also powered the Slater and Sons woolens mill downstream and flowed through or under the entire complex. This large mill had twenty boilers spaced throughout the structure, indicating a greater dependency on the more reliable steam power. Adjoining Webster to the northeast, next to Webster Lake, is the Slater & Sons Bleaching, Dying and Printing facility. This too originally had water power from a small stream but had shifted to mostly steam power by 1892. Today, the interchange of Exit 2, I-395, covers this site, and Webster Lake is submerged beneath a much larger reservoir.

1. Prude, *Coming of the Industrial Order,* 176.

Bird's-eye perspective of Webster, Massachusetts, 1892

Stevens Mill, Webster, Massachusetts

A contemporary industrial building now occupies the in-town site of the former Bates Shoe Factory. The small brook that powered the earlier shoe factory drains through a culvert beneath the city before emptying into the French River. Many of the Slater & Sons mill structures have disappeared, but their flat sites support trucking and storage facilities. With the exception of remnants of the tailraces, the canals have been filled in. The milldam still holds back the flow of the French River upstream. Some older annexes sit empty, including a beautiful boiler house with its massive chimney. Railroad tracks still parallel the river, but these are for today's long-haul trains only, as all local goods are trucked onto nearby I-395. Fragments of abandoned rail sidings, switching yards, and trestles lie forgotten in the woods along the banks of the French River.

Webster, Massachusetts, is a beautiful palimpsest, an urban narrative inscribed by each generation and then partially wiped clean. One mark in the landscape proved immune to cultural erosion: the glacial knob that forced the French River to twist twice and then drop over steep ledges. These natural features brought the mills here, and the town followed. Unfortunately in the late nineteenth century, the textile industry moved to the American South, leaving dark chimneys, empty crumbling brick structures, and rusted railroad bridges. The fine buildings of Webster's Main Street, the library, the churches, and the commercial blocks tenuously resist a similar fate because they are repositories of memories rather than economic engines like the mills. The grand monument to the soldiers and sailors from Webster who fought in the Civil War sits on the lawn of City Hall at a curve in Main Street. The beauty of its sculptures reminds us that layers of the palimpsest are missing; that our reading of the landscape yields only parts of the narrative. Gone are the families whose daughters labored in the mills nearby and whose committed sons swelled the ranks of the soldiers and sailors remembered by names encircling the stone obelisk. Webster's graceful Main Street and determined neighborhoods are emptying husks, cast aside in that most casual of gestures—economic progress. Webster has become a haunting memorial to America's industrial past.

To fully understand Webster's history within its context of hundreds of other mills in southern New England, one must turn back fifteen thousand years to the final retreat of the great glaciers. Blue ice once lay thick across New England. Spreading outward from Arctic Canada, thick ice reached as far south as Long Island Sound. For over two million years the immense bulk of these Pleistocene glaciers weighted down the earth's surface, submerging the entire coastal plain of the eastern United States and its many river systems beneath the Atlantic Ocean. As the edges of the ice ground

Boiler house, Slater Mill, Webster, Massachusetts

Cavalryman, Civil War Soldiers and Sailors Monument, Town Hall, Webster, Massachusetts, 1907; Finn Haakon Frolich, sculptor

southward, they pushed up mounds of earth hundreds of feet deep and miles wide. Narrow ridges called terminal moraines marked the furthest margins of the glaciers' successive advances. Several of these terminal moraines remained as the ice advanced and retreated from its maximum extension at present-day Long Island. The forked ends of Montauk and Orient Points on the eastern end of Long Island mark two such advances. These same moraines continue under the sea and reappear as ridges that form Block Island and the islands south of Cape Cod. The ice advances also formed the arms of Cape Cod itself through consecutive advancements and retreats. Rivers ran through and beneath the glaciers, acting as giant conveyor belts that transported rock fragments from northern New England and deposited them at the ice's southern margins. Sometimes the fragments were mixed and tumbled beneath the ice sheets; sometimes the melt water streams differentiated the rock particles into the increasingly finer grains that formed the beautiful sand beaches of Cape Cod, Long Island, and the southern shores of Rhode Island.

The successive advances and retreats of the glaciers heavily scoured the surface of New England. The immense weight and constant movement of the ice acted like giant sheets of sandpaper rasping across the landscape. Much of the rock material carried southward remained behind after the glaciers retreated, filling valleys and lowlands as the ice melted. Along the coasts of southern New England, these gravely deposits formed earthen dams that obliterated entire drainage systems and diverted rivers into new channels. Instead of flowing through valleys and gorges cut over millions of years, these rivers and streams were forced to tumble over recently exposed rock as they searched for the shortest path to the sea.

Over millions of years, streams and rivers usually carved ravines and valleys through the underlying rock and accommodated themselves to the irregularities of topography and bedrock. In regions subjected to glaciation, these channels were filled with glacial till, forcing the drainage patterns of an entire region to readjust by finding new routes after the glaciers were gone. The rapid flow of melt water from beneath the glaciers hastened this process. A colorful surface geology map of northeast Connecticut illustrates these deposits of glacial debris within several branching stream systems. Unstratified gravel and boulders deposited by the glaciers are rendered in bright colors of orange and reds. The more uniform green of the surrounding hills indicates a topography rubbed bare of all but the thinnest layer of soil.

The branching pattern of rivers betrays their origins in a glaciated landscape on the margins between the rocky upland Piedmont and the narrow New England coastal plain. Because the gradient from the uplands of southern Massachusetts to Long Island Sound or Narragansett Bay is steep, the stream pattern is regularly branched in a uniform dendritic system. Unlike a drainage pattern in the very wide coastal plains of the southeastern United States, these rivers do not have the broad bends or deeply recursive loops of a typical flat gradient. The branches of rivers in a northern glaciated landscape are sharp, often right angles, indicative of a flow against resistive surface strata. These abrupt changes of direction

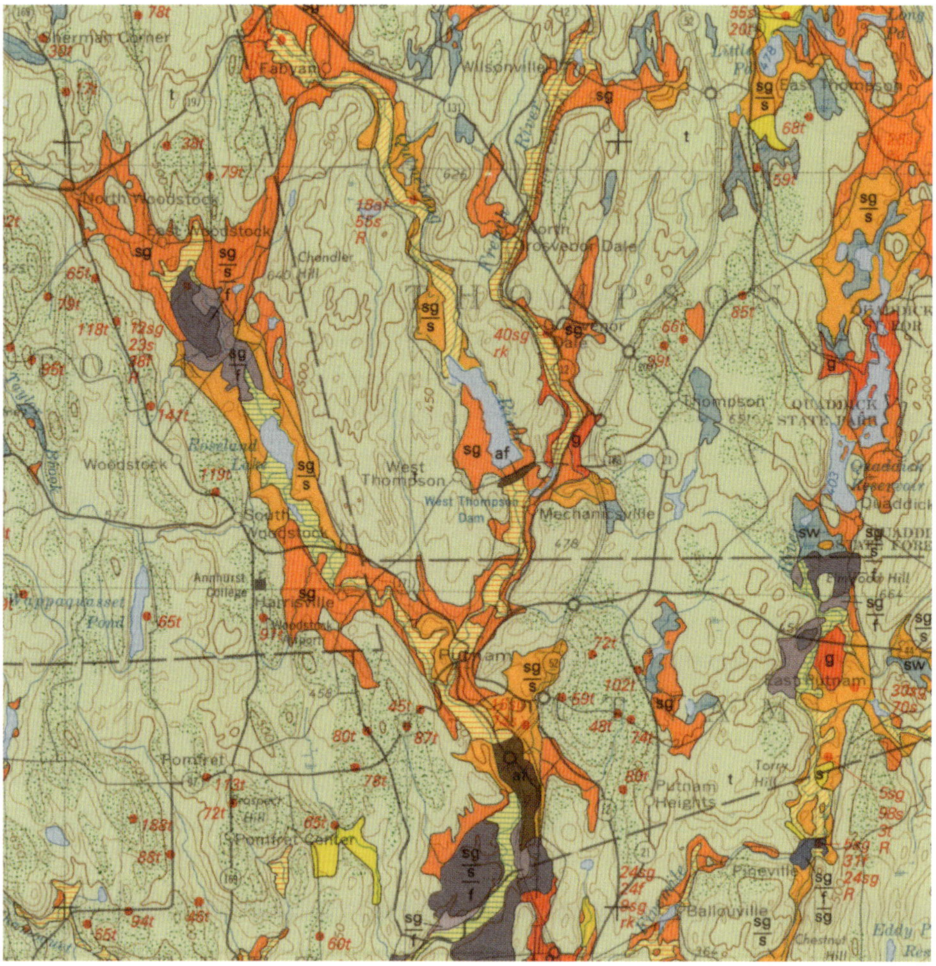

This geology map encompasses the upper drainage basins of the Thames River system and two of its main tributaries, the French and Quinebaug Rivers. In the lower center is the town of Putnam, Connecticut. One of the mill sites discussed later in this chapter is North Grosvenor Dale on the French River, just above the middle center of the map.

with rapids or falls are characteristic of newly formed drainage channels searching for accommodations as the current moves swiftly between steep banks and low hills. Many of the settlements, like Webster, considered in this chapter sit on a series of acute twists in a river's direction. These frequently occurring topographic and geologic features caused the tight congestion and concentrated structures of multiple mill complexes that often shared a series of crowded water rights.

In southern New England, these rechanneled rivers flow relatively short distances from the low hills and mountains of the Piedmont uplands across the narrow coastal plains to the ocean. Compared to the broad southeastern coastal plains of Georgia discussed in the next chapter, the coastal plains of Massachusetts, Rhode Island, and Connecticut are very limited, for the juncture between the uplands and the coastal plains occurs less than fifty miles from the ocean. In deeply indented coasts such as Narragansett Bay of Rhode Island or the Thames estuary of Connecticut, the break between the uplands and the coastal plain happens within a few

Map of the Thames, French, and Quinebaug River watersheds in Rhode Island and southeastern Connecticut *(opposite)*

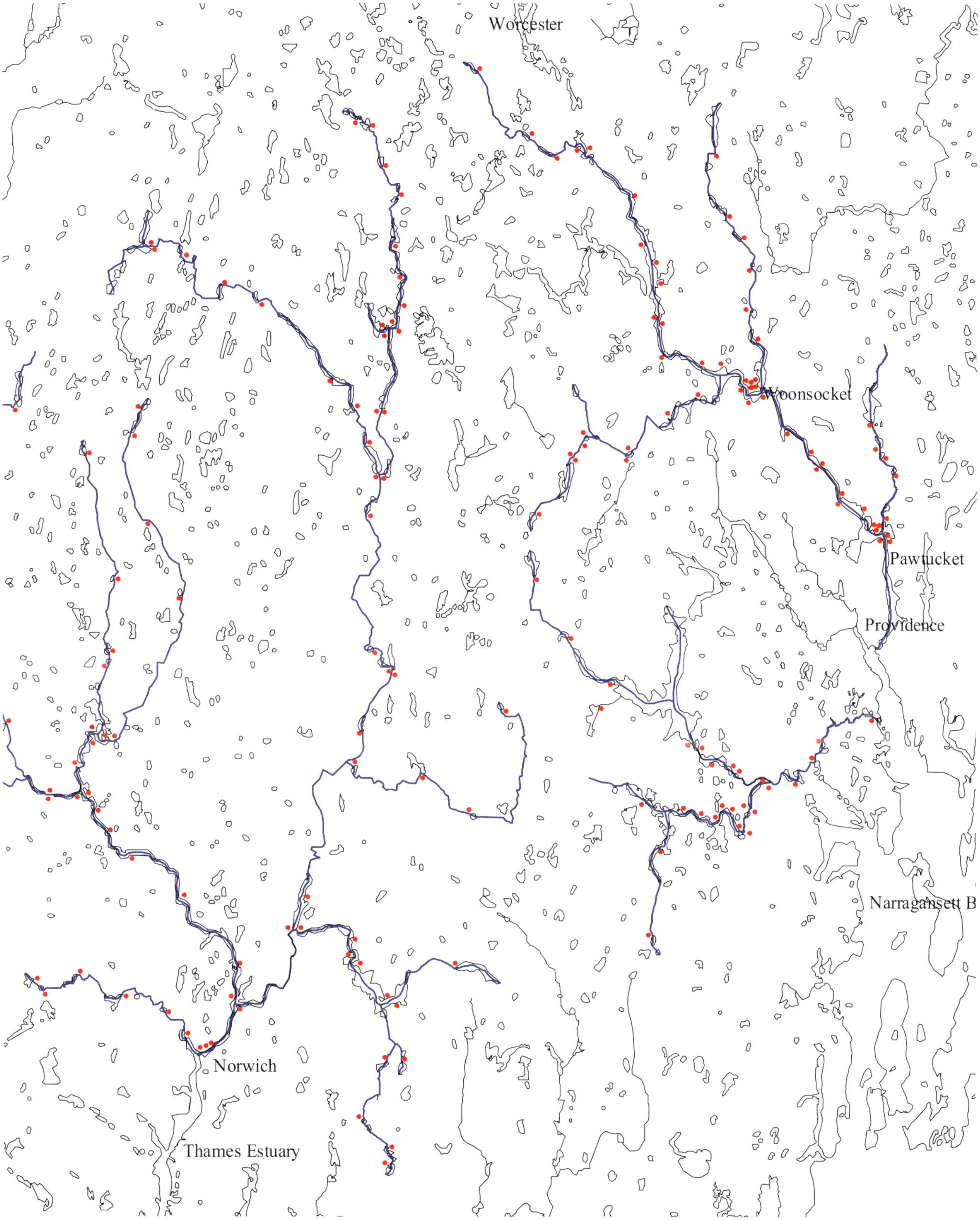
Worcester
Woonsocket
Pawtucket
Providence
Narragansett B
Norwich
Thames Estuary

yards of tidal and navigable waters. This transition from the rounded hills and upland forests to the flatter coastal plain is known as the fall line and is evidenced locally by steep drops such as rapids or water falls, ideal locations for water-powered mills.

Generally, the fall line parallels the shoreline, but in southeastern New England it veers northward along the Connecticut–Rhode Island state boundary and into central Massachusetts and then follows the coast of Maine northeastward into maritime Canada. The place where the fall line shifts direction in southern New England corresponds with the watersheds of the Blackstone, Pawtuxet, and Thames River systems. Thus, the streams and rivers of these watersheds are forced to drain parallel to instead of perpendicular to the harder substrate. This makes for many more rapids and exposed ledges than a perpendicular intersection, creating more opportunities for mill dams and flumes. After the thick ice retreated from New England at the end of the Pleistocene, it left behind a series of geological phenomena perfectly placed for a distant future of harnessed waterpower.

Other aspects of these three watersheds of southern New England were equally fortuitous. The topographical gradient across their entire surface is a constant slope, so that falls occur more or less evenly spaced along the full length of each river and its tributaries. Precipitation is frequent and copious throughout the year, furnishing a relatively constant flow of water from spring through late fall. Summer and fall flow was especially important during early settlements so that gristmills could grind harvested grains. The configuration of the rivers and their tributaries are compact dendritic patterns that afford a maximum number of evenly spaced mill sites. As villages grew around mill sites, they, too, were tightly spaced, as seen on the earlier illustrated 1935 Texaco road map.

In a new and rapidly developing country, mills were important communal institutions. Sawn lumber was necessary for all types of building and for the construction of ships that served the coasts of the new colonies. Grinding corn and other grains into meal is vitally necessary for any culture; thus, gristmills have a history as long as the history of agriculture. Mill stones are mentioned in the Bible: "No man shall take the nether or the upper millstone to pledge: for he taketh a man's life to pledge (Deuteronomy 24:6). The Romans had mills throughout their empire for grinding wheat and developed laws regulating their placement on waterways. Early mill technologies were simple, requiring only a few horsepower of water flow.

The American colonies in the seventeenth and eighteenth centuries had abundant local mills that served a growing density of population. Because mills were such necessary components of early settlements, mill owners were granted concessions and advantages in both the placement and construction of their mills and millponds along rivers and streams. These early mill rights or water rights were uncomplicated inducements to encourage the development of the best sites. The title of this section, *Aqua currit,* is a concise summary of the concept behind these rights. *Aqua currit et debet currere ut currere solebat* means literally that water flows and ought to flow as it customarily flowed. This simple principle formed the common-law foundation for mill and water rights in eighteenth- and nineteenth-century America.[2] Essentially, water in streams should flow as it has always flowed with no disruption. No dam should cause the flooding of another person's property upstream or should deprive a property of downstream flow. Later in the nineteenth century, water rights would become contentious as waterpower and water courses developed into complicated infrastructures for industrial expansion and private profit.

To put in perspective the importance of grist-, saw-, and early textile mills in the early period of the American states, consider that in 1840, New England had a population of 2.2 million people and 7,994 mills.[3] This is an incredible ratio of one mill for every 275 people. These mills were distributed in a dense network to serve widely scattered population centers because overland travel was difficult on muddy or frozen roads. The grinding of grain takes time, so gristmills naturally became gathering places as people waited for their grain to be ground and bagged. A painting of a New England gristmill by the American artist George H. Durrie (1820–1863) romanticizes this image with its peaceful and bucolic winter landscape. The mill owner clears ice from below the water wheel while another sleds bags of grain across the bridge. The log dam provides a water drop, or head, of about eight feet from the millpond behind. The exposed boulders in the middle of the dam and to its left are evidence that this site was a waterfall before the mill construction. The water wheel is visible behind the mill owner. The main building has the characteristic clerestory windows in its roof found on later wooden mills throughout southern New England.

As the mills grew beyond local use and changed to the manufacture of textiles and related goods, the location of their sites became important for other reasons. Ideally, they needed to be near the sea for ease of bulk transportation. Cotton arrived from the south by boat in unwieldy five-hundred-pound bales, and finished cloth was shipped up and down the coast and into the western states by canal barges. One of the earliest textile mills in southern New England at Central Falls in Pawtucket, Rhode Island, was perfectly sited at a milldam where the Blackstone River met the tidal limit of Narragansett Bay. Ships could tie up within a few yards of the mill. An aerial photograph shows this site today: the white

2. Steinberg, *Nature Incorporated,* 141.

3. Hunter, *History of Industrial Power,* 38, table 2.

Old Grist Mill in Winter, 1853, by George Henri Durrie (1820–1863); oil on canvas, 25 3/16 × 36 in.

clapboard structure is the Slater Mill where Samuel Slater began his career. The stone mill to its left is the Wilkinson Mill. Both are part of the Slater Mill Museum. The open parking lots above the museum were once packed with mill structures. To increase the reliability of water transportation, a canal was dug parallel to the Blackstone River from Worcester to Providence. Soon, one of the first railroads in America followed the same route. Mill sites upstream from Central Falls on the Blackstone River were less than fifty miles from the sea by canal or rail. The Thames estuary in nearby Connecticut was navigable to Norwich, allowing that city to develop into a major port as it gathered products by rail from several extensive watersheds to the north.

The textile mills of southern New England soon usurped the best sites as they grew into larger and more complex establishments surrounded by growing communities. By the late nineteenth century, the Blackstone River had 222 mills along 56 miles of river.[4] These mills were grouped in a watershed of 458 square miles that generated 19,994 water-driven horsepower.[5]

4. U.S. Dept. of the Interior, Census Office, *Reports of the Water-power,* tables 68, 69, and 70.

5. Ibid., 39.

Slater and Wilkerson Mills, Pawtucket, Rhode Island

The Blackstone River ranked number one in the United States in generated water horsepower per square mile, far ahead of other river systems such as the Hudson, Delaware, or even the mighty Potomac. Far behind the Blackstone, but still ranked number two, was the nearby Thames River system, with a drainage area of 1,458 square miles.[6] The Thames River basin, which includes the Willimantic, Natchang, Quinebaug, French, and Yantic Rivers, had an astounding 420 mills in an area that encompasses 25 percent of Connecticut.[7] This works out to one mill every three square miles and is especially amazing when one considers that each mill, with its attending flume, millrace, and millpond, crowded its neighbors along rather modest water courses. A corresponding pattern of settlements resulted along other rivers and streams as they branched northward from Long Island Sound through Connecticut and Rhode Island into south-central Massachusetts.

Not all mills on these watersheds were textile mills—some manufactured shoes, and some supplied products to other mills, such as wire or spindles or even mill machinery. The manufacture of cloth is a complex multistepped process. Some mills performed specific parts of the total manufacturing operation, such as spinning yarn or carding cotton, and then furnished their product to other mills for the final weaving on a power loom. The 1885 *Reports of the Water-power of the United States* lists several hundred types of manufacturers, including cotton, woolen, fire arms, furniture,

6. Ibid., 39.
7. Ibid., tables 214, 215, and 216.

paper, cooperage (barrels and casks), shoddy (a type of inferior wool), tools, wire, spectacles and eye glasses, flour and grist, and even silk.[8]

These mills were grouped in close proximity to streams because of the specifics of their traditional waterpower technology. The simplest and earliest water wheels sat in the water flow and let the force of the current turn the wheel. Fluctuations in flow during spring floods and late summer droughts limited the consistency of power. A far more efficient force could be generated if the water dropped into buckets or troughs attached to the wheel and the weight of the water turned the wheel instead of the current. The most prevalent wheel in southern New England was the breast wheel, where the water came in midway, or breast high, on the backside of the wheel, dropped in buckets or troughs, and discharged in the same direction as the turn of the wheel. The highly efficient and technologically advanced water turbine was developed mid-nineteenth century. With turbines the water dropped vertically through a tube, generating power at an astounding 80 percent efficiency. Total horsepower ranged from under one hundred at individual mills to over a thousand horsepower at multimill complexes such as those at Woonsocket and Pawtucket.

The entire site—mill, pond, and waterworks—was called the "mill seat." The waterwheel was only a small part of the engineering necessary to deliver power. A dam was required both to form a reservoir or millpond that ensured a constant supply of water throughout the seasons and to increase the distance the water dropped. A millrace or flume would direct the water from the pond to the wheel. These flumes eventually became great gated stone canals that diverted water to several turbines located beneath or inside the mill in a protected space to avoid freezing in the cold New England winters. Elaborate gates regulated the flow in these channels and hence the speed of the waterwheel or turbine.

The wheel mechanism stood below the mill. Because power was transferred directly upward through metal gears to belts and pulleys, the mills were compact tall structures, often rising four or five stories above the power source. A detailed section through the Slater Mill in Providence shows its position above the turbine immersed in the water below. The power transfer through belts and pulleys was much shorter vertically through multiple floors rather than horizontally through long single-story buildings. Often the flume and wheel machinery were integrated into the building's massive stone foundations. Mill buildings blend into the landscape because the structures had to be integrated closely with the stream beneath. Water flows right through the structures and gives the sites their characteristically romantic setting. Accompanied by a reflecting millpond, with flumes constructed of native stone and water rushing beneath the

8. Ibid., tables 214 and 215.

buildings, mill sites have always had an idyllic picturesque quality. Even as ruins, they retain this quality, perhaps made even more romantic as leafy forests and rampant vines dissolve their ruins into settings of shadows. The sound of water from a millpond rushing over a dam and gushing through a dilapidated stone building imbues these sites with a tragic sense of the passage of time. The familiar composition of remote buildings reflected in a millpond overhung with brilliant orange autumn leaves is the quintessential rural New England vision of past industriousness.

Mills required durable construction materials of heavy stone foundations, brick exterior walls, thick timber beams, and columns with heavy plank flooring because the textile machinery was both heavy and constantly vibrating. The entire structure acted as a composite frame with the wooden beams bracing the brick walls and the tongue-and-groove plank flooring acting as a diaphragm holding everything together horizontally.

The design of these early mills was typical throughout southern New England. They were well-proportioned tall and narrow buildings two to

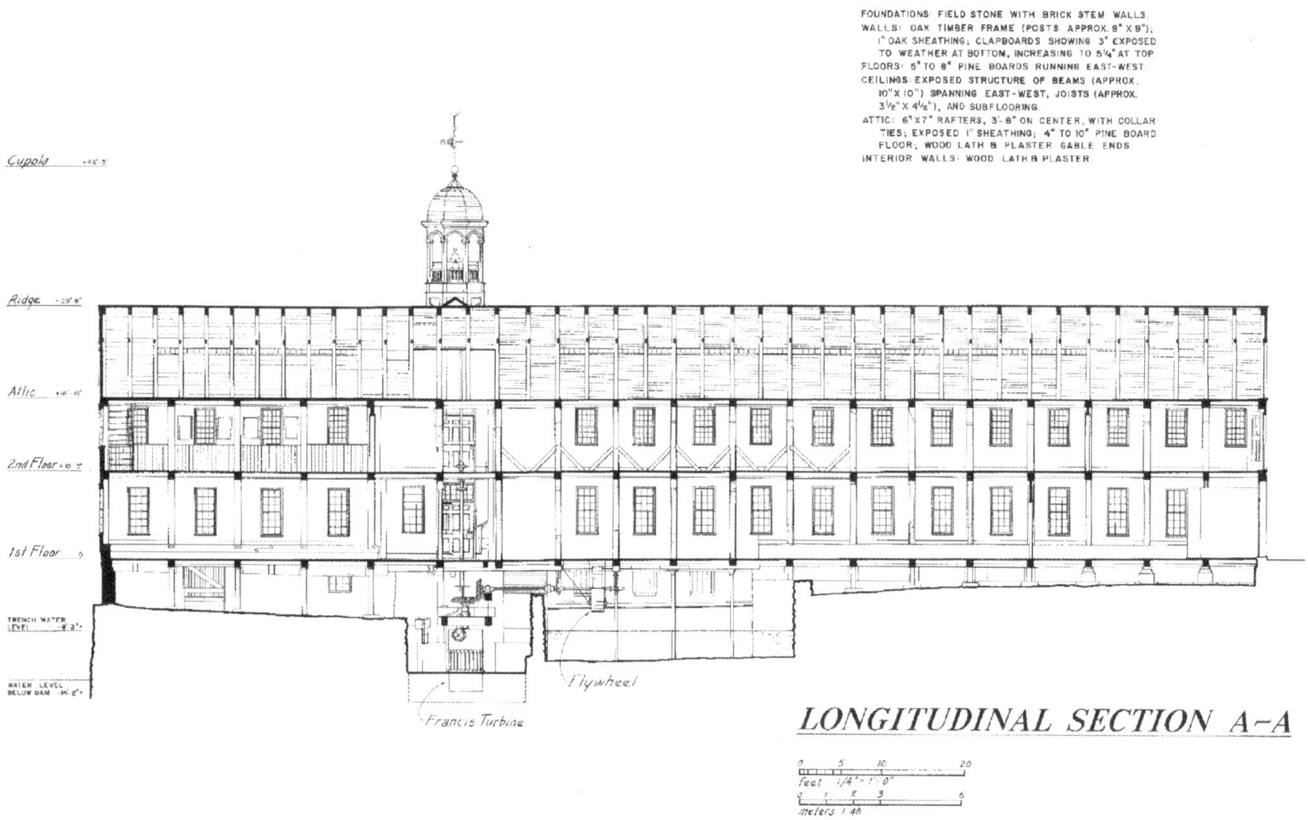

Longitudinal section through the Slater Mill, Pawtucket, Rhode Island

Crown and Central Mill, North Uxbridge, Massachusetts, 1967

three bays wide with high floor-to-floor heights to allow the operations of pulleys and belts above the workers and machinery. The exterior walls were heavily fenestrated for natural light. Steeply pitched roofs often had continuous attic dormers that gave a distinctive silhouette. Many early shingled mills had beautifully proportioned towers capped by finely detailed cupolas that gave them a decidedly domestic scale, in contrast to later brick or stone mills of northern New England in the Merrimack River Valley. In the second half of the nineteenth century, heavy timber floors and masonry exterior bearing walls continued to be used, even as the mills grew to enormous size. With the increase in size, the tower and roof designs reflected the continuing eclecticism of late-nineteenth-century American architecture.

A drawing by S. B. Cushing captures the composition of an earlier mill village. In 1840, Cushing surveyed the Factory Village of the Georgia Cotton Manufacturing Company located on the Woonasquatucket River that drains south through Smithfield Township and Providence into Providence Harbor. The present-day town of Georgiaville and the Georgiaville Mill Pond are located where the Georgia Cotton Manufacturing Company once stood. The mill took its waterpower from the millpond through a trench that the map indicates was relocated when the pond's water level was raised. The water went through the mill building and then out another trench or tailrace back into the Woonasquatucket River.

The village has two orderly rows of numbered houses similar in size and shape. Each row faces a street and has a vegetable garden and a barn for animals. These accommodations housed working families whose members performed all tasks in the mill, as well as growing crops and hay. As these villages were placed on available falls remote from existing town centers, it was difficult for mill owners to attract adequate labor for the mills without furnishing housing. Because of its dark and exploitative history in England, factory work in America had an undesirable reputation. Labor issues would resurface later in the century in large company towns such as Lowell, Lawrence, and Fall River, Massachusetts. In the early years of manufacturing

Map of the factory villages belonging to the Georgia Cotton Manufacturing Company, Smithfield, Rhode Island, 1840; ink on paper

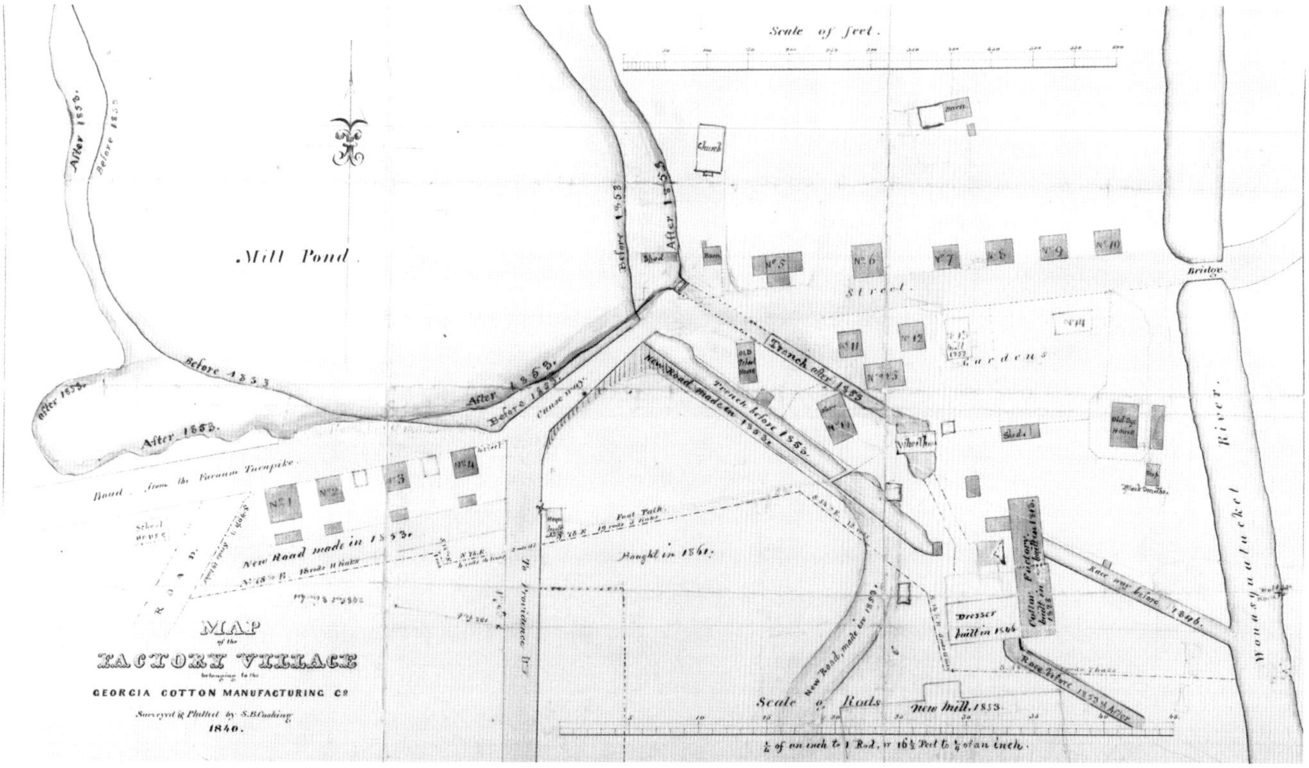

in Rhode Island, however, the scale of operations of family-owned mills was smaller. As children provided a majority of the labor force, large families were desirable, with the father perhaps working the fields, the mother maintaining the home, and the four or five children from age six or seven to teens working in the mill. Late-nineteenth-century struggles over child labor reinforces our incredulity at these appalling arrangements. Often, however, work in a local mill saved a family dependent upon the unproductive farmland of New England. The Factory Village of the Georgia Cotton Manufacturing Company was obviously self-contained and remote from neighboring Providence. Besides the housing, the sketch shows open agricultural fields, an abandoned and a replacement schoolhouse, a store, and assorted sheds and outbuildings. Most importantly, there is a church, an essential part of any New England community. The mill had an old dye house for coloring fabric or yarn, a building labeled "dresser" for dressing or smoothing the cloth, and, at the bottom of the sketch, a considerably larger new mill building.

A delightful hand sketch of Danielson, Connecticut, done by John Warner Barber in 1835, captures this picturesque quality of the idealized Yankee mill village that still captivates our imaginations. The Danielson Cotton Mill is the tall building in the middle with a tower surmounted by a weather vane. The mill tower was an essential marker of the community not unlike the church steeple. All too soon, however, its enforcing clock that measured mill time would become an unwanted symbol of oppression. A bridge over the Quinebaug River provides the approach to the mill between other industrial buildings and housing. Above the drawing are two partial sketches that illustrate the characteristic domestic scaled clerestory roof structure of these early-nineteenth-century New England mills.

Danielson benefited by being at the crossroads of the overland route between the two state capitals of Hartford and Providence. Today I-395 passes just east of Danielson's center with an exit that runs through a confusing off-ramp commercial strip like Exit 2 less than twenty miles to the north at Webster. I-395 parallels three earlier desire lines down the Thames River Valley: the desire of water to seek a new course to the sea; the commitment of Route 12 to connect the mill sites along the river; and the alignment of the railroad as it sought out freight opportunities; yet I-395 does little to acknowledge these corresponding tracings in the same landscape. Because the interstate is a bypass, its right-of-way avoids all the towns and villages by shifting either east or west away from their connecting infrastructure of river, road, and tracks. I-395 is a shortcut to somewhere else, and only for a moment does its alignment parallel the rich regional histories of industrial New England.

Sketch of west view of Danielson, Connecticut, 1835; ink on paper

Flumes, Falls, and Fleams

As with so many obsolete industries, the language and archaic terms for the components of a water-powered mill have slipped from usage and memory. The alliteration of three forgotten terms, flume, fall, and fleam, from mill construction, provided the title for this section. The "flume" was a canal, also called the headrace, usually lined with cut granite, for diverting water from a stream to the mill waterwheel. The tailrace returned the water to the stream on the other side of the mill. The "fall" measured the action or weight of water in the wheel buckets or turbine that forced the mechanism to turn. The "fleam" was the final passageway, often a very large closed pipe, that pressurized the water just before it hit the turbine blades.

Sketches and paintings of gristmills and intimate villages re-create nostalgic images of late-eighteenth-century New England, but they capture a moment that lingered briefly. By the early decades of the nineteenth century, industrial expansion overtook this region. Mills became larger, and towns and cities grew more dense. The great cities of Lowell and Lawrence, Massachusetts, eclipsed the smaller mill towns of southern New England. The 1885 *Reports of the Water-power of the United States* documents this change in comprehensive detail. This section of the chapter discusses the growth and density of textile mills in southern New England between the 1840s and 1900. The comparison of two maps, the 1838 Newell Nelson map of Cumberland Township in Rhode Island and the 1870 *Beers*

Atlas of Rhode Island, gives an accurate picture of the number and development of mill villages and towns across the region. Each mill village or town recorded on these two maps was a highly engineered site that joined waterpower, textile production, and bulk transportation. Several of these sites expanded into factory cities of incredible complexity, such as Woonsocket and Pawtucket. The expansion of the textile industry gave southern New England a finely textured landscape of mills, villages, and towns whose diminished presence still rewards exploration and discovery.

After the comparison of these two maps, this chapter then examines specific mill towns and several abandoned mill sites using both historic documents and field research. The field investigations involved hiking through the woods of southern New England searching for deserted foundations and rusted flume gates to reconstruct graphically the original mill complexes. Often tranquil ponds and overgrown dams in unanticipated locations provided the only remaining clues. The barely discernible paths of abandoned railroad rights-of-way occasionally led to sites far from existing towns, but once important enough to warrant their own freight siding. These trails are beautiful leafy tunnels whose smaller maple and birch saplings contrast with the surrounding white pine or oak forests. Along with the newer forest growth, the rotted timber ties beneath one's feet provide the camouflaged evidence of the former iron rails.

Two of the largest mills discussed are in Connecticut on the Shetucket and French Rivers: one at Taftsville, and one at North Grosvenor Dale. Further upstream on the French River, a series of connected mill sites just above Webster, Massachusetts, between Oxford and North Oxford, illustrates the close coupling necessary between the structures and the local topography. A mill in Blackstone, Massachusetts, shows the complexity of a typical mill seat. For orientation, all these places can be found on the 1935 Texaco road map included at the start of this chapter. Together with hundreds of other sites, these nineteenth-century representative examples of the growth of southern New England's textile industries serve as perfect illustrations of cultural emergence. They all responded simultaneously and similarly to a defined regional geology and topography in their placement and utilization of waterpower.

Cumberland Township sits in the upper northeast corner of Rhode Island, tucked against the Massachusetts boundary. The Blackstone River defines Cumberland's western border as it flows south from Worcester, Massachusetts, through Pawtucket, Rhode Island, and into the Seekonk River and Narragansett Bay. The 1838 map prepared by Newell Nelson locates all the corn, saw-, and cotton mills throughout Cumberland. At the top and bottom of the map, nine miles apart, are the two most important mill and urban complexes, Woonsocket Falls and Valley Falls, today Woonsocket and Pawtucket, respectively. Woonsocket Falls is at the top left of the map and in the larger-scale inset. The thick line along the Blackstone River on Nelson's map is the Blackstone Canal, opened in 1828 to provide transportation of bulk goods between Worcester, Massachusetts, and the port of Providence, Rhode Island. The black hatch marks represent locks as the canal paralleled the fall of the river itself. Two mill villages are noted on the Blackstone River, Man Ville (*sic*) and Albion. Both villages exist today without their mills. A flume from a dam on the Blackstone powered Mannville's cotton and corn mills. Two orderly rows of worker housing sit across the river. The last house in the row is labeled Arlcu Mann, the mill owner and the town's namesake. Behind his dwelling is a drawing of a meetinghouse and schoolhouse that served this small community.

Albion is about a mile and a half further down river, partially obscured by a blotch on the original map. A large dam across the Blackstone provided enough head to power a corn mill and three cotton mills. Across the Blackstone Canal are two formal rows of dwellings and a schoolhouse. The Blackstone Canal actually used the level slack water impounded behind the dam instead of running water through a separate channel. The canal shifted back and forth from constructed locks and impoundments to the river itself.

On the far right side of Nelson's map, a tributary of the Blackstone River named Abott Run drains the eastern part of Cumberland Township. It flows into Rhode Island from Massachusetts in a question mark–shaped sweep before turning back into southern Rhode Island and joining the Blackstone River just before it empties into the Seekonk River and Narragansett Bay. Five mill complexes are located along Abott Run on the Nelson map. Most of their ponds now lie beneath the waters of the twentieth-century Diamond Hill and Pawtucket Reservoirs. There is still a small town on the Rhode Island–Massachusetts border called Abott Run. Much of this settlement pattern has now disappeared, but it was important enough in the nineteenth century to be served by its own railroad, the Rhode Island & Massachusetts line, which connected Valley Falls and Arnold Mills to Boston.

Thirty-two years later the second map, a page from *Beer's Atlas of Rhode Island* (1870), shows the changes in Cumberland Township. The mill villages along the Blackstone River have grown in both size and number. Woonsocket has separated to become its own township. Along the Blackstone River, other mill complexes have developed. Importantly, the Providence and Worcester Railroad parallels the river to offer more reliable transportation than the canal. Trains take raw cotton to the mills

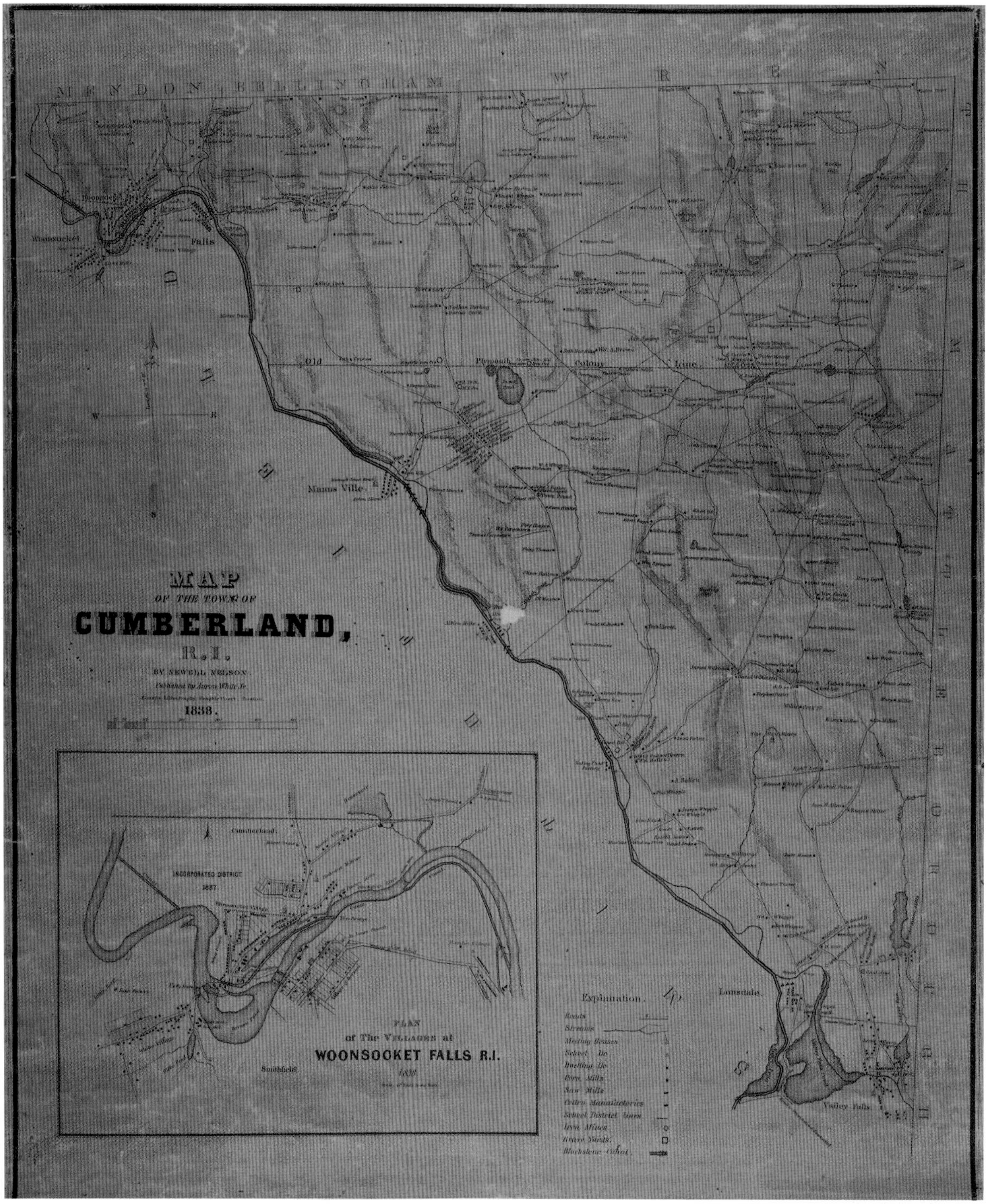

Map of Cumberland Township, Rhode Island, 1838; ink on paper

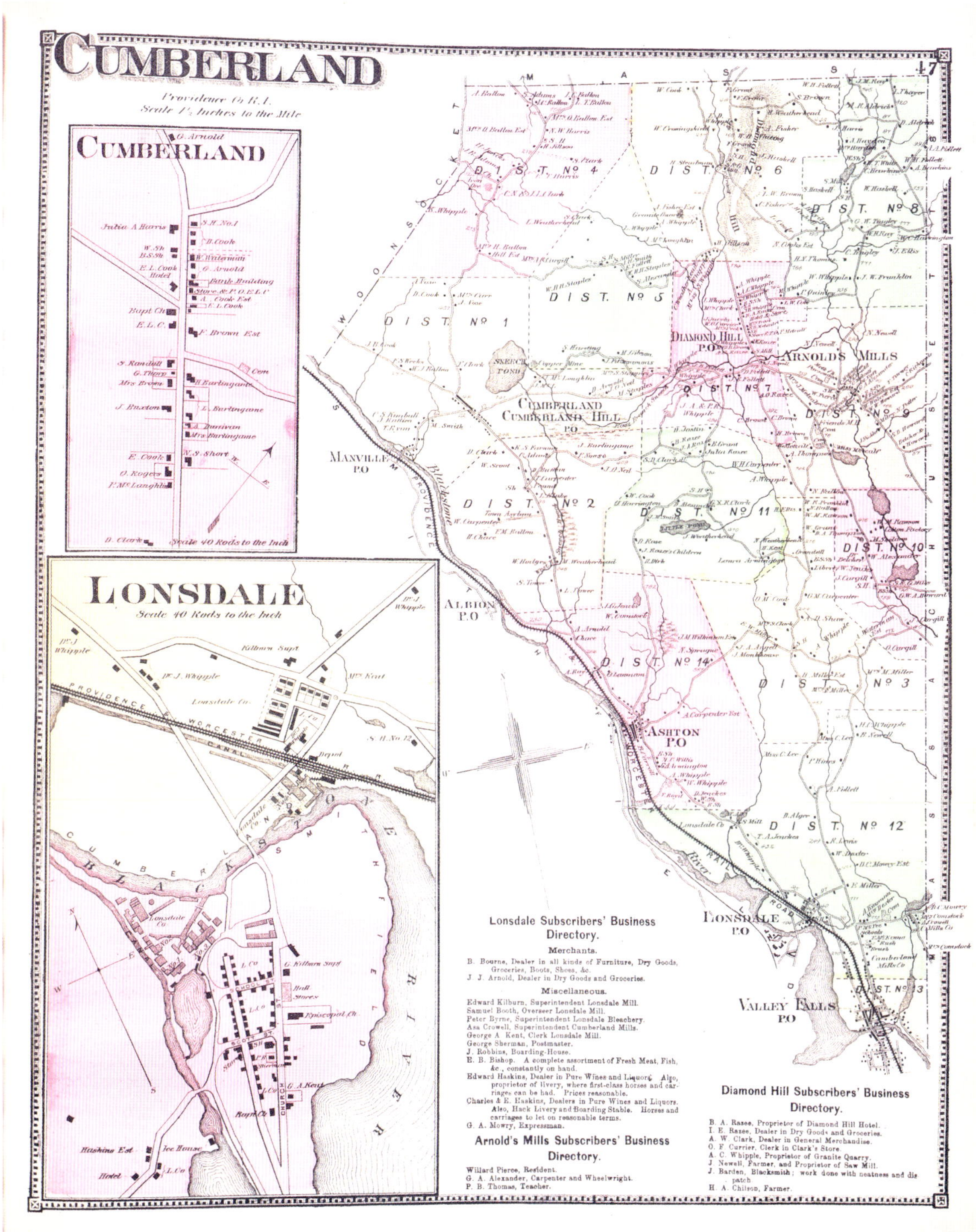

Map of Cumberland Township, 1870

and finished products from the mills to waiting ships in Providence Harbor. Mannville and Albion have prospered by their rail connections, and a new mill complex has appeared at Ashton. Lonsdale and Valley Falls have grown considerably. Diamond Hill and Arnold Mills along the Abott Run watershed have developed in the east in districts labeled 7, 9, and 10. Settlements surround all mill seats.

Maps from other pages in *Beer's Atlas* provide useful comparisons of representative mill seats along the Blackstone and Pawtuxet Rivers in Rhode Island. Detailed plans of individual villages show specific buildings and mill structures. Albion and Mannville include more elaborate dams, flumes, and raceways and communities growing around the mills. Georgiaville, the site we saw in the sketch earlier in the chapter, has become a town with many roads and houses. Several new mill communities have appeared along the Blackstone River: Ashton has two rows of brick worker housing across the railroad tracks by the mill. Mill, tracks and housing still exist today.

Many other small towns have grown into substantial mill seats across the Blackstone and Pawtuxet River watersheds. Blackstone, Massachusetts, and its neighbor Waterford, Rhode Island, have multiple mill complexes that use extensive canals off the Blackstone River. Blackstone has a tiny urban grid next to its mill waiting for worker housing expansion. Slatersville, another entire town owned by the energetic Samuel Slater, has three mills. One of these mills still exists, a beautiful empty stone building slowly collapsing into weed-filled parking lots. It is an exceptionally handsome cut granite structure with well-proportioned double-hung windows. Missing glass panes and broken muntins gape open in random grids.

A full-page map of the Pawtuxet River towns of River Point, Clyde, Lippitt, and Phenix shows the incredible density of mills within a single watershed as they all competed for water rights. The distance on the map from River Point to Harris is less than a mile. The stone mill and worker housing at Arctic, located at the bottom of the drawing, still face each other across an open space of grass. The "crow's feet" of three radiating paths gathered the workers each morning from the tiny street grid of houses. Today, the partially empty mill no longer provides employment, yet the houses are fully occupied along tree-shaded streets. Like the Slater Mill, the Arctic Mill is a solid granite building with thick lintels and finely fitted stones. This type of "mill construction," masonry walls tied structurally to an interior of heavy timber frame and thick plank floors, was found throughout New England. When the exterior walls were dressed granite blocks, the flat building elevations, with evenly sized and spaced wood-framed windows, created a beautiful warm texture.

Slater Mill, Slatersville, Rhode Island

A reconstructed topographic drawing of the North and South branches of the Pawtuxet River situates these same mill sites within the rolling hills of southern Rhode Island. The drawing shows the sharp turns and twists of both rivers as they sought to accommodate their flow within the typical glaciated landscape. The placements of these Pawtuxet River mills illustrate the tight connection between mills, ponds, and topography; it graphically explains how so many mills could gather in close proximity on a single watercourse.

Other early maps of Rhode Island offer similar perspectives on the density of mill towns across this region. Railroad lines and stations increased as the railroads sought out additional freight opportunities. As expected, the railroads served the major mills, and consequently the tracks follow the streams. Tracks of the Providence and Worcester Railroad paralleled the Blackstone River north from Providence to Worcester. Berkeley, Ashton, Albion, and Mannville all had stations as well as freight depots. The

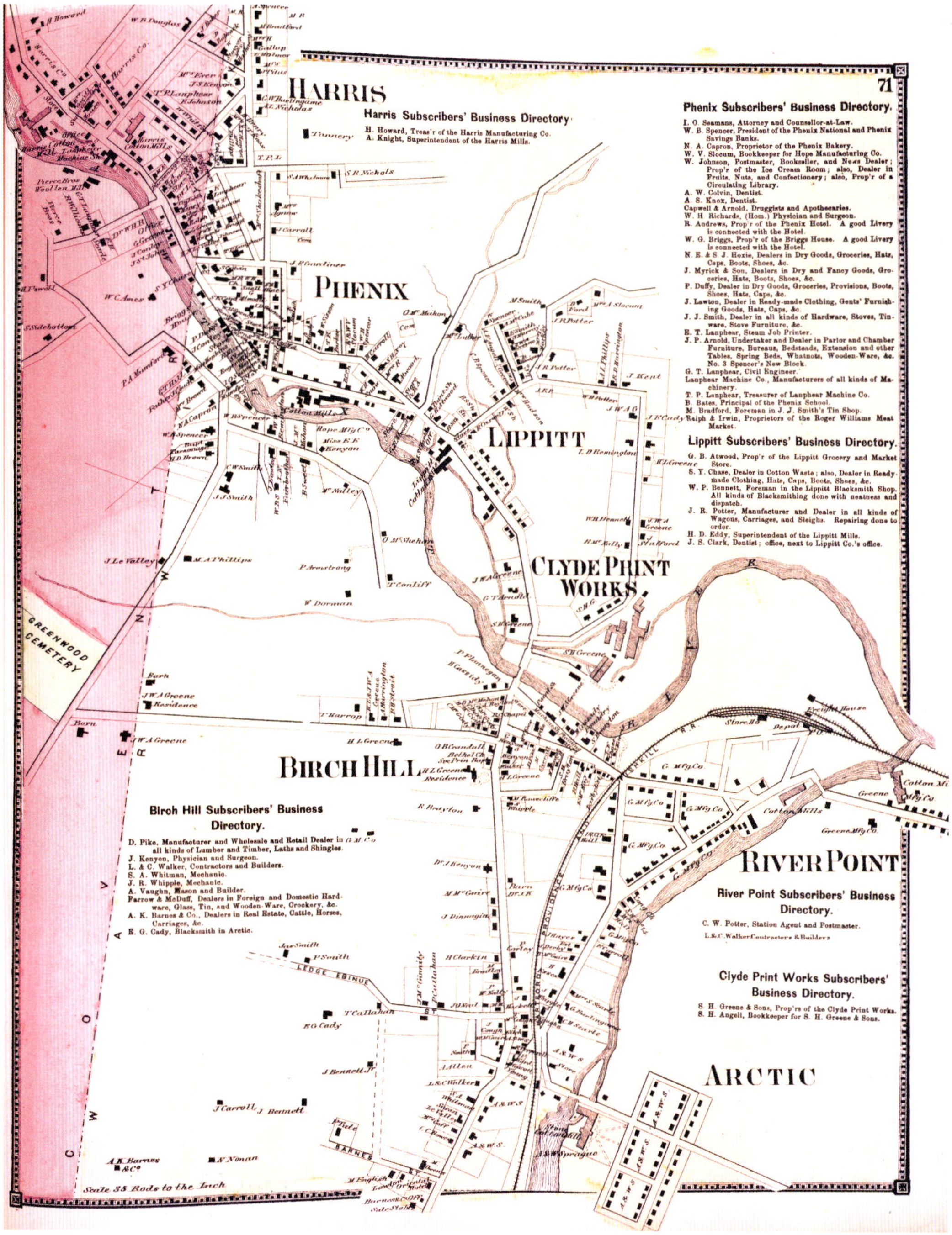

Maps of Arctic, River Point, Birch Hill, Clyde Print Works, Lippitt, Phenix, and Harris Mills, Rhode Island, 1870

Map of mills on the Pawtuxet River watershed, Rhode Island *(opposite)*

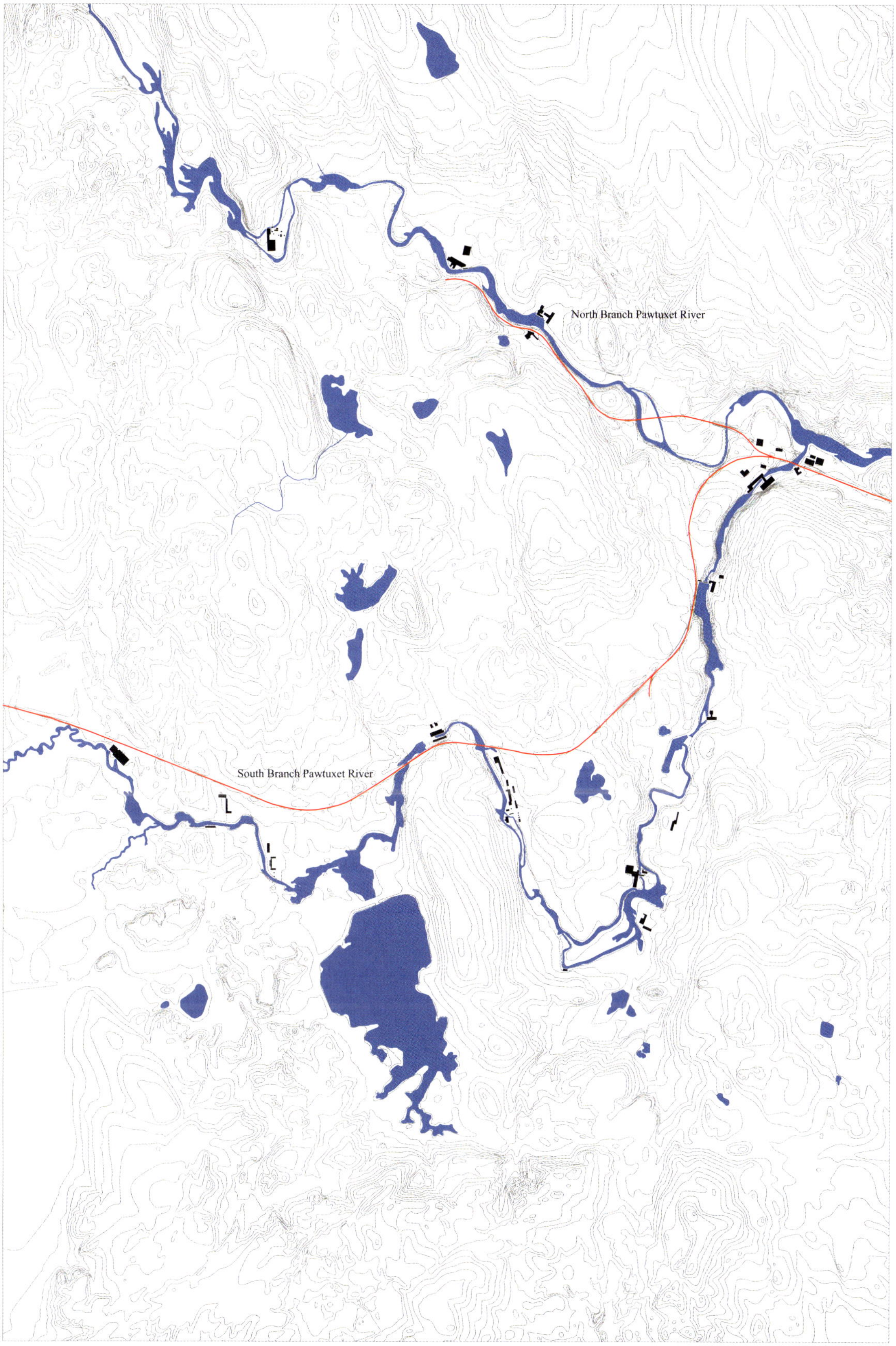
North Branch Pawtuxet River
South Branch Pawtuxet River

Providence and Springfield line followed the Woonasquatuck River northwest through Georgiaville, Slatersville, and other mill towns on its way to Springfield, Massachusetts. The Hartford, Providence, and Bristol tracks paralleled the Pawtuxet River by River Point and Arctic before connecting with the New York and New England line. The New York and New England Railroad traveled up the Thames River watershed through Putnam on the French River along an alignment not very different than I-395 today. Four parallel layers in the landscape have emerged from a single initial response to water power: the watersheds with the engineered dams and millponds, the canals along the rivers, the mills with their surrounding towns, and the railroads with their need for freight and depots. All four systems converged on the ports of Providence and Norwich. Of these layers, only the watersheds remain. The canals exist only in fragments under the dark shadows of bent birches. The mills have closed, and many have been demolished; the tracks have long ago been removed, leaving abandoned rights-of-way hidden beneath fallen leaves and new forest growth, with the occasional granite bridge abutment reflected in a serene river. The discarded mills leave blanks in the middle of towns, desolate spaces whose structures once hummed with belts and pulleys and the noise of hundreds of revolving spindles.

To fully convey the massive size and monumentality of these late-nineteenth-century southern New England mills, this chapter examines the mills at Taftsville and New Grosvenor Dale on the Shetucket and French Rivers, respectively, in eastern Connecticut. A remarkable photograph from the Library of Congress shows the imposing five-story Ponemah Weaving Mill at Taftville sitting in majestic isolation about four miles north of Norwich at the junction of the Shetucket and Quinebaug Rivers. Constructed in 1871 by Edward P. Taft, the mill is over nine hundred feet long—a great leap from the earlier domestically scaled shingled structures with wooden water wheels. The Ponemah Mill is built in an eclectic style with a continuous Mansard attic story, beautiful brick corbeling, and two magnificent bell and stair towers. With its ornate towers rising above the trees, such flamboyant architecture seems incongruous in the rolling topography of rural Connecticut. The scale and size of these late-nineteenth-century masonry structures far eclipsed earlier wood mills of this region and have more in common with the great mill cities of Lowell and Lawrence in the Merrimack Valley than the domestic scale of early Rhode Island mills.

The dramatic and remote mill village of North Grosvenor Dale sits thirty miles upstream on the French River just south of Webster. Like the Ponemah Mill, the mill at North Grosvenor Dale typifies many mill settlements built

Ponemah Weaving Mill, Main Street, Taftville, Connecticut

in the late nineteenth century in southern New England: it is a very large brick structure surrounded by units of associated worker housing. In spite of its fine architectural details, the mill's brooding immensity seems out of place so far from a significant town or city. Its placement takes full advantage of an imposing waterpower site. A long millpond stretches upstream in a narrow valley toward Webster. The mill's isolation reminds us that the necessary coupling of these mill seats with specific geological and topographical constraints determined their location. Until recently, a companion mill stood less than a mile downstream at Grosvenor Dale. Sadly, it was demolished during the writing of this book, leaving a pile of heavy timber beams broken like matchsticks and two rows of worker dwellings facing the highway. The open windows and leaky roofs of empty mills allow the rain and snow to penetrate; the plank floors trap moisture in the joint above the beams that encourages the growth of wood-destroying fungi; eventually the floors collapse. The oil-soaked floors are fire hazards that easily ignite, so in the interest of public safety, the mills are demolished.

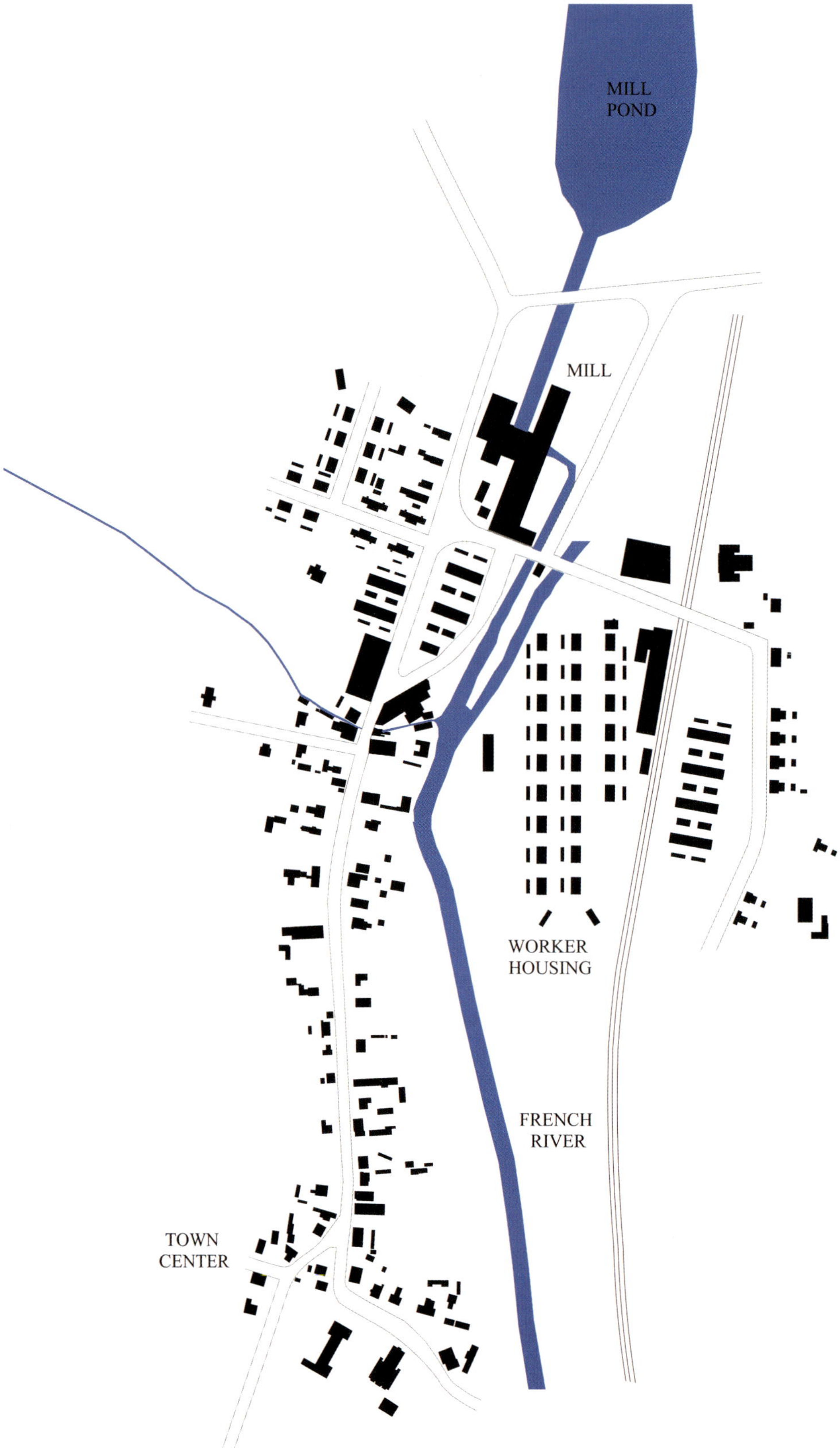

Drawing of the village of North Grosvenor Dale, Connecticut

The mill complex at North Grosvenor Dale is extensive, with many additions made well into the twentieth century. The original nineteenth-century brick structure with its beautiful Victorian towers and tall arched windows is over six hundred feet long. A granite raceway runs beneath the building before rejoining the French River downstream. Two lovely tree-lined streets of worker houses and several large tenement buildings surround the mill. Many of these wonderfully scaled two-family houses have been renovated as affordable housing and are now fully occupied. North Grosvenor is one of the best-preserved late-nineteenth-century mill villages in southern New England. A Main Street leads past the mill to a town center with a post office and several stores. Schools, churches, and other more substantial individual houses are further along Main Street. It is an evocative composition, a marker in the landscape of a diminished industry and vanished way of life. Sadly, the mill may soon follow the fate of its neighbor downstream; its upper-story windows are broken, its roof slates are missing, and its attic spaces are open to bats, owls, and the harsh New England weather.

A series of mill seats along a single watercourse illustrates the organic and sequential organization of mills and ponds unique to this part of New England. Traveling north, or upstream, from the North Grosvenor Dale millpond on the French River as it crosses into Massachusetts, passing the towns of Webster and Oxford, one comes to the former Narragansett Mill Company. This is the first of a group of abandoned mills strung like beads along a one-mile section of the French River. Many of these mills are gone; their sites converted into other uses, and their flumes and headraces eroded into tree-covered mounds. Several 1910 and 1911 Sanborn Fire Insurance map sheets, contemporary aerial photographs, and topographic maps provided the sources for reconstructing these mill seats, for many of the ponds have settled back into the ecology of the river, their banks overhung with maples and their dams camouflaged by soft-green alders. Often the granite headraces or tailraces are leaf-filled depressions in the woods with rusted water gates. The original purpose of a millpond recedes into memory, yet the still water remains as a beautiful element in the local landscape. Many New England towns have large ponds named "the Mill Pond," but few people remember the actual working mill or the pond's purpose as a reservoir for waterpower.

The Narragansett Worsted Company had two mills on the French River that made worsted, a smooth, closely woven fabric used for tailored garments that is known today as gabardine. Water came from a large pond that no longer exists, fed through mill number one, dropped into a smaller pond where it then powered mill number two before returning back to the

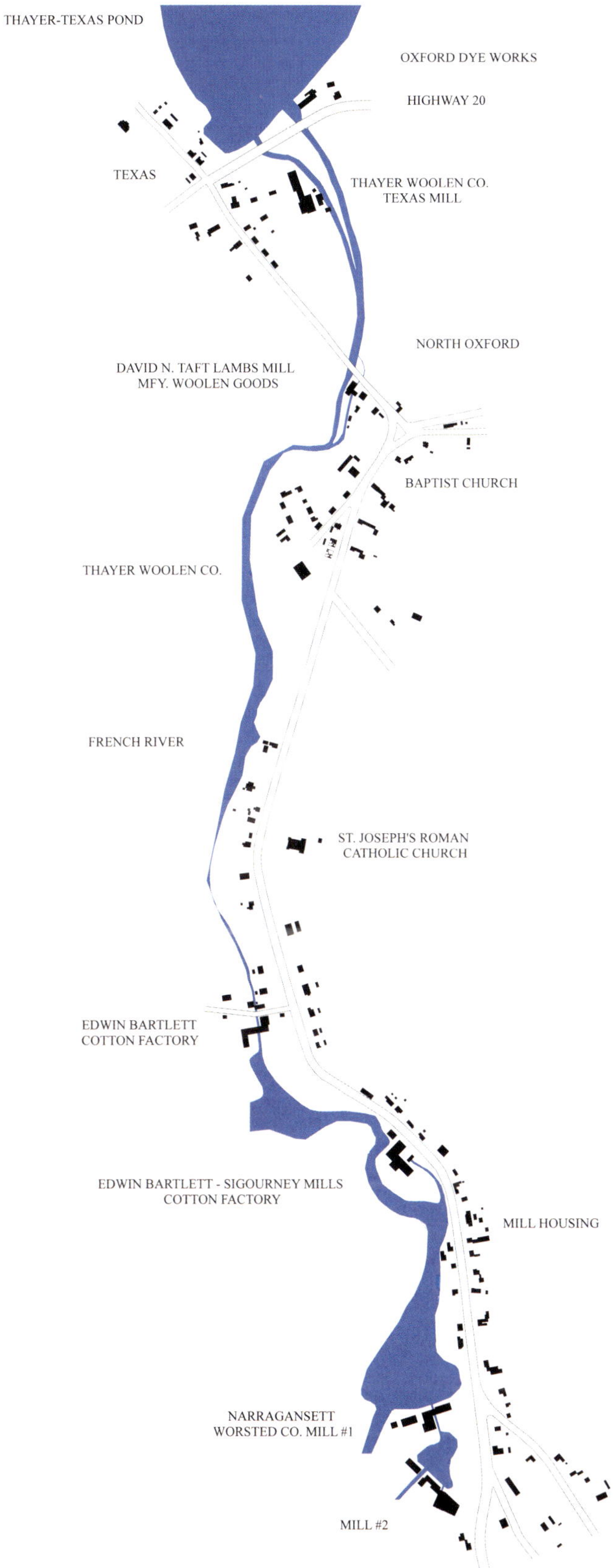

Reconstruction of the mills and worker housing along the French River south of North Oxford, Massachusetts. The distance from top to bottom of this drawing is less than a mile. *(left)*

Worker housing, North Grosvenor Dale, Connecticut *(opposite, top)*

North Grosvenor Dale Mill elevation *(opposite, bottom left)*

Abandoned flume gate, Greenville, Massachusetts *(opposite, bottom right)*

French River through a tailrace channel. By 1911 these two complexes had auxiliary steam power.

The water from the large pond backed up several hundred yards, almost to the next mill, the Edwin Barlett-Sigourney Mills and Cotton Factory. This mill took water from another vanished pond that provided flow through a covered headrace and open tailrace. Main Street parallels the bends in the French River and was lined with dwellings and tenements for workers.

The tiny hamlet of North Oxford lies less than a half mile upstream from the Bartlett Mill and supported two mills. The first mill, the Thayer Woolen Company, took its power from a small brook that still flows into the French River. The mill and several of the two-family worker houses remain arranged in a wonderful small quadrangle. A Baptist Church and the David N. Taft Lambs Mill Mfy (*sic*) Woolen Goods complete the hamlet of North Oxford.

After North Main Street branches west over the French River, it continues to another crossroads town incongruously named Texas. A large pond still exists north of the important east–west Highway 20. On contemporary maps it is labeled Texas Pond, but on late-nineteenth-century maps it is called Thayer Pond. A detailed look at a 1911 Sanborn map resolved the confusion as the mill is labeled the Thayer Woolen Company Texas Mill. Just below the earthen dam that both holds back Texas Pond and provides a causeway for Highway 20 is a small mill, the Oxford Dye Works noted as closed in 1911, a harbinger of the future for the other mills.

All these mills had been retrofitted with steam power by 1911. In 1870, New England textile mills used 75 percent horsepower from water and 25 percent from steam; by 1900 the ratio had reversed, with 33 percent water and 67 percent steam.[9] Millponds could be enlarged for additional storage, mill seats could be repaired, tailraces could be deepened, but none of these could compensate for the seasonal flow of many of these streams. So one after another, mills switched to reliable steam power even though they remained trapped in their original locations, in buildings designed specifically for waterpower.

Mill seats with their division of parts and constituent elements were highly engineered sites. Dams were sturdily constructed to withstand flooding, for if the dam gave way, usually the mill quickly followed. Gates, diverters, strainers, and valves allowed adjustments in flow to conserve water in the dry summers and to lessen the impact of heavier pressures in the winter-spring floods. The gears and power take-offs from the waterwheels had to function smoothly to reduce vibration damage to the structure. As the mills became larger and more complex, the engineering also became more sophisticated. A beautifully rendered 1903 Sanborn Fire Insurance

9. Hunter, *History of Industrial Power,* 494.

map of Blackstone, Massachusetts, illustrates the complexity of this inventive coupling to topography and watercourses. At the town of Blackstone, the Blackstone River makes a series of sharp turns and precipitous drops as it searches for a channel through the hard rocks of the fall line. The Blackstone Manufacturing Company's cotton mill sat immediately on the riverbank, high above the water level. Water for its power was diverted upstream around a tight twist in a cut off from the main river that was, and still is, backed up behind a dam. First the water was impounded in a large pond, and then it was distributed through flumes into four fleams into the mill's cavernous basement. From the fleams, the water dropped forty feet through vertical turbines before being discharged thunderously back into the river. Gates in small buildings allocated the water to different turbines depending upon the power requirements of the machinery in the mill. The mill structure acted like a gigantic dam five hundred feet long and seven stories high. Yellow on a Sanborn map indicates wood frame structures, and blue-gray indicates stone, so as the map indicates, the Blackstone Mfg Co Cotton Mill was an impressive granite structure anchored into the steep bank of the river. Nothing remains of the mill complex except the collecting ponds. A new flood-control structure sits where the former mill anchored the headraces and tailraces. The vacant rights-of-way of the railroad and the old Mendon Road still exist as tree-lined reminders of this mill's original placement.

The immense size and complexity of the Blackstone Mill illustrates the ability of nineteenth-century engineers to derive maximum waterpower from a single source. A constant water supply was vitally important for year-round manufacturing, so a large impoundment was necessary. The ponds and dams required extensive earth works as well as sophisticated calculations of seasonal flow and precipitation. Gates, underground pipes, tunnels, and flumes and fleams all concentrated the water pressure into efficient turbines. The mills themselves had to be substantial structures to withstand the constant vibration and force of the machinery. As these many sites were dismantled and abandoned, the profligate waste of physical resources in buildings, timber, site work, and infrastructure is impossible to calculate. In the end, the water-powered textile industry could neither adapt nor move these physical components, so the mills closed and the towns and cities slowly died.

The study of mill seats in southern Massachusetts raises a question about regionalism generally. One characteristic of regionalism is the tight coupling between a cultural system, of which the southern New England water-powered textile industry is a prime example, and its natural environment. The closer the fit between natural and man-made, the more

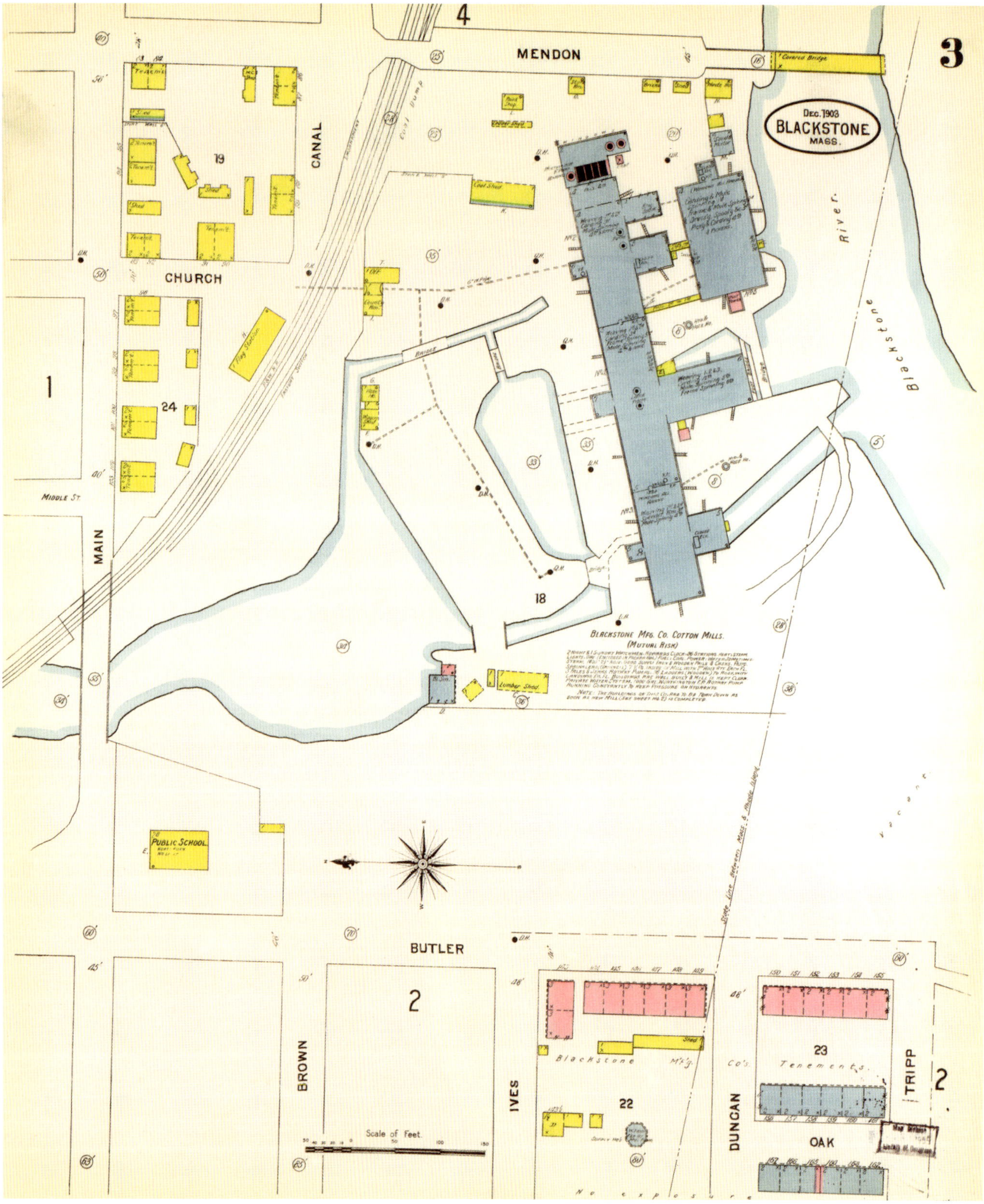
4
MENDON
3
Covered Bridge
Dec. 1903
BLACKSTONE
MASS.
CANAL
19
CHURCH
Coal Shed
Flag Station
1
24
MIDDLE ST.
MAIN
River
Blackstone
18
BLACKSTONE MFG. CO. COTTON MILLS.
(MUTUAL RISK)
Lumber Shed
PUBLIC SCHOOL
BUTLER
2
BROWN
IVES
DUNCAN
TRIPP
2
Blackstone Mf'g. Co's. Tenements.
22
23
OAK
Scale of Feet.

appropriate and timeless appears a region's history. In fact, regionalism takes much of its definition from this integration of social and natural processes. A change in even a small component of the cultural associations or the physical environment risks tragic consequences for both. Regional cultures that depend upon the use or exploitation of a single resource are always susceptible to a complete collapse, as happened with the textile industry. When the resource is place specific because of topography or geology, the industry dependent upon its use or extraction is particularly precarious. The collapse of the Appalachian coal industry and the ruin of the North Atlantic fisheries are two stark contemporary examples. Chapter 6 explores another regional collapse, copper mining, in the mountains of Arizona.

This coupling with the earth that defines much of regionalism contrasts with the apparent lack of specificity of the interstate highway off-ramp towns. Off-ramp towns are not site specific and require little adaptive modifications. Off-ramp towns require no extensive earth moving beyond a level site, nor do they need contiguity with any physical features besides the road and its constant flow of traffic. The ubiquity of the settlements spawned by the interstates would seem to ensure their survival. The obvious risk, however, for the entire highway system is its total dependence on a single resource—oil. Already as this book is being written, the Highway Trust Fund, the tax on gasoline discussed in chapter 2, is in decline. As the worldwide demand for oil increases, its price goes up, fewer Americas can afford to drive, and gasoline tax revenue goes down.

The exodus of the textile industry to the South because of its cheaper labor also left behind another residue in New England besides empty mills. Because so many of these mills were in rural locations, mill owners built housing to entice families to settle and work in their mills. These houses were within walking distance of the work place and often had associated civic buildings such as schools or churches. Mill owners also provided company stores with the usual problems of inflated prices and wage garnishing. When the mill closed, the housing was sold to private individuals and outlasted the mill structure itself. With today's transportation mobility, people can still live in these relatively remote places and commute to work in nearby cities. The regularity and uniformity of worker housing and its gridded streets has an urban quality that sets them apart. These remnants of neighborhoods remain remarkable for their consistency and fineness of detail. Their durable brick or stone construction is unusual in today's suburban landscapes. Even the nicely scaled clapboard and wood-trimmed former tenements have an evocative beauty. Webster, for example, has streets of the classic New England "triple-decker" houses. A triple-decker contains

Sanborn map of Blackstone, Massachusetts, 1903 ***(opposite)***

three housing units, one on top of the other, with open porches or decks on each level. More than the dark empty mills, these modest dwellings capture the poignancy of the displacement of those who struggled in a dwindling industry.

If one discovers a row of similarly scaled houses while driving though New England today, one can be certain they are the fragmentary remains of an erased mill village. A 1910 Sanborn map provides an example of one of these residential villages in Whitinsville, Massachusetts. The Whitinsville Machine Works still operates within walking distance of this most extensive neighborhood of alphabetized streets. The satisfying domestic scale and persistent repetitive street facades of this and smaller communities remind us that people inhabited this rich and complex industrial culture. Places of dwelling can outlast places of labor, testimony to the obdurate attachment we all have to our home.

Our journey has spanned three watersheds encompassing an area barely fifty miles long. We return to Pawtucket, Rhode Island, where the textile factory system in America started with Samuel Slater's innovative machinery design. Pawtucket, as the village of Central Falls, was settled in 1800 as a small separate mill center before becoming a manufacturing city. The physical complexity of Pawtucket's mills is now familiar: a dam across the Blackstone River at a series of sharp bends and rapids that diverted water through two flumes into water turbines in the basements of multiple mills. Twin gatehouses regulated the water flow through the mills and were arranged in sequence on the open canal. In a detail from a nineteenth-century bird's-eye perspective, the Blackstone River flows from the top horizon down through the city to the bottom of the page. The first mill just below the Mill Street Bridge was the enormous five-story brick Stafford Manufacturing Company that produced cotton thread. This building spanned the dual raceways and connected to an island that anchored the dam. Next came the Central Falls Cotton Mill that by 1900 was vacant and closed. The flume then powered the Central Falls Woolen Company and the Pawtucket Hair Cloth Company, the latter of which faced Central Street just after it crossed the river on the second bridge. Its tall tower fronted onto a wide-open space. Across the river with a separate power source loomed the huge mill of Greene and Daniels, Thread and Cotton Yarn Manufacturer. Central Street, lined with modest shops and various commercial endeavors, turned perpendicular to Mill Street and connected to residential neighborhoods. Boarding houses, wooden dwellings, tenements, and several churches and schools surrounded the mills. It was the typical mill village settlement pattern that was repeated hundreds of times across the region.

Sanborn map of worker housing, Whitinsville, Massachusetts, 1912 ***(opposite)***

DEC. 1910
WHITINSVILLE
MASS.
5
D ST.
C ST.
EAST C ST.
B ST.
A ST.
MAIN
BORDER
SUTTON
ARCADE
104
105
106
107
108
109
110
111
112
113
114
Boarding
Boarding
CAR BARN
Machine Works
Pond
Pond
Scale of Feet.

Today, the canal has been filled in and paved, although the dam still exists. The Stafford Mill no longer seems to connect two islands like a great bridge. Many of the smaller wooden structures are gone, replaced by empty parking lots. The composition is depressingly open with a few beautiful buildings in a field of pavement. Like so many existing mills, these remaining structures are used mainly for bulk storage while waiting for a future of renovation and rehabilitation—or demolition.

The textile industry marked its presence across southern New England with a dense texture of mills and villages. When I first started this chapter, I did not fully realize how incredibly numerous and ubiquitous these mills were. Their remains are everywhere as ruins, empty lots, or great

Detail from a bird's-eye perspective of Pawtucket and Central Falls, Rhode Island, 1877

hulking structures with boarded windows. Sometimes they appear as renovated well-proportioned housing complexes. The solid architectural quality of these mills surprised me. Some are elegantly detailed, and most are finely proportioned buildings whose repetitive elevations of brick and stone weathered well over the last hundred years—even when unused. Their well-lit interiors frame perspectives of seemingly infinite bays of heavy timbered columns and beams. The wood for these beams and columns was harvested from the longleaf pine forests of the American South discussed in the next chapter. Ironically, it was this same southern region that captured the entire textile industry because of its cheaper labor.

Several times in my travels through southern New England, I returned to a mill I had earlier photographed, only to find it destroyed, demolished into piles of rubble, great heaps of dimensioned timber. One hundred and fifty years after cutting, these timbers still smell of pitch and sap so characteristic of southern pine. In one instance, I found just the open flume in a flat site with its round opening for the water turbine filled with a bubbling brook still diverted from the main river. Other times, I would find an isolated row of uniform worker houses but no evidence of the vanished mill. Even more evocative, I would happen upon a town or village center of distinguished buildings and grand residences but no other evidence of their source of wealth. But the clues are always there, punctuating every small stream or creek with old foundations or eroded dams.

Nineteenth-century industrial manufacturing used resources intensively including the most significant resource, human labor. The textile industry of New England was no different. Even though textile mills emerged slowly over a hundred and forty years, their reversal—the collapse and closing of the mills—took less than three decades, from 1890 to 1920. So many people were dislocated that whole cities like Woonsocket and Pawtucket never recovered. The great number of laborers required to run the complicated textile machinery could neither migrate elsewhere or be absorbed into other manufacturing jobs. Like many manufacturing centers in America, poverty and unemployment remain embedded in these mill cities that are sadly resistant to any economic development strategy.

One could travel on I-395 oblivious to the region's industrial history hidden from view in the landscape just beyond the right-of-way. After a quick stop at Exit 2 for gas or a Big Mac, one returns to I-395 South and within an hour leaves behind all evidence of a once vibrant industry. If, however, one ventures that short distance into Webster, one discovers histories beyond imagining that contain lessons and meaning that the unbroken expanse of smooth highways cannot erase.

The complex geological and topographical features of southern New England afforded many potential mill sites. Nearness to the sea fostered easy transportation. Agricultural settlements spreading outward from the early colonial cities of Boston and Providence required a density of small local gristmills and sawmills. The Embargo Acts of the early nineteenth century provided the economic incentive for a burgeoning textile industry to expand beyond domestic production. Existing mill sites were rapidly developed into larger complexes with associated worker housing whose inhabitants soon required schools, churches, and other facilities. Small hamlets grew around mills into larger towns such as Webster, and even into major cities like Woonsocket or Pawtucket. With no centralizing government guidance, these many mill towns emerged simultaneously and uniformly across an entire region, all driven by the same economic imperative. Conversely, the collapse of the entire New England textile industry remains shocking in its definitive suddenness. Once the cheaper labor of America's South beckoned, and the industry was freed from the geographical constraints of waterpower, nothing could arrest its eclipse. So perfectly wedded to topography, the darkening mills had no further use, and their empty ruins scattered across the landscape. Only the rushing sounds of streams unfettered from their stone flumes and channels chronicle the silenced spindles of a thousand mills.

4

LANDSCAPES AND COURTHOUSE SQUARES OF SOUTHERN GEORGIA

THE BEAUTIFUL COURTHOUSE SQUARES of southern Georgia owe their existence to a vanished forest and a uniquely sinister history of county government. One of the world's most distinctive ecological biomes, the longleaf pine forests, once stretched across the south from Texas to Virginia. Within a generation after the Civil War, this extensive forest had been clear-cut for timber and naval stores. The resulting economic boom stimulated the construction of the many elaborate courthouses across the region. In the final years of the nineteenth century and the opening decades of the twentieth century, each tiny county enhanced its county seat with its own elegant and finely detailed structure. The courthouse of Moultrie, Georgia, provides an exceptionally handsome example. Georgia's county representative system favored the division of the state into more and smaller counties until today Georgia has the most number of counties of any state except Texas. The purpose of this county system, however, was not to foster wider representation, but rather to firmly maintain the supremacy of the white population over a deeply segregated society. The political strength of Georgia's grip on segregation lasted until the 1960s and restrained the cause of civil rights across the entire nation for decades. Ironically, this pernicious legacy remains embedded in a landscape of great beauty.

Vanquished Forest

Interstate 75 begins in the far north at the Canadian border port city of Sault Saint Marie; after crossing six states and just over 1,700 miles, it terminates outside Miami, Florida. On its way south, I-75 cuts through the center of several large cities, including Cincinnati and Atlanta. North of Atlanta, I-75 twists through the lower Appalachian Mountains; south of Atlanta, the highway follows the rolling topography of Georgia's Piedmont that levels out onto the flat coastal plains and wide vistas of agricultural fields. Along the highway right-of-way, the lush greenery of enclosing upland hardwoods gives way to the tall, thin trunks of loblolly and slash pines. These topographic and vegetation changes announce the footprint of the once great longleaf pine forests whose trees shaped a region and culture.

I-75 does not connect town center to town center but rather bypasses each. The underlying older road system forms a pronounced web with county seats at the nodes of radiating roads. I-75 severs this network first on one side and then on the other. While the smaller local roads still continue over or under the interstate, every exit off the interstate generates its own cluster of new development that interrupts the older settlement pattern of tiny urban villages surrounded by open agricultural fields. Prior to the interstates, the landscape of the rural south was uncompromising in its juxtaposition of built form, exemplified by the county seats, and the extensive unbroken expanses of row crops of corn, cotton, or peanuts. There was no sprawl. Now, however, these extruded commercial strips at each highway intersection dilute the ordered spacing of Georgia's remarkable rural towns.

As an example, Exit 39, I-75, between Tifton and Valdosta, gives direct access into one such commercial development. It is a typical off-ramp town of fast foods, overnight accommodations, gas stations, and empty lots. A figure-ground study illustrates the random spacing of the buildings arranged in apparent disarray along the access road. Each large structure sits within an empty space, obviously parking lots. The food choices are many: Huddle House, Wendy's, Burger King, IHOP, Captain D's, Taco Bell, McDonald's, Waffle House, and Smokies Barbecue. Four gas stations offer self-service: BP, Shell, and two Citgos. Accommodations include a Hampton Inn, Pays Inn, Super 8 Motel, Budget Lodge, and a Scottish Inn. A long partially vacant shopping mall surrounded by huge empty paved open spaces gives a feeling of abandonment. The widely spaced and haphazardly placed buildings sit next to the exit ramp like an appendix to the great tube of space of the interstate that stretches south across Georgia. There is an order here, of sorts, but it is the order of expedience. To clearly understand the difference in urban form between a pedestrian center and one oriented solely to the automobile, one has only to compare this figure-ground with those of courthouse-square towns later in this chapter. The facilities at this off-ramp town serve only the interstate traveler. The two-lane Route 37 continues west from the off-ramp town and into rural Georgia. Suddenly, there are plantations of pines, fields of tobacco, corn, cotton, and great rotating pivot irrigators. Resigned red barns and starkly simple churches punctuate the expanses of green crops. The swampy bottom lands of the Little River and the tracks of the Georgia & Florida Railroad mark the eastern boundary of Colquitt County. Crossing a recently constructed bypass, the

Location map of Exit 39,
I-75 in southern Georgia

road enters suddenly and dramatically into Moultrie's courthouse square with its monumental and stunningly beautiful courthouse.

The journey from I-75 and the off-ramp town takes ten minutes, but it is as though one travels through a time warp into another world. The disjuncture between the unrelenting ribbon of space of the interstate and the serene courthouse could not be more total. With its silver dome and Corinthian porticoes the white building embodies the mythic antebellum south. Disconcertingly, however, closer inspection of the marker on the shaded lawn that surrounds the courthouse reveals that it was constructed in 1902—thirty-seven years *after* the Civil War. The reason for this apparent contradiction lies in a vanished forest. For answers, we must turn back into the distant past of that same ice age whose glaciers shaped the landscape of Massachusetts and Rhode Island.

The extended arc of the North American coastal plain parallels the Appalachian Mountains southward from New England down the Atlantic seaboard. The sandy deposits of the coastal plain form most of southern New Jersey with its extensive

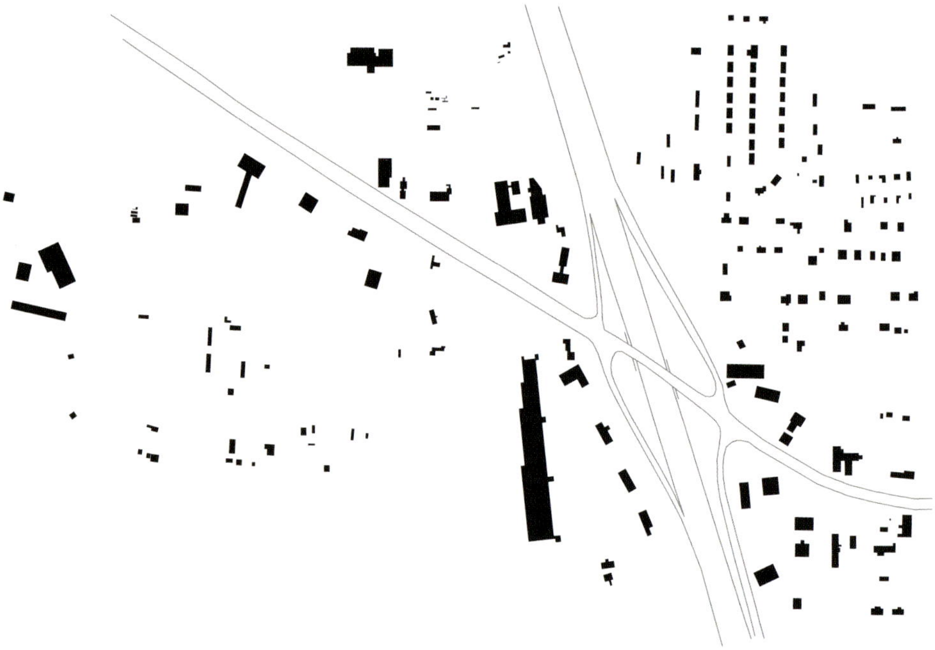

Figure-ground study of the off-ramp town at Exit 39 *(right)*

Map of Moultrie, Georgia, in relationship to Exit 39 *(below)*

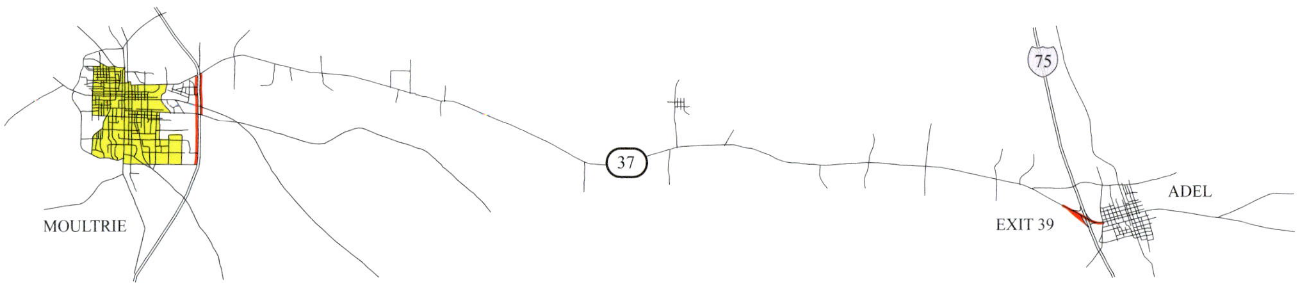

Red barn, Colquitt County, Georgia

pine barrens and wide beaches. At the Chesapeake Bay, it bulges out into the ocean to form the Eastern Shore of Maryland and Delaware and the Tidewater regions of Virginia and the Carolinas. Before sweeping into Alabama and up the Mississippi River Valley, the coastal plain widens to several hundred miles across the southern half of Georgia. Deep sand from ancient shorelines and beaches underlies most of these areas from the tide line inland to the hard rocks of the once mighty Appalachians. During the expansion and contraction of the Pleistocene glaciers, the world's oceans were alternately locked in the thick polar ice caps or released to inundate the continental margins. The deeply indented shorelines of marshes, swamps, and streams of the mid- and south Atlantic coasts record these fluctuations in their serrated outlines and protecting barrier islands.

As the seas rose and subsided, North America's coastlines moved back and forth across what is now the coastal plain, leaving wide sandy terraces as remnants of these former shorelines. Like a deck of cards fanned across a gaming table, these layers tilt from the forgotten fingers of Georgia's Appalachian Mountains far out onto the continental shelf, forming a band of low relief several hundred miles wide. At almost any place in this region of Georgia today, fresh road cuts yield thirty-foot sections of undifferentiated beach sand deposited long ago by drifting dunes and crashing waves.

South portico of Colquitt County Courthouse, Moultrie, Georgia

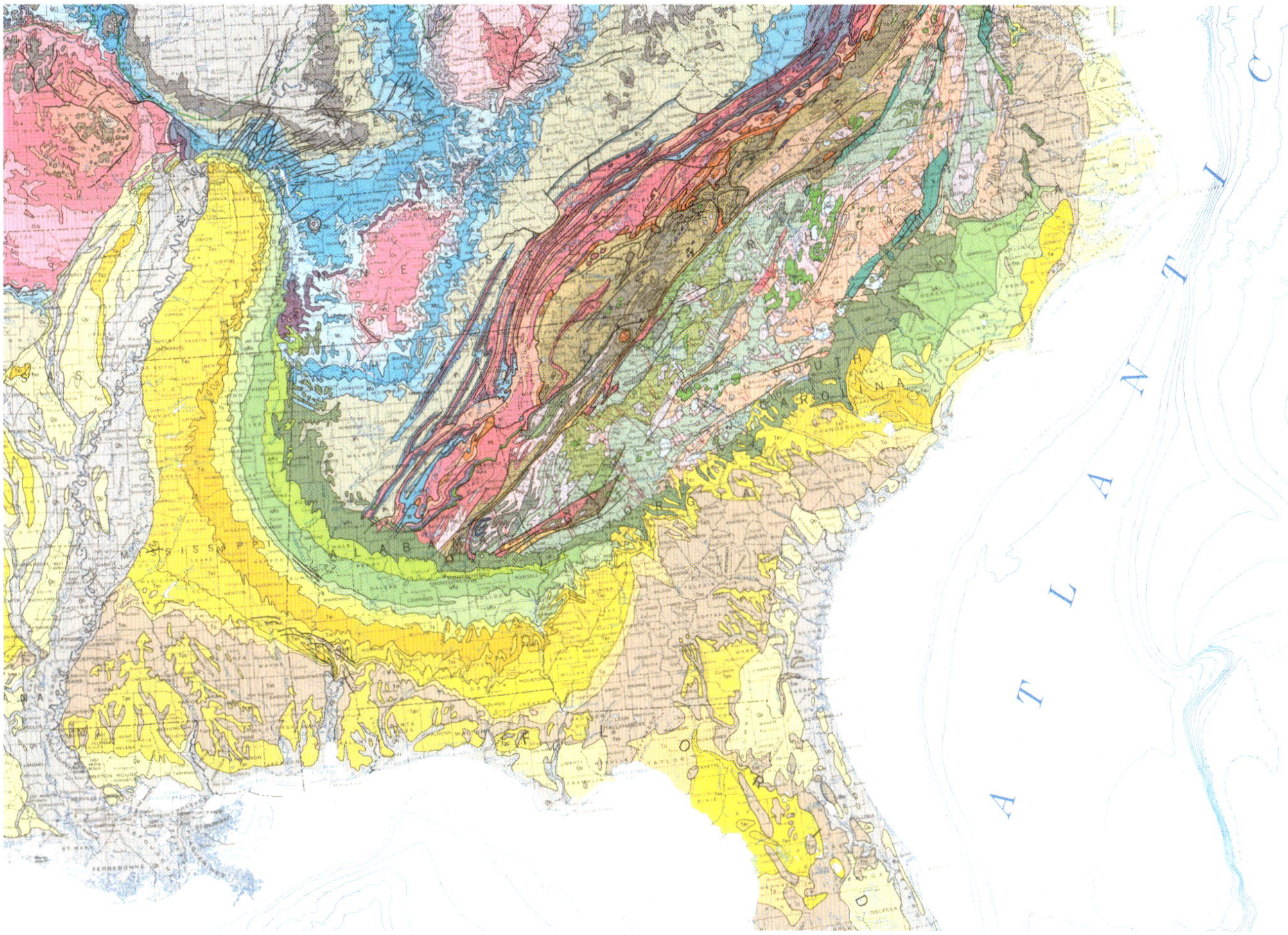

Detail from geology map of the southeastern United States

The fall line in Georgia marks the inner edge of its wide coastal plain. Fragments of the worn Appalachian Mountains form rolling hills of fertile soils before dipping beneath the coastal plain's sandy terraces. The firmer substrate of the fall line hills made rapids in south-flowing streams that hindered navigation. Augusta, Macon, and Columbus, Georgia, were settled at these falls, and the three together punctuate a diagonal across the state that clearly outlines the separation of the upland piedmont from the coastal plains.

The relief above sea level corresponds to the underlying geology. The coastal plain rises barely eight hundred feet in a hundred and fifty miles. Then at the fall line, the elevation climbs quickly above one thousand feet to eventually gain almost five thousand feet in the Great Smoky Mountains in the northwestern corner of Georgia. The gradual gradient of the coastal plain allows rivers and streams to take lazy, widely coiled routes across the sandy soils. These drainage systems meander back and forth within their own wide flood plains of rich alluvial soil.

The extensive longleaf pine forest once stretched for thousands of miles from Virginia to Texas following the exact footprint of the coastal plain.[1] Tragically the

1. The longleaf pine is also known as the Georgia pine or southern pine. Its scientific name, *Pinus palustris,* from the Latin *palustris,* suggests that it grows in wetlands. It does prefer and will thrive in moist rich soils, but over most of its former habitat it was associated with sandy soils.

Longleaf pine forest

longleaf pine forests no longer exist, reduced to stumps within decades after the Civil War. The destruction of these forests was one of this country's greatest ecological disturbances, overwhelming in its scope and frightening in its finality. Ironically, out of this devastation a cultural network of some of the most beautiful courthouse-square towns in America emerged to organize a different and unique settlement pattern across southern Georgia between 1870 and 1920. This chapter traces this emergence before concluding in the court square of Moultrie, Georgia.

The great expanse of longleaf pine forests had spatial characteristics unlike any other woodlands of North America—tall straight trunks evenly distributed across open savannah-like grasses. A remarkable sepia photograph shows a man dwarfed by these great trees. Filled with filtered sunlight and the sound of wind in their long-needled branches, these forests must have seemed limitless. The wonderful fragrance of pine needles soft beneath one's feet and the moaning of the wind through the tree tops impressed travelers through the longleaf pine regions in the eighteenth and nineteenth centuries.

An overlay map of the longleaf pine forest's range illustrates its correspondence with the coastal plains. Adapted to the sandy soils, these grand trees and their associated plant and animal communities expanded into the coastal plains about ten thousand years ago after the last retreat of the ocean. The deep taproot of the longleaf pine enables it to survive in the quickly draining sandy soils. It grows in association with wiregrass (*Aristida stricta*), and sometimes this region is referred to as the Wiregrass. This wiregrass carpeted these forests with a

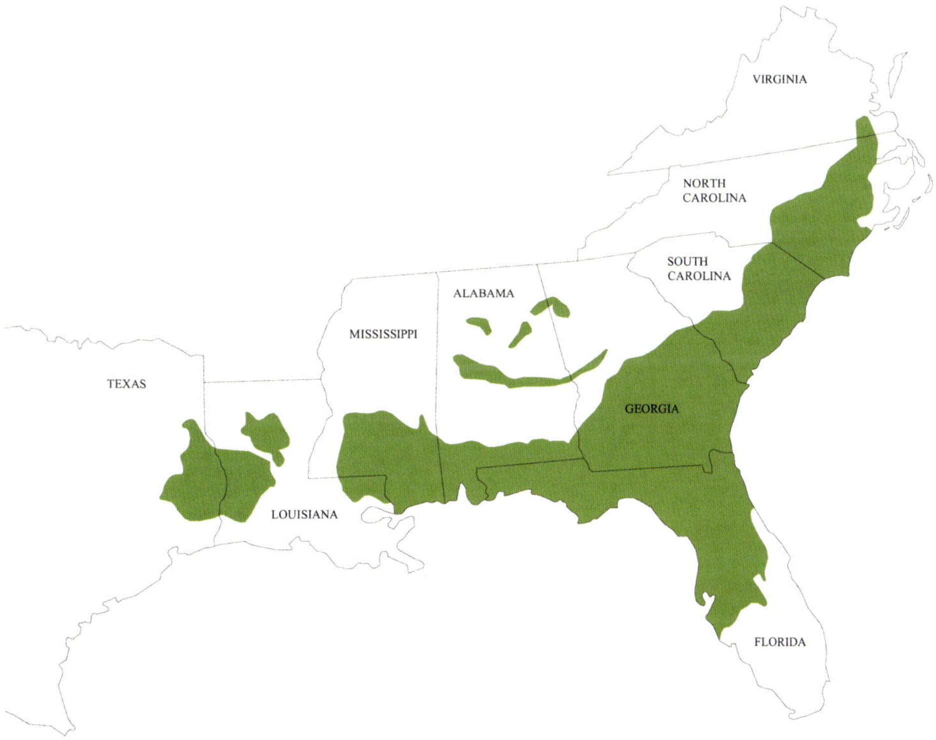

Map of the extent of the longleaf pine forest ecology before the Civil War

beautiful orange color in fall and winter and dark green in summer. These forests must have been magical places full of light and space, truly a unique ecosystem unlike any other in North America.

Hundreds of other grass and flower species intermixed with the wiregrass, such as the rare pink lady slipper (*Cypripedium acaule*) or the carnivorous hooded pitcher plant (*Sarracenia minor*). The longleaf pine ecosystem was diverse with many endemic plants that are rare today, but whose natural histories suggest a stable ecosystem that emerged over thousands of years, allowing plant communities the time to diversify and adapt to specific and unique niches. Sadly, as the longleaf pine forests disappeared, many species of plants and animals that were once an integral part of its ecology became endangered or extinct. Cavities in the longleaf pine trunks provided nesting for the rare red-cockaded woodpecker. This woodpecker has a complex life cycle that must include sap-draining nesting cavities in live longleaf pines. Other similarly endangered species are the gopher tortoise that barrows in the sandy soil and the beautifully iridescent indigo snake that inhabits these same holes.

Longleaf pine forests are fire dependent. They require frequent burning of the ground litter to provide the necessary opportunities for their seedlings to germinate. Their thick bark protects the mature trees from heat, as does the grass-like foliage of seedlings. Fire eliminates competing understory vegetation and thus aids in maintaining the forest's open, park-like spatial qualities. Before the establishment of humans in North America, lightning strikes started these fires. After Native Americans arrived, fires were intentionally started to promote an open habitat conducive to game and hunting.

In 1774, William Bartram, the intrepid explorer and naturalist, traveled extensively in the American Southeast. His journeys took him along the coast of the Carolinas, Georgia, and Florida. He traveled overland from Augusta to present-day Montgomery, Alabama, and descended to Mobile. Significantly, this trip followed the fall line from Augusta to the Ocumulgee mounds near Macon to the crossing of the Chattahoochee near Columbus. He skirted the great longleaf pine forests along their northern boundary. He did, however, make a series of adventures into longleaf pine territory by crossing the upper Florida peninsula from the Atlantic to the Gulf and left several descriptions of these unique forests: "Now the pine forests opened to view. We left the magnificent savanna and its delightful groves, passing through a level, open, airy pine forest, the stately trees scatteringly planted by nature, arising straight and erect from the green carpet, embellished with various grasses and flowering plants; then gradually ascending the sand hills, we soon came into the trading path to Talahasochte; which is generally, excepting a few deviations, the old Spanish highway to St. Mark's."[2] The very specificity of the longleaf pine's ecology allowed it to adapt to the coastal plains. Its preference for sandy loam, its tolerance of frequent fires

2. Bartram, *Bartram Travels*, 188.

that suppressed competition, and its ability to sustain a mature and stable population over thousands of years made these forests dominant across the Southeast. This specificity, however, proved the pine's undoing. Once logged, longleaf pine could not easily regenerate nor could it compete with the rapid growth of other species of pines such as loblolly and slash pine. Fire as a natural part of the ecological processes cannot be tolerated in dense urban and agricultural areas, except as small prescribed burns to maintain private hunting habitats. The few isolated stands of longleaf pine in existence today are managed through burning and thinning in arboretums and forest preserves. The beautiful spatial qualities and soft colors of these small stands are all that remain of once magnificent forests of thousands of square miles.

Early-eighteenth-century Georgians stayed out of the great forested coastal plain, using the extensive longleaf pine and wiregrass ecosystem as pasture for cattle and hogs. Longleaf pine made excellent masts and yards for ships; when timber was cut, trees were located within easy distances from rivers so the logs could be rafted and barrels of turpentine shipped to the Gulf or Atlantic coasts. Lack of seasonably reliable river transportation, however, spared most of the forests until after the Civil War. The few towns in the piney woods of south-central Georgia were river ports or ferry landings; most settlements were widely spaced, self-sufficient cattle ranches as the grasses beneath the trees were ideal for grazing, but the sandy soil was unsuitable for extensive field agriculture such as cotton. Limited crops could be grown on the fertile "bottoms," the rich alluvial soils of river flood plains. The great cotton plantations we associate with antebellum Georgia were located to the north above the fall line and well out of the longleaf pine forests.

Prior to the American Revolution, settlements in Georgia clustered in a few parishes (forerunners to counties) along the Savannah, Ogeechee, and Altamaha Rivers on the Atlantic coast. Quickly valuable property along the coast and fertile bottomlands along the rivers became scarce, and settlers began moving into the interior of the colony. In 1773, the Creeks agreed to relinquish 2.1 million acres inland of the previously settled areas and upriver from Augusta. The British governor immediately sent surveyors to mark the new boundaries and to determine the quality of the acquisition.

These land exchanges and treaty negotiations between the Native Americans and Europeans were often fractious. The Europeans negotiated with tribal chiefs who were not necessarily representative of their populations. Sometimes Europeans offered bribes of prime land to favored leaders as incentives for signing over ever more land. At other times, the state received land from Native Americans to settle grossly inflated trade debts. Most often, white settlers just moved into unsettled areas, initiated hostilities with Native Americans, who then retaliated. The state militia would mobilize, and during the ensuing negotiations, the

Native Americans inevitably relinquished more land. Disputes with the Native Americans continued for decades as their lands were relentlessly taken away, surveyed, and sold. In the bitter end, the remaining Native Americans were forcibly removed from all of Georgia and the Southeast and resettled in the West during the infamous Trail of Tears.

Raw land with no system of boundaries could not be sold or even given away, so the very first step and expense was for the government to have it surveyed into parcels for distribution to individuals. Survey crews fanned out across the immense territory of Georgia to record each new cession. Swamps, heat, and hostile Creeks were all hazards that made their work extremely difficult. Compasses established bearings and chains measured horizontal distances. Astronomers took bearings from the sun and stars to set the survey positions while ax men blazed trees and located stakes. Artisans transcribed everything on drawings and maps for recording in a rustic nearby county courthouse. A simple survey grid was most often employed in such huge tracts of land. The intent was to get as much land into private ownership as quickly as possible. The fledgling American government, just after its separation from Great Britain, was cash poor and land rich. Unimproved land, however, yielded no revenue for the owner or taxes for the state or federal government.

To settle the entire state in the decades after the Revolutionary War, all land had to be surveyed and boundaries established, so that it could be conveyed from public to private ownership. To successfully record the many land lotteries, counties had to be carved out of the newly acquired territories. Primitive log courthouses were built to organize and store the thousands of deeds and land titles. As new counties became more populous, they were subdivided into several smaller political units, new counties with new county seats, until from just a few large counties the number increased to 161 small counties. The characteristic landscape of southern Georgia with its fine grain of lovely county seats emerged out of this process from east to west.

Unlike states admitted later such as neighboring Alabama, Georgia's land was doled out piecemeal as each Native American cession became available. Neighboring Alabama, by contrast, was gridded out in its entirety and aligned by meridians and parallels. Eventually the large western states such as Nebraska, discussed in chapter 5, were surveyed as a whole based upon the very regular national survey grid. Georgia was done in increments called districts, and each newly acquired district was surveyed differently. The size of the grid was different in each area, and the grids were not oriented to meridians or parallels. Often the surveyors would mark individual lots in new districts with the predominant forest cover to aid prospective buyers. A detail from a map of a Georgia district along the Florida line shows these notes. In parcel after parcel, "pines" is repeatedly written, indicating a region of extensive longleaf pine forest.

Detail from Irwin County, District 15, 1820

All this survey work required a convenient repository for records and deeds. These places had to be centrally located for easy access in a region without roads. The 1777 Georgia Constitution contained the following provisions concerning county affairs:

Art. L. Every county shall keep the public records belonging to the same, and authentic copies of the several records now in the possession of this State shall be made out and deposited in the county to which they belong.

Art. L II. A register of probates shall be appointed by the legislature in every county for proving wills and granting letters of administration.

Art. L III. All civil officers in each county shall be annually elected on the day of the general election, except justices of the peace and registers of probates, who shall be appointed by the house of assembly.

Art. L V. A Court-house and jail shall be erected at public expense in each county, where the present convention or the future legislature shall point out and direct.[3]

The emphasis on the depository of public records and the building of a courthouse are especially important, for these provisions contain the humble origins of the courthouse-square towns that spread across the state.

Land acquisition took place in Georgia from east to west in broad increments that ran in north–south cessions that paralleled and were bounded by major rivers. Exceptions to the natural boundaries were the large tracts along the bottom of Georgia above the Florida panhandle as well as the last cession in the northwest that was part of the Cherokee Nation.

3. Hughes, *County Government in Georgia*, 11.

Known as the 1814 cession, the piece along the south was created because of the disastrous defeat suffered by the Creeks at the Battle of Horseshoe Bend on the Tallapoosa River in Alabama in March 1814. As a result of the defeat, the Creeks ceded half their territory in Alabama and Georgia to the United States. Significantly, no responsible leader of the Creeks would participate in this land grab. General Andrew Jackson persuaded a shadowy figure named McIntosh to stand in for the Native Americans and sign as proxy for all four chiefs of the Lower Creeks. Settlers of Georgia complained, nevertheless, as the acquired territory in Georgia was poor soil and unprofitable. This unjust and infertile cession comprised thousands of acres of longleaf pine forests that would be exploited in another eighty years. By act of the legislature, the 1814 cession was divided into three large counties: Early, Irwin, and Appling. Peter Early and Jared Irwin were governors of Georgia; Daniel Appling was a hero of the War of 1812. All three counties remain in name only today as they have been subdivided, altered, and reduced in size.

Before new counties in southern Georgia could be surveyed and subdivided, the line between Georgia and Florida had to be established. By royal proclamation in 1763, by the Treaty of Paris in 1783,and the treaty between the United States and Spain in 1795, Georgia's southern boundary had been fixed at a line beginning in the center of the Mississippi River on the thirty-first parallel. Thus in 1795, Georgia included all of Alabama and Mississippi. The line ran eastward along that parallel to the center of the Chattahoochee River and dropped southward down the center of that river to its confluence with the Flint River. From that point the line ran straight 158 miles to the "head waters" of the St. Mary's River and followed the centerline of the St Mary's to the Atlantic Ocean. This explains the reverse curve boundary line at the southeastern corner of Georgia. Since the headwaters of the St Mary's River lie somewhere in the vastness of the impenetrable Okefenokee Swamp, the bearing from the Chattahoochee east was surveyed several times, each time with different results. Even a slight compass deviation could move substantial land from one state to another—even from one country to another, as Florida in 1795 still belonged to Spain and remained so until the Adams-Onís Treaty of 1819, when Spain ceded Florida to the United States, with actual possession taken in 1821. Fifty years would pass before the boundary was settled between the State of Florida and the State of Georgia by adjudication of the United States Supreme Court. This example illustrates the serious problems and expenses confronting a new state in surveying its holdings. In 1814, this part of Georgia was empty wilderness full of hostile Indians who stole equipment and horses and removed markers. There were swamps, streams, incessant rain, heat, insects, and numerous venomous snakes. These impediments were typical of southern Georgia in the summer months, yet the state had to be surveyed expeditiously and accurately.

At the beginning of the nineteenth century, Georgia made two fundamental changes to the way public land was to be distributed in the remaining two-thirds of the state. First, as each new cession became available, it was to be surveyed in a rectangular grid that facilitated division into lots for sale. There was nothing new about this system; it had already been adopted by the U.S. Congress in the Northwest Land Ordinance of 1785 and was used in parceling out the newly emerging states in the Midwest. For Georgia, this represented a significant financial commitment as the survey work had to be finished and recorded before the state could realize revenue from land sales.

Second, Georgia adopted a lottery system for distributing its public lands. Two great land frauds had already soured Georgians against earlier distribution attempts. As a cession became part of the state's public land, it was surveyed at public expense into small lots of between two hundred and four hundred acres, depending on the cession. Lots within a cession were mostly uniform in size. Each lot was marked in the field, numbered, and mapped. The surveyors' field notes and maps were recorded in a central place, most likely a simple structure in the newly designated county seat. A public lottery presided over by commissioners selected by the legislature was held and lots distributed by chance. The lottery eliminated most of the temptations and means for fraud, for it no longer made any sense to bribe or influence the surveyors or the commissioners, as no one could know what lots would be taken or by whom. The lottery gave everyone a fair and equal chance at obtaining land.

This is not to say that the system was free of difficulties. Surveys could be erroneous. Specific lots could vary greatly depending upon the luck of the grid on the land: a lot could be in a fertile river bottom, in a continually wet swamp, or in a sandy pine barrens. There was no way to know until one had drawn the number and walked the ground. Record keeping of survey maps, lot numbers, and the names of new owners was vitally important. The state mandated rigorous recording procedures that required safe depositories within reasonable distances of the land being sold. And thus was institutionalized the county seat with its courthouse.

County size decreased and the number of counties increased through the complex process of cessions transference. Counties began large, but as their populations and land transactions increased, the larger counties were subdivided into smaller and smaller counties. The county boundary shifts occurred again and again through an even more complex system of surveys, land sales, and ownership deeds. In the vast majority of cases, these were very local and specific transactions that allowed a political and governmental subdivision to emerge over time until the state was complete with 161 (later reduced to the present 159) evenly spaced counties, each manifested in the landscape by a tiny urban core of commercial establishments framing a courthouse in the middle of an open space.

The system of cessions, surveys, and lotteries that enabled Georgia to transfer over twenty-six thousand square miles of raw land into private ownership is truly remarkable. Of equal significance is the way these accumulated transfers are marked across the state with county seats and courthouses, each in the geographic center of its county. If each county seat is marked by a dot, their even spacing across the whole of Georgia becomes obvious. This even spacing required years of survey work, land transferences, and county boundary adjustments. The county seats represent a clear example of an emergent settlement pattern; one that has many analogies in the natural world: the open spacing of desert plants in the competition for water, the nests of pelagic birds on rocky promontories, and the spacing of individuals in a school of fish. No overall plan dictated this settlement order in Georgia, just a multitude of similar, seemingly random, local responses over time. However, as the second section of this chapter explains, this emergent pattern of numerous small counties had far reaching and tragic consequences for the United States African American population.

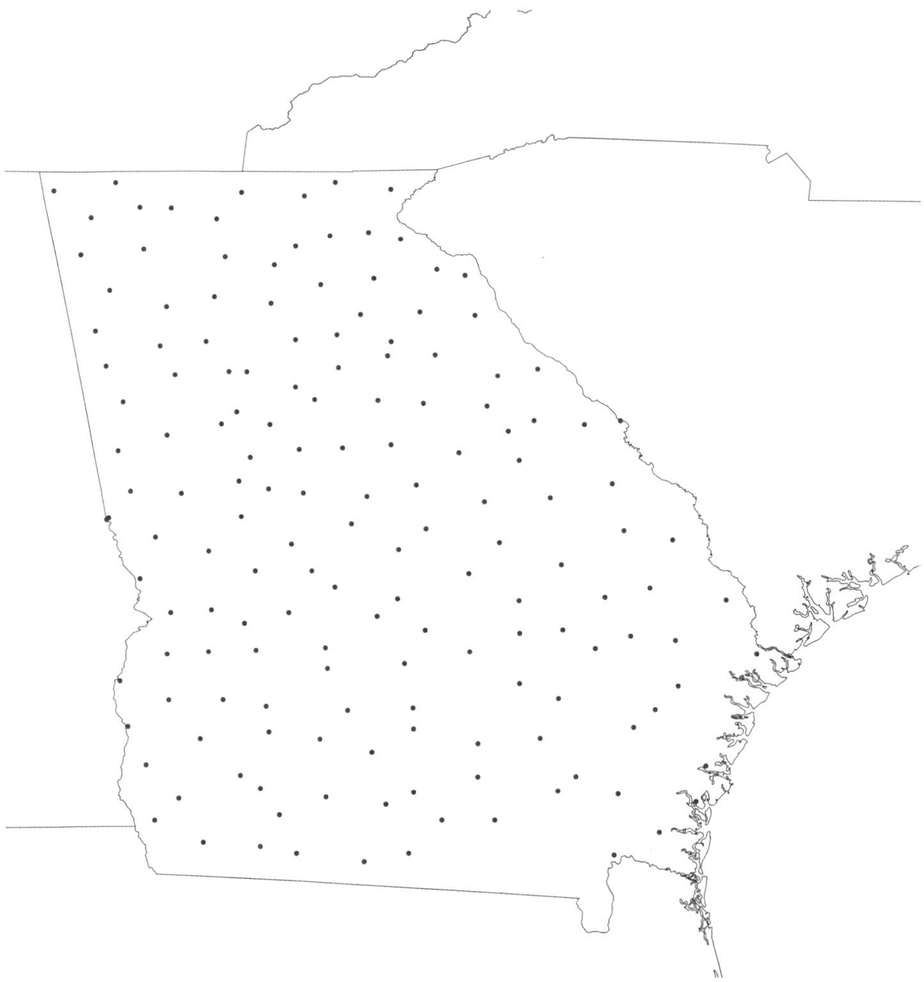

County seats of Georgia

Great costs were involved in this process, and at the end of the Civil War a defeated Georgia had few economic resources remaining. Its agriculture was decimated; its railroad infrastructure in ruins. Its single greatest natural asset lay in the unexploited forests of longleaf pine. A demand for naval stores propelled by a worldwide expansion in shipping coupled with an increase in timber demand as the United States experienced a building boom in the North and West gave Georgians every reason to harvest the longleaf pines. The sale of timber created a tremendous economic boost in Georgia and, in the process, helped substantially increased its railroad trackage.

Two commodities, both obtained from pine trees, have always been essential to the building and maintenance of ships: tar and pitch. Pitch is used with oakum, or loose fiber, to caulk seams between planking; tar is used to coat lines and rigging to protect against salt corrosion. Book Two of Homer's *Iliad* describes the gathering of the Achaians and the cataloging of their "black" ships. The Greek ships, like all wooden vessels from the beginning of seafaring, were covered in black pitch to protect the hulls and seal the seams. Pine trees are burned to produce tar. Turpentine and rosin derive from cutting or "tapping" the trunks of live pine trees. The gummy sap runs from the wound to a shelf cut into the trunk and then is ladled into containers to be distilled as turpentine. Of course, tapping of live trees caused irreparable damage to the trunk. Because of its high sap content, longleaf pine is one of the best trees for producing these products, known collectively as naval stores. In the nineteenth century, before the wide use of synthetic petroleum-based products, naval stores was an extensive industry in the longleaf pine forests of the Carolinas and Georgia. The familiar moniker "tar heels" derives from the adherence of tar and straw to one's shoes. As demand grew for naval stores toward the end of the nineteenth century, the forests of southern Georgia became a previously untapped resource for exploitation and profit. A photograph of the docks at Savannah conveys the immensity of these operations as barrels of turpentine stretch into the far distance.

After the Civil War, Northern capitalists and bankers quickly realized the profits to be made from cutting the longleaf pine forests of southern Georgia. Railroads were built deep into the flat pine country to bring barrels of tar, pitch, turpentine, and rosin to market and logs to sawmills. Between 1870 and 1920, freight trackage in southern Georgia increased dramatically, and passenger service soon connected to every small town. Lumber from Georgia built homes and barns across Iowa, Kansas, and Nebraska. Longleaf pine timber of great girth and strength made possible the plank and heavy timber construction of the New England textile mills. To satisfy these demands, thousands of acres of longleaf pine forests disappeared within twenty years. The destruction was so fast and so complete that people could not recognize the landscapes of their childhood. North Carolina's eminent botanist and ecologist B. W. Wells recounted this

Barrels of pine resin

devastation: "Like a fine old aristocracy destroyed by war, the original longleaf pine forest of our sand hills has been completely cut and burned until the entire scene has so changed that no person of the rising generation may now gain any real idea of the majesty and glory of the original forest."[4]

With a clear-cut landscape and the exposed earth uncultivated, property owners of Georgia turned to the old standbys of southern agriculture, cotton and corn. Mechanized farming and heavy chemical fertilizing rendered the sandy loam of the former longleaf pine forests able to support cotton, at least in the short term. Cotton production in Georgia peaked in the first two decades of the twentieth century. Most of the new acreage occurred in the coastal plains of southern Georgia on the land cleared of longleaf pines. Tenancy farmers and sharecroppers struggled in subsistence living, scratching out an existence in the bare sandy soils. Finally many poor blacks and whites gave up and migrated to urban areas such as Atlanta or Chicago.

4. B. W. Wells as quoted in Early, *Looking for Longleaf,* 171.

Savannah docks loaded with barrels of turpentine and resin

Cutover land, Heard County, Georgia, 1941

Spreading suddenly across the southern United States from Texas, the boll weevil arrived in Georgia in 1915 and destroyed cotton as the predominant row crop. After 1920, cotton became just another agricultural product significant only in a few counties. Georgia's coastal plain still dominates the state's contemporary cotton production, but it is barely 15 percent of diversified rotations of peanuts, soy beans, cattle, poultry, and timber. Artificial irrigation and mechanization have changed the landscape from one of small farms to large farms with enormous combines.

The naval stores and timber obtained from the destruction of the longleaf pine forests provided an economic boost after the terrible toll of the Civil War. World War I increased demand for cotton cloth as the cleared land of the former forest came under extensive cotton cultivation just before the boll weevil epidemic shut down cotton production. During the decades between 1870 and 1920, wealthy landowners of southern Georgia allied with northern capitalists to decimate the longleaf pine forests. Then as cleared land produced cotton, the same southern landowners supplied northern mill owners with quantities of cotton for their mills. During the same time period for African Americans, however, segregation and Jim Crow laws meant unrelenting poverty, disenfranchisement, and fear. As the twentieth century unfolded, southern Georgia entered into dark decades of racial strife fermented by white supremacy.

Built during these booming decades of growth and exploitation between 1890 and 1920, the many beautiful courthouses remain today evenly spaced across the southern Georgia landscape. Their beauty came at the cost of an entire ecosystem, and their original intent was not justice for all. Beneath their masked myth of a democratic ideal, the courthouses were not beacons of equality, but rather symbols of racial imperialism. Today, their urban compositions still haunt us with their elegant facades and elevated domes all within a space surrounded and framed by arcaded storefronts. Some are very graceful, treasures of architecture to be preserved. A closer reading of this landscape, however, discovers relicts of other narratives as southern Georgia's counties emerged from the ghost of the longleaf pine forests.

One Standard of Justice

There has to be a reason for so many counties in Georgia: its 159 counties are the most of any state except Texas, which is five times larger than Georgia and has 254 counties. Neighboring Alabama, slightly smaller than Georgia in area, has just 67 counties. Dividing and subdividing areas into smaller and more numerous counties was costly and time-consuming, yet Georgia continued to create more counties until 1924, when the final formation of Peach County brought the total to 161. (Two counties, Campbell and Milton, merged with Fulton in 1929 and 1932 to bring the total down to 159.) A line drawing of Georgia's counties within

Abandoned sharecropper home, Colquitt County, Georgia

a matrix of its neighboring states' counties illustrates the scale of its many small governmental units. Even without the state boundaries delineated in a bolder line, the tighter textures of divisions make Georgia's area apparent. Georgia's present county and state governments conceal a past that privileged property ownership and white dominance above racial equality or representative government.

In the Georgia State Constitution of 1789 and in amending conventions thereafter, the state provided for a county unit system of representation. The two largest counties then in existence, Chatham and Liberty, were given four state representatives each; the seven next largest counties were allocated three representatives, and the remaining counties two. One state senator was selected from each county. Thus began a long history of government by county unit rather than by population, which would have far-reaching and hurtful consequences. Not until the civil rights struggles of the 1960s was this pernicious system eliminated. While the destructive political system of unit representation has disappeared, it left behind a fascinating landscape that contains examples of great architectural beauty and wonderfully ordered urban spaces. Here we explore the mechanisms for county formation and end with a detailed discussion of one representative county seat, Moultrie, Colquitt County, and its extraordinary courthouse.

Map of Georgia's counties within the context of neighboring states of Alabama, South Carolina, North Carolina, Tennessee, and Florida

In 1877 Georgia adopted a new Constitution that further entrenched the county unit organization. Article III, Section 3 stipulates the allocation of representatives: "The House of Representatives shall consist of representatives apportioned among the several counties of the State as such counties are marked and defined and as the same may be hereafter created as follows: To the eight counties having the largest population, three representatives each; to the thirty counties having the next largest population, two representatives each; and the remaining counties, one representative each." This meant that a tiny county with a population of 700 had one vote while a much larger county with a population of 100,000 had three votes. Or put differently, a small county had one vote per 700 people; a large county had one vote per 33,300 people—hardly representative. From 1880 to 1940, the urban population of Georgia, primarily African Americans and poor whites fleeing the awful conditions of rural poverty, increased from 9.4 percent to 34.4 percent, while the rural population decreased from 90.6 percent to 65.6 percent.[5] Obviously the rural areas stood to gain most from the perpetuation of the county unit system, and so, not surprisingly, the number of rural counties increased significantly between 1877 and 1940.

Calculating the actual votes in the state legislature shows the inequities: the eight largest counties with 30 percent of the state's population had 24 representatives or 11.75 percent of the 205 seats in the House. The next thirty counties had 60 representatives combined. The remaining small rural counties had 121 representatives or a majority of the House and control of the state government. In an even more convoluted effort, the primary elections for U.S. senators and congresspeople used the same system, except the county units were multiplied by two as passed in the Neill Primary Act of 1917: "The candidate who receives the highest number of popular votes in any given county shall be considered to have carried such county and shall be entitled to the full vote of such county on the county unit bases, that is to say, two votes for each representative to which each county is entitled in the lower House of the General Assembly." Since Georgia was a one-party Democratic state, a small group of people maintained control of the state's political, economic, and social agenda. Hidden within the county lines of a map of rural Georgia are the means for significant racial dominance. With support from neighboring southern states, a small group of powerful individuals strongly influenced the national political course. For almost a hundred years Georgia's rural white population maintained a totally unrepresentative form of government that enabled it to subjugate an African American minority. The same local political system enabled Georgia to return senators year after year to the U.S. Senate, where they built up seniority and monopolized committee chairmanships that enabled them to successfully challenge and block all civil rights legislation at the national level for decades.

In 1962, the federal government ruled the county unit system unconstitutional and required the Georgia General Assembly to reapportion on the basis of population. Shortly thereafter, the U.S. Supreme Court ruled that Georgia's ten U.S. congressional districts were to be reapportioned based upon population. Thus ended an inequitable political system that fostered the creation of small counties. The counties themselves, however, remain, specters of power mapped upon the landscape.

We see this landscape in southern Georgia in the county courthouse squares

5. Hughes, *County Government in Georgia*, 47.

County courthouse domes, southern Georgia ***(left to right from top: Turner, Jeff Davis, Appling, Wilcox, Worth, and Jenkins County courthouses)***

and courthouses sitting serenely aloof in their imperialistic splendor, monuments to a discredited political system layered upon a vanished longleaf pine ecosystem. The very architecture of the buildings themselves speaks of conquest. Forms borrowed from Roman imperial buildings such as pedimented temple fronts, columned porticoes, and imposing domes all command attention. These courthouses in southern Georgia were not built in a wave of antebellum neo-Palladianism; rather, the courthouses discussed herein were all constructed between 1890 and 1920—during the height of white supremacy and Jim Crow laws. Wealth and power concentrated in the hands of white landowners, not the poor African American tenant farmers. An agricultural society based upon land ownership and property rights requires depositories for the records of these

Dome of Early County Courthouse, Blakely, Georgia

rights and places to adjudicate disputes and thus the need for courthouses. Whites controlled the government, the allocation of public funds, and even the judicial system. Harper Lee's classic novel, *To Kill a Mockingbird,* exposes the racial injustice played out in hushed courtrooms across the South. These extravagantly ornate buildings in evocative squares poignantly mark the failure of our country to honor our pledge "With equality and justice for all." The beauty of these courthouses today belies their imperfect inaugurations one hundred years ago.

Shifting county boundaries consumed time and money. Before 1877, these spatial manipulations required acts of the State Legislature. After 1877 and continuing to this day, differences and overlaps are usually handled at the local county level. Discrepancies still arise, such as the same property being recorded in two adjacent counties resulting in two individuals owning the same piece of land and paying taxes to two different counties. In the nineteenth century, much of southern Georgia was originally unimproved land, and survey lines could be rather permissive.

The formation of Georgia's counties is so remarkable a process of emergence that it needs be described in detail. The explanation of the process itself buttresses the hypothesis that emergent settlement patterns arise from many incremental local decisions. Even without overall guidance, a cohesive whole can arise from a myriad of continuous small adjustments. In the case of rural Georgia, the greater whole was political power and white supremacy; the tiny adjustments were one hundred years of boundary alterations.

As discussed in the first section of this chapter, when Native Americans ceded land to white Americans, the different cessions were surveyed into several large counties. These counties were partitioned into smaller districts that were further divided into regular parcels for potential sales. An 1819 survey drawing of the original Irwin County, District 4, shows the regularity of lines with little regard for local features, except where the lines meet a major river, the Ocmulgee. (This area is now in Ben Hill County, northeast of Fitzgerald.) Where possible, the county's external boundaries were straight and oriented to the cardinal points of the compass. Where an unfordable river delineated the edge, the boundary reflected the irregularities of the stream course. During a ground survey all manner of discrepancies would appear. Different survey parties could proceed from different cadastral bases, so lot lines would not line up. Streams would bisect parcels making them less—or more—than the 250 acres a buyer had purchased. As southern Georgia is crossed by many creeks, parcels could end up either larger or smaller than the idealized size purchased on paper. In a landscape of flat gradients, such as Georgia's coastal plains, streams meandered back and forth, constantly changing course, adding or subtracting area from parcels.

A new county was usually taken from several already existing settled counties, and land holdings could be cut in half—one part in one county, the other in another

Detail of Irwin County, District 4, 1819

county, causing several problems. Since the paying of taxes was time-consuming, often requiring a day's drive to the county seat—having to duplicate this effort was onerous, especially if the tax rate was higher in one county than another. An elected official in an existing county could have a county redistribution put all his land into a new county, and his constituency would disappear. These and many other very local concerns caused difficulties as boundaries were again and again redrawn. By necessity, changes would follow the original deeded and recorded parcel lines from maps such as the 1819 Irwin County survey. The resulting irregular adjustments, called "crenellations," are particular to Georgia (and parts of Alabama).[6] The northern boundary of Calhoun County contains two examples of crenellations, parcels added by bumping the county boundary up and around parcels in a neighboring county. Crenellation is evidence of local adjustments based upon entirely specific circumstances that arose during and after the subdivision

6. Vanderhill and Unger, "Georgia's Crenelated County Boundaries," 59.

of counties. A large-scaled map of Georgia consists of straight county boundaries, excluding, of course, those delineated by watercourses, but at the local scale, the county edges are full of inconsistences and specifics. These offsets and jogs are wonderful examples of local accommodations, hundreds of very detailed and individual responses resulting in a complex puzzle of interlocking pieces across the areas of the state allocated by land lotteries.

Detailed county boundary problems were adjusted on the scale of individual parcels. The statewide map of Georgia was in constant flux as counties were reconfigured by adding or subtracting areas from contiguous counties, or entirely new counties were formed from larger existing ones. A comparison of two maps of the entire state that record these changes shows the constant recalibration of county boundaries. In the older map of 1831, the state has not yet taken the last cession in the northwestern corner belonging to the "Cherokee Indians." Counties in the lower part of Georgia, the area of the longleaf pine forests, are large. A map of 1856 shows far more counties, especially in the lower third of the state. Colquitt County, site of the county seat of Moultrie, has come into existence along with many neighboring counties. The Cherokee have lost their land in the north. A close reading of these two maps uncovers a wide range of county boundary adjustments, yet these maps represent only twenty-five years in a hundred-year process. Although these are simple lines on a map at the scale of the entire state, at the local level, the time and cost of survey work must have been extensive. But if

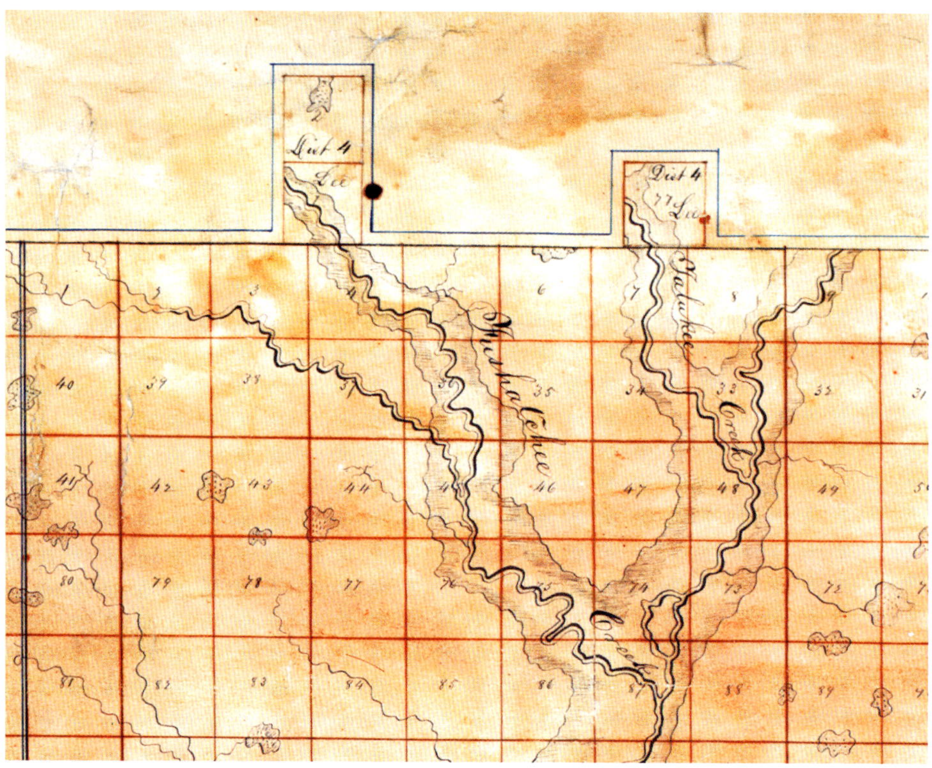

Detail from the north boundary of Calhoun County map, 1867, showing the crenellated extensions of three parcels

the ultimate goal was to maintain political power for whites through segregation, one can understand the motivation, especially if those same whites who benefited most controlled the legislative purse.

In order to make the pieces of the puzzle fit across the entire state, the shape of counties underwent constant change and realignment. These realignments were not minor shifts in boundaries, but substantial reconfigurations of entire counties. The reconfigurations of Pulaski County illustrate the extent of these significant changes. These simple line diagrams are based upon historic maps and represent four major shifts in Pulaski County's boundaries. Pulaski County was created in 1808 and named, like so many towns and counties in southern Georgia, after a historic figure in American history. Count Casimir Pulaski of Poland fought on behalf of the American cause in the Revolutionary War. He was mortally wounded in 1779 during the assault on British positions around Savannah. His exploits are commemorated by a lovely monument in Monterey Square in the city he died trying to recapture.

Eighteen separate acts in the Georgia laws were required before Pulaski County assumed its present boundaries. The first in 1808 took land from Lauren County, which no longer borders Pulaski; the last in 1912 gave land belonging to Pulaski to Bleckley County. The first two diagrams indicate Hartford as the county seat. Hartford was a river port town on the Ocmulgee River, which bisects Pulaski County. In 1839 the county seat was moved across the river to Hawkinsville, and Hartford was abandoned. What is even more astounding is the change in the counties surrounding Pulaski; these are not minor adjustments in boundaries, but rather a complete reshaping of the entire area. By comparing the four drawings, one can see that many of the neighboring counties are different, indicating a corresponding change in their shapes and areas. Similar shifts were taking place all across the state, in an arduous effort to increase the number of counties.

As the repository of all property deeds and marriage, birth, and death certificates within a county, the courthouse is the guardian of civic order. Ideally, the courthouse should be located in the geographical center of the county to afford equal access to all surrounding businesses and farmers. Streams and rivers should be kept to the perimeter of a county to avoid ferry crossings and spring floods on the journeys to and from the county seat. With the construction of contemporary highway bridges, we easily forget the difficulties of wagon travel over distances of eighteen or twenty miles of unpaved roads and uncrossable streams. As a county's boundaries changed, often the courthouse and its entire surrounding commercial context would be moved to another location better situated in a new geographical center. Consequently, Georgia has many abandoned towns that are little more than somnambulant crossroads; others are just forgotten names on old maps.

Each seat usually began early in the nineteenth century on a single road that crossed the region. These roads were often Native American trading routes that

Georgia, 1831

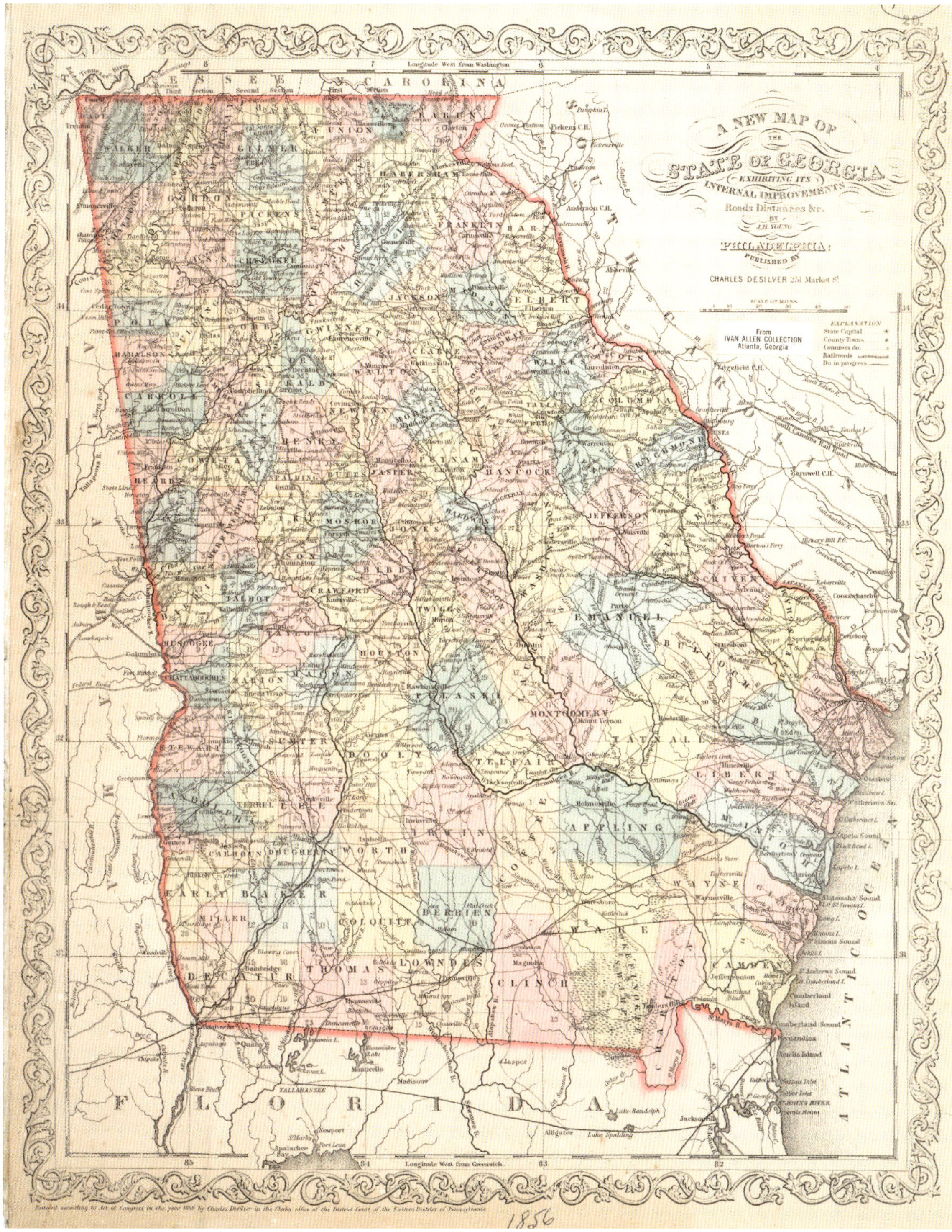

"A New Map of the State of Georgia Exhibiting its Internal Improvements Road Distances &c, 1856"

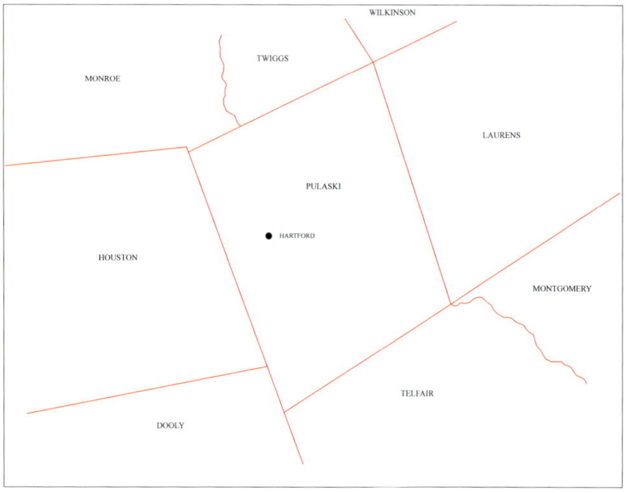

1822

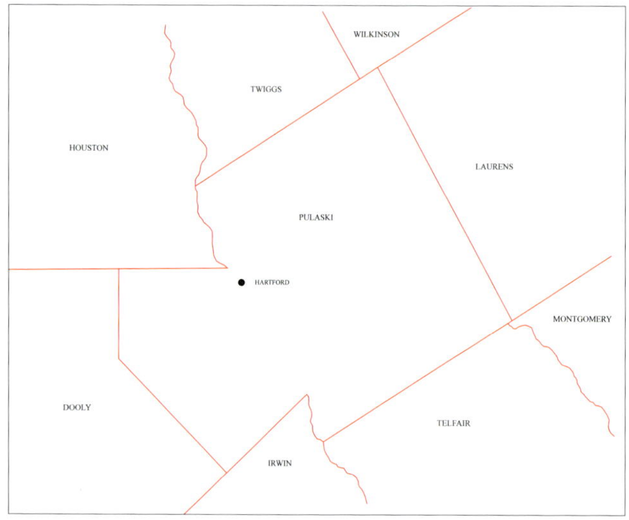

1839

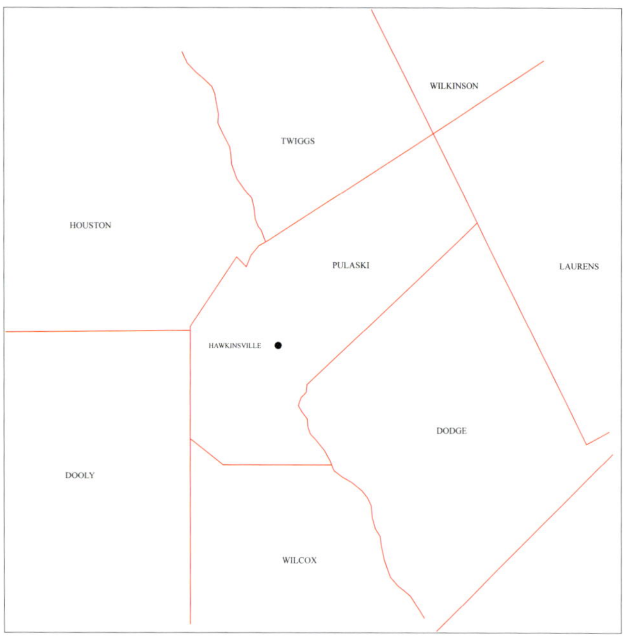

1885

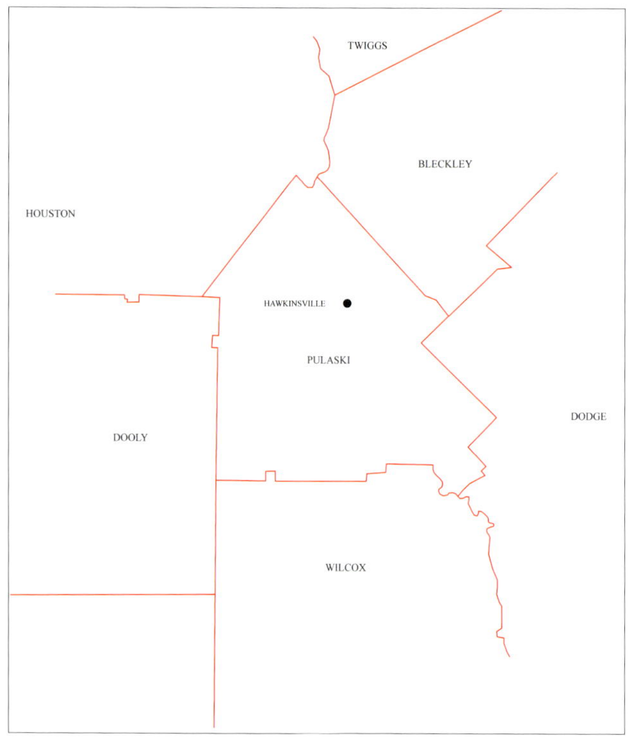

2009

Changes to the boundaries and shape of Pulaski County, Georgia

traced the easiest path across swampy lowlands to fords or later to ferry crossings. As neighboring seats became more numerous with the increasingly smaller division of counties, other crossroads intersected these single roads and thus developed the characteristic hub and spoke road infrastructure of southern Georgia. Some towns were the center of four, six, or even a dozen radiating roads. Travel by horse or wagon was through a town's center, from county seat to county seat. A farmer with a team of mules could transport produce to a town and return home in a single long day if the distance was less than about twenty-four miles, so a day's ride or about eighteen to twenty-four miles separated towns. This, too, was the convenient distance for a circuit judge to drive between court sessions. Today, as one drives by automobile across southern Georgia, the ubiquitous mileage signs for the next town announce these consistent distances once measured by a team of mules.

With the advent of railroads into this region in the decade after the Civil War, the movement of bulk freight switched from less reliable rivers to rail. The rail lines connected to the ocean ports of Savannah, Brunswick, and the Gulf port of Apalachicola. The railroad's introduction corresponded with the wholesale clearing of the longleaf pine forests as naval stores and lumber could be moved in great quantities to the docks of ocean ports. In most cases, maps of the 1870s–1880s show a single line or spur pushing through to a small town. Soon these tracks mimicked the radial pattern of the roads with four or more lines connecting county seats. During the apex of railroads from 1900 to 1930, over 95 percent of all long-distance travel, either freight or passenger, was by rail. If, in the late nineteenth century, a U.S. congressman living in Hawkinsville wished to travel to Washington, DC, he went first to Cochran, then to Macon, up to Atlanta, where he caught the main line from New Orleans through the Carolinas and western Virginia into Washington.

Rail transportation dominated travel throughout southern Georgia as agriculture shifted to cotton after the destruction of the longleaf pine forests. Trains served the region through the boll weevil epidemic and both world wars. The density of trackage connected every town with a web of steel tracks and regular timetables. Towns such as Jesup became important rail junctions that gathered freight, timber, or naval stores, or later cotton or peanuts, and distributed them in extensive marshaling yards to long-haul trains that carried them to distant ports or to the expanding cities and towns of the American West. Today, almost all towns in southern Georgia contain empty spaces, ghosts of former tracks, abandoned stations and freight terminals. Except in still functioning rail junctions such as Sylvester or Jesup, freight trains are overshadowed by automobile and truck movement. Railroads have left behind forgotten infrastructures whose timetables and schedules recede into memory, recalled only by mournful freight whistles in the night heat of the rural South.

By the first decade of the twentieth century, the longleaf pines were gone.

The lumber sawmills and turpentine stills were dismantled, and the temporary boomtowns associated with the naval stores industry disappeared. Southern Georgians saw an expanse of cleared land that could be made suitable for cultivation with chemical fertilizers, so they turned to the South's traditional cash crop, cotton. Statistics from the 1900 lower Georgia agricultural census show a landscape of small farms of four to eight improved acres per inhabitant. Most farmers owned a horse and at most a team of mules. Over 30 percent were sharecroppers or white tenant farmers; close to 50 percent of sharecroppers were black. Not surprisingly, zero percent lived in towns of more than 2,500 people.[7] This was a very rural region. The county seats, no matter how small, were the largest urban complexes most people would ever experience.

In the early twentieth century, southern Georgia's unpaved roads brought wagons of cotton and other farm produce to the county seats. The radial network of roads came together at a square in the town center within the larger geometry of a regular street grid. The contradiction between a dynamic and redundant weblike transportation system and the static completeness of the square gives this landscape of southern Georgia its unparalleled impact. One travels across open fields on roads that hug a ridge line; then the road dips and twists to avoid a swamp before entering abruptly into a completely enclosed urban space. This spatial sequence repeats in almost every town. Figure-grounds of six representative county seats from across the region show the consistency of this urban model of concise form. There was no statewide agency mandating conformity to this model; each county government followed its own design. Often the creation of a county seat was an unrestrained and deliberately speculative venture. A property owner would donate the land for the courthouse itself, realizing it would be a magnet for surrounding commercial development. The landowner would then anticipate a profit on the sale of desirable commercial lots framing the square. Because each retail establishment built on its own parcel, market logic suggested self-aggregation, especially in the pedestrian precinct of a small town. Commercially, the courthouse square functioned as an open-air mall with a continuous shaded arcade and the courthouse as its anchor. The construction of the courthouse would be funded from county tax revenues authorized by county commissioners elected and influenced by white landholders.

The placement of the courthouse as an architectural object in the middle of a space is one of the unique aspects of American vernacular urban form. Urban history is full of examples of civic open spaces, from the Greek agora to renaissance piazzas. Often, these spaces have a prominent building framing one side, such as the Temple of Jupiter in Pompeii's forum or the Palazzo Pubblico in Siena's Piazza del Campo. But it is unusual to find the important building in the actual center of the open space allowing for four equal elevations. Placing the building in the center opens the formal design question of which side is most important,

7. Harper, "Development of Agriculture," 329.

Abandoned railroad bridge, Ocmulgee River, Jeff Davis County

so the solution is a four-sided structure with all elevations and entrances equal. For its antecedent, southern vernacular architecture turned to that supreme paradigm of bilateral symmetry—a building on a hilltop outside Vicenza, Palladio's striking Villa Capra. This building has gripped the imagination of architects for centuries, but why a renaissance villa provided the prototype for the courthouses of the Wiregrass region of the American South remains a mystery of Western cultural thought. Not just one such structure, but many spread across the landscape of the South. Like Palladio's Villa Capra, the bilateral temple fronts and four

Lumpkin

Blakely

Statesboro

Buena Vista

Wrightsville

Butler

Figure-ground studies of six representative Georgia county seats

equal entrances of each courthouse are resolved in a round space at the center of the interior beneath a high dome—the ultimate symbol of ecclesiastical or civil authority in Western civilization. The very center of the weblike transportation network that spreads across this vast agricultural landscape of fields and crops becomes a circular three-stored balconied space, filled with mellow wood railings, gracefully curved stairs, hushed voices, and filtered light. The juxtaposition between the hardscrabble poverty of the surrounding flat landscape of southern Georgia and the rich cultural thread of the domed courthouse collects, with a single powerful symbol, all the disparate parts—of rich and poor, of powerful and disenfranchised, of the distance between an idealized democracy and the harsh reality of a sharecropper's tin shack. The disjuncture between the symbol, with its long intellectual history and timeless image, and the intimidating conditions for African Americans in southern Georgia at the turn of the last century is overwhelming.

Not every one of the eighty-five courthouses in this region is a neoclassical four-sided structure. Some are great feats of towers and turrets, combinations of Romanesque and neoclassicism; some are Georgian revival, an architectural style named for the same king as the state of Georgia. Sometimes the courthouse has been torn down, replaced by an undistinguished modern building. Not every town contains a centralized courthouse square. Rail junctions such as Jesup or Sylvester have more linear urban forms with well-defined commercial streets. Their courthouses are placed in a square to one side. But in all cases, these county seats are very dense concise urban complexes spaced regularly across an open landscape that was once white with cotton.

The archetypal courthouse-square town of Moultrie sits in the center of Colquitt County in southern Georgia. Named after one of Georgia's early U.S. senators, Walter T. Colquitt, the county was formed in 1856 by taking land from neighboring Lowndes and Thomas Counties. Moultrie sits almost perfectly in the geographical center at the confluence of nine radiating roads that connect to nine neighboring county seats.

The town was first settled as Ocklockoney on the river of the same name, but its name was changed in 1857 to honor William Moultrie, a wealthy planter from South Carolina. General Moultrie was a hero of the American Revolution known for his defense of Charleston against the British. He served two terms as governor of South Carolina. In southern Georgia, the names of places represent a common and distinctive understanding of the region's position within the larger struggles of the fledgling nation. Most counties, towns, and county seats are named after Revolutionary War heroes or political figures. Inhabitants knew about historical figures and events, even those that took place in distant lands, such as Stephan Decatur's naval battles in North Africa, which are memorialized by Decatur County. Georgians placed importance on the historical continuity of

Aerial photograph of Moultrie, Georgia, 2008

their political system and its defenders and proponents. To say this is indeed a political landscape one needs only to recite the place-names. This rich history of white America, however, is only part of the narrative of the South. Only three counties in southern Georgia have Native American names: Seminole, Chattahoogee, and Muscogee. The early European Americans felt it imperative to legitimize their usurpation by marking a network of place-names firmly emblematic of their different and distinctive heritage.

The timber and naval stores industries discovered Colquitt County's untapped forests in the late nineteenth century. Colquitt's population exploded between 1890 and 1910 from fewer than five thousand people to almost twenty thousand. Railroads proliferated with lines coming into the county from north and east; these were boom times for Moultrie. After the longleaf pines were depleted, cotton followed as the cleared land was transformed to row crops. Colquitt County was typical of the change in southern Georgia from longleaf pine forest to agriculture fields, and Moultrie serves as a perfect example of an early-twentieth-century county seat in the Wiregrass.

Until the boll weevil infestation in the second decade of the twentieth century, cotton was brought into town by wagon for ginning and shipment to the north or to ocean ports. While in town, farmers picked up the necessary bags of fertilizer for their return trip and shopped for necessities such as shoes or cloth, tools or farm implements. Banking and government business could be accomplished at the same time. Luxuries might be a bag of candy or a fancy hat. Because farmers traveled by horse or mule, every town had several liveries or stables to rest,

Colquitt County Courthouse,
Moultrie, Georgia

water, and feed draft animals for a day or overnight. These were large structures located on side streets within a short walk to the courthouse square. The cotton gin and perhaps a sawmill and lumberyard were near the tracks. These were large shed-like structures covered with corrugated tin sheets. Inside, they were hot, noisy, and dusty, filled with either cotton lint or sawdust. Next to the livery was a farrier or blacksmith and perhaps a carriage shop for the more affluent judge, doctor, or banker. The passenger and freight rail depot was nearby, for the station was the town's main portal to the larger world.

Banks were always the most substantial structures after the courthouse. They were placed on a prominent corner of the square; their neoclassical architecture implied stability, strength, and power. Surrounding the square were specialty shops that made these towns self-contained mini-regional centers. Each shop was housed in a separate structure with a full sidewalk display shaded from the hot Georgia sun by deep and continuous arcades. Together, the stores formed an uninterrupted frame for the open courthouse square. Individual shops might sell stationery and paper products, groceries, hardware, women's hats, or shoes with an adjoining cobbler. There would be a drug store and the multipurpose general store or dry goods store. There was always a barbershop for haircuts, shaves, and shoeshines. Even the smallest town had one or two hotels. Visitors on business arrived and left town on the railroad's schedule, and this often meant overnight stays. When court was in session, the circuit judges and the entourage of lawyers and other interested parties needed a place for meals and accommodations for the night.

Other civic and community places included churches, a post office, perhaps a masonic lodge, and, of course, a jail. There were doctors and lawyers for the wealthier farmers. Leading away from the town center were streets of large homes with deep porches on shaded lots for those professionals who worked in town. With its repetitive small dwellings and separate churches, the African American part of town was located across the tracks or down by the mill. Segregation was firmly embedded in the physical form of these small towns.

Unlike today's large chain stores, courthouse-square towns were wonderfully specialized in response to their greater rural market. They were tight urban clusters that fostered levels of social discourse from shopping to business to politics. Their uniformity of size and spacing across the region in a tightly woven net of roads and railroads meant a redundancy in both form and content that gave consistency to an entire region.

A beautiful composite Sanborn Fire Insurance map from 1908 illustrates the wonderful composition of Moultrie's courthouse square. The town is platted in a grid oriented to the cardinal points of the compass, with the open space of the square occupying a central block. The surrounding blocks all face the square with solid facades of brick buildings. The buildings enclose the open space with a continuous arcade. In the center of the space sits the four-equal-sided courthouse surmounted by a dome. It is a classic urban grouping of courthouse, square, and retail frame, all within a grid of residential streets. On the town's periphery are warehouses, a railroad maintenance shop, and cotton gins. Roads and rails radiate away from the square into open agricultural and forested lands and neighboring county seats.

Moultrie's commercial core had an amazingly complete inventory of services and stores in the 1908 map. The train tracks were laid right into the town center. The Georgia Northern depot contained a ticket office, an express office for fast freight, segregated passenger waiting rooms, and a baggage room, all only one block away from the square. There were two hotels in Moultrie, one across the street from the railroad depot and the other on a prime corner anchoring the courthouse square. Everywhere on side and back streets were large liveries. Around the square itself were dry goods stores, drug stores, groceries, a bakery, a clothing store, and a millinery shop. There were three barbershops. We forget that in the man's world of the late nineteenth century, before the invention of electric and safety razors, a straight razor shave was an hour-long sitting hopefully accompanied by a boot shine and the latest local gossip. Barbershops were "Whites Only" clubs with easy chairs and wood-paneled walls.

Moultrie had its own opera house with a stage and flies for scenery. Most small towns had opera houses to take advantage of the many traveling entertainment troupes, vaudeville acts, or magic shows that plied rural American. There are two banks, with classical temple fronts, ready to loan money to farmers against the collateral of their next harvest. Besides the courthouse, other civic structures included a city hall and three churches—Methodist, Baptist, and Presbyterian—placed discreetly one block away from the commercial center. The beautiful library building with its classical facade remains, although today it is a law office.

Toward the town's edges were lumber sheds and cotton warehouses, which were serious structures because of fire danger, often with steel shutters on windows and doors. As cotton warehouses increased in Moultrie in the next decade, merchants built compartmentalized, fire-walled structures for additional safety. All this storage capacity enabled Moultrie to function as an economic, civic, and retail node for a defined agricultural region in the Wiregrass. It was a successful distribution center and celebrated this role with a wonderfully scaled urban space. A 1946 photograph shows the courthouse square filled with people celebrating the Tobacco Fair. Colquitt County was, and still is, a large producer of tobacco. The light poles are draped with the tobacco leaf emblem; spectators hang out of the courthouse windows; and adults and children mull around their cars and trucks. A large group stands on the base of the monument to the Confederacy topped by a Confederate soldier. Not surprisingly, this is a completely segregated crowd.

Moultrie is the final piece in the kinetic puzzle of shifting boundaries, changing

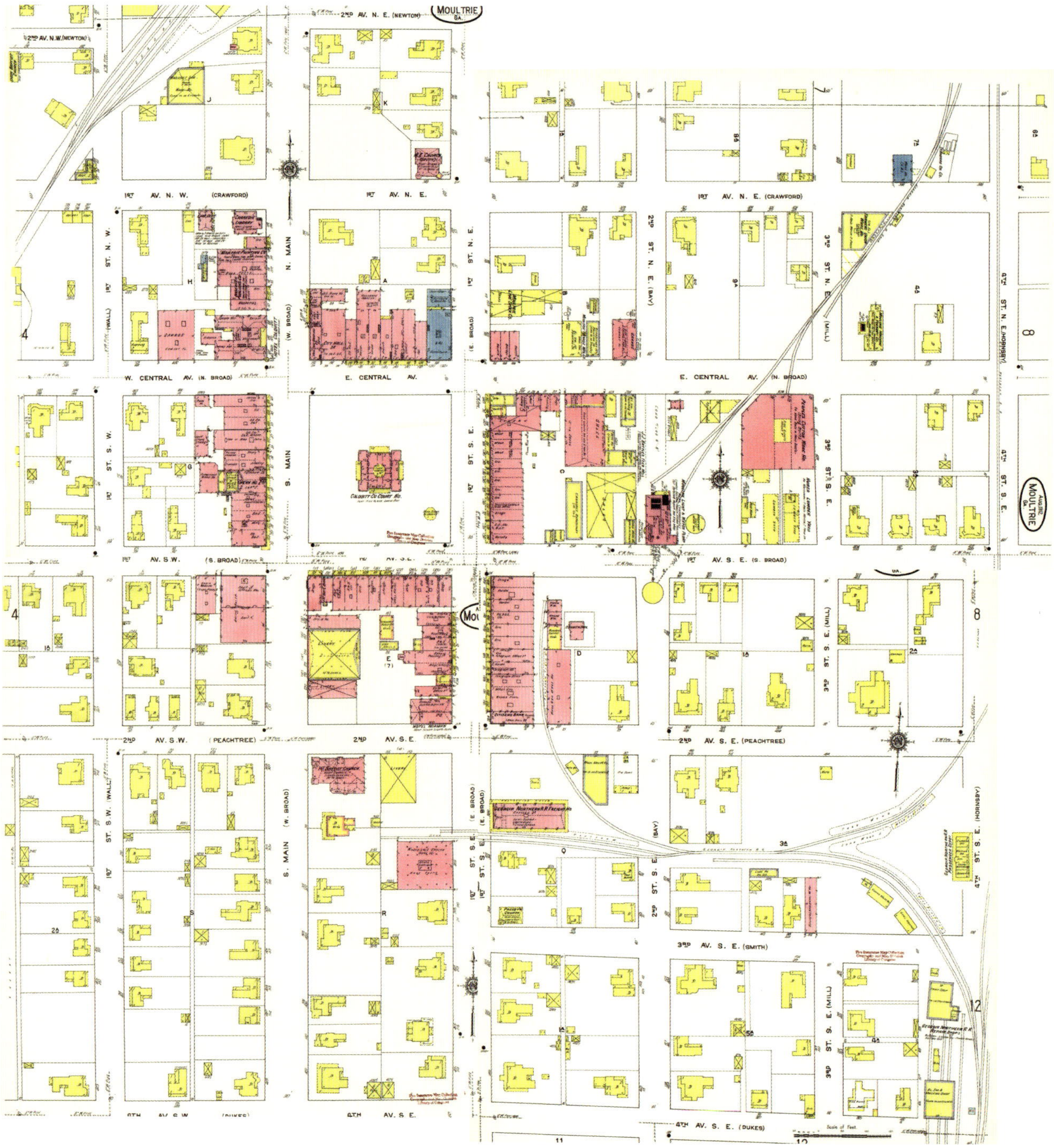

Composite Sanborn Fire Insurance map of Moultrie, Georgia, 1912

ecosystems, and evolving social organizations of southern Georgia. Moultrie's silver courthouse dome caps the end of our investigations of the network of towns and counties spread across this region. The courthouse's splendid architecture of painted brick and wood replaces the seemingly limitless longleaf pine forest that once covered this landscape with a different architecture of its own,

Cotton warehouse, Moultrie, Georgia

"an architectural symmetry. . . . no means unlike that of some gothic cathedral." These words were written by the brilliant British naval officer Basil Hall in 1829.[8]

The weighty dome of the courthouse shares the square with another monument erected just a few years after the courthouse's completion. In 1906, the local chapter of the United Daughters of the Confederacy dedicated a tall obelisk surmounted by a Confederate soldier in the square's southwest corner. Over a hundred years later, beautiful crepe myrtles, the quintessentially southern tree, surround this monument to the past. The soldier with his bold chin and steady

8. Hall, *Travels in North America*, 175.

Moultrie, Georgia, 1946. Note the Confederate Monument on the right.

gaze stands for many things: states rights, a noble cause, the death of so many similar young men. He can also be interpreted as part of a larger history—of segregation and racial inequality. Even the grand architecture of the courthouse cannot hide the contradictions and ambiguities that have passed through its doors. Its four imperial temple fronts pay mute tribute to the hope of triumphant civil rights and racial equality. The haunting beauty of the courthouse in its square mocks many veiled narratives while silently accepting the passage of time. It is all that remains of a complex history, the only marker in a forgotten landscape.

Heading south again through Georgia's coastal plain, I-75 lies straight as a ruler upon the gently seaward sloping topography. It passes through county after county with little acknowledgment except for tiny signs along the shoulder. All the discussions of boundaries and political divisions of this chapter have been about lines unseen on today's maps. From the highway, broad vistas of green agricultural fields belie the fact that one travels through only recently constructed

Colquitt County Courthouse
and Confederate Monument

landscapes. Forgotten are the great forests and the despicable tragedy of racial strife. Perhaps this will be the legacy of the interstate: that access to its long distances are free to all regardless of race or color. The interstate system is the most democratic of infrastructures, allowing travelers to pass over our differences. That is our Faustian bargain: that to bind the nation with easily accessed ribbons of roads, we relinquish the past by erasing our darkest, most wretched histories.

5

LANDSCAPES AND FARM VILLAGES OF THE GREAT PLAINS

THE SPREAD OF THE CADASTRAL GRID across the Great Plains and the subsequent rapid development of railroads determined the pattern of Nebraska's agriculture. The Land Ordinance of 1785 initiated one of the largest land transferences in human history, from federal government control to private ownership. The measurement of this cadastral shift remains indelibly etched across the vast landscapes of the western United States. The survey grid determines road direction, field distribution, and irrigation arrangements as well as town plans. Using an entirely different ordering system, the great railway expansion of the second half of the eighteenth century encouraged the intensive agricultural development of the fertile Great Plains. The intersection of the two systems in the centers of western towns, the orthogonal lines of the cadastral grid with the diagonal routes of the railroads, creates some of the most evocative spaces in the American landscape. The urban design of Nebraska's farm communities joins the infinite space of the Plains with the finite form of small villages. The imposition of the interstate highway, a different system of bypasses and off-ramps, over the two historical patterns of the grid and the railroads, creates a new settlement pattern while erasing the old.

Winds of the Pleistocene

In the early twentieth century, the Lincoln Highway traversed the United States from New York City to San Francisco and offered the most direct route for automobiles crossing the continent. The Lincoln Highway was not a separate dedicated road; rather, it was a named route that utilized existing roads of differing surfaces as it threaded its way across twelve states.

Bright red, white, and blue signs with a distinctive blue "L" painted on telephone and telegraph poles marked the route. Highway maps from the 1920s directed the motorist, "Follow the painted poles to your destination."

The Lincoln Highway began and ended in specific and well-known places: from its eastern terminus in Times Square it stretched 2,600 miles to San Francisco's Legion of Honor in beautiful Lincoln Park on the Pacific Ocean. It was America's first transcontinental highway, and its two ends bracketed the vast interior of the continent between the frenetic congestion of Times Square and the majestic headlands of the Golden Gate.

Today Interstate 80 follows an almost identical path across America, but the interstate begins in the East as an exit off I-95 just west of the George Washington Bridge in New Jersey and ends in the West as I-80 merges with the I-280 spur into San Francisco. The earlier specificity and scale of the Lincoln Highway's two ends contrasts with the nebulous locations of I-80's beginning and end. Both Times Square and the Legion of Honor, then and now, are defined and familiar places with architectural enclosure and pedestrian activities. By contrast, I-80's lack of any understandable connection with an identifiable beginning or end in New York or San Francisco reinforces its detachment from its physical context. An off-ramp in New Jersey or a merge lane in San Francisco is not a comprehensible place.

Like the Lincoln Highway, I-80 crosses twelve middle-tier states coast to coast. In the East, parts of I-80 trace earlier toll roads such as the Ohio Turnpike and the Indiana Toll Road. Leaving Chicago and the Mississippi River, I-80 crosses the farmland of Iowa. A bridge over the Missouri River brings I-80 into Nebraska at Omaha before connecting south to the state capital of Lincoln. West of Lincoln, I-80 runs ruler straight to a crossing of the Platte River at Grand Island. For over one hundred miles or almost two hours' driving time, a car's steering wheel remains fixed as the road follows an undeviating east–west survey line. After Grand Island, I-80 abandons its linear and unbending direction to conform to the wide sweep of the Platte River until both the river and the highway exit Nebraska into Wyoming. A Standard Oil Company of Nebraska road map of 1922 shows the middle segment of the state with a black dotted line of I-80 superimposed over the road system of 1922. On this early map, the Lincoln Highway, marked with dark squares surrounding the number 34, sweeps down just north of the Platte River. The interstate traces two important nineteenth-century narratives of America's westward expansion: the immigrant wagon trails along the Platte River that headed to California through the Rocky Mountains and the public survey grid that facilitated one of history's great land transferences. Like a black pen stroke upon the landscape, I-80 highlights both the cultural construct of the survey grid and the influence of the

Platte River geography on transcontinental travel. In spite of its inauspicious beginning outside New York and its confusing end in San Francisco, the interstate does connect to our heartland's histories.

The gentle double curve of the Platte River across Nebraska owes its existence to the natural processes that formed the Great Plains. To begin, the first half of this chapter turns back several million years in time, to explain its title, "Winds of the Pleistocene," before exploring the pattern of the Great Plains in a defined area of south-central Nebraska. Detailed descriptions of the cadastral survey of America's West lead to an investigation of railroads in Nebraska in the second half, "The Plow Follows the Ox." Ultimately these two sections reveal separate narratives, one the making of the survey grid and the other the westward expansion of railroads, that join together to make a distinctive space found in most Great Plains towns.

During the 2.5 million years of the Pleistocene Epoch, glaciers advanced and retreated across the northern plains. These thick sheets of ice pushed and shaped the earth's surface as far south as eastern Nebraska. The freezing temperatures and massive weather systems associated with the towering ice fronts generated fierce storms that transported the newly turned and barren soils at the margins of the glaciers hundreds of miles east across central North America. The Pleistocene winds swept fine silt across Nebraska and Iowa and into Illinois and Ohio. Over millions of years, these wind-borne, fine-grained particles produced a thick layer of well-drained topsoil as deep as eighty feet. Known as loess, these soils cover much of the Great Plains from Texas to Manitoba and eastward across the central states of Iowa and Missouri and across the Mississippi River into Illinois and Indiana. Evidence of these eolian landscapes still appears as long dunes running north–south in western Nebraska's Sand Hill region. From an airplane, this evenly rippled surface of the Sand Hills looks much like corrugated beach sand at low tide, with wind instead of water as the fluid

Exit 353 on I-80 in Nebraska

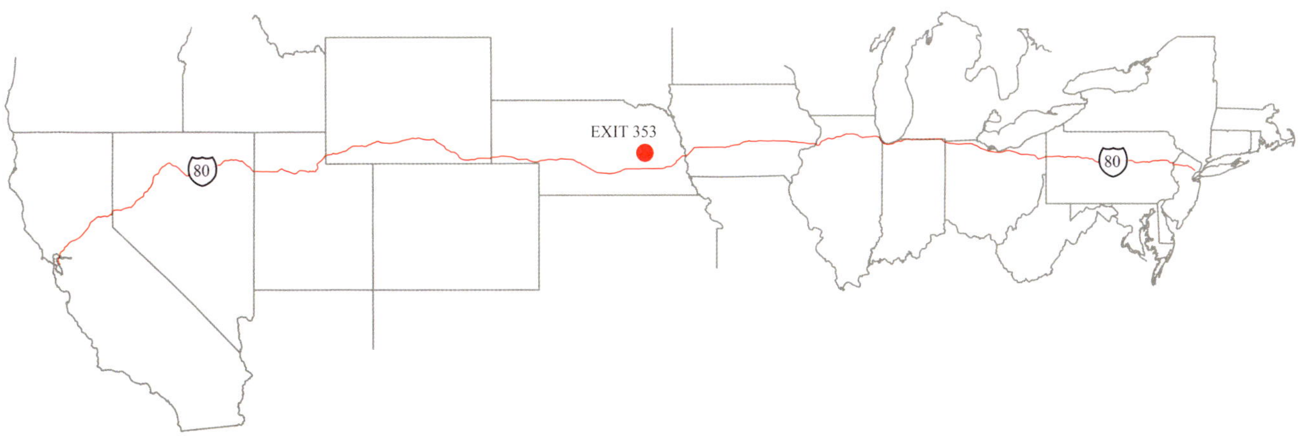

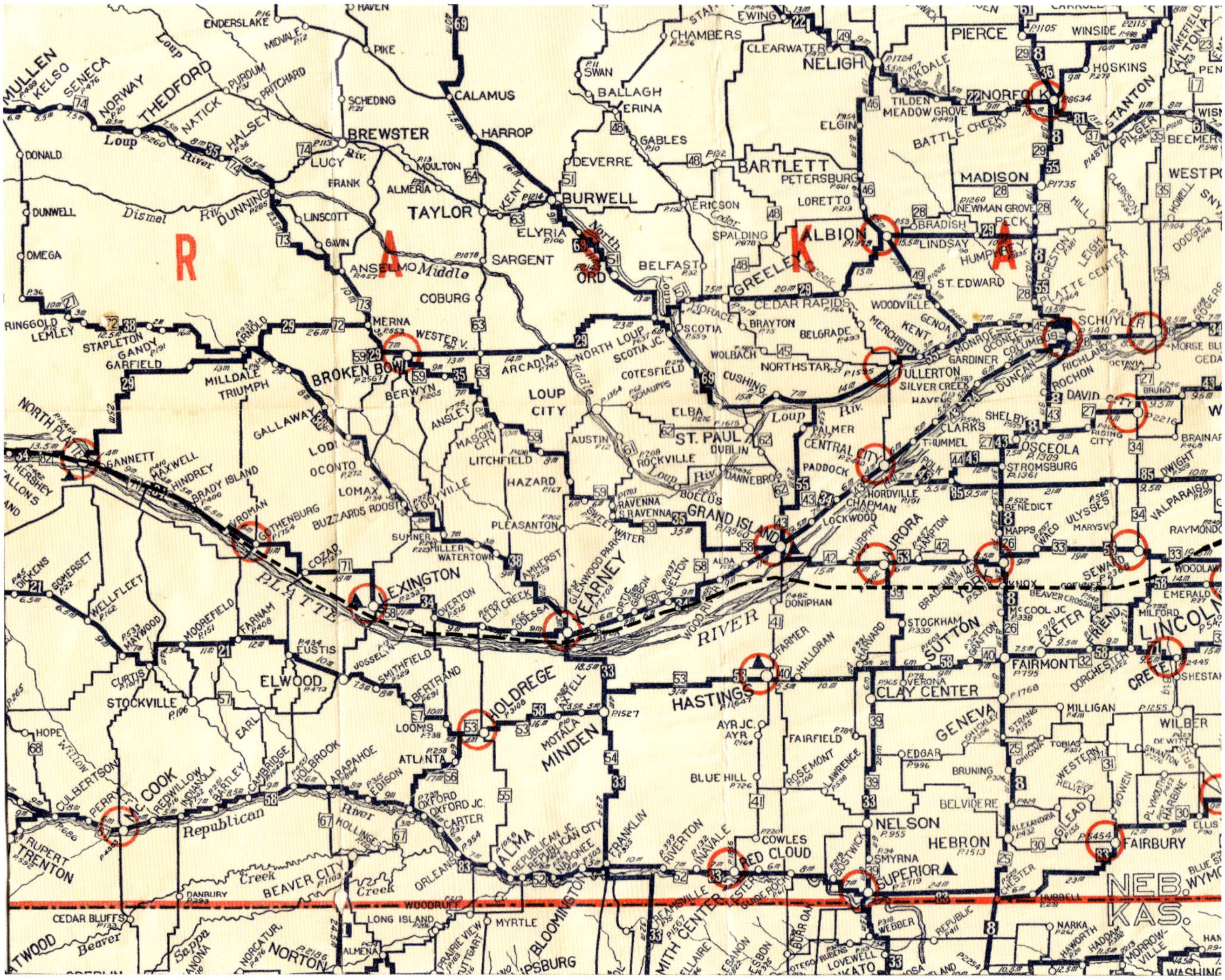

Detail from a 1922 Standard Oil road map of Nebraska. The dotted line represents the right-of-way of I-80.

agent. Loess soils have no boulders or even small stones. They appear relatively flat, are well drained, and are extremely friable when devoid of vegetation. With adequate moisture, loess soils support thick, dense mats of plant growth. Without vegetative cover, however, these same soils revert quickly to their eolian origins and can be blown again over long distances. The disastrous dust bowls of the 1930s across Texas, Oklahoma, Colorado, Kansas, and southern Nebraska resulted from the removal of native vegetation through extensive plowing and cultivation coupled with inadequate rainfall. The wind-borne soil particles traveled so far east that ship decks in the Atlantic were covered in fine layers of dust from Nebraska.

Water easily percolates through the tiny homogeneous particles of loess soil. A shallow-gradient river or stream that flows through loess soils takes its drainage pattern from this same porosity as the water's channels spread out into braided-like stream beds that separate, rejoin, and intertwine in a broad shallow floodplain. The Platte River floodplain comprises multiple channels that constantly separate and rejoin along its even gradient. Early travelers along the Platte banks commented on the river as being a mile wide and a foot deep. The Platte, the Missouri, and other rivers that flow across the Great Plains carry a heavy sediment load of eroded loess silt beyond the water's capacity to keep it in suspension, so a single deep channel cannot form. As the excess sediment is deposited, sand bars divert and twist the watercourse into many interlocking channels. The wide curves of the Platte across its entire length in Nebraska indicates that it flows through a homogeneous surface with little resistance, in contrast to the Blackstone River with its abrupt shifts and turns through granite rocks discussed earlier in chapter 3.

Water and wind rapidly erode loess soils, causing steep gullies and sharply edged dendritic patterns in a stream's floodplain. A constructed map of two streams in south-central Nebraska illustrates this organic hydrological pattern. The recursive courses of both streams bow and turn back on themselves, indicative of both a flat gradient and a homogeneous substrate. The one-mile-square grid overlay represents survey section lines that highlight the disjuncture between the rigidly linear cultural system for ownership demarcation and the underlying ribbon-like drainage organization with its fractal-edged floodplain.

Loess soils of the Great Plains supported the vast treeless grassland ecologies that covered much of America from the Mississippi River to the Rocky Mountains. Agriculture easily replaced these ecosystems, provided there was adequate and regular precipitation. A constant annual rainfall of twenty inches during the spring-summer growing seasons is the minimum for large-scale farming of cereal crops; the history of the success and failure of human settlement on the Great Plains closely follows the cycles of annual precipitation.

The Rocky Mountains form a continental-long barrier to easterly flowing moisture-laden winds. Along their eastern slopes and continuing out into the plains, precipitation is dramatically reduced, forming a "rain shadow" of far less than twenty inches of rain. Precipitation increases as one moves east across Nebraska and Kansas and into Iowa and Missouri, fed by moisture-laden fronts pushing north from the Gulf of Mexico. The line at which agriculture becomes viable without artificial irrigation, the line of more than twenty inches of rain, occurs around the hundredth meridian that runs through central Kansas and Nebraska. Further east, Iowa, Illinois, and Indiana have one enormous advantage: plentiful moisture that, coupled with perfect soils for agriculture, makes perhaps the best conditions for farming on the planet.

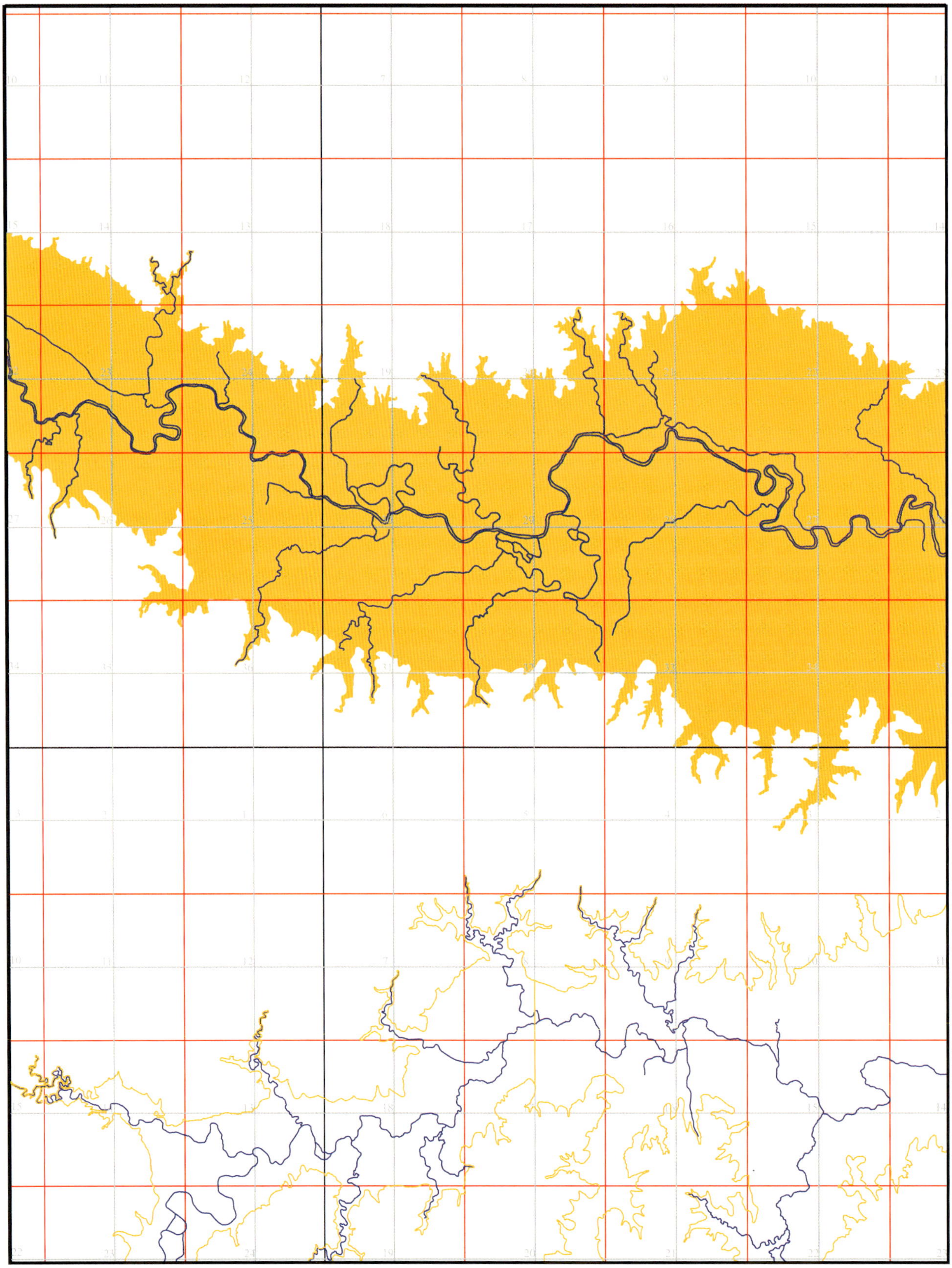

As the moisture gradient increased from west to east, so did the height of the native prairie grasses. The tallgrass prairies once spread across Iowa and Missouri into eastern Nebraska and Kansas. Mixed grasses bracketed the hundredth meridian, and west beyond this point the short grasses predominated. Each of the three height categories of grasses describes three different, very complex, and unique ecologies within the larger Great Plains, now all but eradicated by agriculture except in a few tiny protected areas.

As European-American settlers ventured westward out into this vast featureless expanse, they required some system of marking to record ownership. If the Great Plains, along with the earlier settled states of Ohio, Illinois, and Iowa, were to be fully occupied for agriculture, a clear and efficient method for parceling land ownership had to be invented. Soon after becoming independent from Britain, the fledgling American Congress developed the remarkable Public Land Survey System. Working westward from eastern Ohio across the continent, this particularly American land survey system expedited the largest transfer of land from public to private ownership in human history and, in the process, indelibly marked our western landscapes for succeeding generations.

Prior to the Revolutionary War, the King's charter for his American colonies granted land all the way west to the "China seas." As the interior of the continent and even its Pacific Coast was unknown and unexplored by Europeans, little attention was given to these overly ambitious boundaries. After the American Revolution, however, the young nation found itself in possession of all lands to the Mississippi River, and the issue of ownership had to be addressed. Each of the original thirteen colonies, now states, relinquished any claims to "the China Seas" and agreed to western limits of their boundaries approximately as they are today. All lands outside the boundaries of the original thirteen colonies were to belong to the federal government. As discussed earlier in chapter 4, Georgia, for example, gave up title to all lands from the Chattahoochee River to the Mississippi River, land subsequently divided into the states of Alabama and Mississippi.

At the end of the Revolutionary War, America was land rich and cash poor. The Continental Congress passed two pieces of legislation, the Land Ordinance of 1785 and then the Northwest Ordinance of 1787, to control the survey, sale, and settling of the new federal lands. These ordinances stipulated the mechanics of surveying work so that the land could be transferred from the public domain into private ownership and established the guidelines for large areas becoming states. (The discussions of surveying in chapter 4, while similar, were for lands internal to and owned by the state of Georgia and were not part of these federal land ordinances.) In the late eighteenth century, the United States had not yet gained the vast area

Streams in south-central Nebraska *(opposite)*

of the West: the Louisiana Purchase, the lands taken from Mexico in the Treaty of Hidalgo, and the true northwest states of Oregon and Washington. Nevertheless, the same Ordinances of 1785 and 1787, with several modifications, governed land transfers all the way to America's eventual Pacific Coast. The intention was for the U.S. government to make money on these enormous land sales, but events and the ingenuity of American frontier individualism conspired against any great federal profit. Land was not to be given outright but was to be sold at prices ranging from twenty-five cents to two dollars per acre. It is difficult to imagine land in the United States so plentiful that it could be almost given away, but raw, unimproved land was considered practically useless in the eighteenth century.

In the late eighteenth century, settlers began moving through the Appalachians into the fertile Ohio River Valley, an area then called the Northwest Territory, made up of the future states of Ohio, Indiana, Illinois, Michigan, and Wisconsin. At the time, these states actually comprised the northwest of the then bounded United States. Immigration had swelled the population of America, and in a newly formed democratic government, many legislators complained that we were essentially giving the land to ourselves. Later in Nebraska under the Homestead Act, the federal government did give away land, the only required payment being proof of improvements. The story of the transference of three-quarters of a continent from the public domain to private ownership is one of the most fascinating aspects of America's westward expansion, for it required a substantial reconceptualization of public-private property.

In Europe at the time of America's independence, the sovereign or king owned all land in a country and its colonies. Land titles could be transferred to favored individuals for finite periods of time, but the ordinary citizen could never own land outright. Many of the original British colonies in America were created by such grants: Pennsylvania to William Penn and Georgia to John Oglethorpe being two of the most notable examples. The public domain, or Crown lands, as they came to be called, belonged to the king. The fledgling government of the United States, in a remarkable stroke of insight, declared that the vast lands beyond the original colonies belonged to the government, hence the people. This public land, separate from government-owned land such as military reservations, was to be transferred from the public domain as quickly and expeditiously as possible into clearly titled private ownership. The methods for acquiring title varied over time from preemption purchase and soldiers' military bounty land warrants to lotteries and outright sales. In the end, much land was given to veterans of various wars, to the railroads, and to speculators. In the vast spaces of the western states, land was given free to railroads as a way of capitalizing their construction, for, as the second section of this chapter explains, railroad transportation was absolutely integral to the expansion of agriculture. Fairly or unfairly, the survey and transfer of land continued until by the early twentieth century, in little over one hundred years, all lands in the public domain were disposed of.

As thousands of immigrants spread westward beyond the Appalachians and then across the Mississippi, there were several ways for an individual American, or soon-to-be-American citizen, to acquire title to land. The first was through public auction or lottery after the land had been surveyed. Second was by a soldier's military bounty land warrant. Since land warrants had been issued to American soldiers since 1776, essentially free land anywhere available was given as payment for military service. These straightforward grants rewarded soldiers who fought for a cash-strapped nation. As the Nebraska Territory opened, settlement ran ahead of the land surveys, causing the federal government to pass the Preemption Act of 1841. This act provided that settlers in Nebraska and some other western states in the Louisiana Purchase could settle on unsurveyed land, improve it, and then be permitted, when the land was surveyed, to select and purchase the 160 acres whose boundaries most closely corresponded with their improved acres.

The price of land was adjusted as the westward formation of states continued. Often, prices were graduated downward as the best land sold quickly and less desirable land remained unsold for longer periods of time. The most valuable land was that along existing and future railroad rights-of-way. Prices distant from tracks dropped from $1.20 to as low as 10 or 12 cents an acre. In 1862, the federal government passed the first Homestead Act. Applicable mainly to Nebraska, the Homestead Act permitted a U.S. citizen at least twenty-one years of age to claim 160 acres of land for free. After five years of residence, the homesteader had to "prove up" his or her claim by demonstrating improvements to obtain title. Eventually about 30 percent of Nebraska, or over twenty-five thousand square miles, was transferred into private ownership through this process. The Homestead Act attracted thousands of settlers to Nebraska and hastened its admission to the Union as a state in 1867.

Another way for a person to obtain land was to purchase it outright from the railroads. In order to privately finance the construction of the transcontinental railroads completed in 1869, the federal government gave free land from the public domain to the Union Pacific through Nebraska and westward and to the Central Pacific eastward from California. These were very substantial grants of ten square miles per linear mile of track laid, allocated in a checkerboard pattern on both sides of the right-of-way. In

1870 the federal government provided additional grants to a second railroad through Nebraska, the Burlington and Missouri Pacific. As the tracks followed the river valleys, the land itself was more fertile and especially valuable. Consequently, it sold quickly, and Nebraska soon became crisscrossed with a fine network of railroad tracks.

The method for surveying the thousands of square miles of the United States was refined and amended over time. As settlement moved west, and a defined area became first a territory and then a state, its external boundaries were set. Some boundaries were straight lines; some followed the irregular course of a major river such as the Mississippi. All states up and down the Mississippi or along the Ohio River have at least one side bounded by either river. The Great Lakes caused the irregular shapes of the upper midwestern states. As one moved into the arid and mountainous West with fewer large rivers, state boundaries became more regular, as is the case with the true rectangle shape of Colorado. While the north, west, and south boundaries of Nebraska are straight, the Missouri River makes its eastern edge a great curve.

To survey a state, even an irregularly shaped state, the *x* and *y* survey axes were established by a north–south meridian and an east–west parallel. A meridian or line of longitude is an imaginary arc on the Earth's surface that runs from pole to pole. Each meridian is perpendicular to any intersecting line of latitude, yet all meridians converge as they approach the poles. As we shall see, this particular attribute of spherical geometry caused difficulties with on-the-ground orthogonal surveys. Lines of latitude, by contrast, parallel the equator, decreasing in diameter as one nears either pole.

Within a newly formed state, the meridian was usually located parallel to the longest possible north–south dimension. States might designate several lines of longitude as meridians to fill out an irregular shape. Some meridians run through contiguous states; for example, Nebraska's Sixth Principal Meridian runs south through Kansas. Meridians were numbered or named east to west across the United States. Many were given names based upon towns or major geographical features. A baseline, a designated line of latitude, intersected the meridian at right angles. Often a state would have several baselines to make it easier to fill out an irregular shape. Many baselines formed multiple state boundaries, as is the case along the southern boundaries of Kansas, Colorado, and Utah.

A beautiful map prepared in 1867 for the General Land Office summarizes the extent of the land survey work already accomplished across the United States. The original thirteen states plus Kentucky and Tennessee had already been surveyed earlier under a different system and have no grid. Texas, originally part of Mexico and then briefly an independent country, followed the land grants of the original Spanish occupants, so it had no survey grid. Some states do not yet exist, such as the Dakotas and Wyoming. Other states have only a portion completed, usually a fertile river valley, such as New Mexico's Rio Grande Valley or California's flat Central Valley. Nebraska is only partially surveyed in the fertile and wetter east. Moving westward from its eastern terminus at the Missouri River, Nebraska's baseline is the state boundary with Kansas that runs along the fortieth parallel. The perpendicular principle or prime meridian continues south into Kansas. The two cross at a point on the Nebraska-Kansas line 108 miles west of the Missouri River; a memorial constructed over the original nineteenth-century stone monument still marks this point today at 97°22' west. The magnitude of the undertaking evidenced by this map is overwhelming. These baselines and meridians are not short lengths but run to hundreds of miles. The line that delineates the southern boundary of Kansas from the northern boundary of Oklahoma runs though the Four Corners of Colorado, New Mexico, Arizona, and Utah for over a thousand miles. The perpendicular meridian passing north–south through the Four Corners is 700 miles long. These survey lines were grand gestures across vast distances.

On the 1867 map, all the irregular shapes in the more settled and surveyed midwestern states are completely filled in with squares in continuous grids. These squares are six miles wide by six miles long and are confusingly called townships, although they have nothing to do with towns. The east–west increments are known as ranges. The American Public Land Survey came to be known as ranges and townships. The prime meridians are marked off in six-mile increments numbered north or south from the baselines. Baselines are marked off into six-mile increments numbered east or west from the meridian. Any given six-mile square can be designated and located by these numbered coordinates. The thirty-six-square-mile townships were further divided into thirty-six one-mile-square pieces called sections. In the flat states of the American West such as Nebraska, the survey grid of the nineteenth century shaped and continues to influence the landscape we see today. County boundaries are based upon meridian and latitude lines, and property divisions and agricultural fields fill out the spaces outlined by township sections. County roads and state and federal highways align with sectional and township boundaries. Highway maps such as the one illustrated at the beginning of this chapter clearly show the step-like movement of roads as they cross the landscape in straight lines and make right angled turns to follow section boundaries. Interstate I-80 between Lincoln and Grand Island runs along a section line parallel to latitudinal lines, which, of course, makes it also parallel to the equator.

Map of the United States and territories, showing the extent of public surveys and other details/constructed from the plats and official sources of the General Land Office, under the direction of Jos. S. Wilson, commissioner, by Joseph Gorlinski, draughtsman, 1867; Department of the Interior, General Land Office, Oct 15th, 1867 ***(overleaf)***

PACIFIC OCEAN
WASHINGTON
OREGON
CALIFORNIA
NEVADA
IDAHO
MONTANA
DAKOTA
NEBRASKA
UTAH
COLORADO
KANSAS
ARIZONA
NEW MEXICO
LOWER CALIFORNIA
MEXICO
TEXAS
Explanations

MAP
of the
UNITED STATES
and
TERRITORIES,
Showing the extent of Public Surveys and other details,
CONSTRUCTED FROM
the Plats and official sources
of the
GENERAL LAND OFFICE,
HON. JOS. S. WILSON,
Commissioner,
LAKE SUPERIOR
LAKE MICHIGAN
LAKE HURON
LAKE ERIE
LAKE ONTARIO
UPPER CANADA
MAINE
NEW YORK
PENNSYLVANIA
OHIO
ILLINOIS
WISCONSIN
MICHIGAN
IOWA
MISSOURI
KENTUCKY
WEST VIRGINIA
VIRGINIA
TENNESSEE
NORTH CAROLINA
SOUTH CAROLINA
GEORGIA
ARKANSAS
MISSISSIPPI
LOUISIANA
FLORIDA
ATLANTIC OCEAN
GULF OF MEXICO

To understand the indelible influence of the survey grid on America's western landscapes, I explore an area of south-central Nebraska in greater detail. This portion of Nebraska is representative of the common attributes of the entire eastern half of the state and several neighboring states. It contains differences, however, important to the discussions of this chapter on Nebraska. South-central Nebraska lies in the Corn Belt east of the one hundredth meridian. Because of the potential bulk freight of harvested corn, the Burlington Northern Railroad still serves the region with a dense network of trackage. The Platte River, the former Lincoln Highway, and I-80 run through the center of this area. And lastly, it contains a manageable sampling of small- and medium-sized towns whose tiny urban grids each contain one of the most evocative and existential spaces of any American small town.

The selection of such an area raises an important question about the word "regionalism." While a gridded area of Nebraska may be representative of the larger ecological unit of the Great Plains, the boundaries are cadastral lines that can be extended almost infinitely in any direction—for example, along the meridian line into Kansas or along the baseline through different moisture gradients, either east or west. The two earlier discussions of southern New England and southern Georgia posited regional boundaries defined by ecological limits, the watershed; or by the extent of longleaf pine forests; or by political considerations and the county unit voting mechanism. Like the longleaf pine forests, the grasslands of the Great Plains have been replaced by agriculture, so an ecological dimension to this region no longer applies. Today south-central Nebraska is a segment of an immense grid with seemingly infinite limits; the less than satisfactory definition of this area must be a series of squares within a survey grid. This fractal quality of the Great Plains' boundaries gives the American West a sense of unlimited amplification and space, yet towns of the Great Plains sought the exact opposite: to enclose and restrain the far horizons through tree cover and concise urban compositions.

More than any other region, the Great Plains owes its physical characteristics to linear abstractions. Because the orthogonal grid determined Nebraska's landscape, the following paragraphs carefully review the process of surveying the state. Nebraska's baseline is its southern boundary with Kansas at forty degrees north of the equator. More accurate modern survey technology positions the Nebraska-Kansas boundary at 40°00'07". From a known location, called a reference point, on the baseline, a meridian was extended north and south. In Nebraska and Kansas, this point is 97°22'08". The extended meridian was designated the Sixth Principal Meridian. Together, the baseline and meridian established an x–y axis marked in six-mile increments within Nebraska (and Kansas) from which all subsequent land subdivisions were referenced. Any of the six-mile squares could be designated by its relationship to the prime meridian and baseline such as Range VII east, Township 7 north. Standard parallels every twenty-four miles parallel to the baseline and guide meridians every twenty-four or thirty miles parallel to the prime meridian provide verification that the survey lines are parallel to those of the larger grid. Most counties in Nebraska are stacked up in square tiers of sixteen townships each beginning from the baseline; those of Kansas to the south are slightly different in size. The study area of this chapter on Nebraska comprises the nine named counties on the diagram: Hamilton, York, Seward, Clay, Fillmore, Saline, Nuckolls, Thayer, and Jefferson.

Lines of longitude, however, are not parallel, but rather converge until they meet in a point at the north and south poles. While not an issue over short distances, at the greater distances across an entire state, this was a significant problem, for theoretically all townships and sections should be

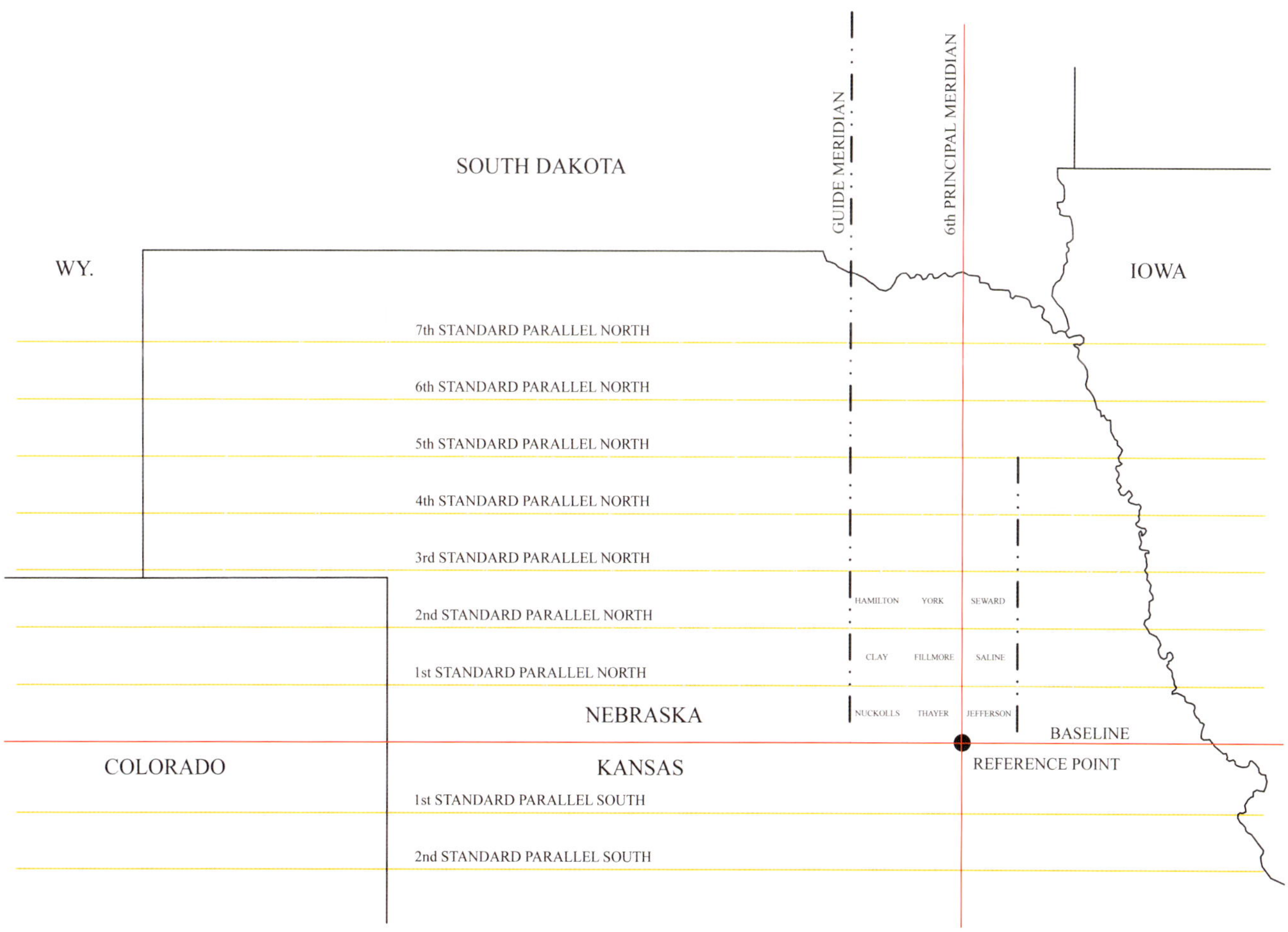

Drawing of Nebraska illustrating the way the state was surveyed and the positions of meridians and parallels. The baseline is the boundary between Nebraska and Kansas. All meridians and parallels relate to the reference point at the intersection of the baseline and the sixth prime meridian.

the same area. Eighteenth- and nineteenth-century surveyors were aware of this discrepancy and compensated through offsets and adjustments visible in today's landscape from an aerial perspective or experienced on the ground as a sharp series of right angle turns in county roads.

A detail from a beautiful map prepared in 1874 by Asher & Adams illustrates the application of these cadastral lines. The selected area of the 1874 map corresponds with the same nine named counties in the previous diagram. The baseline border with Kansas is highlighted in red and marked off in ranges east and west with roman numerals. The perpendicular north–south principle meridian is marked with Arabic numerals. Each square is six miles on a side or thirty-six square miles; each county is four townships on a side (thirty-six times sixteen) or 450 square miles. With some minor boundary modifications, these county boundaries remain today. Closer study of this map reveals that as one moves west or east from the principal meridian along the baseline, the north–south lines that delineate the townships begin to offset, indicating corrections due to convergence of longitudinal lines.

Detail from the "New commercial and topographic rail road map & guide of Nebraska"; prepared by Asher & Adams, 1874

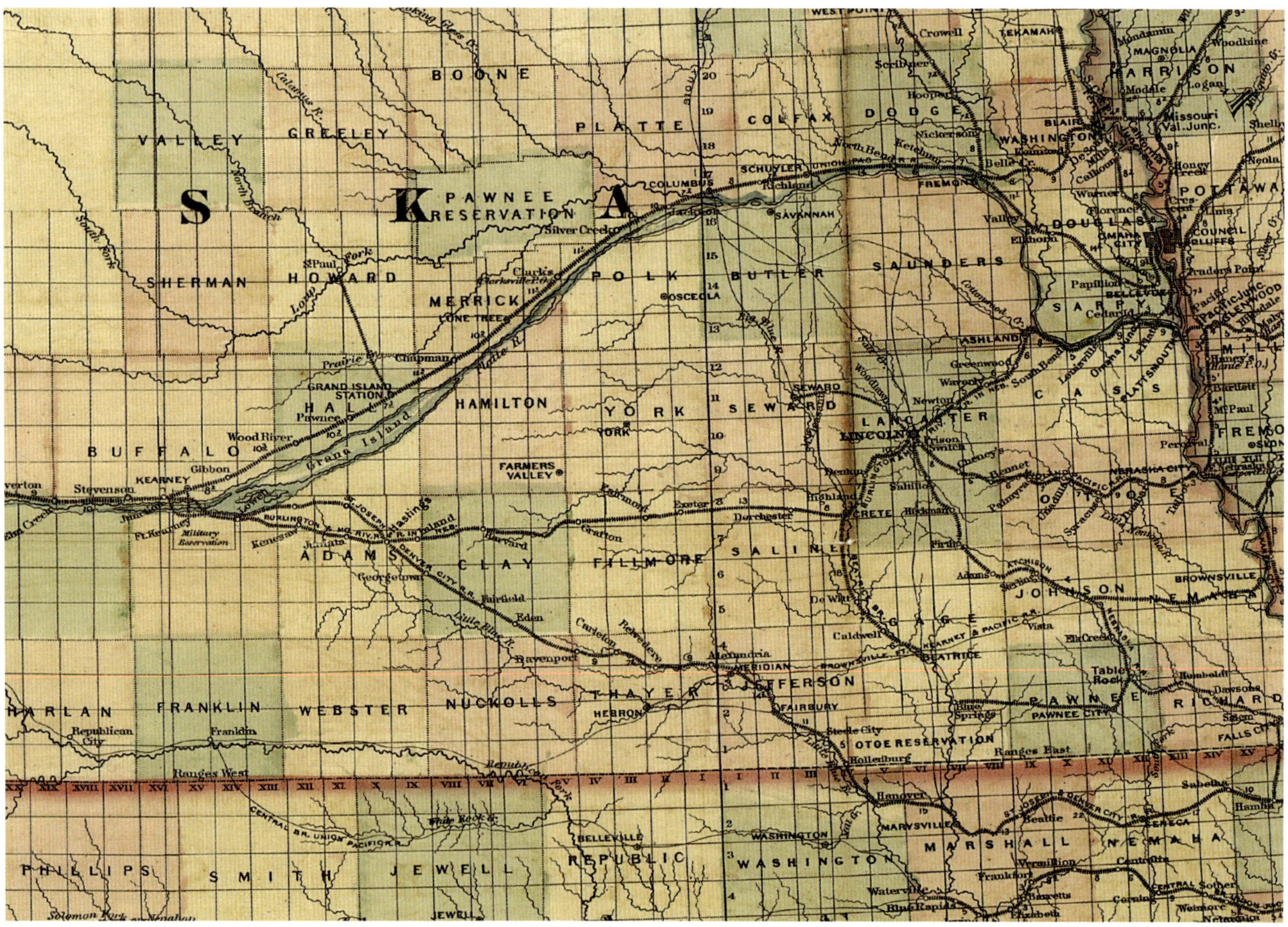

Squares corresponding to counties are subdivided into townships. Each township was again subdivided into one-mile squares, thirty-six to a township, called sections. Sections within a township are numbered from the upper right corner, right to left in a sequence particular to the American survey grid.

The numbering sequence of the sections has an interesting history unrelated to nineteenth-century American survey methods. Modern English texts read from left to right; modern Hebrew and Arabic from right to left. The reading of a text or numbering system alternately from right to left and then left to right is found in ancient scripts such as archaic Greek or Safaitic. Such texts are referred to as "boustrophedon" from the Greek meaning "as the ox turns." When plowing a field with a team of oxen or other draft animals, one walks down a furrow and then reverses direction,

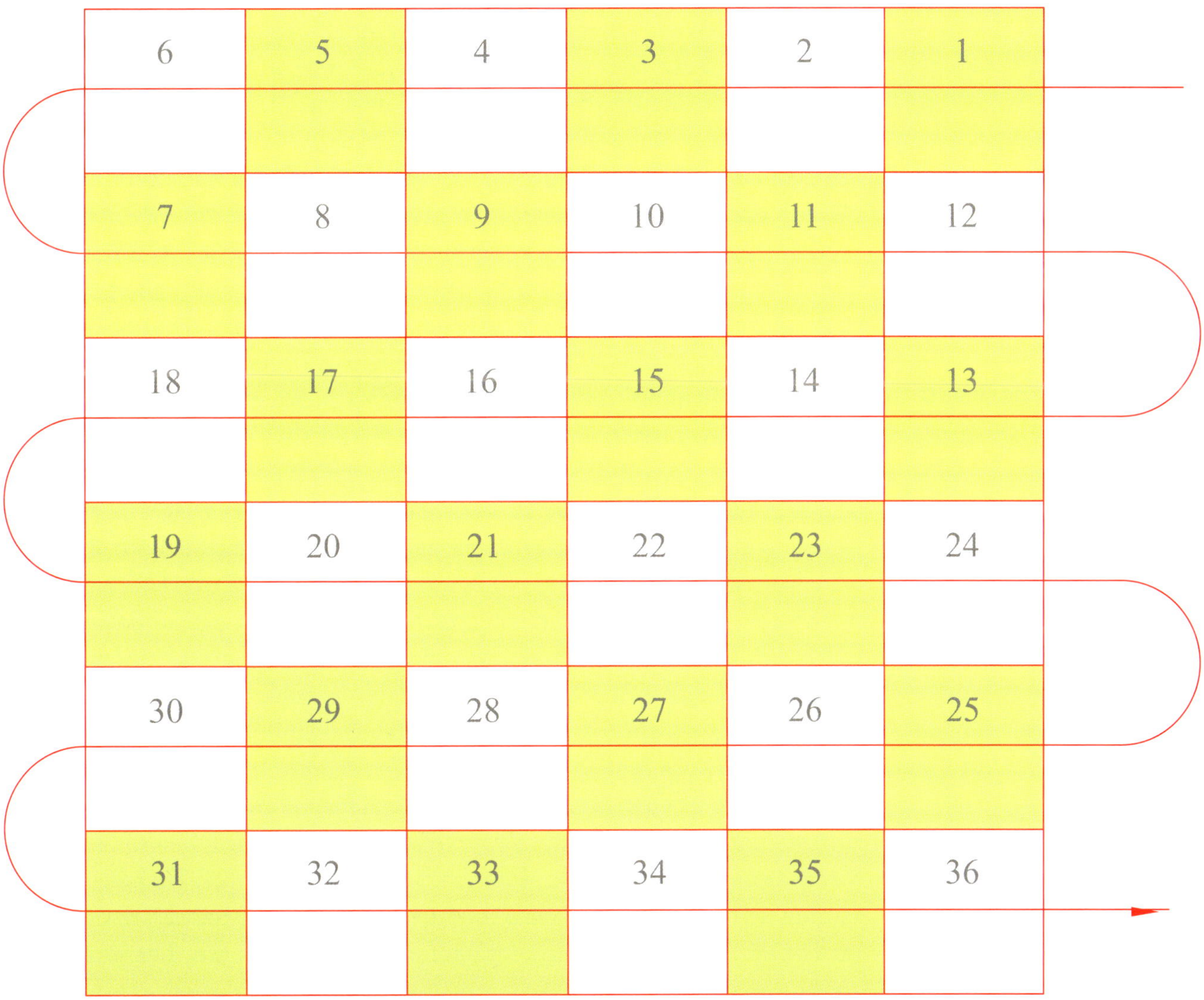

Diagram of a typical township illustrating its division into thirty-six sections

back and forth. Oxen were difficult to maneuver so the turn would be wide in order to return parallel to the first furrow. In boustrophedon script, the hand of the writer goes back and forth like a team of oxen pulling a plow. This numbering sequencing for sections in the American survey system allowed a survey team to mark off a township line in one-mile increments, then turn and return along another line in the direction from which they came. This would make more sense than going one way and returning without marking anything. Also, one of the attributes of boustrophedon sequencing is that all odd- or even-numbered sections occur in a checkerboard pattern. This was advantageous in designating every other section as public or railroad land, a particularly American adaption.

The square-mile sections of 640 acres were subdivided into increasingly smaller areas in a consistent and logical way: the half section, divided north–south, of 320 acres; the quarter section of 160 acres formed by an east–west line across the tall half section; the half-quarter section of 80 acres; and finally the smallest unit, the quarter-quarter section of 40 acres. These were the only sizes and shapes that were available for sale. "Forty acres and a mule" became the maximum that a small family or individual could reasonably farm in certain parts of the country. This small acreage unit also upheld the notion that America would be populated by small yeoman farmers spreading across the continent, as opposed to large landholders with ranches or plantations spanning thousands of acres. This idea of the individual farmer owning and improving his or her land was important to Thomas Jefferson and other early congressional supporters of the American survey system. For this and other reasons, the American survey grid has been called the "Jeffersonian" or "democratic" grid. In practicality, because the soil types and moisture gradients are different across the enormous areas of America's West, these salable lot dimensions were subject to much discussion as the survey work moved into the more arid spaces of the Great Plains. For example, in the Sand Hill Country of western Nebraska, forty acres makes little sense as the lack of rain makes anything other than large pasture grazing impractical. Nevertheless, these standard sizes remain embedded in the landscape, regardless of changes from ownership consolidation, local topography, or modern irrigation technology.

The imprint of the American survey grid is one of the most enduring cultural landscapes in the world. Flying west from Chicago, one sees, from thirty thousand feet, mile upon mile of gridded, cultivated landscapes stretching in every direction to the curvature of the horizon. The organization of the grid is such a ubiquitous facet of everyday life that westerners accept such things as the constant right-angle sectional road intersections,

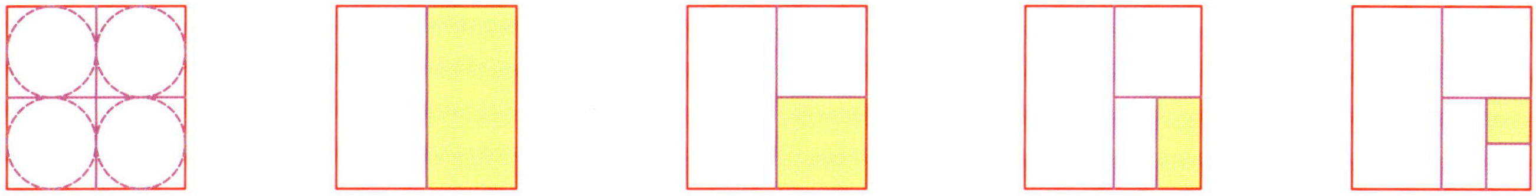

Diagrams of the possible divisions of sections

and the consistent reorientation of sun and shadows as one drives along roads that only orient to the cardinal points of the compass.

To examine in more detail the fascinating impact of the rigid reality of the survey grid on Nebraska's landscape, we climb again to thirty thousand feet above the same area of south-central Nebraska to look down in a satellite image on a small selected portion southeast of the town of Edgar. A line drawing on the facing page explains the geometric figures found in the aerial photograph. The one-mile-square north–south, east–west survey grid is readily apparent across the entire landscape. The grid is so obvious because each section boundary is usually a dirt county road or even a wide paved state highway such as Route 4 across the bottom of the image. Route 4 corresponds to the bottom-most horizontal line on the facing drawing. This is the boundary between Nuckolls and Clay Counties and is the first standard parallel north of the baseline boundary with Kansas. Three squares above this road, there are clear offsets in the north–south alignments of section boundaries and roads indicating the correction for converging lines of longitude.

The one-mile sections are especially evident because of the green circles inscribed by pivot irrigators. These circles are uniformly one-half-mile diameters and thus are perfectly inscribed into a quarter section of 160 acres. Four circles delineate a one-mile section. Because these immense sprinkler systems provide much needed and constant moisture, they outline an area of intense green crop growth in contrast to the ochre-colored fallow fields. Linearly plowed sections and partial sections are also irrigated and consequently green. The pivot irrigator has transformed farming in America from southern Georgia to California's Imperial Valley. As one moves west closer to the hundredth meridian and the moisture gradient of less than twenty annual inches of rain, irrigation requirements increase, and the green circles proliferate. Pivot irrigation exists even in isolated pockets in the arid regions of Nevada's Great Basin.

The pivot irrigator's great insect-like exoskeleton structure of struts, wires, and pipes with wheeled towers pivots around a deep well driven several hundred feet into the earth. The entire motorized structure automatically swings in a full circle a quarter mile in radius according to sophisticated computerized controls that monitor soil moisture and ambient

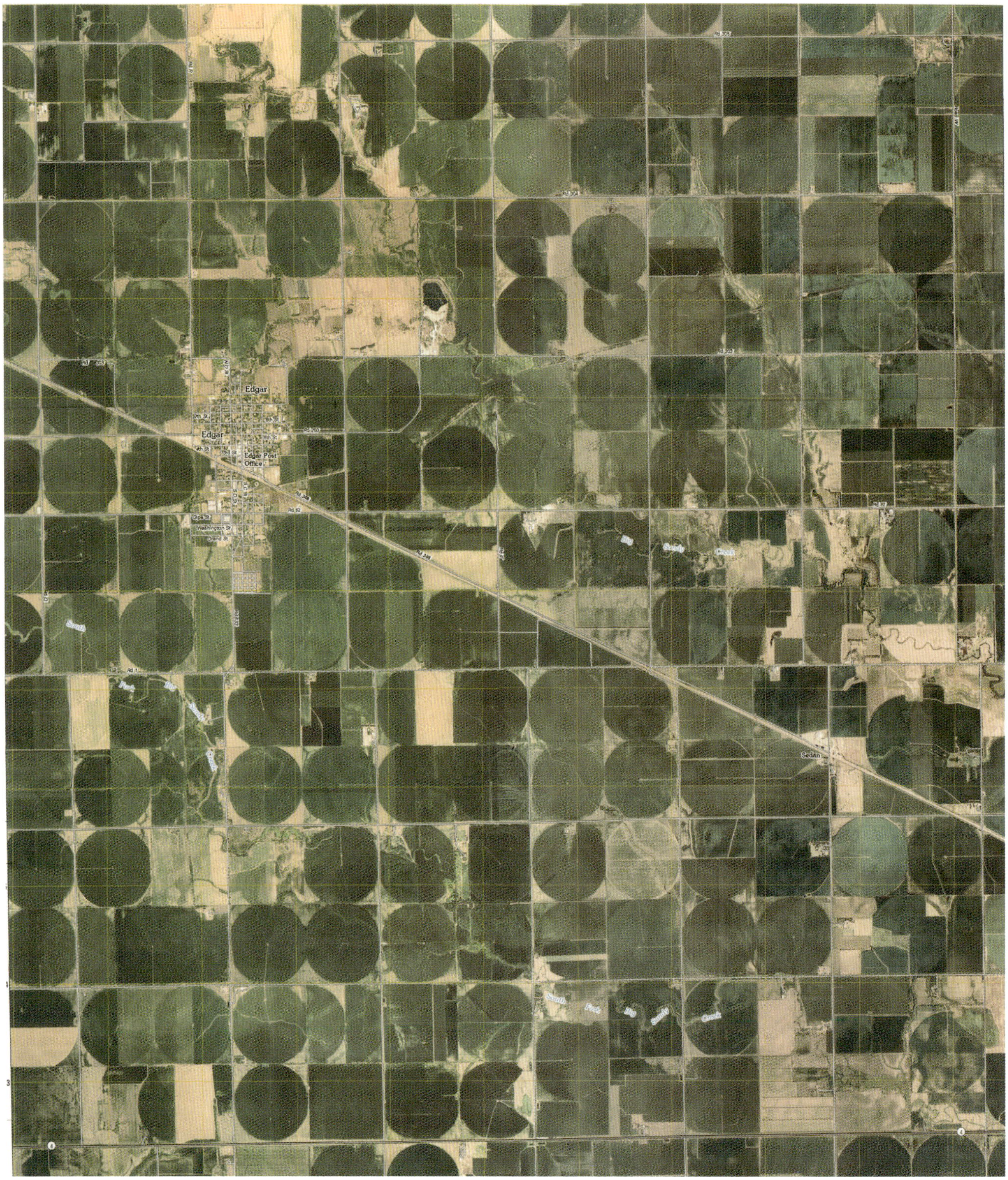

Aerial photograph of the landscape around Edgar, Nebraska

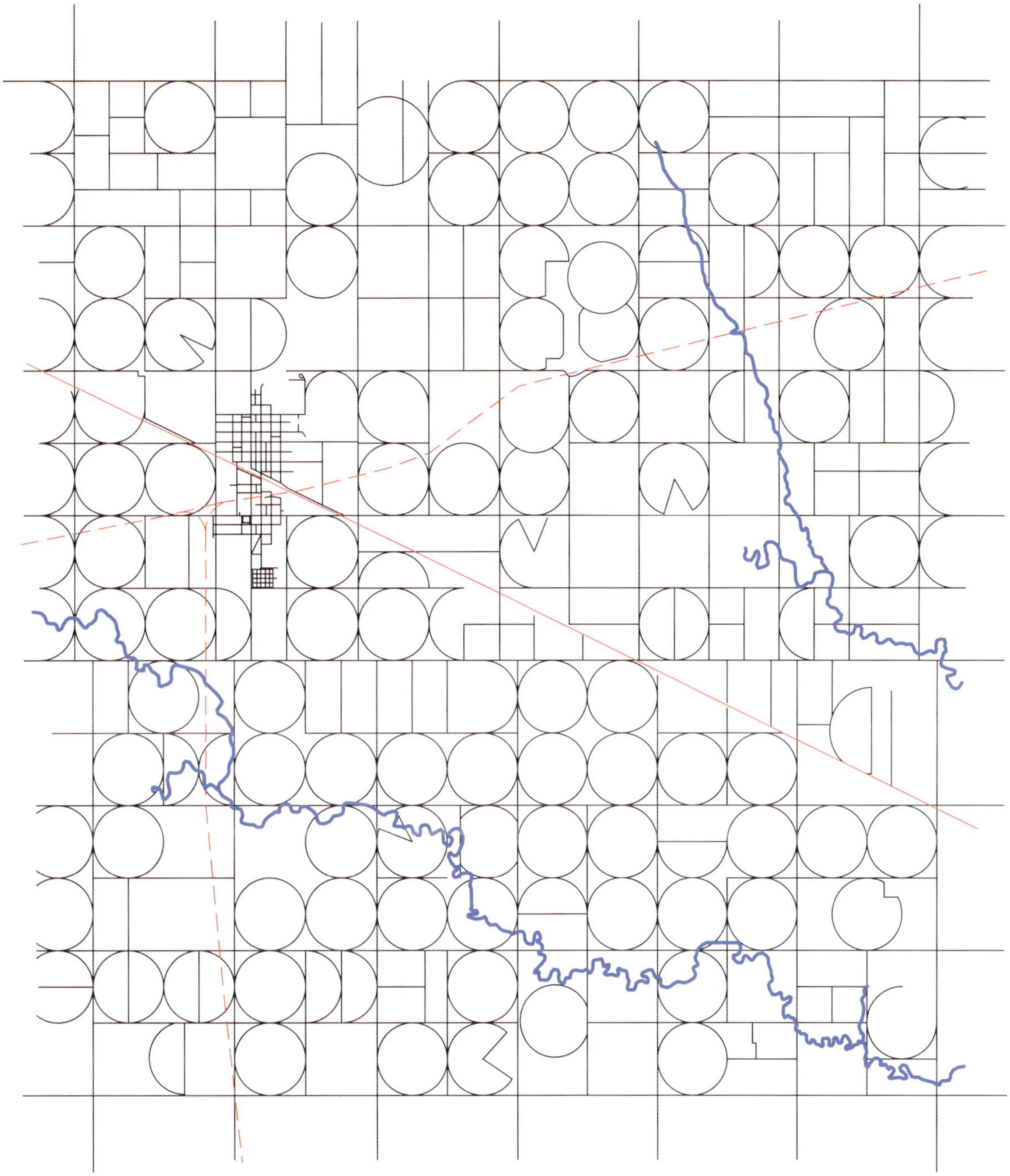

Diagram of the landscape demarcations illustrated on the facing page. The red line represents existing railroad tracks. The dotted red line represents abandoned track rights-of way.

weather conditions, so as to conserve water. These giant sprinklers make agriculture possible in soils beyond the constraints of inadequate precipitation. The aerial photograph indicates that Nebraska farms are heavy users of pivot irrigation. The tremendous increase in crop production resulting from pivot irrigation is not, however, without cost. Nebraska sits atop one of the most extensive aquifers in the world; the Ogallala runs from South Dakota, beneath Nebraska, Kansas, and Oklahoma, to the Texas Panhandle, covering almost 174,000 square miles. Constantly increasing agricultural demand on marginal lands for irrigation across this aquifer has withdrawn water faster than it can be replenished, and underground levels have dropped dramatically. It is questionable whether such irrigation practices are sustainable, even in the short term. Already in some areas of Nebraska, well-water capacities have dropped below levels where it is economically feasible to pump, and surrounding fields remain fallow.

In the aerial photograph, the center pivots and pump housings are visible at the end of thin access tracks across each circle. Because the wheeled towers can move over uneven topography, natural surface drainage patterns appear beneath the circular furrows. In some places, the natural drainage and topography are too steep to allow the application of a pivot,

Pivot irrigator

and partial sections remain uncultivated. Linear furrowed fields follow the subdivision of sections interspersed around the circular fields. Half, quarter, half-quarter, and even quarter-quarter sections can be identified. The original survey grid persists in the landscape, even with the introduction of modern irrigation technology.

One line, however, across the landscape escapes the grid: a narrow diagonal swath cutting southeastward through the center of the small town of Edgar, beginning in the upper left of the image and exiting at the lower right. As this line cuts across the square sections, it leaves areas too irregular for a circular pivot, and the many resulting triangular plots have been plowed in linear rows. This diagonal line is the track right-of-way of the Union Pacific Railroad that runs from the main intercontinental line north of the Platte River, through Hastings, then southeastward through Edgar and Fairbury and on into Kansas. If one looks very closely at the photograph, there is the faint line of another intersecting diagonal cutting northeast to southwest where the Union Pacific tracks cut into Edgar's urban grid. This is the recently abandoned track of the Burlington Northern that connected towns across south-central Nebraska.

These anomalous diagonals in an otherwise rigidly orthogonal landscape suggest another order, that of the rapid expansion of rail lines across the vast distances of the Great Plains. Railroads made possible the bulk transportation of corn and other grains to distant markets. As the dense web of tracks spread across Nebraska, farmers increased their production of cash crops to quantities unimaginable by those who surveyed the American West fifty years earlier. Soil, irrigation, survey lines, and railroads have converged to make the Great Plains the world's richest agricultural region. The bold, relentless progression of a uniform grid across thousands of square miles appears as a farsighted and successful promotion of individual land ownership that quickly transferred into extraordinary agricultural wealth.

The second section of this chapter explores the expansion of railroads into south-central Nebraska and their influence on the urban form of each town they served before returning once more to I-80, Exit 353, for a final disturbing perspective on the shift from rail transportation to highway travel and the corresponding changes to Nebraska's small towns.

The Plow Follows the Ox

Since the beginning of human inhabitation of the Great Plains, people crossing its vast spaces have closely followed its streams and rivers. Native Americans shadowing the seasonal migrations of buffalo, fur trappers headed to the Rocky Mountains, and immigrants' wagons traveling to

California have all followed the wide sweep of one of the most important waterways across Nebraska, the Platte River. In the nineteenth century, the transcontinental tracks of the Union Pacific Railroad traced a similar route along the gentle gradient on the north side of the Platte River Valley from the Missouri River west across the prairies and onto the plateau of Wyoming. The golden spike driven at Promontory Summit, Utah, on May 10, 1869, symbolically closed the rail connection across the continent and ended one of the riskiest construction ventures in America's history. Laying tracks through sparsely inhabited land generated little income for the railroad because there was insufficient demand yet for freight or passengers. The federal government acknowledged the risky and extensive start-up costs of railroads in the West by granting substantial free land to private railroad corporations. Sale of this land by the railroads helped defray their capital expenditures for engineering, tracks, bridges, and grading. Proximity of these free grants to the new rail lines increased the value of both immediately and encouraged the development of more agricultural cash crops that potentially provided more bulk freight. With more revenue-producing freight, the railroads committed to additional track in a cycle that stimulated both farming and railroads. The railroads developed towns and promoted settlement. Nineteenth-century railroads depended upon, and made their money from, bulk transport. While passenger service and local businesses were important promotional aspects of rail access, real profits lay in long trains of hopper cars full of grain. Throughout America's West, trains and farming have a uniquely symbiotic relationship: without rail transportation, agricultural produce could not get to market; without extensive agriculture, railroads had little incentive to build tracks into remote areas of the Great Plains. So while towns and town building established important trade centers along the tracks, it was the spreading fields of wheat and corn that lured the railroads west.

From the middle of the nineteenth century onward, track lines stretched net-like from Chicago out into the plains states of Illinois, Iowa, Wisconsin, and Missouri. Longer single strands of tracks probed even farther to the banks of the Missouri River at Council Bluffs, Iowa, searching for potential business. Immediately after the Civil War, as the Union Pacific began its race with the Central Pacific to link the coasts, another railroad, the Chicago, Burlington and Quincy, laid tracks across the rich farmland of southern Iowa toward the Missouri River crossings at Plattsmouth and Nebraska City. A map of the state of Nebraska published in 1876 shows the federal lands given to the Burlington and Missouri River Railroad, a subsidiary of the Chicago, Burlington and Quincy. The orange-colored checkerboard areas are the alternate sections in every township granted to the railroad. These sections totaled 2.5 million acres. As can be seen from this map, the boustrophedon system of numbering sections facilitated the allocation of alternate sections. Rather than the epic engineering feat of continental expansion, the Chicago, Burlington and Quincy headed into the fertile Corn Belt of south-central Nebraska with the goal of capturing as much corn haulage as possible. Soon carloads of corn moved east to Chicago, and tall grain elevators punctuated the prairie horizon. Begun in 1848 as the Aurora Branch Railroad and then merged as the Chicago, Burlington and Quincy, today, after many consolidations, the railroad is called the Burlington Northern Santa Fe (BNSF). The Burlington Route, as it became popularly known, ran through southern Nebraska to Denver. With the acquisition of the Great Northern Railroad, the Burlington Route carried freight north through Wyoming and Montana to the port of Seattle. Today, after a merger with the Sante Fe, the BNSF serves both the Northwest and the Southwest through Texas and New Mexico and transports freight east to Chicago or to Mississippi River ports. Its orange and black locomotives are a familiar sight in many small western towns and county railroad crossings.

In the late nineteenth century, the Burlington and Missouri line was one of twelve railroads operating in Nebraska. Today, most of these lines have

Map of the state of Nebraska showing the lands of the Burlington and Missouri River Railroad in Nebraska, 1876

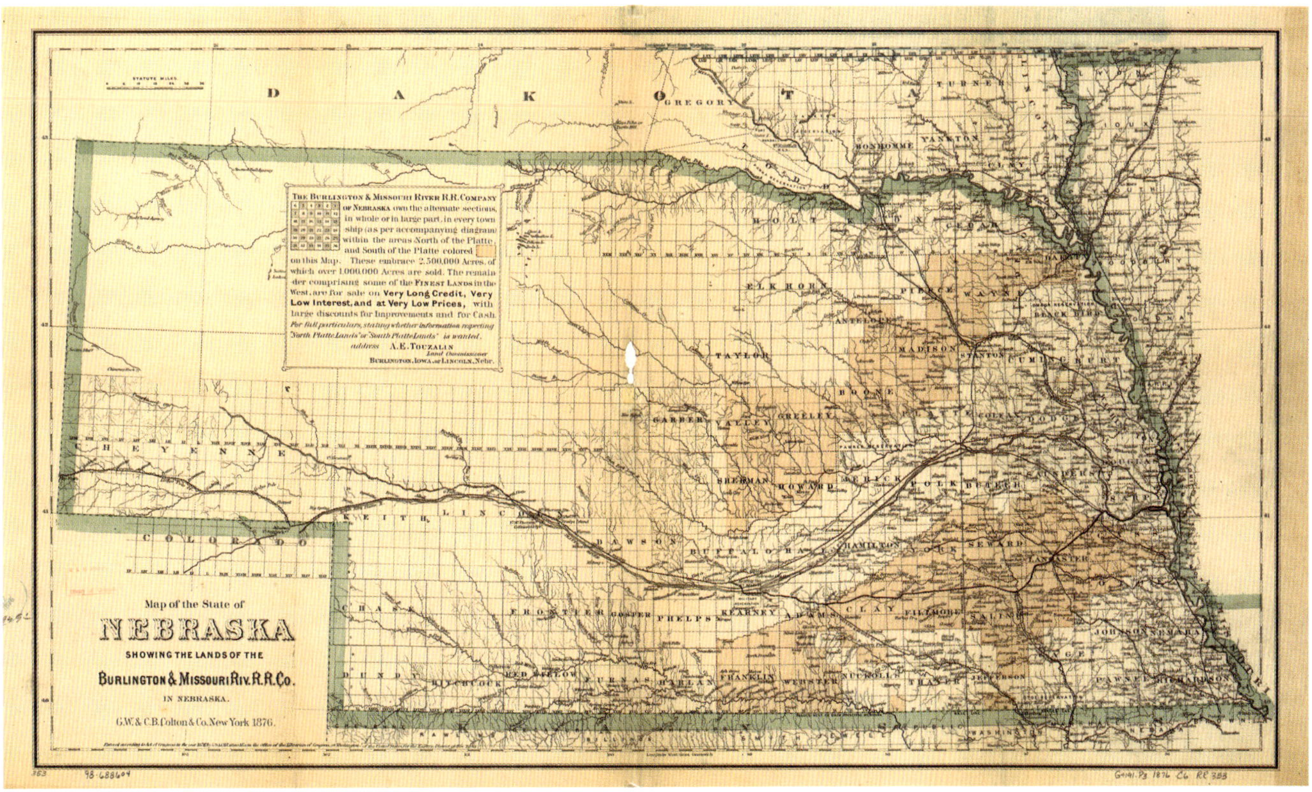

merged with either of the two twenty-first-century giants: the Union Pacific or the Burlington Northern Santa Fe. A few short-track regional railroads remain in Nebraska, such as the Nebraska Central serving the freight needs of local communities in the central part of the state. Nebraska Central's distinctive red and white livery can be found on deep rumbling locomotives idling on sidings in such towns as Cedar Rapids or Madison, a rare reminder of the days of many competing railroads throughout the state.

In 1897 Frank H. Galbraith, a Chicago railway mail clerk, designed an informative map to help employees of the Railway Mail Service quickly locate counties and post offices throughout Nebraska. As the post offices were always located in towns, details from this beautiful map provide inventories of the state's rail service. The dense network of tracks across south-central Nebraska radiated outward from the major hubs of Hastings and Lincoln to every surrounding small town. The map has some amusing graphics to aid in identifying and remembering places: a picture of a pig at Hoag; a tree trunk at Oak; and a camel at Campbell. The different color rail lines are coded in a side chart: among the twelve then existing railroads, black is the Union Pacific, red the Burlington and Missouri, and red with a squiggly overlay is the Pacific, Joseph and McCook, a subsidiary of the Burlington and Missouri. Today's Burlington Northern Santa Fe resulted from many mergers and consolidations of railroads within the areas it serves.

While the federal government had granted free land to the railroads for construction capitalization, the railroads were required, in exchange, to provide mail service for fixed rates to every small town and large city. In the nineteenth and early twentieth centuries, passenger trains included a mail car, a kind of post office on wheels for sorting, delivery, and pickup. The Railway Express Agency, the UPS and FedEx of the time, carried local domestic freight in separate baggage cars. Because it was a monopoly, REA transported everything that was not bulk cargo, including animals, general merchandise, and small packages. Before going out of business in the early 1970s, the REA's familiar diamond-shaped logo was a fixture on railroad cars and offices in every small-town station. Larger towns and cities had separate REA depots from which cargo was distributed by trucks to outlying farms. All these rail delivery services traveled over a dense network of tracks connecting all of small-town America. The Burlington and other railroads, however, were more interested in profitable long-haul freight opportunities than in local passenger or mail service, so they aggressively promoted developing agricultural areas and then captured the resulting grain trade. South-central Nebraska became prime corn country. As the Galbraith map illustrates, the Burlington and its subsidiaries had a tightly interconnected web of tracks throughout the nine-county study area delineated in the previous section.

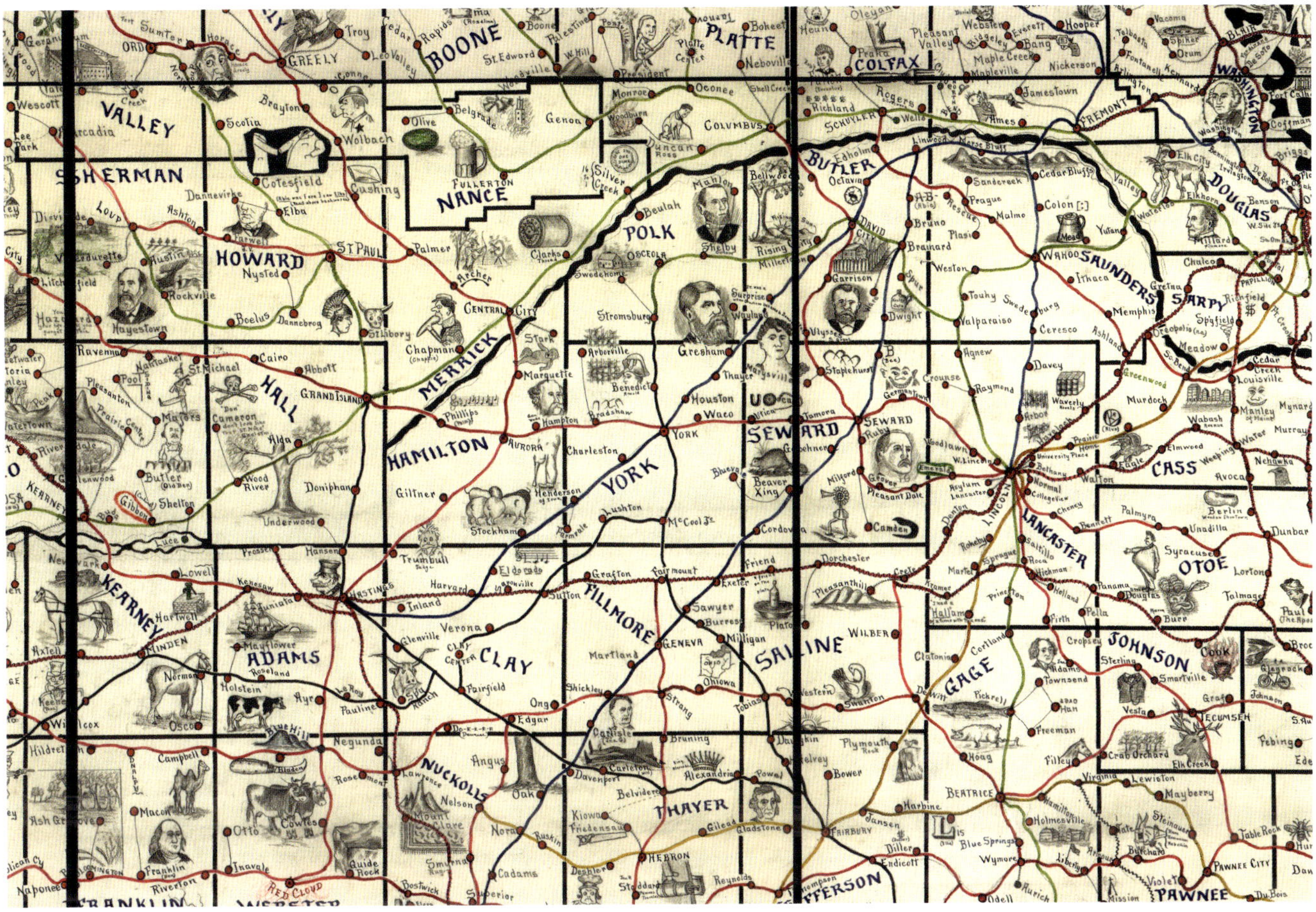

Detail from Galbraith's railway mail service map, Nebraska, 1898

Before motorized vehicles, corn was harvested and carted by wagon to the nearest grain elevator. Grain elevator operators, usually separate from railroads, bought, and still buy, grain from farmers either for cash or contracted prices to be sold for anticipated increases in bulk prices known as "futures." The difference between the farmer's price and the profit for the grain elevator operator is called the "basis." This buying and selling is a very complicated series of transactions worldwide, made even more intricate by local ethanol plants in the prairie states that also consume corn to produce fuel. Of course, rather than team-drawn wagons, today corn is trucked longer distances to grain elevators or ethanol plants.

In the nineteenth century, grain elevators provided bulk storage of corn before loading it into rail hopper cars for shipment to distant cities. Railroads typically leased land for the track siding in front of the elevator and often owned the elevator itself, although more common was a special elevator owner-operator arrangement. A wagon team was able to make a round trip journey from fields to elevator and back in a day if the distance was around eight miles. Shorter distances facilitated more frequent trips. Obviously there were constant negotiations between farmers and railroads over the spacing of elevators across the landscape, with farmers wanting closer spacing and railroads wanting greater distances between. A new rail spur and elevator generated its own grain catchment area from surrounding farms and encouraged farmers formerly more distant from tracks and elevators to switch from subsistence farming to cash crops.

The farms served by a grain elevator were at the mercy of both elevator prices and railroad freight rates. If two railroads competed against each other for the freight from a single highly productive agricultural region, farmers benefited. Railroads did market analyses and calculated the placement of elevators and track spurs throughout Nebraska and other prairie states to maximize grain tonnage and minimize overlapping catchment areas. When forced by competition to protect a market share, railroads would slice a track through a rival's area to provide more frequent elevator access.

The railroads actively promoted increased settlement and population growth to stimulate increased crop cultivation and eventually expand shipping opportunities. Railroad companies encouraged immigration from the East or even as far as Europe, providing free transportation across the country to Nebraska for potential land owners and farmers. Several years of above normal precipitation in the late nineteenth century helped railroads advertise the advantages of farming and fostered settlement growth. When several bad years inevitably followed, it spelled disaster for farmers, railroads, and bankers. Nebraska's settlement history showed population growth during wet years followed by a determined exodus during dry periods. This boom and bust cycle was especially prevalent along the marginal twenty-inch rain gradient mentioned in the previous section of this chapter.

Railroads also actively promoted towns along their tracks, often platting out street grids on lands given as part of federal grants. Towns served several purposes: First, they were a concentrated destination for goods distribution. From general merchandise, coal, and lumber to mail and passengers, towns were tiny commercial centers advantageous to railroads. Second, the placement of grain elevators generated the growth of towns' retail centers because farmers could accomplish multiple transactions when bringing loads of corn to the elevator. They could empty their grain and load up with supplies for the return trip. Towns offered all those services necessary to a developing agricultural community: land offices for survey work, governmental centers with courthouses, doctors, lawyers, and other professionals all centered on a main street a short walk from the tall grain elevators.

The 1897 Galbraith map offers clear evidence of the Burlington's efforts in town building. Heading west out of Lincoln toward Hastings and beyond, the railroad laid out ten evenly spaced towns in alphabetical order from *C* for Crete to *L* for Lowell. The predominance of New England names in this list was probably because the chief engineer of the Burlington at this time was Thomas Doane, originally from Massachusetts.[1] These ten towns are uniformly eight to ten miles apart, easy day trips of four or five miles one way for a team-drawn wagon to deliver grain to each town's elevator. The distances farmers were willing to transport corn may have been determined by sectional orthogonal road networks that did not allow roads to cut shorter diagonals across the agricultural landscape. Nevertheless, as delineated by Galbraith's map, grain elevators were numerous, and rail transportation in this area of south-central Nebraska made them very accessible.

Many of the railroads and their tracks shown in Galbraith's map have disappeared. The smaller railroads have been absorbed by bigger rail companies, and much trackage has been torn up and their rights-of-way abandoned. At least 50 percent of the towns indicated on Galbraith's map with freight access no longer have it, and only five towns have Amtrak passenger service. Railroads are still the most efficient and cost effective means of transportation for bulk haulage of cereal crops to distant markets and coal for local power plants, but the advantages of trucks for short distances spelled the end of local trains. Many of the grain elevators have been closed as rail companies, and farmers' cooperatives consolidate storage facilities. Since all corn is now trucked directly from the field to the elevator, elevators can be larger and farther apart. Today, railroads are only interested in grain collection and storage facilities that can generate at least one hundred carloads of grain. Contemporary catchment area circles would be much greater than the four- or five-mile radii of the nineteenth century, reflecting both the consolidation and wider spacing of grain elevators. Another type of catchment area with wide circles surrounds ethanol plants, for corn is trucked straight from fields to ethanol plants over considerable distances, depending on the cost per bushel of fuel versus food.

Galbraith's wonderful and informative map illustrates that the placement of railroad tracks across the landscape of Nebraska resulted from very specific market forces. Tracks cut across the survey grid without regard for the orthogonal lines of survey sections. Railroads shortened distances to maximize grain collection, to minimize miles of expensive tracks and rights-of-way, and to discourage encroachment by competing rail companies. The ghostly diagonal through Edgar in the aerial photograph and the

1. Overton, *Burlington Route*, 287n58.

corresponding line drawing at the end of the previous section remind us that little remains of the dense web of railroads serving every small town in this region of Nebraska. The forgotten right-of-way is a spectral scratch on an agricultural palimpsest; it has been all but erased by the revolving styluses of pivot irrigators automatically turning round and round.

Edgar itself, like so many small Nebraska towns, exists today as a diminished armature of a once sustainable trading center. Fewer than five hundred people live along its shaded residential streets, and its Main Street is mostly vacant. In 1921, however, Edgar's population was over one thousand, its shops were open for business, and its three churches were the focus of a vibrant community. The town was fortunate to have two railroads and consequently two depots with different destination choices: the Saint Joseph and Grand Island Railroad connecting to the Union Pacific and the West Coast and the Burlington and Missouri River Railroad connecting to the state capital at Lincoln and points east to Chicago. Along the two intersecting sets of tracks and multiple rail sidings were three grain elevator companies, as well as lumber and coal storage. Edgar even boasted two small hotels for visitors required to stay the night to accommodate train passenger schedules. The main commercial street, C Street, had at least twenty shops, a bank, two garages, and, surprisingly, a "motion picture" theater. These establishments clustered along the two blocks running north, within a short walking distance from the train depots. Spreading out of the commercial core were blocks of substantial residences on broad tree-lined streets. Edgar was the very model of a viable agricultural trade center siting in the immensity of Nebraska's Great Plains.

Within the nine counties of our study area in south-central Nebraska, there were over forty small towns. All once had grain elevators served by at least one railroad. One of the alphabetized towns named by Thomas Doane mentioned earlier, Exeter, offers a similar example to Edgar, with the same downward demographic shift. In 1933 Exeter's population was 960; by 2008, it had dropped to 641. Formerly, Exeter was served by two railroads, the Burlington and Missouri River and the Fremont, Elk and Missouri Valley Railroad. Today only the Burlington travels through Exeter while, five blocks south, Route 6, a major east–west highway that parallels the Burlington tracks across south-central Nebraska, follows a section line through residential streets. In the general lexicon of western railroad towns' typologies, Exeter would be considered a modified parallel railroad town with the urban grid parallel to, and clamped on both sides of, the railroad tracks. In Exeter's case, however, two duplicate sets of tracks and sidings once ran through the town with dual stations and multiple storage facilities. Like Edgar, Exeter had two grain elevators, one on each

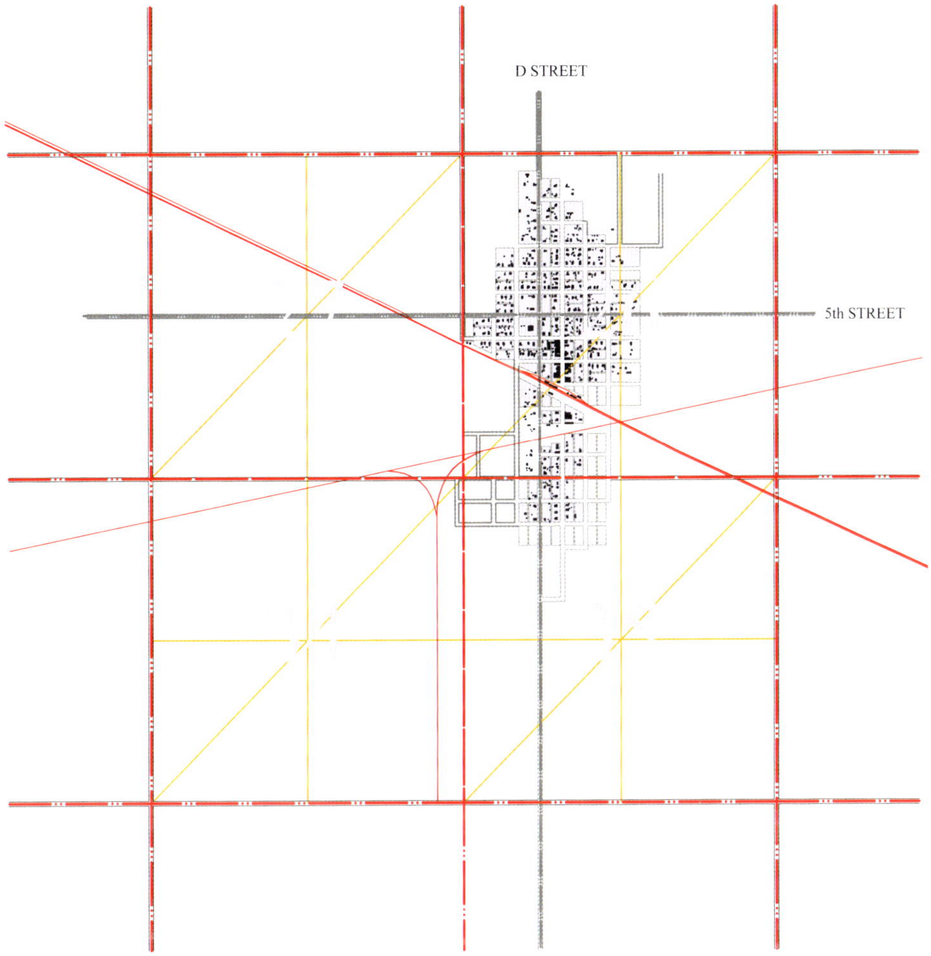

The town of Edgar, Nebraska, located within the range and township grid. The town is primarily in Section 26. 5th Street runs along a half-section line; D Street follows a quarter section.

railroad, giving local farmers competitive options on grain futures and freight rates.

Lumber and coal were essential imports for Great Plains states: the coal for domestic winter heating and lumber from eastern forests for building construction. Exeter Avenue, the main street perpendicular to the tracks, had two blocks of stores and a small manufacturing concern, Smith's "Adjustable Metal Indexes" (most probably small labels or tabs for filing dividers) at the corner of Exeter and Seneca Avenues. Like Edgar, Exeter also had a movie theater and north of the tracks a small hotel. Exeter, too, was a small thriving trade center, but today, sadly, Exeter exists as a shadow of its former self. Many storefronts are boarded up and empty, their fine trim details slowly weathering in the corrosive prairie sun.

Typical of all small plains towns, Edgar and Exeter have beautiful tree-lined residential streets. Because the residential blocks are three hundred feet square, houses can be set back from the street, allowing for large trees to thrive in the front lawns. Garages are entered from back alleys in

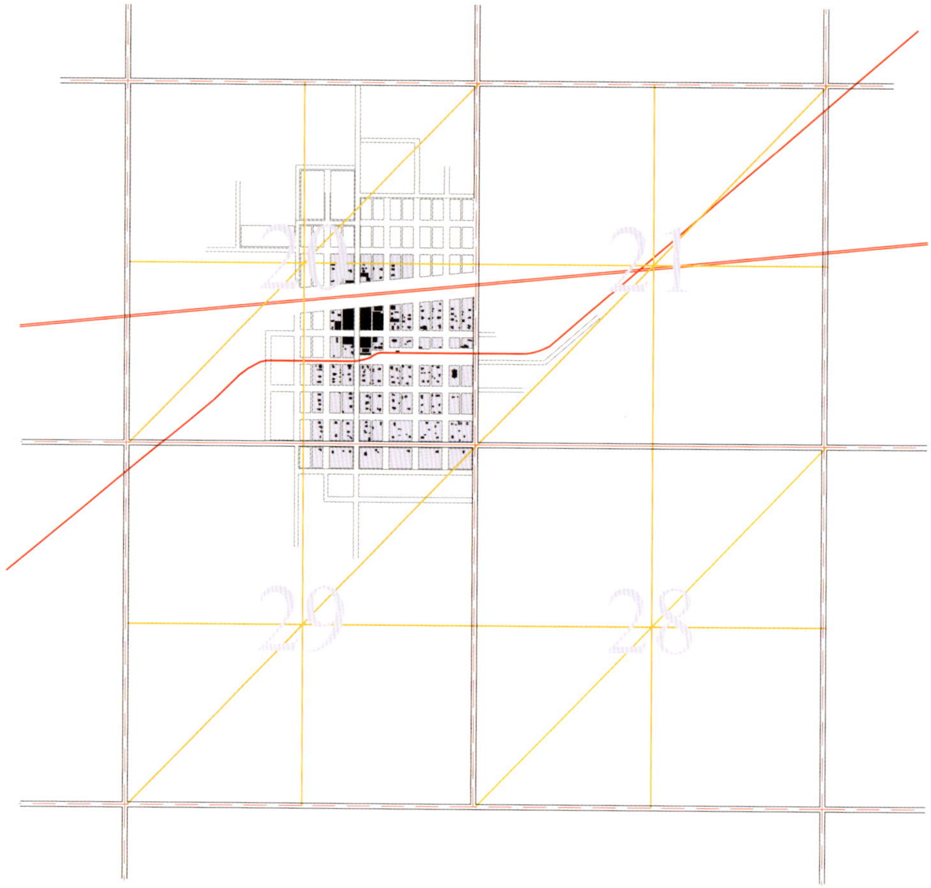

The town of Exeter, Nebraska, located within the sectional grid

the interior of the blocks; thus the houses fully address the street, unencumbered by the blank garage doors and asphalt driveways so prevalent in today's suburban developments. Sidewalks are separated from the street pavement by grass planting strips eight or ten feet wide that hold trees whose branches join high over the street. Within the treeless immensity of the Great Plains, it is as though the inhabitants wanted to bring the forest to them: most small towns have far more trees and shade cover than towns in other more forested places in the eastern United States. The scale of houses, the amount of tree canopy, the expansive lawns—all give Nebraska small-town residential streets a beauty and an enviable tranquility missing from newer towns across America.

Occasionally a town's street grid and urban pattern readjusted its orientation to correspond to the diagonal tracks. Central City north of the Platte River has two grids: one that orients to the township and sectional lines and one that shifts forty-five degrees in response to the Union Pacific's main transcontinental line. More often the tracks reorient slightly to conform more closely to a town's street grid, which by itself orients to township and sectional lines. The different arrangements suggest the order of

Abandoned storefront, Exeter, Nebraska

construction: first the tracks and then the town's platting or vice versa, with the rail line extending to an existing town. Almost always, however, a town's entire grid, or partial grid, in the case of Central City, corresponds to, and integrates with, the cadastral survey.

In contrast to Central City, Edgar's tiny urban grid orients north–south to the cadastral grid; its boundaries are contained mostly by Section 36. Its street grid is numbered east–west and lettered north–south. D Street follows a quarter-section line through both Sections 26 and 35; 5th Street, the major cross street that ends the three blocks of commercial buildings, is a true half-section line east–west. Gipe Street south of the railroad tracks is the southern boundary of Section 26. Together all these survey correspondences illustrate a town grid firmly embedded in the matrix of the larger grid of sections, ranges, and townships. What is readily apparent, however, is that the two diagonally crossing railroad tracks slice through Edgar with no regard for its street pattern.

Edgar's main commercial street, C Street, runs north after crossing the tracks, lined with a continuous facade of storefronts and business establishments positioned on twenty-five-foot-wide lots. Hotels, a bank, and

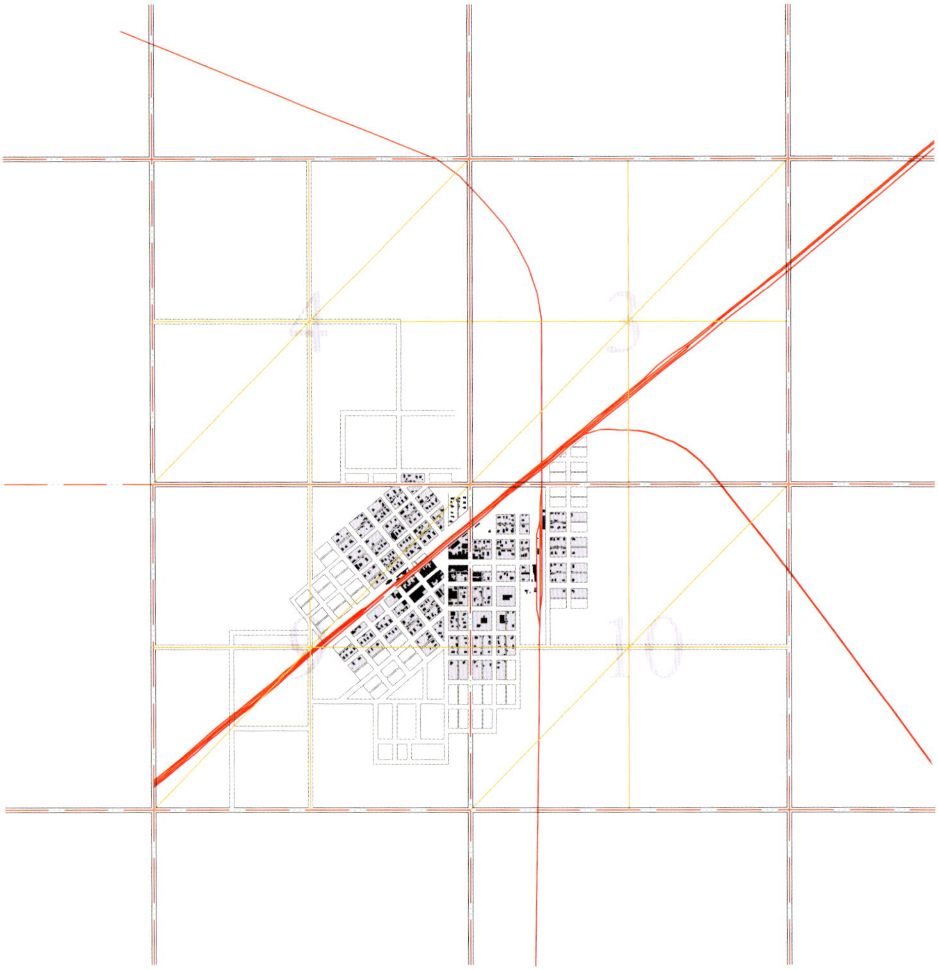

The town of Central City, Nebraska. The town has two different street grids that orient to two different railroad tracks. The Union Pacific's main transcontinental line cuts almost forty-five degrees across the drawing.

a garage anchor the important corners. Like so many western towns, Edgar fits the typology of a modified *T* layout: the main commercial street perpendicular to and forming a *T* with the tracks. Often the tracks were pushed to one side of a town to lessen the on-grade hazards of vehicles crossing in front of moving trains. In Edgar's case, the blocks on the southern side of the tracks are residential, except for the Chicago Lumber Company with its dedicated siding.

Exeter's placement within the matrix of the survey grid is similar to Edgar's: its platted blocks fill a half section; its easternmost street, appropriately named East Boundary, lies along the edge of Section 20; its lower South Boundary Street also follows the south sectional line between Sections 20 and 29. Many of its east–west streets carried Native American tribe names such as Arapahoe or Cheyenne. The main line of the Burlington enters the street grid almost parallel to the survey lines and severs all but two of the town's north–south streets. Two streets run along either side of the three tracks, named, appropriately, South and North Depot

Streets. The main commercial street, Exeter Avenue, occupies two blocks next to the tracks of a defunct subsidiary of the Union Pacific. As these former tracks approached Exeter, they swung parallel to the street grid and occupied a full block across the entire town before exiting and turning southwest toward Geneva. The tracks no longer exist, but the space remains, a grassy expanse filled with weeds and saplings, abandoned foundations, and rotten railroad ties.

Like most commercial streets found in Great Plains towns, Exeter's streets are shaped by continuous facades of single-story brick buildings decorated with finely scaled details. In nearby Kenesaw, Nebraska, as in many Nebraska towns, a tiny bank's neoclassical front, rendered in sculptured stone columns, breaks the continuity of these typical main street storefronts. Classical symbolism of solidity and permanence cannot disguise the bank's blank and broken windows, its empty interior forlornly hidden behind the triumphal arch.

Like all towns in the Great Plains, Edgar and Exeter are announced in the distance across open fields by their tall-silhouetted grain elevators. The dark green of the densely planted residential streets envelops the giant cylinders and anchors them to the earth. Surrounded by boundless cornfields, the trees enclosing every town evidence the community's need to shelter itself against the harsh winter winds and furnace-like summer sun. In the forested regions of America, settlers cleared land for towns; in the immense space of the Great Plains, settlers brought the forest with them.

The bases of grain elevators' repetitive vertical storage tubes sit alongside the linear open space of the tracks that slice through each town's tiny urban grid. Joined together like giant organ pipes for ease of loading cars on sidings, the grain elevators mark a vertical counterpoint to the horizontality of the tracks. Up close they dwarf the trains like the landscape in which they exist. Draped rounded shadows heighten the relief of the silos' sensual repetitive rounded forms. Like enormous proboscises, dangling chutes swing between the towers waiting to pour grain into open hopper cars.

The openness of the track space contrasts with the pedestrian-scaled enclosure of a town's perpendicular main street. Crossing the tracks from the single-storied brick facades of the main street, one comes into a long extruded space enclosed on one or both sides by the giant cylinders of the silos. Looking either right or left, the single point perspective of steel rails and ties vanishes into infinity. It is at this space, existential in its grandeur, disconcerting in its emptiness, that the two narratives of this chapter on Nebraska meet: the projection of the survey grid and the necessity of railroads to seek out markets. The diagonal swath of railroad tracks interrupts

Abandoned bank, Kenesaw, Nebraska *(right)*

Grain elevators
(above and left)

the continuity of the American survey grid as manifest in the urban form of a small town. Unlike any other urban spaces in America, these tiny places in Nebraska towns mark over and over again the intersection of our capitalist culture with the immensity of the prairie landscape.

The deep rumble of locomotives pulling long lines of either grain or coal cars briefly animates these empty spaces several times each day. Suddenly, the tracks are filled with noise, color, and motion as gigantic engines, two pulling and two pushing, blast through the space. The shrill bell of the crossing gates conflicts with the mesmerizing jolts of car after car clacking across the street guard. It is a moment of excitement, of full-throttled power that thrills the child in all of us. For a short moment we are connected to other histories and faraway destinations by the train's dramatic passage through this place where sky and earth forever converge but never meet. And then silence, the space is again empty, and the tracks stretch to the horizon. The town, too, is quiet.

Grain elevators along tracks

In the early twentieth century, the tracks and sidings in towns like Edgar and Exeter would have been filled with activity. A passenger depot would collect the arrivals and send off the departures of people several times daily. The arrival of mail was an event for the entire town. The Railway Express Agency stored packages and freight for pickup or distribution to remote farms. Coal and lumber cars stacked along sidings in the process of unloading. Hopper cars pulled beneath elevator chutes to be loaded with grain. Squat round water tanks waited to replenish steam locomotives. All these activities required buildings, storage sheds, offices, platforms, and people. Rather than deserted or abandoned, these railroad places were a town's busy portal to the wider world. A detail from a 1922 Sanborn Fire Insurance Map of York, Nebraska, illustrates the density of activities within just such a space. There are two lumber companies, the E. S. Clark & Company and J. F. Grosshans Grain and Lumber. Both have block-long sheds that parallel the track siding and front onto Fourth Street, allowing dimensioned lumber and milled stock to be unloaded from one side

Nebraska Central Railroad locomotives

and retailed on the other. Both companies also have sheds for coal storage and for lime and cement. There is both a passenger station and a freight depot. The freight depot has a long platform to handle large quantities of packages. Grosshans has a tall grain elevator for storage of twenty thousand bushels of corn. A track siding bends south to serve the York Milling Company's elevator and flour mill. The complex of buildings includes a fifty-foot elevator, hay storage for draft horses, a mill, a brick steam plant, and a generator.

A photograph on a postcard mailed from Pawnee, Nebraska, a town east of Exeter on the Burlington Line, shows a similar space during a passenger train stop. People crowd the station platform, a baggage cart sits to the right, and young boys hawk newspapers. A grain elevator and windmill are in the distance. The windmill would have powered a pump that filled an elevated water tank beside the tracks. It was a busy, bustling space with pedestrians mingling in the long narrow area between the train and the station.

A much larger town of six thousand people in 1922, York is a county seat not far from Edgar and Exeter. One could take a train linking all three towns, albeit with several changes of railroads. The through track of the Chicago and Northwestern Railway in York is the second from the bottom on the Sanborn map connecting northeast to David City and southwest to Hastings, both significant rail junctions. A second railroad, the Burlington, Chicago and Missouri, also served York. Several important features are apparent from the Sanborn map besides the many structures within the railroad right-of-way. The tracks are fully integrated into the fabric of the town's street grid. The tracks into town makes a sweeping turn from the northeast, line up with the grid, and bisect an entire three-hundred-foot-wide swath of lots before exiting out the opposite side of the grid. Unlike today's train tracks that are segregated from traffic and streets, these tracks and sidings are easily accessible as part of the town's activities. Remarkably, the county courthouse and surrounding commercial core is just one block away. From the depot, one could walk to the courthouse or McCloud's Hotel in less than three minutes. The entire urban composition is similar to that of Moultrie, Georgia, discussed earlier in chapter 4, but at a slightly larger scale. In both towns the train is an instrument of concentration: collecting all urban functions into a well-defined pedestrian precinct filled with commercial and retail stores, supplies, transportation, accommodations, restaurants, entertainment, and government activities. To read these different activities around York's square is a lesson in successful civic composition. Beginning in the square's southeast corner at McCloud's Hotel and walking clockwise around the beautiful courthouse, one would have encountered all the myriad parts of a well-established commercial

Composite Sanborn map of York, Nebraska, 1922

Burlington Station, Pawnee City, Nebraska, 1912

core. There are several bakeries, hardware stores, creameries, wallpaper and paint stores, print shops, agricultural implements stores, wholesale groceries, and tobacco shops. A business college occupied the space above a corner drugstore on the second and third floors at the corner of Lincoln and 5th Streets. Across the street was a motion picture theater next to Dean's Hotel. On the west side of the square a continuous elevation of eight stores, two drugstores, and a barber shop were all anchored on the corner by a sturdy bank built of limestone. The block running north from the square on Lincoln Street was bookended by two additional banks. More stores, a YMCA, a second barbershop, and another drugstore filled in the block between. The north side of the square had ten stores, yet another druggist, and a fourth bank. One block north was the York Opera House opposite the granite post office. Similar to the other three sides of the square, the eastern block contained more stores: two hardware stores, two cobblers, another creamery, and a printer. Over fifty different commercial establishments surrounded and framed the square in 1922, while more stores, churches, and fraternal organizations filled out the blocks a few streets distant. It was a remarkable fragmentation and specialization of businesses that contrast starkly with the big-box retailers of today—like the Walmart Supercenter just south of York at the interstate intersection. The number of possible transactions and individual conversations within York's square must have been extraordinary as each store stocked and sold different merchandise within a short walking distance. Add to this the governmental functions of the courthouse, the garages in the back alleys, the different clubs, the hotel dining rooms, and the York Hospital Clinic, and downtown York was a complete urban center affording many levels of human discourse and interaction.

All this has disappeared. York is a textbook lesson, instead, in urban destruction. First the railroad left town, leaving behind empty blocks now filled with weeds. Next the beautiful nineteenth-century courthouse was demolished in 1980 to make way for a bland red brick structure constructed right to the sidewalk edge, thereby destroying the planted frame of the square. Next, automobile traffic has been routed through town on one-way streets, changing the main streets of York from congested hubs of activity to arteries of speeding traffic. A bypass has recently been constructed completely around York's historic center, swinging out into farmland to the west so that the major north–south Route 81 can avoid any downtown congestion. Soon this bypass will be lined with the inevitable malls and big-box chain stores. The decision to place Exit 353 of I-80 just south of York set all these changes in motion. Exit 353's placement connects two heavily traveled roads, an interstate and a regional federal highway. There is nothing local about Route 81, for it eventually connects north to I-29 in South Dakota and south to I-135/35 in Kansas. A small self-contained regional trade center, York could not withstand the centrifugal forces of a national highway system with interstate destinations.

Exit 353 has quickly become the quintessential off-ramp town with an astonishing collection of services. There are eight motel/inn establishments, ten fuel/truck stops, fourteen restaurants/eateries, and a giant Walmart Supercenter. These buildings scatter along two service roads that parallel Route 80 both south and north of the I-80 overpass. Parking lots surround each building, making it imperative to drive from one to another. A random pedestrian walking between the open lots would appear odd. A figure-ground study of this off-ramp town illustrates the lack of spatial cohesion. Unlike the train, the automobile is an instrument of dispersion. There are no other community components in this off-ramp town, no institutional or civic structures, no housing. There is no connection to the past or to other histories. Even the survey grid remains unacknowledged. Individual franchises may be familiar to interstate travelers, yet the whole composition is divorced from its local Nebraska landscape.

Like the railroads before, Walmart undoubtedly did a market study before locating at this intersection, which is convenient for the long-haul trucks carrying goods to stock long rows of shelves. A Walmart catchment or market circle is based upon a driving-time radius and must swing wide, far into the surrounding farmland, to capture the dwindling populations of many tiny towns. Exeter, Edgar, and York are within such a circle and cannot resist these modern economic forces.

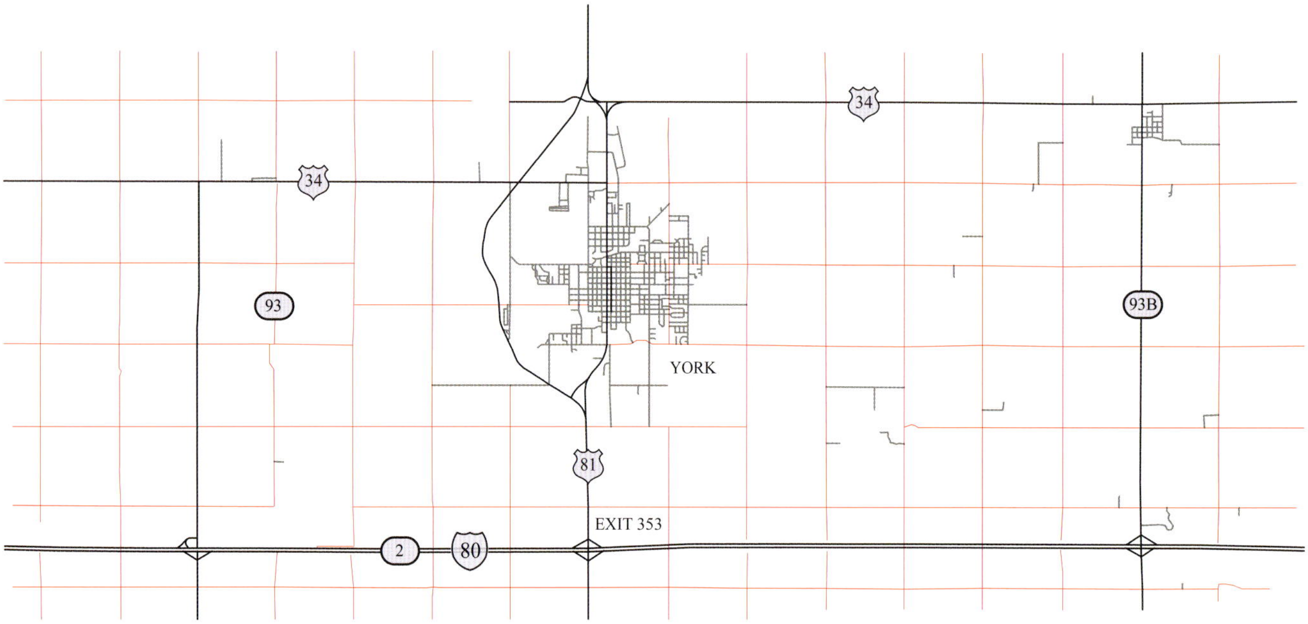

Bypass roads around York, Nebraska

Nineteenth-century urbanism was measured by the pedestrian. The courthouse square in York was only five hundred feet across; the commercial main streets of Edgar and Exeter are just three blocks long. The distribution of goods and services took place in multiple, separate stores arranged around a common public space, either a square or street. Daily transactions of all kinds required human dialogue, hundreds of disparate, brief encounters with shared purpose. The twenty-first-century off-ramp town at Exit 353 offers different, opposing choices: familiarity within isolation, anonymity coupled with ease of accessibility, and spatial confusion surrounded by controlled and branded identity. Unlike Edgar, Exeter, and York, off-ramp Exit 353 is growing, extruding motels, fast-food vendors, and big-box retail along Route 81 in both directions, draining the economic vitality from all neighboring small towns. People come to Lowes and Walmart from as far away as the expanding peripheries of Lincoln or Hastings.

The derelict and empty track spaces of prairie towns like Edgar are depressing and melancholy monuments to our profligate disposal of human and cultural resources. Vacant, receding into an indefinite and narrowing horizon, these hundreds of towns mark our inability to sustain even the most modest connection to our past or with each other. These dissolving towns are not the result of an economic imperative beyond ourselves, but are rather the result of a willful disregard for our heritage and our landscapes. To attribute the neglect of these towns to autonomous outside economic influences or to the automobile is too easy. We,

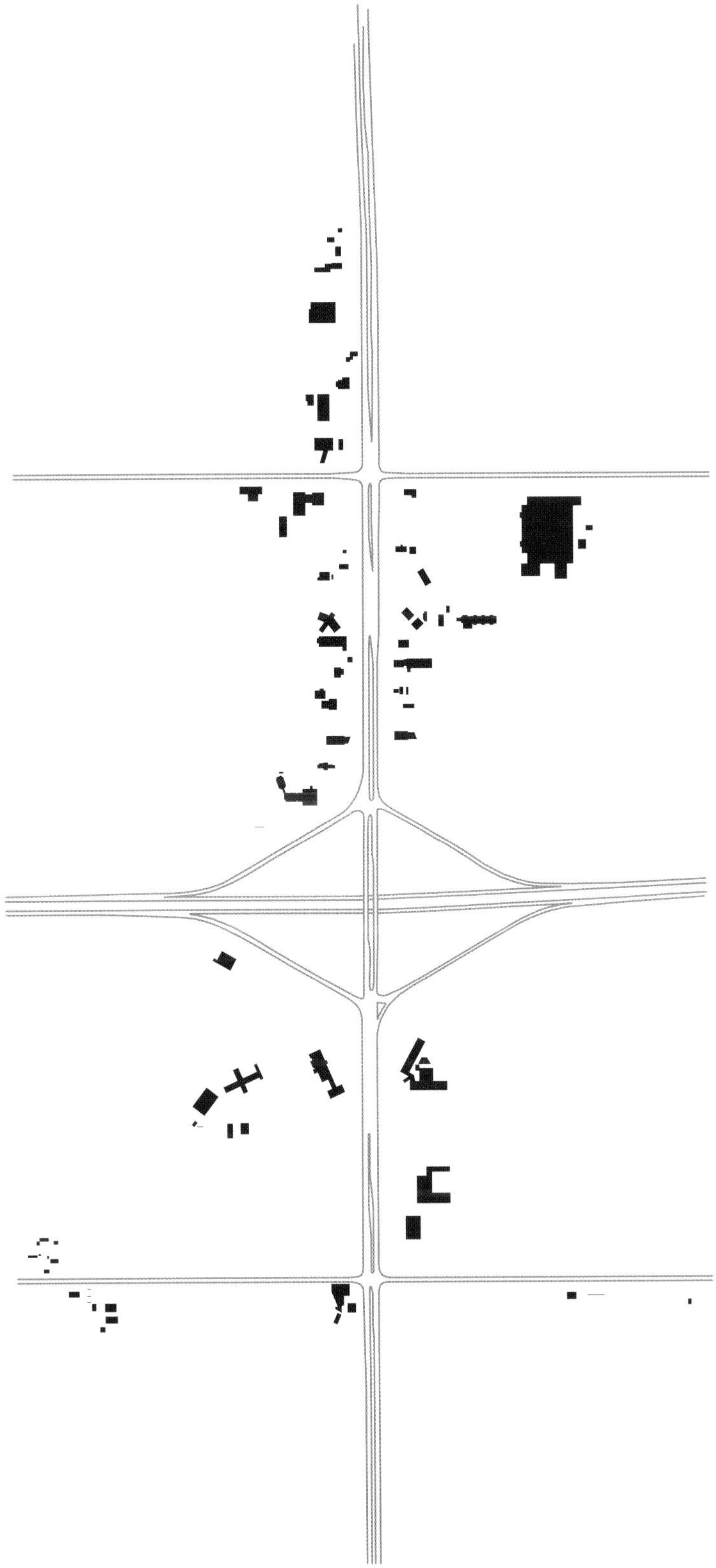

Figure-ground study of the off-ramp town south of York, Nebraska, at Exit 353, I-80

Abandoned grain elevator in the ghost town of Houston, Nebraska

alone, are responsible for our daily choices, not the automobile or the interstate, for these are both only instruments of our desires.

The open road stretching west beyond Exit 353 offers a false promise, for prosperity and success do not always lie westward on the open road. From the grim mill towns of New England to the despondent courthouse squares of Georgia to the wasted farm communities of Nebraska; all across the United States lie the ruins of that promise, for there is nothing out there through the Golden Arch. Only more emptiness. The fault lies not in our quest for more speed and shorter distances, but in our failure to recognize the innumerable, invisible strands of shared histories and intentions and our inability to persist in our attachments to landscapes and to respect places that tie us to each other and tell us who we are.

6

LAND ROUTES AND MINING TOWNS OF THE SOUTHWEST

GEOGRAPHY INFLUENCED nineteenth-century wagon trails and then railroad routes across the American West. Twentieth-century interstates trace similar lines across vast spaces and through steep mountains. Several mining towns provide examples of places left behind by these sequential route choices. The spaces between interstates in the American West are immense, reflecting the enormous size of the states and the sparsity of cities compared to the East. Along the interstates, towns such as Holbrook, Arizona, struggle to reinvent themselves in response to new transportation shifts. Holbrook was first a railroad town, then a major stop along the legendary Route 66. Now it has become an off-ramp town for Interstate I-40. In the voids between interstates, however, towns deprived of their original reasons for existence such as copper-mining communities in eastern Arizona cannot survive and quickly become exhausted and desolate places. Miami and Superior, Arizona, have broad streets and few inhabitants. Globe, Arizona, serves as a county seat and attracts visitors heading into Apache National Forest. Clifton, Arizona, abandoned next to one of the largest open-pit copper mines in the world, exists as a shell, its collection of beautiful vacant buildings filled with the brilliant sunlight and deep shadows of the desert.

Warren's Map

As the interstate highways stretch westward across America's heartland, the spaces between their routes become greater and the uninterrupted distances between cities longer. This broadening of the density of the interstate network from east to west results from the dramatic increase in the landmass of the American continent west of the Mississippi River. Although common perception of U.S. geography places the Mississippi River at the country's midpoint, in actuality more than two-thirds of America's land area lies west of this great north–south waterway. The western states are considerably larger than the eastern states; consequently their state capitals are farther apart. Since the original legislation for the interstate system mandated that all state capitals be connected, the western interstate highways spread out to link these far-apart cities. Most people who drive coast to coast soon realize that distance calculated in the west has a different meaning than that in the east. One crosses a small state such as Massachusetts in less than two hours; one traverses Nebraska in a very long day. A cursory glance at the topographic map of the entire country in chapter 2 shows the tight network of interstate routes eastward of the Mississippi River quickly giving way to immense spaces between interstates in places like Texas, Arizona, Wyoming, and Nevada, to name but a few of the states of the American West. A second glance at the same map reveals the strong horizontal or east–west bias of interstate travel across the country. Wide-open spaces and ever-westward expansion are deeply embedded in America's history. Writers, painters, and artists have acknowledged this salient aspect of America's geography. The West is big; it is far distant from the East Coast. California, or the Pacific Coast, the golden land, is the prize won. Between California and the Mississippi River lies something early settlers named the "Great American Desert" because precipitous mountains and vast desert spaces formed impenetrable barriers to westward expansion. In its exploration of one of these spaces, located in Arizona, this chapter contrasts with the two earlier discussions about Massachusetts and Georgia. Towns in the eastern and smaller states are almost always close to a neighboring interstate. In this area of Arizona, by comparison, many of the towns lie far removed from the interstates. The interstates' influences are still recorded, however, in the shifting patterns of settlements necessitated as towns respond differently to changing highway alignments and scales. When the interstates circumvent such large areas, they monopolize all continental through traffic, reinforcing the isolation of the bypassed regions. Towns connected to the interstate grow and flourish; towns distant from the interstate generally wither or develop a localized industry such as mining or tourism. This chapter explores examples of both conditions: Superior, Miami, Globe, and Clifton are Arizona towns deep within this area well away from interstates; Holbrook is positioned at the periphery and connected to three interstate exits.

The part of Arizona that forms the basis for this comparison lies between I-40 in the north and I-10 to the south, and between I-17 to the west and I-25 to the east in New Mexico. The rugged topography of the Apache-Sitgreaves National Forest covers much of this area in eastern Arizona and reaches into New Mexico. This is a huge sparsely settled region of approximately forty thousand square miles east of metropolitan Phoenix. Few towns exist within this region's dramatic mountains and canyons. Because its emptiness, like that of other great spaces in the West, results from the constraints of geography on travel, we turn first to the histories of America's routes of westward expansion.

The growth of America's population in the nineteenth century westward across the continent emphasized the importance of east–west routes across the Great Plains and through the Rocky Mountains to California. Few overland routes connected south to north from Mexico into the United States or to Canada beyond. There was little need for such routes as the Mississippi River provided the best north–south highway from the Gulf to the Great Lakes. Before 1848 when the America West belonged to Spain and then Mexico, there was a much stronger south to north orientation up the Rio Grande Valley into what became New Mexico. The Spanish traveled from their capital of Mexico City northward following rivers through the arid Sonora and Chihuahua Deserts. One of the major routes to Albuquerque and the important outpost of Santa Fe traced the course of the Rio Grande from El Paso and Las Cruces north, just as I-25 does today. Maps of North America, prior to the Treaty of Guadalupe Hidalgo in 1848, tell a completely different story of two countries' histories. For Mexico, the frontier lay to the north; for the United States, the promised land beckoned far to the west. Sadly, both countries claimed the same land in the Mexican-American War that resulted in our usurpation of 50 percent of Mexico's territory. It is our history, not Mexico's, and our obsession with east–west routes of travel to California that dominate our continent.

As we have seen in previous chapters, most of America's interstates follow established routes of earlier federal or state roads that in turn followed unpaved ways and trails. These lines of travel, desire lines, between important points usually trace their origins back to Native American trading routes. The construction and wide rights-of-way of modern-day roads and highways have erased most evidence of earlier trails. The Natchez Trace that cuts diagonally across Mississippi on its way from Nashville to Natchez remains one example that has not been obliterated by subsequent highways. Its route has been so eroded by footsteps over hundreds of years that in many places it is a wide trench between high banks. Today, the Natchez Trace is a national park. Trails across the American West have similar histories: first as Native American trading routes, then as trails for European fur traders, and finally as wide swaths of tracks carrying thousands

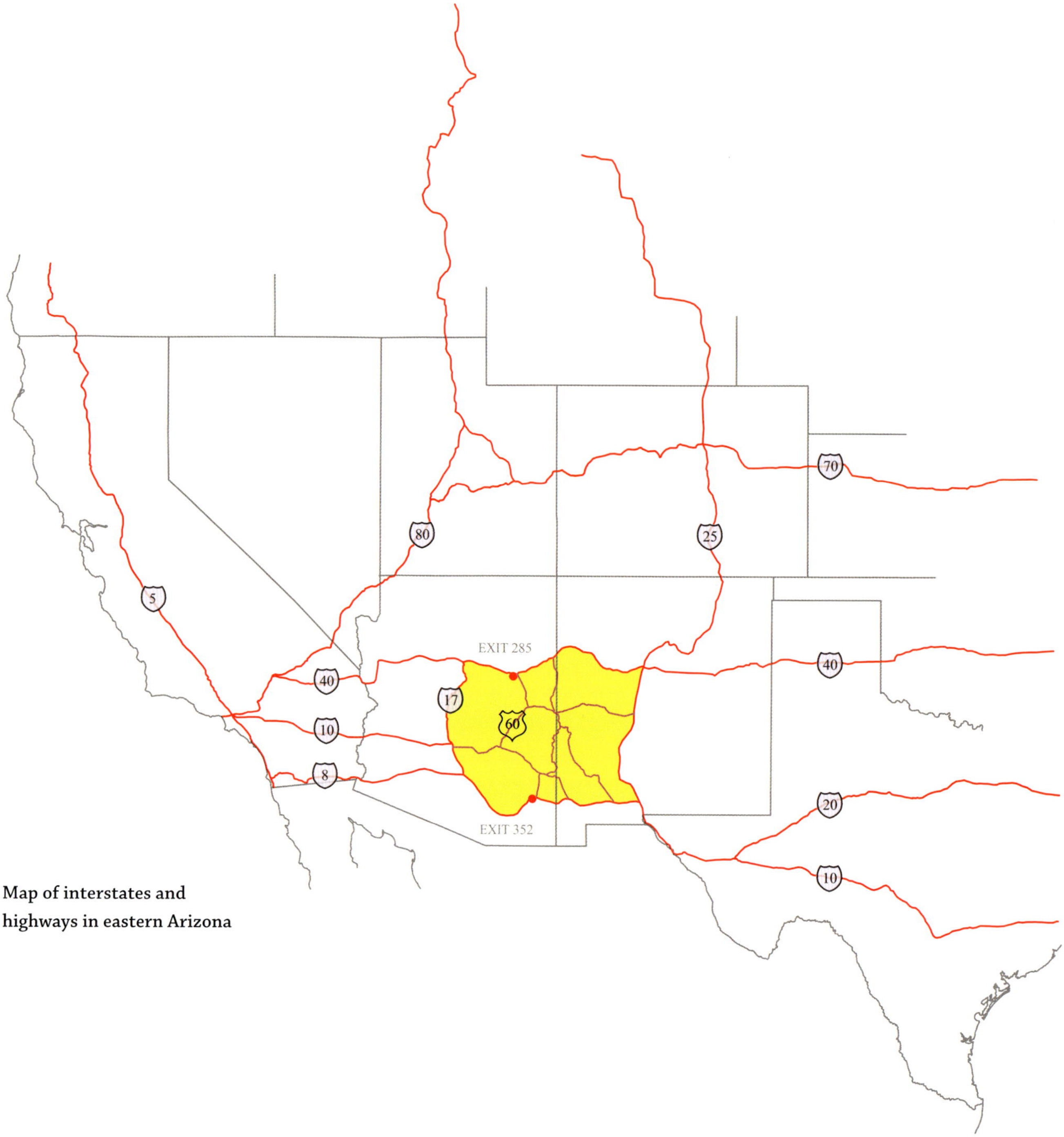

Map of interstates and highways in eastern Arizona

of emigrants ever westward to the promise of better lives. Names such as the Santa Fe Trail, the Oregon Trail, the California Trail, and the Mormon Trail embody important chapters in our history. The National Park Service preserves accessible segments of these western trails distant from modern roads, providing interpretive maps and directions for the interested explorer. In several locations, the ruts made by hundreds of heavily laden wagons still exist, worn into stone hillsides as poignant testimony of the tenacity and struggle of families moving west.

Another easily overlooked fact of the geography of the United States that influenced routes across the West was the lack of deep water harbors on the Pacific coast. There are only three major ports, and consequently three important connecting routes radiate out from Salt Lake City: one to Seattle, one to San Francisco, and one to Los Angeles/San Diego. Between these ports lie a thousand miles of beautiful but inhospitable coast. The three interstates that today form this "crow's foot" of three spreading highways, I-84, I-80, and I-15, traverse some of the most spectacular scenery in America—scenery that was miles and miles of empty, parched landscapes of unbelievable hardships for the earliest emigrants on foot.

All routes to the West begin at navigable waterways: usually St. Louis on the Mississippi River or at some jumping-off point on the Missouri River such as Omaha, Nebraska. Lewis and Clark started in St. Louis and followed the Missouri, the Yellowstone, and then the Columbia in their futile search for a direct water route across America. A map of the American continent demonstrates that the broad watershed of the Mississippi River not only reaches far north but also stretches west along the Missouri, Platte, and Arkansas Rivers. Goods and supplies could be ferried relatively easily up or down these rivers across great distances before being loaded onto wagons for long, arduous overland journeys. In fact, one could begin at Pittsburgh, go down the Ohio, up the Mississippi, and up the Missouri to Omaha before heading across the Great Plains along the Platte. This water journey covered almost one-third of the continent. Unfortunately for early pioneers, Omaha was only halfway across America. Once one arrived by boat at Omaha, there were still fifteen hundred hard, toilsome overland miles to San Francisco.

Another fact of western travel in the early nineteenth century that we forget today was its dependence on draft animals, mainly hardy mules or even hardier oxen. Horses were found to be too fragile for such harsh conditions as well as tempting prizes for the excellent horsemen of Great Plains Native Americans. Draft animals required water and forage daily if they were to survive to constantly pull heavy loads. By necessity, then, these early overland trails clung closely to streams and rivers. River flood plains also offered abundant vegetation for forage and a gradual gradient for easier travel. As we saw in the discussions of Nebraska, the Platte River was a widely used thoroughfare across the Great Plains for all three reasons: water, forage and gradient.

Four remarkable geographical features impede westward travel across America: the expanse of the Great Plains, the majestic heights of the Rocky

Mountains, the forbidding wastes of the Great Basin, and the sheer peaks and deep snows of the Sierra Nevada. All four constraints run thousands of miles north–south in successive waves blocking all routes of travel westward. The history of westward travel involved discovering passages and threading trails safely through these dramatic and beautiful geographical barriers.

The first railroads across the West followed these same historical overland wagon routes, not so much for the water, although water was necessary for steam engines, but for the long gradual gradients along rivers. The first transcontinental railroad, the Union Pacific, left the Missouri River at Omaha and followed the Platte River across the Great Plains of Nebraska and into the Laramie and Medicine Bow Ranges of Wyoming before meeting the Central Pacific at Promontory Point, Utah. Early settlers heading west by wagon on the California and Oregon Trails had followed the same route. From Promontory Point west, the Central Pacific continued along the California Trail and the Humbolt River in the Great Basin of Nevada, up through the Sierra Nevada and down into the Central Valley. Today, Interstate I-80 runs along the same Union Pacific Railroad tracks most of the way from Omaha to Oakland. Driving I-80, one sees long train sets running parallel to the highway, pulled by two engines front and pushed by two engines rear, carrying freight to distant cities. All transcontinental railroads and all subsequent interstates across the West replicate earlier wagon routes that began as solutions to two facts of geography, either aridity or topography, and sometimes to both.

In the late 1850s, Jefferson Davis, secretary of war under President Franklin Pierce, commissioned studies of possible transcontinental railroad routes across the American West. He gave this daunting task to a brilliant recent West Point graduate, Second Lieutenant G. K. Warren in the Topographical Engineers. In 1855, Lieutenant Warren produced one of the first comprehensive maps of the American West. Although his initial effort was an outline sketch map designed to illustrate the relationship of five different routes to each other, a more detailed and larger scaled map followed in 1858 with a full report.[1] Jefferson Davis strongly favored a southern route across Texas and the New Mexico Territory to Southern California. He hoped this would bind California more closely to the South with the possibility of drawing at least Southern California into the orbit of the slave-owning states. Because the different routes carried such importance to both the future North and South in the years preceding the Civil War, the U.S. Congress could not decide on a single route, and the entire project was soon abandoned. With the end of President Pierce's term in 1858, Davis returned to the U.S. Senate and, of course, was subsequently

1. For a detailed discussion of this map and the men who surveyed the different routes see Cohen, *Mapping the West*, 172.

elected president of the Confederacy. In one of the many ironies of American history, Lieutenant G. K. Warren became a high-ranking officer in the Union Army, reaching brigadier general. He is credited with recognizing the strategic importance of Little Round Top on the undefended left flank of the Union Army during the second day of the Battle of Gettysburg. Along with support from intrepid Joshua Chamberlain and the courageous Twentieth Maine, Warren's quick action at twilight on July 2, 1863, foiled Lee's attempt to turn the Union's left flank and prevented a major disaster for the North. Warren continued as a respected officer in the Union Army until late in the war when, at the Battle of Five Forks, he reputedly was not aggressive enough for his commanding generals Phil Sheridan and Ulysses S. Grant. Sadly, Warren resigned from the Union Army in disgrace, although he was exonerated of all wrongdoing after his death in 1882.

The maps and reports Lieutenant Warren compiled at the request of Jefferson Davis to study railroad expansion across the West still exist in the superb and accessible map collection at the Library of Congress. The first section of this chapter examines a detail of his initial draft map done in 1855 to better understand the routes eventually taken one hundred years later by the two interstate highways across Arizona. The full map, about twenty by twenty-three inches, has been folded, with the fold creases clearly visible. Nineteenth-century state and territory limits on Warren's map were outlined in red, a graphic addition that greatly aids a comparison with today's boundaries. All five routes Warren chose across the West for potential railroads correspond to the routes of subsequent transcontinental railroads and, coincidentally, the five major east–west twentieth-century interstates. Few good passes cut through the mountains forming the Continental Divide and the Sierra Nevada further west, so both railroads and highways took parallel advantage of the same few openings. In short, wagon trails became railroad routes that became highways that became our modern interstates; all mark similar and deeply engraved paths across fifteen hundred miles of the rugged, desolate, and incomparable landscapes of the American West. The story of these paths of travel is the history of the settlement of the West as much as it is the history of the vast open spaces between.

Lieutenant Warren compiled the information on his map from five separate survey groups sent west by Jefferson Davis. These survey teams were to gather information for five possible transcontinental rail routes; the fifth team also investigated possible north–south routes in California's Central Valley. Warren's map should be closely compared to the map of the entire interstate system in chapter 2. The northernmost route along the forty-ninth parallel roughly corresponded with today's I-90/94 from

Map of routes for a Pacific railroad, compiled to accompany the report of the Hon. Jefferson Davis, sec. of war. G. K. Warren, Lt. top. engrs. 1855

Minneapolis–St. Paul to Seattle. I-80 follows the middle route along the forty-first parallel beginning at Omaha, through Salt Lake City to San Francisco. Another route slightly south followed the thirty-ninth parallel through Denver and corresponds to today's I-70. The fourth route followed the thirty-fifth parallel through Albuquerque, across Arizona to Los Angeles and corresponds to today's I-40. A shorter proposed rail route connected Houston on the Gulf with Los Angeles along the thirty-second parallel close to the Mexican border on a route similar to I-10. This southernmost route required that the Gadsden Purchase, a large piece of Mexico's territory, be acquired in 1858 after the ratification of the 1848 Treaty of Guadalupe Hidalgo. Without this additional land, the southern route could not pass through several mountain ranges on acceptable grades for railroads. Even though President Lincoln chose the middle route from Omaha through Nebraska and Salt Lake City as the first transcontinental line, eventually all proposed routes would be developed by competing railroad companies. As we saw in the previous chapter on Nebraska, America's rail network expanded very quickly in the decade after the Civil War all across the open spaces of the West, adding track density and freight to the longer armature of the transcontinental lines.

Our explorations will concentrate on the two southern routes that I-40 and I-10 follow across present-day New Mexico and Arizona. A detail of Warren's map shows the two rail routes running parallel to each other through the New Mexico Territory approximately two hundred miles apart. On Warren's nineteenth-century map the New Mexico Territory stretched from Texas to the California border. A connecting north–south rail line follows the Rio Grande north, as does I-25 today.

Several familiar place-names on Warren's map help orient one to present-day landmarks. Albuquerque and Isleta on the Rio Grande were both early Spanish settlements. Although Albuquerque has far eclipsed Isleta as a city, Isleta was initially a more important rail junction. Santa Fe is just above Albuquerque and the map's fold line. West of Isleta, the proposed rail route splits around the Zuni Mountains before paralleling the River Puerco of the West. Holbrook, Arizona, sits where the Puerco

Detail of Warren's map

forks north from the Little Colorado River, called Colorado Chiquito on the map. The rail path follows the Little Colorado, then climbs through the Mogollon Mountains between San Francisco and Bill Williams Peaks, the latter named after an explorer, trapper, and colorful mountain man of the early nineteenth century who traveled much of the Southwest. The Flagstaff metropolitan area sits today in this same spot. The sweeping arc of the Mogollon Rim, an edge of the Colorado Plateau, divides Arizona into two large ecological zones discussed in the next part of this chapter. Warren essentially took his route across the high, flat Colorado Plateau from Texas to California, avoiding the Grand Canyon further north. His route then makes a short dip to thread through the Grand Wash Cliffs, before making the large loop below the Black Mountains and crossing the Colorado into California. I-40 takes a shortcut south of Warren's proposed route, although today's BNSF tracks still follow his line. Interestingly, Route 66 followed Warren's proposal and remains today, between Seligman and Kingman, as one of the best-preserved stretches of that historic road. Warren's proposed route established a remarkable congruency across a hundred years and hundreds of miles, testimony to the power and determinacy of geography, and to one man's accuracy and thoroughness.

The southernmost proposed rail line connecting El Paso with Tucson on Warren's map follows a route that reflects the different concerns of travelers in the mid-nineteenth century, namely the hostile Chiricahua Apache. East from Tucson, his route skirts around the word "Cienaga" (Spanish for "marsh") on the map, which probably refers to the Willcox Playa, a dry lake south of Willcox. He then heads through El Dado Pass or the "Pass of Chance." This mountain pass through the Chiricahua Mountains, now part of Coronado National Forest, was the center of the U.S. military campaign against the Apaches and their fierce and able leaders, Cochise and then Geronimo. The U.S. Army established Fort Bowie at this strategic location, and the Butterfield Overland Mail and Stage used the fort's protection as it traveled through the Pass of Chance in the 1850s. Warren's route then continues east to the Spanish settlement of Dona Ana, near Las Cruces, New Mexico, then through El Paso and Fort Bliss, Texas. Old Route 80 (not to be confused with the much more recent I-80 far to the north) cuts across southern Arizona connecting Tucson with El Paso by way of the mining town of Bisbee and the border crossing at Douglas. Today's I-10 follows Route 80's alignment except it shortens the loop to Bisbee and connects instead with Willcox. Both the interstate and Route 80 stay on the desert floor to avoid the Chiricahua Mountains, a small but significant victory in the twentieth century for the memory of Cochise and his warriors.

These congruencies and minor shifts in route alignments corroborate four hundred years of foot and wagon trails, then rail tracks, then highways, and finally today's interstates, all marking the same lines through a vast landscape. Our movements act as a stylus. We etched the earth, first tentatively, then more and more firmly until a deep groove of our desire marks layers of sedimented histories. Today, these layers are fragments of past conversations, interrupted or silenced, discoverable only to those who listen carefully, or study old maps.

Before the construction of interstates I-40 and I-10, the road network within the state of Arizona, and any state for that matter, had numerous and equally improved routes carrying through traffic in many directions. One had multiple choices depending upon seasonal weather, regional amenities, and final destinations. A page from a Phillips 66 road map from 1940 shows the road network within the southeastern quadrant of Arizona. On this map, Route 66 comes down from Gallup, New Mexico, heading west; Route 60 travels across the state through Phoenix; and Route 70 comes up from Lordsburg, New Mexico, through Duncan and Safford, Arizona, to Globe and then joins Route 60. Lastly, Routes 80 and 86, also from Lordsburg, go more southerly through Tucson. Roads indicated as a solid red line are two-lane paved highways; anything else, such as Route 60 east of Springerville, shown dotted, was "improved—gravel, stone, shell, topsoil-sandclay." U.S. federal highway numbers are within a shield, state highway numbers within a circle. Phoenix's population in 1940, according to the Phillips 66 map legend, was sixty-three thousand; both Globe and Miami were five to ten thousand people. Towns along these federal highways competed with each other for automobile and truck traffic. Globe especially was a major overnight stop with a hotel, motor cabins, and several home-cooking-style restaurants.

Route 66 has become the most famous of the early federal highways. Ironically, its promoters wanted Route 66 to be numbered 60, but settled for the subsequently more graphically identifiable double 6's. With the construction of I-40 in the 1950s, much of Route 66 disappeared. Where the two were congruent, I-40 was constructed right over the older route's right-of-way. When closely parallel with each other, Route 66's pavement was torn up and planted with vegetation. Occasionally, one sees an isolated and lonely row of telephone poles stretching into the distance, evidence that the pavement of Route 66 once existed next to the poles. Several segments of Route 66 still remain; far from I-40, they are meccas for avid explorers of America's early highways. Perhaps more than any other road, Route 66 symbolized the American myth of the open road heading west to a better life.

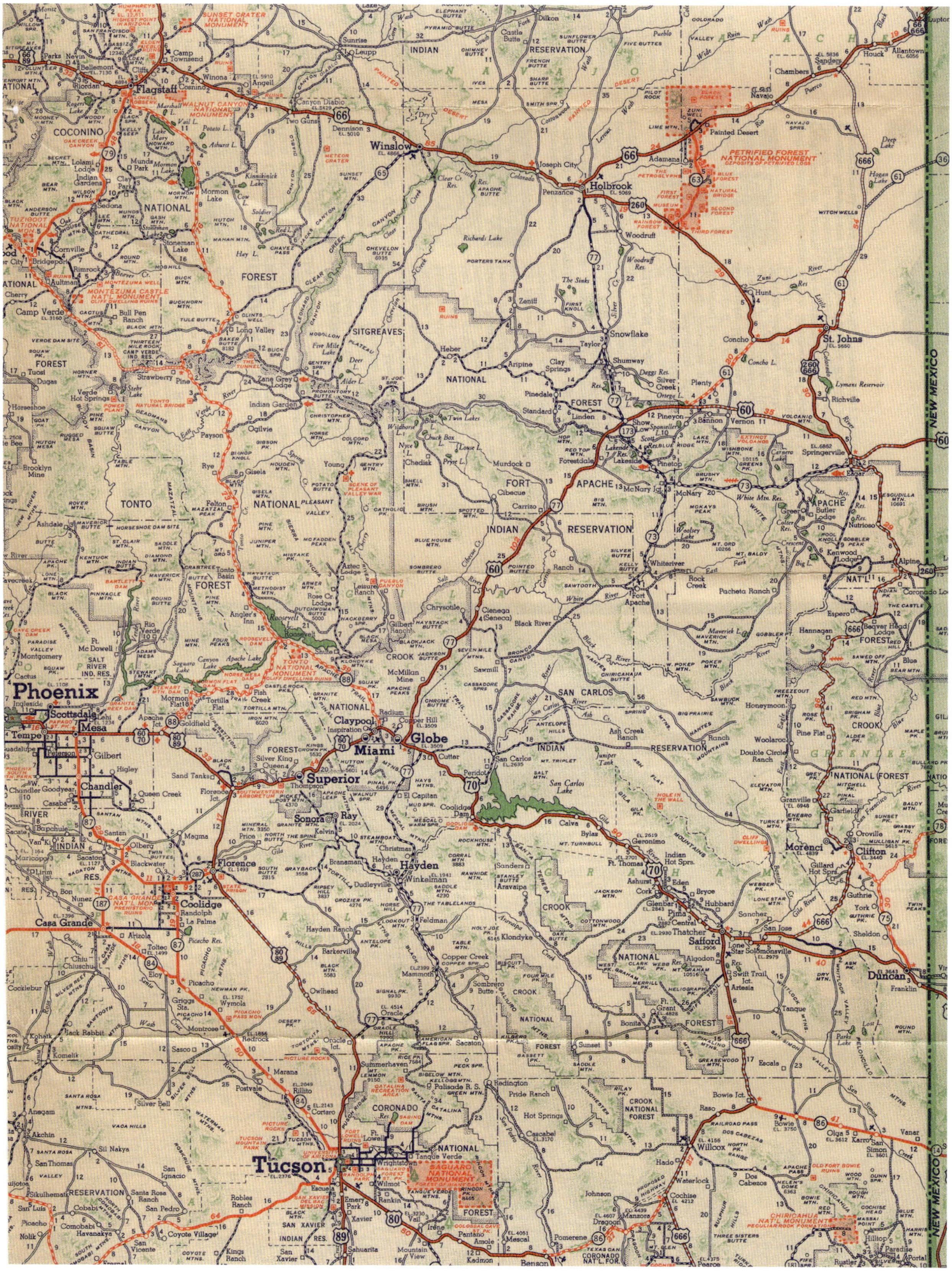
Flagstaff
Winslow
Holbrook
Phoenix
Scottsdale
Mesa
Tempe
Chandler
Globe
Miami
Superior
Florence
Coolidge
Casa Grande
Hayden
Tucson
Safford
Clifton
Morenci
Duncan
Willcox
St. Johns
Snowflake
Showlow
Springerville
Payson
COCONINO
NATIONAL
FOREST
TONTO
SITGREAVES
APACHE
CROOK
CORONADO
FORT APACHE
INDIAN
RESERVATION
SAN CARLOS
PETRIFIED FOREST NATIONAL MONUMENT
SAGUARO NATIONAL MONUMENT
CHIRICAHUA NAT'L MONUMENT
WALNUT CANYON NATIONAL MONUMENT
SUNSET CRATER NATIONAL MONUMENT
MONTEZUMA CASTLE NAT'L MONUMENT
CASA GRANDE NAT'L MON.
TONTO NATIONAL MONUMENT
NEW MEXICO
San Carlos Lake

Other routes like Route 60 have remained, sometimes renumbered or improved; some routes have been discontinued. Route 60 has become a secondary highway from metropolitan Phoenix to Globe and then into the dramatic Salt River Canyon. East of Phoenix it begins as a six-lane expressway connecting the city's expanding suburbs before narrowing to a two-lane highway. As illustrated on the Phillips 66 map, other roads access this region of Arizona, some to serve the interior mining towns, others as scenic byways to remote recreational opportunities in the mountains of Apache National Forest. For example, Route 666, today renumbered Route 191, transects eastern Arizona for nearly three hundred miles. This narrow twisting scenic road is also known as the Coronado Trail, for it supposedly traces the route the Spanish explorer followed north looking for gold. If true, Coronado traversed some wildly rugged terrain, for Route 191 climbs six thousand feet from the Chihuahua Desert at Douglas, Arizona, through the Mogollon Rim up onto the Colorado Plateau. He would have bisected two spectacular and awesome physiographic regions of the West, the Range and Basin Province and the Colorado Plateau, as well as the dramatic geological transition zone between. As discussed in the second section of this chapter, this mountainous transition zone is famous for its copper-bearing ore deposits. Ironically, Coronado should have been looking for copper instead of gold. Today, Route 191 actually passes through the huge Morenci open-pit copper mine before winding through the Apache National Forest Wilderness Area. Route 666 ended at Route 66 on the flat high plains of the Colorado Plateau. As today's Route 191, it joins I-40, east of Holbrook.

Three different narratives describe Holbrook: first it was a stop on the Atlantic and Pacific Railroad's main east–west line; then it became a main street town providing all types of services to travelers on Route 66; today it is an off-ramp town at Exit 285 on I-40.

The Atlantic and Pacific Railroad was originally incorporated by the U.S. Congress in 1866 as a transcontinental rail line connecting Springfield, Missouri, with California. Two portions were completed, one from St. Louis to Tulsa and a second from Albuquerque to Southern California. The swath of land given to the Atlantic and Pacific across the New Mexico Territory was excessive, even for the generous federal land grants to railroads of the time. The impoverished soils of the high desert made land like the Painted Desert relatively valueless, even for ranching, so railroads demanded more acreage as compensation. As the A&P tracks extended across the high Colorado plateau from Albuquerque into Arizona, the railroad added a surprising density of "end of track" towns. These temporary towns at the end of a segment of track construction often became permanent settlements.

Detail of eastern Arizona from a Phillips 66 Petroleum Company 1940 Official Road Map of Arizona *(opposite)*

Many of these closely spaced towns still exist, if in name only, evidence of the railroad's slow progress across the flat landscape. Nineteenth-century railroad schedules of the Atlantic and Pacific list Carrizo, Billings, Navajo Springs, Sanders, Allantown, Mamielite, and Defiance east of Holbrook, and St. Joseph, Hardy, Winslow, Dennison, Canon Diablo, Angell, and Cosnino west of Holbrook toward Flagstaff.

As was often the case, larger railroads soon purchased smaller ones like the Atlantic and Pacific. First the Atchison, Topeka and Santa Fe Railway, which then became the Santa Fe; then all these former lines were merged into the enormous Class 1 Burlington Northern Santa Fe Railway we saw in the second section of chapter 5. As a reminder of this acquisition sequence today, the old red sandstone 1892 Santa Fe station sits next to the tracks in Holbrook as a BNSF maintenance storage building.

A portion of a U.S. Geological Survey map of 1888 locates Holbrook next to the Little Colorado River. This historic map is notable for the very few settlements it shows across a wide expanse of flat topography. It is a beautiful example of cartography that starkly renders an immense unoccupied landscape. St. Joseph is west of Holbrook, and the tracks stop at Hardy in the middle of nowhere. All three communities, Holbrook, St. Joseph, and Hardy, were "end of track towns," places where the track construction crews stockpiled wooden ties and iron rail before the next push west. Often the construction ceased at one of these towns, pending more funds. Such towns were little more than temporary camps until the surrounding lands were populated and generated critical freight for the railroad. The dirt roads reaching out into the flat terrain from Holbrook indicate some activity, such as ranching, had already started. Of the three towns, St Joseph and Holbrook remain.

At the turn of the twentieth century, Holbrook was a watering station for steam locomotives on the Atchison, Topeka and Santa Fe's main line as it crossed the high plains of the Colorado plateau. Two large water tanks stood next to the tracks diagonally across from the passenger station. Like so many railroad towns we saw in the previous chapter about Nebraska, the tracks and sidings ran down the middle of the town, parallel to small blocks of commercial buildings. Grocery storage and feed warehouses lined a siding, while the presence of an ice-making facility suggests Holbrook was also an ice stop for trains carrying produce from the sunny valleys of Southern California to Chicago. The three or four blocks of commercial establishments must have served surrounding cattle and sheep ranches. The town's population of slightly over one thousand could not have supported much rail freight. By 1943 a single gas station sat diagonally at the intersection of Central Avenue and Porter Street, and Holbrook had

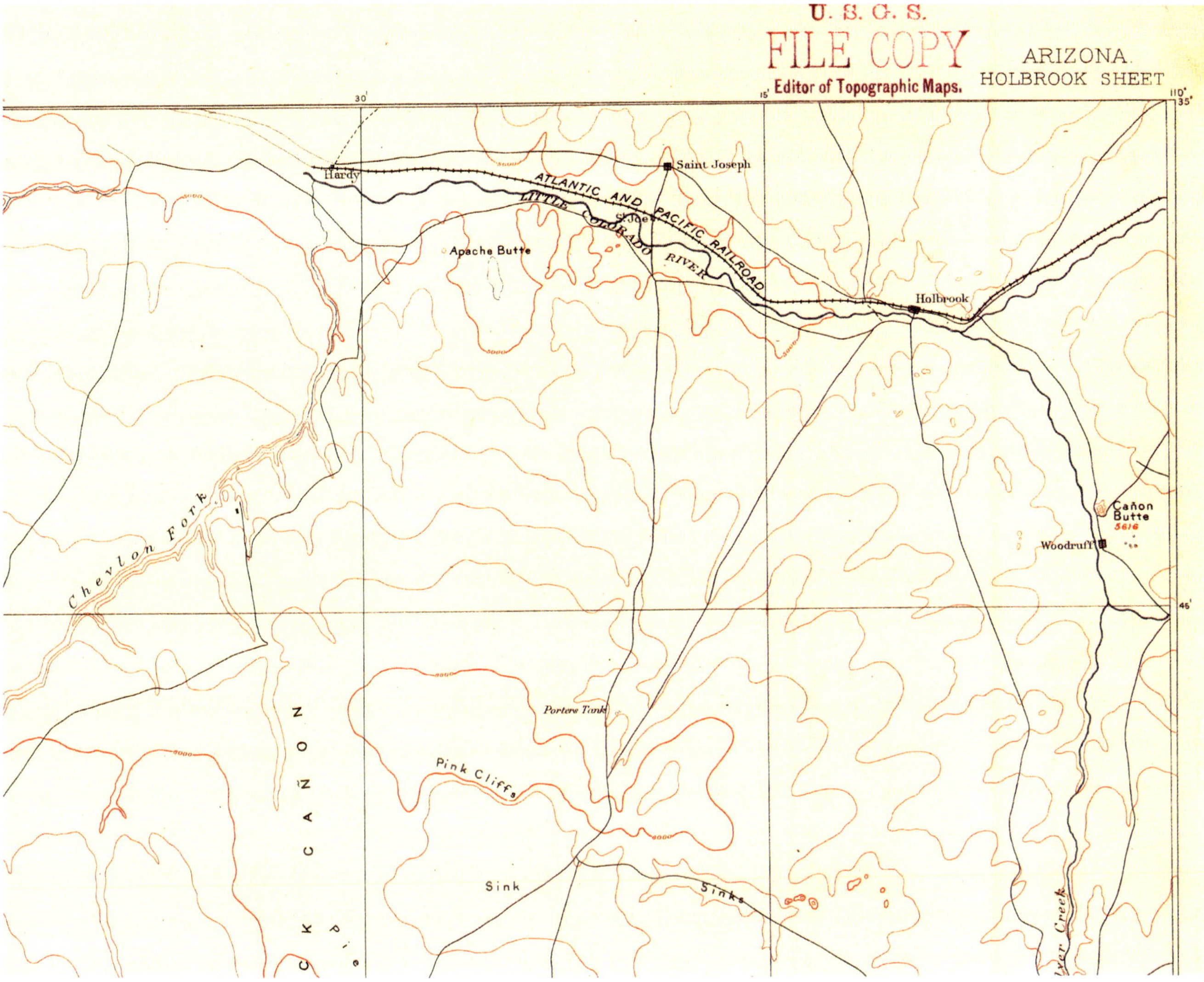

Detail from 1888 USGS map of Holbrook, Arizona

several car sales showrooms. The Arizona Hotel and the Hotel Holbrook indicated a schedule of passenger trains that necessitated overnight stays for the few visitors and traveling salesmen who ventured to Holbrook.

At the time of the Second World War, Holbrook was a minor maintenance stop on the AT&SF, remotely placed in the desert of northern Arizona, yet it had a "moving picture" theater with a stage, a pool hall, and a beautiful new Navajo County Courthouse. Imagine for a moment Holbrook's moving-picture theater filled to capacity. As the movie ended at 9:00 p.m., people flowed out onto the sidewalks and spilled into the street, stopping traffic. Some patrons stayed for drinks or snacks, so the evening's activities would continue. For a brief instant, the town's people would take possession of Holbrook's wide streets. As we have seen in all towns we have explored so far, an active public street is a precious place. The word "place" comes into our language by way of the Latin *platea* meaning street. Unfortunately, we can no longer be nostalgic for places and streets. Nostalgia, from the Greek root *nostos,* means to return home, and these towns, these homes, have disappeared. That era is past, for any present evening at 9:00 p.m. Holbrook is deserted. No one walks its streets, not even the lone woman peering into the empty windows of a Hopper painting.

The 1920s saw the formation of the American Association of State Highway Officials and the beginning of dedicated federal roads across the country. Three routes were designated as federal transcontinental highways across Arizona: Routes 80, 60, and 66. Several factors made Route 66 important to towns like Holbrook. First, the importance of its two ends: the Great Lakes port of Chicago and the growing Pacific port of Los Angeles associated with the agricultural region of Southern California. One should not overlook the obvious fact that this road, and this road alone, directly connected the two largest-growing metropolitan areas of early-twentieth-century America. Because Route 66 traverses almost entirely flat terrain, it was especially advantageous for burgeoning truck traffic. During the Second World War, major military bases developed throughout the southern regions served by Route 66 because of the warm and consistently sunny weather. Military traffic jammed the highway from 1940 to 1945.

Sadly, America's great agricultural collapse, the Dust Bowl of the 1920s, also occurred along this route in Kansas, Oklahoma, and northern Texas. Oklahoma was especially hard hit, subject to one of the greatest migrations in U.S. history. Tenant farmers forced from their land drove or hitchhiked to the empty promise of Southern California. Destitute workers crowded Route 66 through the harsh deserts of New Mexico and Arizona. The songs of Woody Guthrie give voice to these wretched wanderers. Steinbeck's Tom Joad, from *The Grapes of Wrath,* fleshed out the features of so many faceless Americans. Route 66's recognition by Guthrie, Steinbeck, and other artists earned it the nickname "Mother Road of America" and folkloric stature in American history.

The increasing popularity of the Southwest's treasures of natural beauty such as the Painted Desert and the Grand Canyon coincided with America's growing infatuation with automobile touring. In the halcyon days after the Second World War, tourists flocked along Route 66 in growing numbers, headed to Southern California's attractive climate. We forget that before the Los Angeles metropolitan area swallowed all vestiges of its surrounding bucolic landscapes, places such as Palm Springs, Del Mar, and Santa Barbara gripped the imagination of people locked in the gray winters of the north. Route 66 offered the way to sunshine.

Most importantly for towns like Holbrook, the other moniker of Route 66, "Main Street America," describes the highway's salient engineering feature: it ran straight down the main streets of all towns it passed through. There were no bypasses. This single, simple fact gave enormous economic advantages to every small town along Route 66. Cabin courts, restaurants, gasoline stations, and automobile repair stations appeared, each town vying with one another for the tourist dollars with unique signage and distinctive billboards. Some, like the famous "Teepee Villages" Motel, even became the advertising images itself.

Holbrook was no exception, and by the Second World War, it had switched from a railroad town to a "Main Street" town. Route 66 ran through Holbrook one block over from the tracks along Hopi Drive. Tourist courts and gas stations soon lined this new main street and pulled the commercial core away from the tracks and into alignment with the federal highway. Many colorful relics of mid-century highway accommodations still exist along the partially deserted segment of Route 66 through Holbrook. The former Pow Wow Motel sign towers over the street announcing "Rocks." The small lettering at the sign's bottom reminds us of another time when accommodations were advertised with the new "TV" and "refrigeration."

A more recent USGS map surveyed just before the construction of the interstates tells a different story from the map of 1888. Route 66 has been constructed, along with Route 260 to St. Johns and Route 77 down to Show

"Teepee Villages" Motel, old Route 66, Holbrook, Arizona

Rainbow Rock Shop with its green dinosaurs, old Route 66, Holbrook, Arizona *(above)*

Former Pow Wow Motel sign, old Route 66, Holbrook, Arizona *(right)*

Low and Globe. Route 66 makes an alignment adjustment at Holbrook's center and then heads west parallel to the AT&SF tracks. The construction of I-40 around Holbrook brought an off-ramp town into existence separate from Holbrook's commercial streets. I-40 is engineered with three exits at Holbrook, two of which connect like the string on a bent bow, the bow being the interstate, the string a straight boulevard of two and a half miles between exits 289 and 286. One can leave the interstate, travel down a wide strip of modern franchised accommodations and restaurants, and regain the highway without ever going through the historic town center. It is the ultimate bypass, a cruel easy off, easy on, serving just the interstate. The road goes nowhere beyond Holbrook; it starts and ends with the interstate. One could continue beneath the interstate and eventually turn on Hopi Drive, the old Route 66, drive its length and again gain access to I-40. But the new strip of eleven hotel/motels and eight restaurants, bookended by two gas stations, exists separately from the original town and serves only as a series of quick options for through travelers on I-40 or tourists visiting the Painted Desert National Park. Holbrook had adjusted to one shift of its center, from railroad tracks to Route 66 as its main street before this last, and probably final, shift to serve the interstate. As an off-ramp town, this new strip has no commercial or retail services except the three services that are always located at exit towns: overnight accommodations, food, and gas. Holbrook's old commercial core has been left to struggle for whatever tourist traffic ventures beyond the fast lanes of modern interstate travel. Only those intrepid explorers looking for remnants of Route 66 seek out fragments like Hopi Drive for its nostalgic reminders of another past. The stories of the "Mother Road" still resonate with those searching for something beyond easy off, easy on.

Holbrook has always existed as a stop on the way to somewhere else; first as a train watering station, then as a car and truck stop on Route 66, and now as a fragment of a town attached to an interstate off-ramp town. At each shift in its history, Holbrook has served a similar and necessary role, aiding travelers through the hot and dusty deserts of Arizona. Trapped by their past, isolated towns like Holbrook have few choices for reinvention. Its sole function as a nodule or appendage to transportation networks has persisted for 150 years through three transportation changes. Perhaps our bias for more picturesque and charming towns with coffee shops and boutique stores blinds us to the gritty beauty of places like Holbrook. Families on their way to the sunshine, the lonely soldier gazing from a waiting train's window, a battered Ford sedan filled with expectant laborers—all are now faded apparitions from a distant past. Yet today downtown Holbrook's green and yellow spotted dinosaurs that group at the corner, its

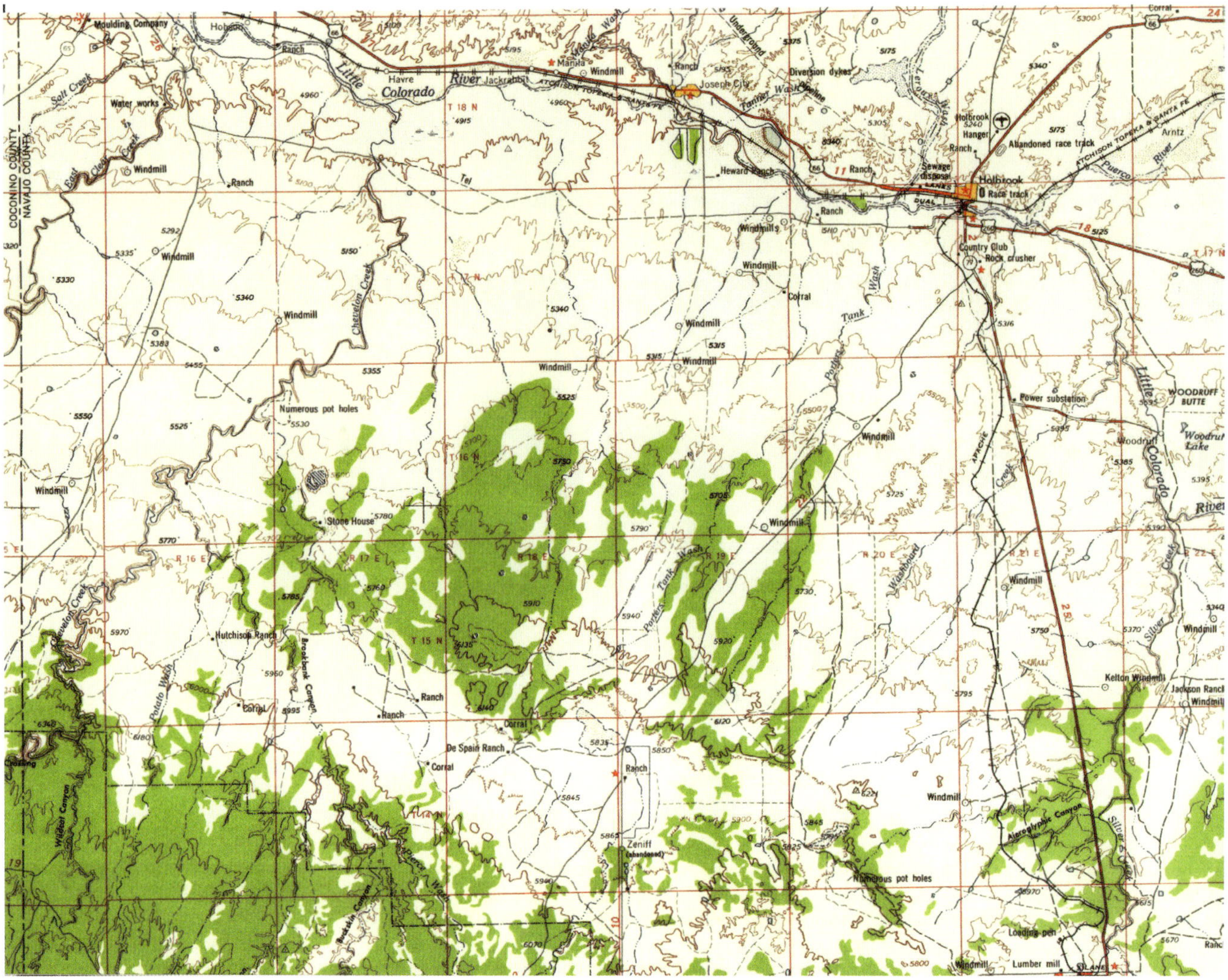

Detail from 1954 USGS map of Holbrook, Arizona

rock shop, its delicious Mexican eating places, the children gathering in its wide streets, and the local sheriff's car paternally patrolling its residential neighborhoods are all vestiges of a place that persists as a community within the overwhelmingly spectacular landscape of the Painted Desert.

Copper Futures

The southwest quadrant of the Colorado Plateau's immense uplifted disk falls as an arc diagonally across Arizona. Six hundred million years ago, this landmass, roughly 130,000 square miles, slowly rose almost two miles above the surrounding continent, forcing its entrenched meandering rivers to cut through the horizontal sedimentary rocks like a buzz saw through layers of plywood. The most well-known and spectacular example of this process is the Grand Canyon sculpted by the Colorado River. The Colorado River and its tributaries drain the Colorado Plateau and, over time,

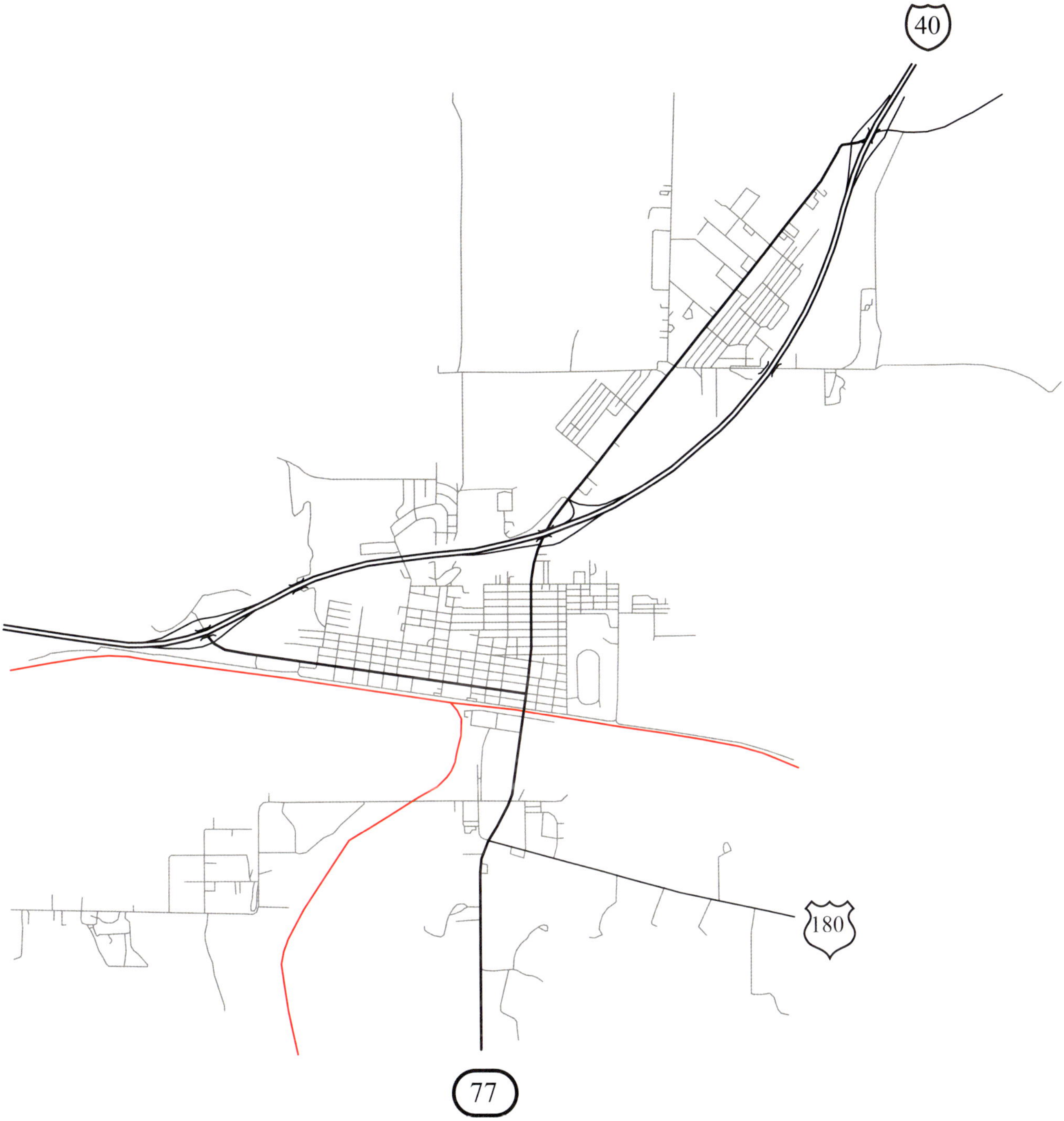

have incised hundreds of step slits into the soft red limestone. Hidden canyons such as the mystical Canyon de Chelly with its famous Anasazi cliff dwellings provide us with several of our most spectacular national and state parks. Zion, Canyonlands, Arches, Bryce Canyon, and Capitol Reef National Parks contain some of the most dramatic landforms on Earth.

Drawing of Holbrook, Arizona, showing I-40 with its three exits as it bypasses Holbrook

Abandoned car along old Route 66 near Holbrook, Arizona

Holbrook, Arizona, and all the towns along the I-40–Burlington Northern Santa Fe Railroad corridor are located on the Colorado Plateau, for both the railroad and the interstate follow the flat easy gradient of the horizontal plateau after rising up out of the Rio Grande Rift at Albuquerque, New Mexico. After Holbrook, I-40 climbs through Flagstaff and then turns south at Kingman, Arizona, before dropping off the plateau and crossing the ubiquitous Colorado River into California's Mojave Desert.

Another geological area, the Range and Basin Province, encompasses a vast area of the American West, stretching from Washington State, through all of Nevada and eastern California, and down through Arizona and New Mexico before reaching far south into Mexico. Its name, Range and Basin, aptly describes its landforms, long parallel north–south mountain ridges alternating with flat arid valleys or basins. The portion of the Range and Basin Province that covers much of southern Arizona is the Sonoran Desert, which reaches north from deep within Mexico. The Sonora Desert's elevation is nearly three thousand feet lower than places like Holbrook on the Colorado Plateau. A symbol of Arizona, and native only to the Sonoran Desert, the familiar organ pipe cactus spikes the arid hills and flat basins for miles in every direction around Phoenix and Tucson. Both Sun Belt cities, Phoenix and Tucson spread across "basins" or wide valleys. Their success is tied to the arid desert sunshine, and they are totally dependent for water on the Salt, Verde, and Gila Rivers that drain down from the edge of the Colorado Plateau. Surely Tucson and Phoenix are both examples of twentieth-century America's hubris: cities with millions of inhabitants and highly productive year-round agriculture are located in a hot, dry landscape.

Between the high Colorado Plateau and the lower Sonora Desert sits another narrow geological transition zone of much older rocks in a mountainous landscape shaped by water erosion. The elevations are lower than the Colorado Plateau, and the geological strata are more severely faulted and more heavily eroded by rivers over the millennia. The Mogollon Rim, the high escarpment that defines the southwestern edge of the Colorado Plateau, runs along this transition zone for two hundred miles, making a great arc from the New Mexican border northwest to Flagstaff. Perhaps the best place to experience the dramatic scenery of this geological transition zone is along Route 60 through the spectacular Salt River Canyon. This remarkably engineered stretch of highway between Globe and Show Low, Arizona, twists and turns through the sheer cliffs and precipitous clefts carved over millions of years by the seemingly insignificant shallow stream far below.

In the nineteenth century, Native Americas took advantage of this inaccessible topography to retreat after raiding settlers in the valleys below. Today, the area is primarily a series of connected national forests, including the spectacular Apache-Sitgreaves National Forest that spreads eastward into New Mexico. Two large Native America reservations span the centers of these mountains: Fort Apache and San Carlos Apache Indian Reservations, both established by President Grant in 1872. The White Mountain Apache Tribe inhabits the Fort Apache Reservation, a land area twice the size of Rhode Island that centers on the historic Fort Apache beneath the shadow of the eleven-thousand-foot Bald Peak. Similar in size but with a smaller population, San Carlos Apache Reservation consolidates various Native American tribes from the region.

Numerous rivers drain down from these remote mountains to flow across the desert through Phoenix. Early in the twentieth century the Salt, Gila, and Verde were dammed for flood control and for a consistent water supply for agricultural irrigation and for the ever-expanding metropolitan area of Phoenix. The Salt and its tributary, the Black River, cut deeply northeastward into this rugged transitional geological zone, reaching all the way to the Mogollon Rim. The Theodore Roosevelt Dam controls the Salt River, protecting Phoenix from the catastrophically disastrous yearly summer-fall floods that would sweep away everything in the flat desert valley below. Artificial Roosevelt Lake shimmers in the desert sun, its intense blue a surreal mirage between cactus-covered hills. No vegetation and no marshes or wetlands exist around the shore of this lake; it floats dreamlike in such an unexpected location.

Tossed, tumbled, and kneaded in the wide mixing bowl of plate tectonics over millions of years, the rocks and strata of this region became a mixture of many kinds of geological formations and processes, some filled with igneous intrusions that contained ore with precious minerals. Subsequent uplifts and folding of strata and millions of years of water erosion cut into and exposed these ores close to the surface, depositing traces of minerals in stream beds. A brightly colored fragment of a geological map of the area around Globe, Arizona, gives an idea of the geological stresses that squeezed and melted the rocks before pushing them up through the earth's crust. The many black lines on the map represent faults, shifts, or sheer displacements in the earth's crust. Severely faulted granitic rocks formed from complex chemical changes in hot magnum deep within the earth pushed up to the surface in wide porphyritic copper deposits. The ore deposits in this area of Arizona are not particular high in copper, sometimes less than 1 or 2 percent, yet they are economically accessible to surface or open-pit mining techniques.

With the discovery of electricity in the late nineteenth century, copper became a necessary and highly valued metal. Telegraph equipment, telephones, electric trains, and streetcars all needed copper wires. The proliferation of manufactured electrical appliances such as radios and refrigerators created such a high demand for copper that during the two world wars, civilian use of copper was rationed. Because of this demand and because 60 percent of all copper mined in the United States comes from Arizona, copper-mining companies greatly influence all aspects of Arizona's political history. Much of the labor force in Arizona's mines came from just across the border in Mexico. Both racism and corporate arrogance caused continuous episodes of worker unrest and injustice throughout the nineteenth and twentieth centuries. Arizona has a long and particularly nasty narrative of disputes between labor and management in the mining industry.

Copper was first discovered in the Southwest thousands of years ago by Native American craftsmen searching for blue turquoise. They encountered the blue azurite crystals that are evidence of copper deposits in the outwash of streams. Deposits of gold or silver were also found together with the copper. All three minerals were used in the making of the exquisite Native American jewelry that was traded throughout South and Central America. It was silver, not copper, that first drew Europeans into the mountains of Arizona. In their search for treasure, the Spanish followed the Gila and Salt Rivers north across the Sonoran Desert but found little to convince them to remain in this inhospitable part of the Southwest. After the American Civil War, federal troops soon subjugated the various Apache tribes and allowed prospectors to explore for gold and silver. Any silver and gold deposits were soon exhausted, but the large copper deposits were noted by knowledgeable miners. As copper's use in manufactured

Geologic map of the Globe Quadrangle, Arizona, by Nels Peterson, Arizona Bureau of Mines, 1954 *(opposite)*

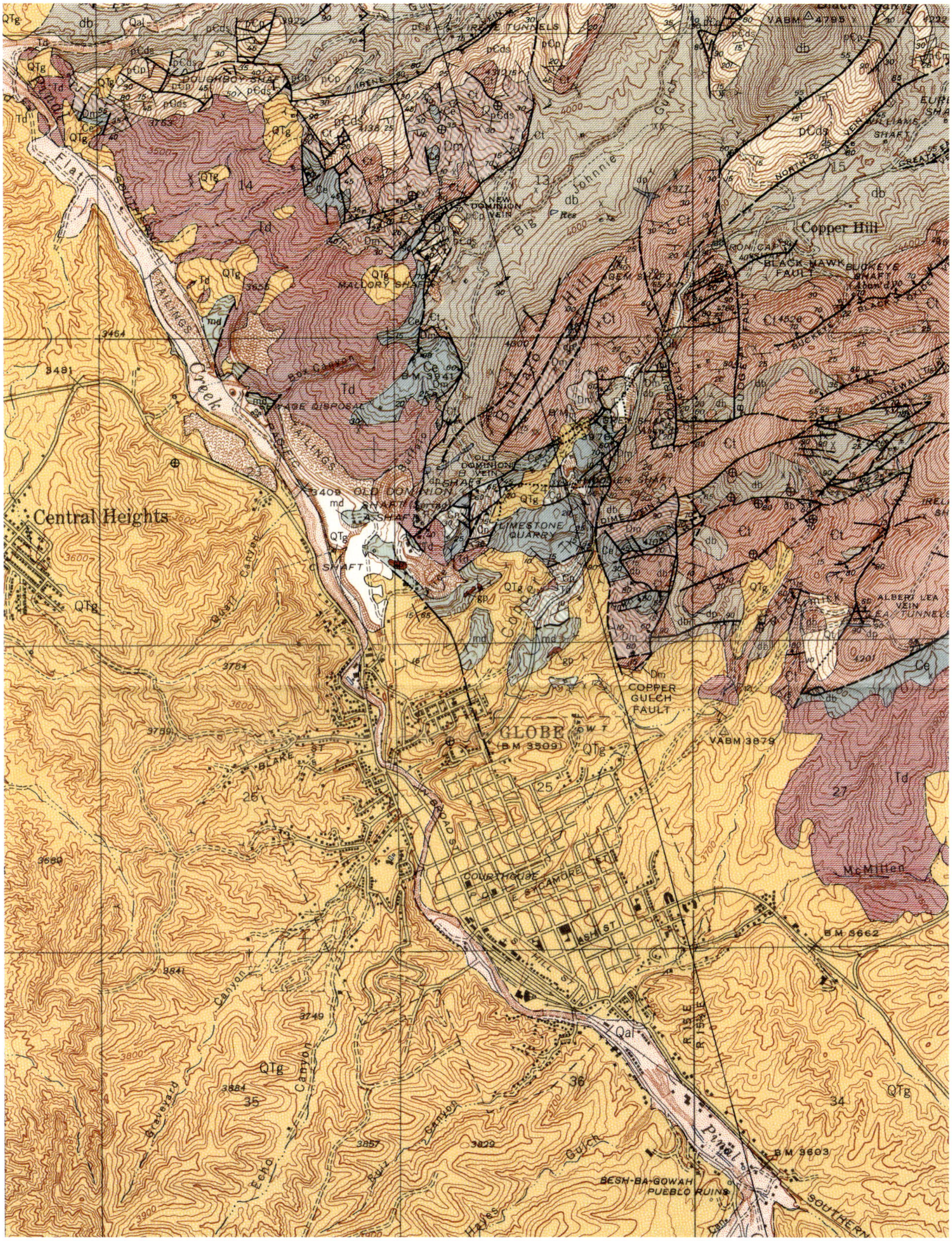
Central Heights
Copper Hill
GLOBE
COPPER GULCH FAULT
LIMESTONE QUARRY
OLD DOMINION
MALLORY SHAFT
BLACK HAWK FAULT
ALBERT LEA VEIN
BESH-BA-GOWAH PUEBLO RUINS
McMillen
COURTHOUSE
SYCAMORE
ASH ST
Pinal
Flat
Creek
VABM 3879
B M 3662
B M 3603

electrical products expanded, demand skyrocketed, roads and railroads were constructed into the remote mines, and Arizona's copper boom began. Mines were opened in Miami, Superior, Globe, and deeper into the mountains at Clifton. At first, ores with high percentages of copper were extracted from underground shafts. Soon, with the development of heavy equipment, open pits became more economical. Within decades, this region of Arizona was pockmarked with ever-expanding terraced pits and their associated tall piles of excavated overburden hauled by enormous trucks the size of houses.

As immense and awesome as these open pits are, there is very little about copper mining that is pretty. The shifting of tons of rock leaves scars on the landscape, the smelting of ore generates toxic acids, and leaching beds release plumes of underground sulfuric acid that destroy streams and water sources. With copper less than 5 percent of the ore, very high quantities of waste materials are generated. There are basically two processes for separating copper from its ore. Both processes begin by pulverizing rocks to the texture of talcum powder. Huge flotation ponds, sulfuric leaching vats, or smelters separate the copper from the unwanted rock powder. All of these processes release potentially fatal toxic fumes, sludge, or acids. The final step involves an electrolytic refinery where an electric current causes pure copper to precipitate out. In all situations a complicated and large flow of heavy materials goes from mine to smelter to final pure copper, leaving great piles of waste across the landscape.

Dump beds of ore trucks, Morenci Mine, Globe, Arizona

By the First World War, copper mining was in full swing in eastern Arizona, both supplying the nation's need and generating huge profits for shareholders. Copper prices, however, proved volatile as they were dependent upon world conditions far beyond the hills and mountains of Arizona. Prices can fluctuate greatly: when demand is high and supplies low, fortunes are made; when demand is low and supply high, mines shut down. When the mines do close, towns and whole regions suffer. Competition from foreign mines, especially in Chile, hurt the U.S. copper industry from the 1930s onward, causing a drop in Arizona's mine output. In fact, the second and third decades of the twentieth century may have been the apogee of Arizona's copper industry. Any graph of copper prices over the twentieth century reveals sharp spikes and steep dips; consistent volatility defines the copper industry across decades. The Second World War only briefly interrupted the constant downward trend of Arizona's market share. It is no accident that the Sanborn Fire Insurance Maps used to illustrate the vitality and prosperity of Arizona's mining communities in this chapter were all created in the 1920s with no subsequent years ever included. Sanborn maps are themselves measures of capital worth. The company usually continued to map most towns and cities into the 1940s. Empty towns with no assets were discontinued.

This extended introduction to copper mining forms the background to discussions of several mining towns located within this remote area of Arizona, far removed from any interstate. The map in the first section of this chapter shows that Route 60, designated a transcontinental federal highway in the early 1940s, runs diagonally across Arizona through three towns, Globe, Miami, and Superior, before connecting to other routes in Phoenix and continuing on to the West Coast. Route 60 was an important east–west highway traveling across the United States from Norfolk, Virginia, to Los Angeles through Louisville, Kentucky, and St. Louis, Missouri. As a key highway, it generated traffic in all the towns through which it passed. Route 60 especially benefited Globe, for it followed its main street, Broad Street. It is interesting to look at the posted travel times from one city to the next on a 1940s road map; obviously, they are much longer than our interstate possibilities today. From Albuquerque to Globe was ten hours, so Globe would have been fortuitously positioned as a day's drive from Albuquerque, necessitating a night's rest before heading west across the deserts of Arizona. With the construction of I-10 and I-40, these three towns lost any through travelers other than people associated with the declining business of copper mining or tourists heading into the mountains for recreation.

Transcontinental traffic switching to the interstates did not cause the collapse of Globe, Miami, and Superior. Their demises followed the steady drop in world copper prices throughout the twentieth century. All three towns were caught in a downward spiral of depressingly obvious economic decline. Their main thoroughfares are now mostly vacant, with stores closed and streets deserted. These tragic empty towns can only corroborate past prosperity. Route 60 has been improved to travel around each town by adding bypasses that slowly strangle any hopes for renewal. Globe manages to hang on as a county seat; it has a beautiful surviving collection of structures lining its main street. Globe has become a center for people heading into the Apache-Sitgreaves National Forest beyond the two large Native American reservations or for tourists searching for artifacts of Arizona's rich mining history, a history everywhere evident in the scarred landscapes surrounding all towns in this, the "copper triangle" of Arizona.

In 1926, the first state highway into this area of Arizona made a right turn into the commercial center of the town of Superior. The highway intersected two of Superior's streets, Main and Magnum. Named for the mining company, Magnum Street ran uphill to the entrance and head structures of the underground shafts. Superior's downtown was a small grid of residential streets with names like Copper and Porphyry Avenues, leaving no doubt about the town's origins. The intersection of Main and Magnum boasted two hotels, the Magnum and the Coleman, a movie theater, auto dealers, gas stations, and several restaurants. A drug store, auto service, a grocery store, and a sturdy bank anchored the four corners. Imagine the traffic generated as a major highway stopped and made a right turn at the town's center. Local merchants must have prospered. Bakeries, a tailor shop, a grocery store and meat market, two cobbler shops, and two barbershops filled out the commercial core. A detailed Sanborn map from 1926 labels the uses of each building and color-codes the construction materials. Pink signified brick, blue indicated stone, and yellow represented wood. Superior's map has a preponderance of pink and blue, which means the town's buildings were well constructed, finely detailed, and substantial structures.

All the structures necessary for processing ore—the head structures, crushers, industrial rail facilities, and the brown, dusty smelter—clustered around the mine shafts on the slopes above the town. Black mounds of waste carried from deep within the earth reconfigured the topography and dwarfed the buildings below. Today, a single brick chimney silhouettes against the sky, a stark punctuation mark in a bleak landscape. The vacant buildings and empty lots of Superior's wide intersection are even bleaker; the boarded windows of the isolated Macpherson's Hotel Magnum are the

Sanborn map of Superior, Arizona, 1926

only remnants of the town's vitality identified by the descriptive labels on the 1926 map.

Economic salvation dangles tantalizingly close to Superior. One of the world's largest copper ore deposits has been discovered over a mile below the earth's surface nearby. Access to this ore will require a tremendous mining operation below and above ground, resulting in extensive environmental changes on the surface. Developing this mine would add jobs and economic stimulus to Superior, but it would also be fraught with complicated environmental issues. A 2,400-acre parcel of federally protected land blocks the full expansion of the mine. This land, known as Oak Flats, was given federal protection by President Eisenhower. A proposed contentious land swap slowly waits for approval from the federal government. This swap pits mining and economic development proponents against environmental and Native American concerns. It is a classic struggle between exploitative financial power and the protection of a beautiful landscape.

The future of derelict Superior hangs in the balance.

Three miles wide, the open-pit Miami Copper Mine looms over the small town of Miami. Below the gray slope of the mine, Miami's commercial center now exists along Sullivan Avenue, two blocks over from an improved Route 60. A beautiful Sanborn map from 1922 shows the incredible density of businesses once fronting Sullivan, Keystone, and Inspiration Avenues. Like the map of Superior, blue is the most conspicuous color on the map of Miami. A close study of this map reveals the rich commercial texture of early-twentieth-century mining towns. Pool halls, barbershops, and cobbler shops predominate. Miami was a rowdy town of bearded men needing frequent shaves, men who wore boots always in need of repair, and men whose recreation consisted mostly of pool and drink. The very few bars or saloons that accepted women had a clearly labeled "Ladies" section, in the broadest sense of the word. Although bearded men in heavy work boots no longer walk Miami's deserted streets, Sullivan Avenue today is worth a detour off Route 60 for its collection of old storefronts—one recycled into the delightful Fine Arts Internet Café serving strong coffee—and several Mexican restaurants. Down an empty grass-covered side street, a VFW Hall commemorates those young people from Superior who served their country in faraway places.

Globe is less than five miles from Miami. Unlike Miami or Superior, Globe has recently experienced a renaissance as a weekend and tourist destination for people from metropolitan Phoenix. As the county seat of Gila County, Globe has an imposing stone courthouse that attracts activity to its downtown. Route 60 once ran straight through Globe's commercial center, framed on both sides by continuous and busy storefronts. Globe's Broad Street was, and still is, an archetypal American main street: wide pavement with angle parking, continuous well-scaled stores tightly grouped together that once provided all necessary services and businesses. While Globe began as a mining town, it has successfully reinvented itself as a stopping place for people heading into the spectacular scenery of the Salt River Canyon or the dramatic topography of the Tonto National Forest and the Superstition Wilderness Mountains. Unfortunately, Route 60 now bypasses the downtown, and a competing strip of newer motels and eateries has grown up outside the historic center. The adobe-style El Rey Motor Court remains from the late 1930s, a reminder of Globe's mid-century's prosperity.

Globe's main street, Broad Street, parallels and crosses the seemingly insignificant Pinal Creek. This intertwined relationship has caused several disastrous floods of Globe's business district. A sepia-rendered 1902 USGS map illustrates Globe's organic relationship with the creek, the valley, and

Sanborn map of Miami, Arizona, 1922 ***(opposite)***

June 1922.
MIAMI
Ariz.
MIAMI AV.
KEYSTONE AV.
INSPIRATION AV.
CHISHOLM AV.
PINTO
ORPHAN
GIBSON
SULLIVAN
CANAL
LIVE OAK
SIKES
FIRE STATION
AUTO REPG
B. P. O. ELKS CLUB
Bank
Moving Pictures
Motion Pictures
Ford Garage
Printing
Hotel
M. E. Church

Side street, Miami, Arizona

the topography. The copper mines climb Block Mountain along the aptly named Copper Gulch, with the town, creek, and railroad entwined in the valley below. The ore could be easily transported downhill to the railroad running along the level banks of Pinal Creek. Globe's main street grew along these same level floodplains while the residential streets curled up the surrounding hills. This historic topographic map of 1902 shows the mountains around Globe just before copper mining literally exploded, recontouring the hills west of Globe into open-pit mines.

A relic of Globe's former luster, the finely detailed Valley National Bank, remains at the corner of Broad and Mesquite Streets. Now empty, this beautifully scaled neoclassical building helps frame an important intersection on Globe's main street, even though a forlorn "Hair-Nail's, Tanning"

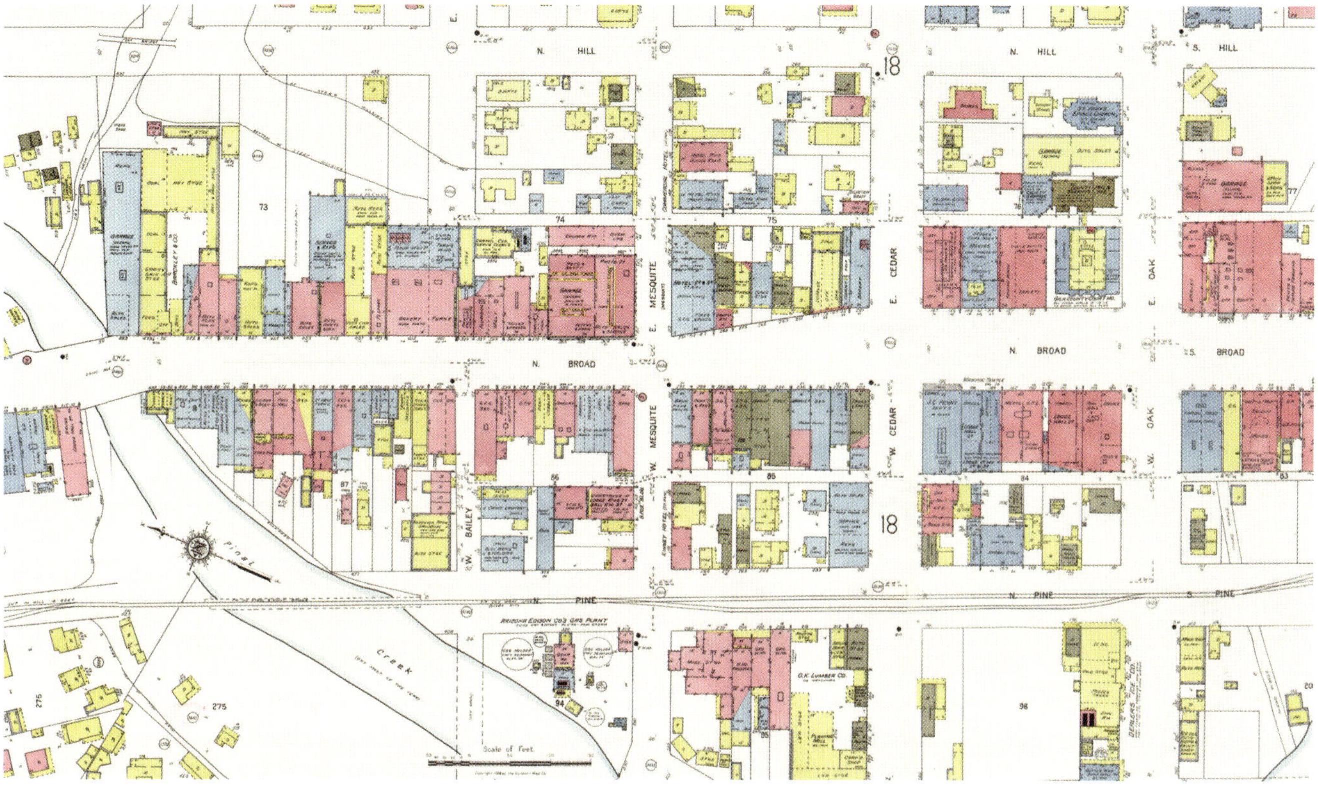

Composite Sanborn map of Broad Street, Globe, Arizona, 1929 *(above)*

Broad Street, Globe, Arizona, circa 1965 *(left)*

Horrell's Ranch
Ramboz Pk.
Sleeping Beauty Pk.
McLean's Ranch
Black Pk.
BIG JOHNNIE MINE
COPPER HILL MINE
GREY MINE
BUFFALO MINE
OLD DOMINION MINE
Black Warrior
MIAMI FLAT
Big Eds Well
GLOBE
BASE
LINE

sign remains pasted in its arched window. Along Broad and hidden down side streets are several excellent coffee cafés and home-style cooking restaurants attempting to recover a past when many visitors traveling along Route 60 stopped for a meal and a night's rest.

Although mining brought Superior, Miami, and Globe into existence, they are not company towns, but rather fully incorporated towns whose governance belongs to their citizens. All three towns have similar physical characteristics: a dense business district surrounded by gridded residential streets. Each town's commercial core rests along a wash or creek, reflecting their origins as outwash mining tent camps. As drift mines developed, they located on hillsides above the towns so ore could move downhill by gravity to railroads. Consequently, railroad tracks ran through each town's business center. Because of the remoteness of the three towns, their commercial centers had to supply most necessities for everyday living, resulting in diversities of businesses and services including hotels for out-of-town visitors. Early in their existence, communication between each town to the outside world was by train only. When the mines slowed or closed, inhabitants moved away, and the buildings remained as empty shells; today, they are mostly urban artifacts, only one-half of a town's composition: forms without content, buildings devoid of use, places of haunting beauty with no purpose.

A comparison of all three Sanborn maps of Superior, Miami, and Globe illustrates each town's dense clustering of well-constructed buildings. These were not temporary or flimsy structures, but rather substantial buildings of brick or stone meant to last. Some businesses such as banks and hotels were finely detailed of quality materials, and since these towns are remote, building materials had to be shipped great distances at considerable expense. When these towns were originally built, mine workers lived in them and walked to work. If the mines reopen, workers will drive from far distances for the few mining jobs left after extensive automation. These beautiful urban commercial cores will inevitably fall into neglect and disrepair. Eventually the elements of desert dusts, sand, wind, and moisture work their inescapable destruction, and buildings will collapse or be demolished. The idea of building entire towns and then discarding them is such a wasteful, unsustainable endeavor.

Towns are repositories of ourselves, our hopes, our aspirations, and our failures, places that encapsulate our lives together, yet we abandon them with such profligate ease. As we discard our towns, we also dispose of the places where we played as children, grew up, and became adults. With their disappearance, we can never return to our past or the spaces and rooms of our memories. We slowly relinquish all connections to where we came from.

Map of Globe, Arizona, 1902 ***(opposite)***

Former Valley National Bank,
Globe, Arizona

Other towns in this "copper triangle" are true mining or company towns. All land is owned by the mining company, including that beneath any commercial or civic structures. Homes may be owned by individuals, but the land under them belongs to the company. More often the company owns both land and buildings. "Out of a job, out of a home" is the rule if a worker gets laid off or fired. More importantly, as an open-pit mine expands to follow an ore vein, it swallows everything in its way, including towns. For some unknown reason a single sheet of a remarkable 1919 Sanborn map exists in the Library of Congress of just one section of Sonora, Arizona. This sheet shows a tight grid with residences very densely packed in short blocks, a large public school, and several commercial blocks. It seems to be one map in a series; all four sides appear to connect with other sheets that no longer exist. Sonora and nearby Ray, Arizona, are two towns that have been devoured by the open-pit copper mine near Kearney. Where these two towns once stood is now a big hole in the ground.

One should look carefully at this map of Sonora, for while it is only a partial sheet, it tells a sad tale that has no end and continues unrelentingly into the twenty-first century. Sonora was a Mexican town, while Ray was a "white" town. The texture of the residential streets on the map of Sonora gives a telling clue: small houses, close together, located on tiny blocks. Ray, by contrast, had larger homes on widely spaced lots. Segregation and prejudice plagued immigrants even though they were all skilled miners and a crucial labor force for the mining industry's success. The few available photographs of Sonora show a lively, vibrant town, despite its brief and fragile existence.

It is conceivable, perhaps, for a town to disappear, flooded behind a dam, buried by a mudslide or a volcanic eruption, but to be intentionally wiped from the earth by giant excavators and replaced by a hole is profoundly disturbing. All the exuberant density of human interactions implied by the Sanborn map is gone, suspended somewhere in the dust of an open pit: the buildings, homes, and streets have vanished, leaving behind no repository for collective memories, not even a place for phantoms to gather.

Two other remote copper-mining towns in the mountains of eastern Arizona illustrate another stark reality of mining, the continuous and debilitating friction between labor and management. Morenci and Clifton sit less than a mile apart below one of the largest open-pit copper mines in the world. Morenci is a company town with repetitive houses, schools, and stores owned and operated by the mining company. Below in a canyon carved by the San Francisco River sits the remains of Clifton, once a thriving incorporated town with buildings strung along the river's riparian shelves and clustered around copper smelters and concentrators. Clifton

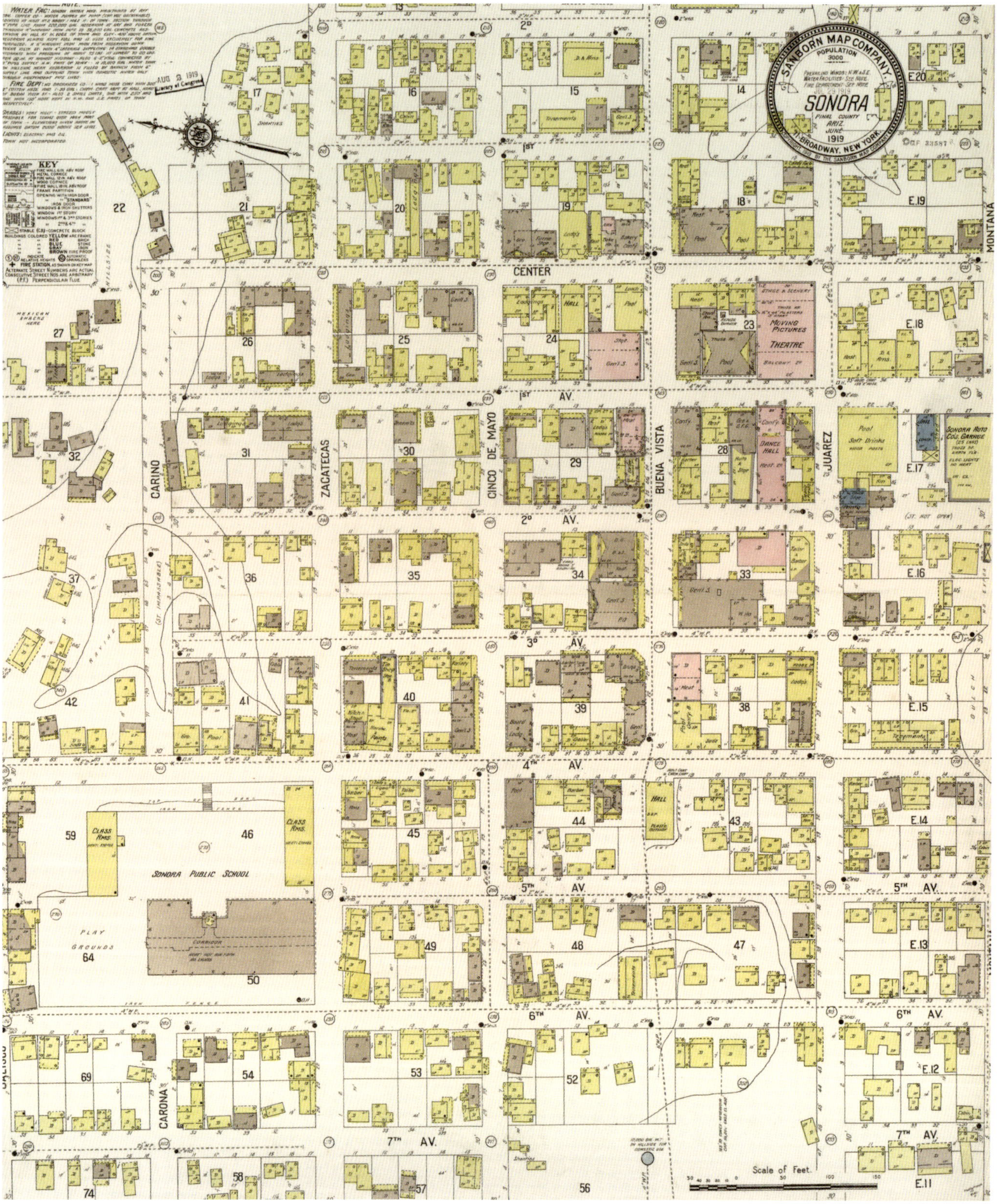
SANBORN MAP COMPANY
POPULATION 3000
SONORA
PINAL COUNTY
ARIZ.
JUNE
1919
11 BROADWAY, NEW YORK
KEY
CENTER
1ST AV.
2D AV.
3D AV.
4TH AV.
5TH AV.
6TH AV.
7TH AV.
CARINO
ZACATECAS
CINCO DE MAYO
BUENA VISTA
JUAREZ
MONTANA
CARONA
MOVING PICTURES THEATRE
DANCE HALL
SONORA AUTO COL. GARAGE
SONORA PUBLIC SCHOOL
CLASS RMS.
PLAY GROUNDS
HALL
Scale of Feet.

is the specter of many things: its perilously beautiful location, the tight symbiotic relationship between generations of workers and copper processing, and the futile struggle of America's labor to wrench decent wages and safety improvements from corporate control. All that remains of this struggle is Clifton's single street, enclosed by empty facades colored warm ochre by the desert sun.

According to local legend, in the mid-nineteenth century a Captain Chase pursued a band of Apache raiders through the canyons of the San Francisco River. Two of his troopers, soldier-prospectors, noticed evidence of copper deposits on the canyon's rock walls. Having failed to capture the Apaches, they instead staked claims and later returned to prospect and mine the high-grade ore. The San Francisco canyon must have originally been beautiful; enclosed by steep walls on all sides, the river was a wide meandering stream twisting through russet sandbars. Cottonwood trees would have provided welcome shade and grass fodder for tired horses. The river ran between high banks that edged narrow shelves the length of the canyon, except where tributary creeks, dry most of the year, joined with

Open-pit mine, Kearny, Arizona *(above)*

Sanborn map of a portion of Sonora, Arizona, 1919 *(opposite)*

runoff from the desert above. The first prospectors would have camped on these natural shelves, especially the broad flat land where Chase Creek, named for Captain Chase, joins the San Francisco River. Subsequent settlements expanded along these banks right up to and sometimes even tunneling into the canyon's rock walls. This idyllic yet precarious settlement pattern would ultimately seal the fate of Clifton.

A USGS map surveyed in 1900–1901 shows Clifton and its railroad, the Arizona and New Mexico, molded into the canyon floor along the San Francisco River and stretching up Chase Creek toward Morenci. The colors of this beautiful historic map's contour lines are rendered sepia against a warm tan background to evoke the desert landscape. The soft blue color of the San Francisco River seems peaceful and unthreatening. Today the entire mountaintop labeled Spring Copper Mountain is gone, removed and replaced instead by a gigantic open-pit mine. Nearby Morenci was a company town that existed for non-union mine workers; it has since been relocated several times as the great pit expands.

A composite Sanborn map of Clifton from 1914 shows the complex structures for crushing, smelting, and refining copper tightly grouped on the canyon floor. It is an amazingly dense cluster of utilitarian buildings perched between the cliffs and the river. The noise, smell, and dust must have been overwhelming in the close confines of the canyon. Although most of this complex has been erased by the improvement to Route 191, vestiges remain: ore bins and a 3,500-gallon water tank shown on the Sanborn map still exist. A photograph taken in 2011 shows this same concrete tank behind the stone ore bins.

More industrial buildings were across Chase Creek. Tracks came into the canyon from the main Union Pacific line to the south, and on a broadening of the shelf along the river, space was made for five tracks or sidings for storage of freight cars. These same tracks continued in the other direction up Chase Creek as the main mining activities followed the ore deposit along the stream to the mountain beyond.

Copper Avenue parallels Chase Creek on the other side, opposite the industrial buildings. Copper Avenue was the center of Clifton, a narrow street enclosed by beautiful brick and stone facades. Walking up Copper Avenue in 1914, one would have encountered first a barbershop, two cobbler shops, a moving-picture theater with a stage next door for traveling vaudeville, bowling alleys, and two saloons, with one noted as "female boarding." Across the street were several restaurants and yet another saloon. Continuing up the street with its high sidewalks were more pool halls, restaurants, and saloons. Clifton must have been an exciting bawdy place in 1914. Remarkably, there was a Chinese laundry on Cooper

Map of Clifton, Arizona, 1902 ***(opposite)***

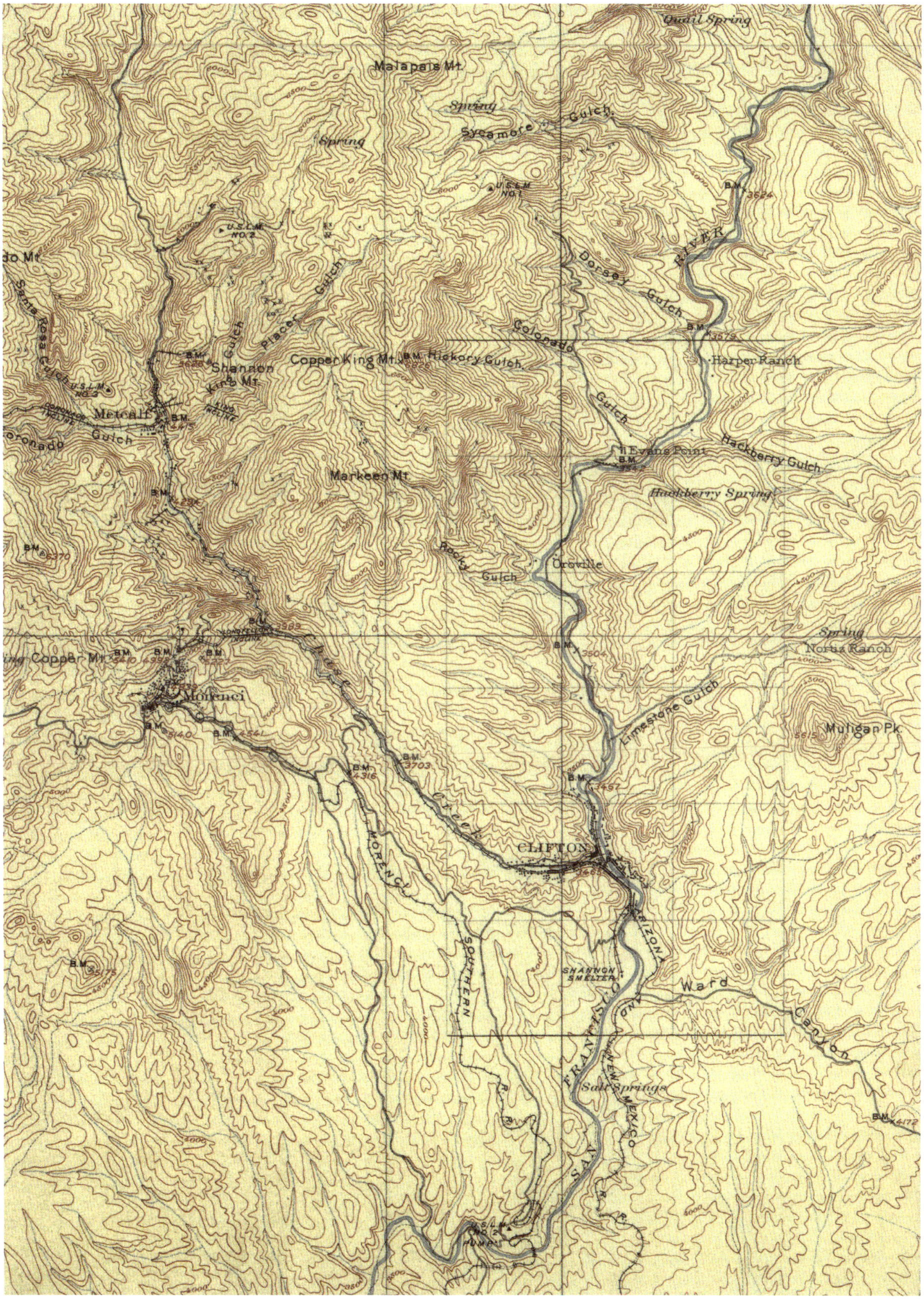
Quail Spring
Malapais Mt
Spring
Sycamore
Gulch
Spring
Dorsey
Gulch
Placer
Gulch
Coronado
Gulch
Harper Ranch
Shannon
King Mt
Copper King Mt
Hickory Gulch
Metcalf
Evans Point
Hackberry Gulch
Hackberry Spring
Markeen Mt
Rocky
Gulch
Oroville
Copper Mt
Morenci
Spring
Limestone Gulch
Mulligan Pk
Creek
CLIFTON
MORENCI
SOUTHERN
SHANNON SMELTER
Ward
Canyon
Salt Springs
SAN
FRANCISCO

Composite Sanborn map of Clifton, Arizona, 1914

Remains of ore bins on the hillside behind Clifton, Arizona

Avenue, indicating that Chinese immigrants had come to remotest Arizona. As we shall see in the next chapter, this was no small achievement in early-nineteenth-century xenophobic America. Meat markets, bakeries, furniture and crockery stores, another moving-picture theater, beer and grocery stores complete this small commercial center. At the end of the street, the Roman Catholic Church, clearly noted in parentheses as "Mexican," obviously served a congregation of Mexican miners who migrated north for work. In Clifton, as in all Arizona mining communities, churches, restaurants, pool halls, and even the miners' showers were segregated. Partway up Copper Avenue, between the Chinese laundry and the church, is a building marked "Lodge Hall 2," above a meat market and storage. Trade unions attempting to gain a foothold in the mining workforce would have met here.

Union-management battles waged throughout the twentieth century across America, in coal mines, in copper mines, and in steel and textile mills. During the staunch Republican years of Ronald Reagan's presidency from 1981 to 1989, political opinion turned against many unions in favor of large corporate owners. In 1981, the price of copper dropped sharply by over 50 percent, and the copper industry laid off thousands of workers

Copper Avenue, Clifton, Arizona, 2011

and closed mines. After two years of failed negotiations, at midnight on July 30, 1983, the union members walked off the job at the Morenci, Ajo, Clifton, and Douglas mines. On the morning of August 19, helped by hundreds of federal soldiers with tanks, the Morenci mine reopened with non-union replacement workers. The strike was effectively broken. Morenci Copper Mine became, and still is, an open shop, with housing and all other facilities owned and controlled by the company. The local unions were defeated by the strikebreakers and labor's failure to secure advantages for its members, coupled with the unnecessarily forceful response of the military.[2]

Because Clifton was not a company town, workers could retreat to the safety of their homes during the strike, relatively secure from the mining company's influence. While they may have been fired from their jobs, the miners at least had their homes, and the merchants had their businesses. Tragically, several months later on October 1, 1983, fate had one final blow for Clifton as an unusual storm dropped as much as ten inches of rain across southeast Arizona. With its residential and commercial buildings built precariously along the alluvial shelves of the San Francisco River,

2. Jonathon D. Rosenblum's accessible and compelling *Copper Crucible* fully explains the Arizona miners' strike of 1983. I am indebted to his clear portraits of the many people involved, from management to workers.

Clifton was literally washed away. Many families, without jobs or homes, left Clifton never to return.

By comparison with an off-ramp town like Holbrook, Arizona, single-resource towns like Superior, Miami, Globe, and Clifton emphasize the fragility of a dependency upon one extractive industry. Remote as these mining towns are, they are completely at the mercy of global forces far beyond their control. The price of copper is set in boardrooms in London with no regard for Clifton's workers or their families. Company towns like Morenci fare no better, for they exist only as long as the mine operates. At least Holbrook has a certain tenacious resilience, reinventing itself in response to shifting transportation changes. Even its new off-ramp town provides some employment opportunities, and its access to I-40 allows a modicum of mobility for its residents. We have seen this same cycle of boom then bust in other towns across America: the mill towns of New England tied to a single textile industry, coal towns in West Virginia and Pennsylvania, port cities, and steel and auto manufacturing cities. None can escape their tight symbiotic relationship with the success and failure of an industry, an extractive process, or transportation mode. The inhabitants have no alternative possibilities for prosperity. Without a diversity of jobs, towns lack resilience in the face of economic or environmental calamity.

Perhaps being tied to a transportation network such as the interstate is not so bad. As we etch our desires for movement more and more deeply into our culture, our routes and highways are more durable than most of the towns they connect. Ironically, the surveyed ways across the American West on Warren's map are more permanent than anything in between. Towns have come and gone, rail lines have been discontinued; only the geography remains.

7

RIVER SYSTEMS AND CHINESE SETTLEMENTS OF CALIFORNIA'S CENTRAL VALLEY

THE INTRACTABLE COMPLEXITIES of the river systems that drain California's Central Valley provide the background for discussions of Chinese immigrants in America. The confluence of the Sacramento and the San Joaquin Rivers forms the mysterious California Delta that teeters on the edge of ecological collapse. The future of one of the world's most productive agricultural regions and distinctive natural environments depends upon the state's ability to resolve this crisis. After completing the construction of the transcontinental railroads, many Chinese laborers moved to the Delta and were instrumental in draining and converting the tule marshes into fertile farmland. Through the exploration of old maps and photographs, four unique Chinese settlements provide detailed examples of places built by tireless workers searching for a better life far from their native shores. The lives of these workers were inextricably bound together with the success of the Delta's development, and yet the remnants of their towns cannot compete with the heavy traffic and off-ramp towns along the great north–south commercial corridor of I-5 that runs the length of California. One of the towns, beautiful tiny Locke, remains as a monument to the persistence of immigrants in the United States and as an unmatched model of modest yet thoughtful urban design.

No Outlet

At first a few light snowflakes drift in the dry wind. As moist air rises, the scattered few become many, a dense, heavy snow that tightly wraps trees and rocks in its brittle silence. For hours, then days, the snow accumulates, forming deep drifts of frozen water that would be released only by the sunlight of a spring day. When the snow melts, each water drop begins its long journey of hundreds of miles. Cascading down granite cliffs into boulder-filled streams that then feed the recursive twists of shallow, slow rivers. Weeks, months later, the creaky twist of a faucet in a Los Angeles kitchen sink releases clear water drops whose origins began as snows in the high Sierras.

The distance water must travel from the deep snows of the high Sierras to the dripping faucet in Los Angeles is the length of California's great Central Valley. Tributaries of the two rivers that flow through the Central Valley, the Sacramento and the San Joaquin, gather snowmelt from the five-hundred-mile-long Sierra Cordillera to the east; they join together in a maze-like delta before squeezing their combined discharge through the Carquinez Strait into San Francisco Bay and the Pacific Ocean. More than 50 percent of all stream flow in California moves through these two rivers and into their delta. Only half of that flow reaches the Pacific. The rest is channeled or pumped southward to irrigate thousands of acres of cropland or to provide water for twenty million people. What makes the flow of water possible naturally to San Francisco Bay and by manipulation to Los Angeles is the table-like flatness of the Central Valley. Flatter than almost any place on earth, topography across the Central Valley is measured in inches; it is so flat that water drains equally in all directions. The five-hundred-foot contour that inscribes the entire valley means that the elevation change north to south is less than a foot over one hundred miles. Both the Sacramento River, which carries most of the runoff from the Sierras, and the San Joaquin River meander in great recursive loops and oxbows that are indicative of rivers sheeting across a flat surface. Where these two rivers unite in a delta, their flow becomes a labyrinth of waterways, sloughs, and hidden back channels. Because of the flatness of the Central Valley, water taken from either river can easily be engineered into furrow irrigation or gentle gradient channels between rows of crops. Water can also be channeled great distances over hundreds of miles.

California's Central Valley is immense: four hundred miles long and a consistent fifty miles wide. To put it into perspective, the Central Valley contains twenty thousand square miles, an area larger than Vermont and New Hampshire combined. A dramatic black-and-white digital relief map of the entire state of California shows the Central Valley surrounded by the Sierras to the east, the Cascades to the north, and the Coast Ranges to the west. The Central Valley is like a giant footprint pressed into the earth's hard granite mantle, its sole flat, its heel in the northern Cascades, its extended toes pushed up against the Tehachapi Mountains north of Los Angeles. Locked into California's interior by mountains, the rivers and their tributaries in the Central Valley have a single restricted outlet to the Pacific located in the center of the state. The Central Valley is isolated from the rest of the United States, cut off by mountains and five hundred miles of desert. This valley is a remarkable piece of the earth's geography that results in the most agriculturally productive portion of California being a virtual island isolated by mountains, clinging to the continent's edge.

California's land mass and the formation of its Central Valley resulted from the inexorable movement of tectonic plates over incomprehensibly vast spans of geological time. Millions of years ago, a piece of the earth's crust, the Farallon Plate, slid beneath the North American Plate, forming a deep trench along the collision zone. This trench corresponds to the northwest-tilting axis of the Central Valley. The Farallon Plate has disappeared into the earth's mantel, to be followed by other plates moving northwestward into North America, the most recent being the Pacific and Gorda Plates. As these plates, and perhaps others, turned downward, they left behind great slivers of land that were peeled off the plates' surfaces much like wood shavings in a pencil sharpener. Over time, these remnant arcs of land formed the Coast Ranges and enclosed valleys that confine the Central Valley and separate it from the Pacific Ocean. Some of these valleys have become lexicons of American culture: Silicon Valley, Napa Valley, Sonoma Valley, and, of course, the Salinas Valley made so famous by John Steinbeck. Ruler-straight fault lines are visible in these mountains and valleys; several disappear beneath San Francisco Bay to reappear to the northwest, including the well-known San Andreas Fault. Viewed from such an altitude, this map of California is a remarkable and clear record of the constant movement of the earth's surface.

Over the eons of geological time, the Central Valley trench was sometimes the edge of the North American continent, sometimes an extensive estuary, and several times an inland sea, all the while accumulating marine and terrestrial sediments. Glacial deposits from the Sierras, volcanic eruptions and lava flows, and more recent alluvial outwash plains have filled the original trench to a depth of over twelve miles. As these layers flowed and settled, their surface became the smooth billiard tabletop valley floor that today supports the richest agricultural land and the most extensive hydrological infrastructure in the history of the world.

I-5 runs the full distance of 1,381 miles up the West Coast from the Mexican border through California, Oregon, and Washington to Vancouver, Canada. It is one of two interstate routes that connect Mexico with Canada across the United States. Within California, I-5 travels the entire

Experimental digital shaded-relief map of California, 1990 ***(opposite)***

DIGITAL SHADED RELIEF
EXPERIMENTAL DIGITAL SHADED-RELIEF MAPS OF CALIFORNIA
By
Kathleen Edwards and R.M. Batson
1990
MEXICO

length of the Central Valley, hugging the slopes of the Coast Ranges before shifting eastward around the intersection of the Sacramento and San Joaquin Rivers. A network of circumferential highways connects I-5 to the two inland ports of Sacramento and Stockton. I-5 continues north, bisecting the Central Valley before climbing through the Cascade Range into Oregon. For much of its length in California, I-5 parallels the older Route 99, once known as California's "main street"; at points, I-5 even assumes some of Route 99's former right-of-way. The decision was made to construct I-5 west of Route 99 to avoid dense urban areas of the Central Valley such as Fresno and Modesto. I-5 was to be a high-speed connection between Los Angeles and the state capital at Sacramento. Through the sparsely settled but intensively cultivated Central Valley south of Stockton, I-5 has few intersections or even exits. West of the state capital of Sacramento, I-5 connects to the Bay Area by a network of other interstates including I-80 discussed earlier in the first section of chapter 5. Heading east onto I-80 would lead across Nevada, through the Rockies, and, two days later, into Nebraska on the way to New York City. Through the Central Valley, I-5 travels above the deepest part of the tectonic plate subduction trench, a thin black double line marking a past tear in the earth's surface. As I-5 shifts eastward at Stockton to avoid the confluence of the Sacramento and San Joaquin Rivers, it intersects at Exit 485 one of the few roads, Route 12, that crosses this great watery labyrinth. To the east, Route 12 heads across the Central Valley's wine-producing region around Lodi and eventually ends in the Sierra foothills. To the west, it runs straight to the town of Terminous, then across several bridges to Rio Vista, continuing around San Francisco Bay, up the Sonoma Valley and the Valley of the Moon to the Pacific Coast.

Terminous is a gated community oriented around a former packing shed converted into a marina, with stores, a restaurant, gas for boats, and boat sales. Quiet tree-lined streets of modular double-wide homes and a trailer RV park complete this small town serving the thriving boating and fishing recreational industry of the Delta. Once Terminous was the end of a track spur of the Western Pacific Railroad's main line from Stockton to Sacramento that ended at Potato Slough and the South Branch of the Mokelumne River. At the beginning of the twentieth century, the Western Pacific advertised a warehouse facility over seven hundred feet long for off-loading agricultural produce from shallow draft barges onto freight cars. Before trucks, almost all produce from the islands of the Delta moved by barge along the maze of waterways to railroad terminals. A 1920 photograph of the interior of a waterside shipping shed shows boxes of celery ready to be loaded into railroad cars. These sheds were long, open structures with loading docks

Map of I-5 and the location of Exit 485 in California's Central Valley *(left)*

Map of Exit 485. The red is the off-ramp town known as Flag City. *(below)*

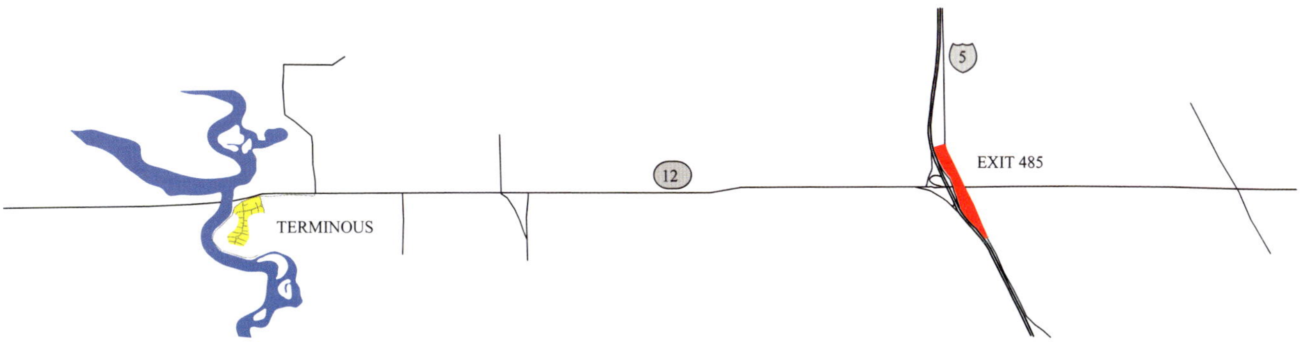

that floated up or down with the water level. The Western Pacific Railroad track spur to Terminous is now gone, and the railroad itself has been absorbed by the giant conglomerate of the Union Pacific.

Canning factories were constructed throughout the Delta alongside warehouses. Before widespread refrigeration, both vegetables and fruit were harvested and canned immediately for shipment east. Boats brought fresh fruit right to the factory, and railroads took the canned produce away. The Delta was best known for asparagus and pears, and several large companies located their canning factories in the towns studied in the next section of this chapter. As we shall see, the canning industry provided many job opportunities for newly arrived immigrants.

Trucks now transport agricultural produce from the Delta and the Central Valley, bringing fruit and vegetables directly to urban areas in California or across the United States on the interstates. Bulk grains such as wheat or rice travel by rail to ships in the inland deepwater ports of

The Western Pacific Railroad Company, Terminous, California. Interior of the dock warehouse with crates filled with celery.

Stockton and Sacramento. At Exit 485, off I-5, the straight line of Route 12 connects forgotten Terminous with the off-ramp town of Flag City; the towns are like two trays at opposite extensions of an unequal balance. One end drops into the past, the other vibrates with the noise of idling trucks.

Flag City sits surrounded by several wide off-ramp access roads that allow easy off and easy on for the enormous rigs that pull into the service area for food, accommodations, and fuel. Strategically located in the center of the long north–south corridor of I-5, Flag City also is a terminus for east to west travel. Trucks from the East Coast park here waiting for an advantageous time to enter the congested traffic of the metropolitan centers of San Francisco, Oakland, or San Jose. Besides the normal services, Flag Plaza has extensive heavy truck maintenance facilities. Heading east or south from the Central Valley into America's vast deserts, truckers have every reason to check the reliability of their equipment.

Long-distance trucking is often a family business, so Flag City has Rocky's Café Family Dining for the husband-wife couples who share driving responsibilities. Most truckers sleep in the airstream-like aerodynamic compartments attached to the truck cabs. These compartments must be constantly air-conditioned in the one-hundred-degree heat of the Central Valley, so the seventy or eighty trucks in Flag City's parking areas keep their diesel motors running constantly.

Motorists traveling I-5 also have many reasons for stopping at Flag City: Taco Bell, McDonald's, Burger King, and Carl's Jr. "Charbroiled" Burgers all offer fast food. For the tired driver, Best Western and Microtel offer

Figure-ground study of the off-ramp town, Flag City, at Exit 485

rest, and Shell and Chevron provide gas and all-night food marts. If one is bold enough to enter the truckers' realm of big rigs and colorful cabs, Flying J offers complete lubrication and maintenance services.

Flag City sits isolated in flat farmland that extends in all directions to the hazy horizons. From the air, its curved appendix shape blends imperceptibly with the sweep of the interstate; its buildings and roads exist in a different time and place from the surrounding fields of crops, but then Flag City's context is the highway and the far web of interstates that stretch across the United States. There are no connections to anything local, for no one dwells in Flag City. No one stays here more than momentarily, a brief rest on the way to somewhere else.

From the individual cabins of the 1930s to the anonymous motels of the 1950s to today's RVs, the lure of the open road defines us. Nomadic Americans carry their homes with them. The new Flag City RV park fills a large rectangular plot just east of the service area. Pull-ins and hookups for cable TV and Internet wrap around a bare central lawn. The site is exposed to both the baking sun of a semi-arid climate and the constant noise of I-5. Flag City encroaches into valuable farmland as it spreads eastward along Route 12 toward Lodi. As with all off-ramp towns, Flag City will eventually expand into a linear strip mall capturing the peripheral expansion of Lodi. Several hundred yards west of I-5 from Flag City across well-cultivated fields is a peculiar rectangular body of water with squared corners. From the air, four more similar excavations can be seen stretching parallel to the interstate. About 250 feet across and 1,000 feet long, they are segments of a forgotten artificial channel, like a large dotted line representing the sweep of the proposed Peripheral Canal. This canal was to carry water directly upstream from the Sacramento River, around the Delta, and into the California Aqueduct and other channels of California's water system to be redistributed to central and southern cities. Due to costs and environmental concerns, construction of the Peripheral Canal remains stalled, at least for the present. The fill dug from these five canal segments was used to elevate the roadbed of I-5 above potential flooding. The Peripheral Canal, I-5, the Western Pacific Railroad, and the California Aqueduct are four parallel pieces of extensive infrastructure designed to route traffic and water north to south along the length of the Central Valley. All four are in this location because it is out of the deep muck of the Delta waterways and on the more stable alluvial soil of the valley floor.

A beautiful soil map illustrates the twisting waterways of the Delta reaching out into the Central Valley. The material represented by a green dashed graphic is peat. The thick red line of I-5 and the railroad tracks swing onto a brighter splash of color representing alluvial clay. Lodi too is situated on the same higher, more stable clay soils. Route 12 runs across this same alluvial clay material before crossing the Delta on a series of bridges. If one looks very closely, one can see that the railroad once came down from the north to connect with several small towns in the Delta before ending at Isleton. There must of have been substantial revenue-generating cargo in these towns to justify the expense of laying track through the peaty soils. The Peripheral Canal was to swing along the edge of the Delta parallel to I-5. Water was to enter the canal just south of the city of Sacramento from the pronounced *D*-shaped westward curve of the Sacramento River, bypassing the Delta completely to be pumped directly into the California and Mendota Aqueducts.

Turning west on Route 12 from Flag City, crossing under I-5, taking the bridges over the South Mokelumne and North Mokelumne Rivers, and turning right onto Jackson Slough Road, one enters into a different place with histories far removed from the fast foods and gas stations of Flag City Plaza. It is a landscape of levees and dikes, of deeply depressed bottom lands and long vistas looking down onto fruit tree canopies. Many roads in the Delta have the descriptive word "slough" attached, meaning a place full of deep mud. Water channels are everywhere, and, in fact, one is almost always on an island. Jackson Slough Road crosses Brennan Island and arrives at the small town of Isleton, which is nestled behind the great levee holding back the Sacramento River. Isleton, like the road across the interior of Brennan Island, rests twenty feet below the top of the levee. As the Sacramento River is constrained on the other side by a similar levee, the town is about fifteen feet below the normal height of the river's water level. Climbing steeply onto the levee road that twists north, one passes in succession the towns of Walnut Grove, Locke, and Courtland, all of which figure prominently in the narrative of the next section. Embedded in the streets and storefronts of these four quiet, beautiful little towns are subtle clues to the layers of history contained in the remarkable landscape of the Delta.

Driving the Delta today on narrow elevated roads along the tops of the continuous levees is to experience a landscape engineered and manipulated to the edge of cataclysmic disaster. The levees twist and turn as they hold back almost every slough and river across the entire Delta. The Delta is composed almost entirely of islands, each completely ringed by dikes. Because of soil subsidence in their interiors, the islands are depressed basins, often twenty to thirty feet below the roads; thus they are islands in name only. Driving on the levee puts one above the tops of the fruit trees growing below on one side and at the level of the water on the other side. Everywhere pumps pull water up from the sunken farmland and dump it back into the waterways. Levees around several large islands failed during

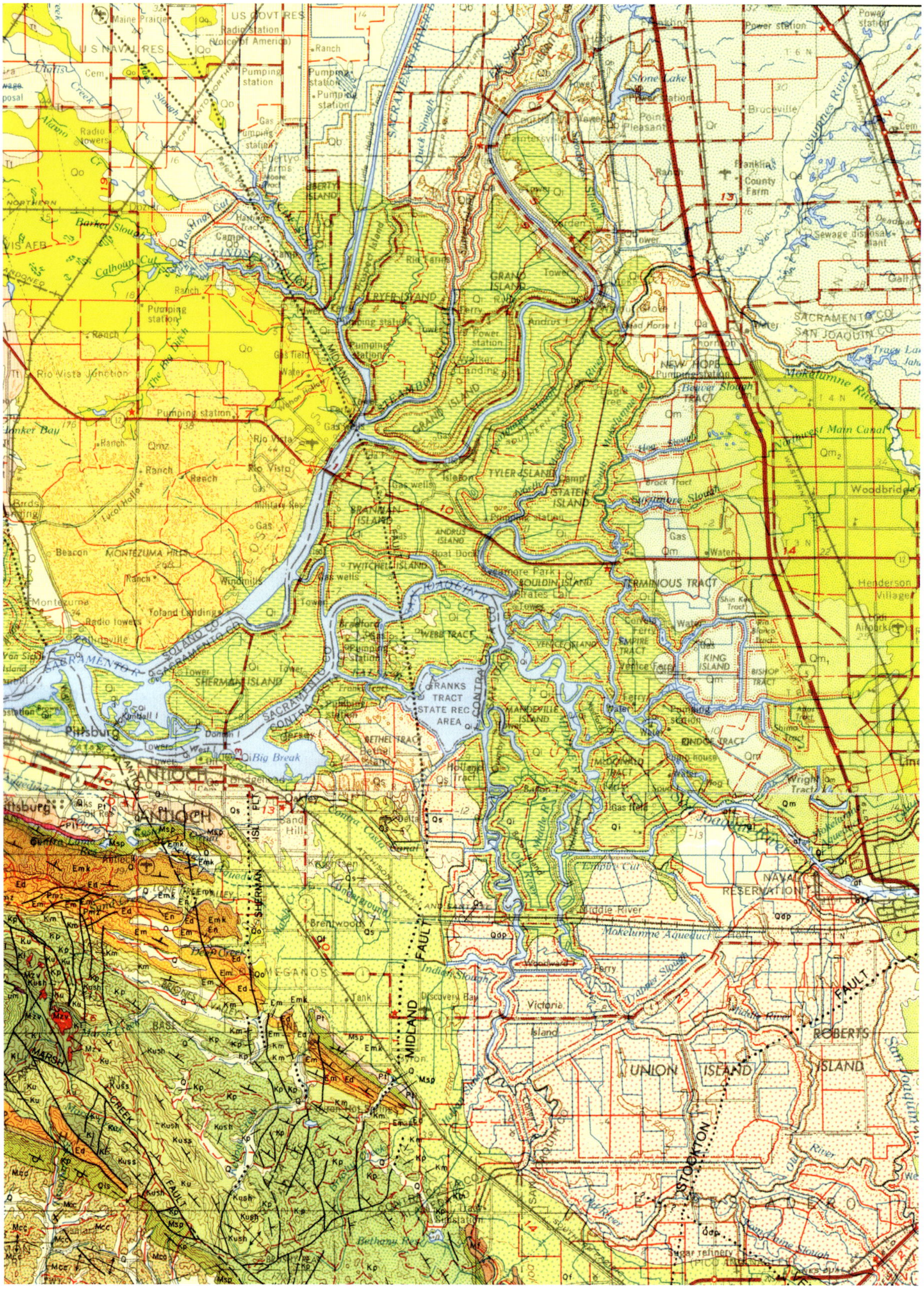
US GOVT RES
Radio station
(Voice of America)
U S NAVAL RES
Pumping station
Bruceville
Franklin
County Farm
Power station
Point Pleasant
Sewage disposal plant
Hastings Cut
Barker Slough
Calhoun Cut
Rio Vista Junction
Pumping station
Rio Vista
MONTEZUMA HILLS
Beacon
Montezuma
Toland Landing
Radio towers
GRAND ISLAND
TYLER ISLAND
BRANNAN ISLAND
ANDRUS ISLAND
STATEN ISLAND
TERMINOUS TRACT
KING ISLAND
BISHOP TRACT
WEBB TRACT
SHERMAN ISLAND
FRANKS TRACT STATE REC AREA
MANDEVILLE ISLAND
BETHEL TRACT
RINDGE TRACT
EMPIRE TRACT
SACRAMENTO CO
SAN JOAQUIN CO
SOLANO CO
SACRAMENTO CO
SACRAMENTO R
SAN JOAQUIN R
Mokelumne River
Woodbridge
Henderson Village
NEW HOPE
Northwest Main Canal
Pittsburg
Big Break
ANTIOCH
Oakley
Brentwood
MIDLAND FAULT
MEGANOS
Middle River
Mokelumne Aqueduct
NAVAL RESERVATION
Victoria Island
UNION ISLAND
ROBERTS ISLAND
STOCKTON FAULT
FAULT
San Joaquin R
Sugar refinery
Bethany Res
MARSH CREEK
Indian Slough
Discovery Bay

past floods, and the interior of the islands have never been pumped dry, so they remain shallow lakes used by the increasingly popular recreational boating and fishing industry of the Delta. Frank's Tract is one such submerged island, now a lake large enough for sailboats. Because the roads follow the dikes, routes are circuitous and indirect. Ferries are the only access to several islands, run by the California Department of Transportation back and forth carrying cars and trucks. Taking a ferry interrupts travel and time, as one steps out of the car to wait before slowly being winched across a slough. To stop and get out of one's vehicle, to stand waiting in the hot hazy sun among flocks of feeding birds and fields of crops, seems a delightful luxury when compared to the bland parking lots and drive-through windows of highway rest stops. It is a verdant agricultural landscape visible from above with vistas stretching over fields of vegetables or converging rows of fruit trees. Waterways always line the sides of the road, either as rivers, sloughs, or irrigation channels.

One edge of the Delta lies against the Sacramento River Deep Water Ship Channel, an artificially dredged waterway that runs straight across the flat landscape to allow large oceangoing ships to dock right in the city of Sacramento. A similar shipping channel brings ships into Stockton. It is a surreal sight to be driving across this region and see, off in the distance, an enormous, stately ship appear to be plowing through fields. Both deepwater channels are enclosed on both sides by high spreading levees. Ships are loaded at both ports with grain for export back out through San Francisco Bay and into the Pacific.

The wonderfully intricate drainage system of the entire state holds the key in explaining this topographical manipulation and the importance of the Delta's water to California. A red diagram of the Central Valley drainage system shows how its many tiny tributaries and rivulets act like some giant circulatory organ for the exchange of fluids. The organic imagery is intentional as the Delta is an ecology of fluid exchanges: of salt and fresh water, of the pulsing of the tides and mountain floods. The Delta's extensive wetlands and marshes distribute and filter the nutrients and sediments from mountain runoff into the once extensive estuary of San Francisco Bay. As the spring meltwater gradually dissipates through the Carquinez Strait into the Bay, the Delta returns to a more normal water level and the Central Valley to its usual hot arid expanse baking under the brilliant California summer sun.

A unique ecosystem of plants and alluvial topography evolved in the Delta to accommodate this seasonal pulsing of water. The principle plant was the tall, dense, rush-like tule (*Scripus acutus*). Over time, these plants died and decayed into thick beds of organic peat-like soil. This soil is incredi-

Soil map of the Sacramento and San Joaquin River Delta, Central Valley, California *(opposite)*

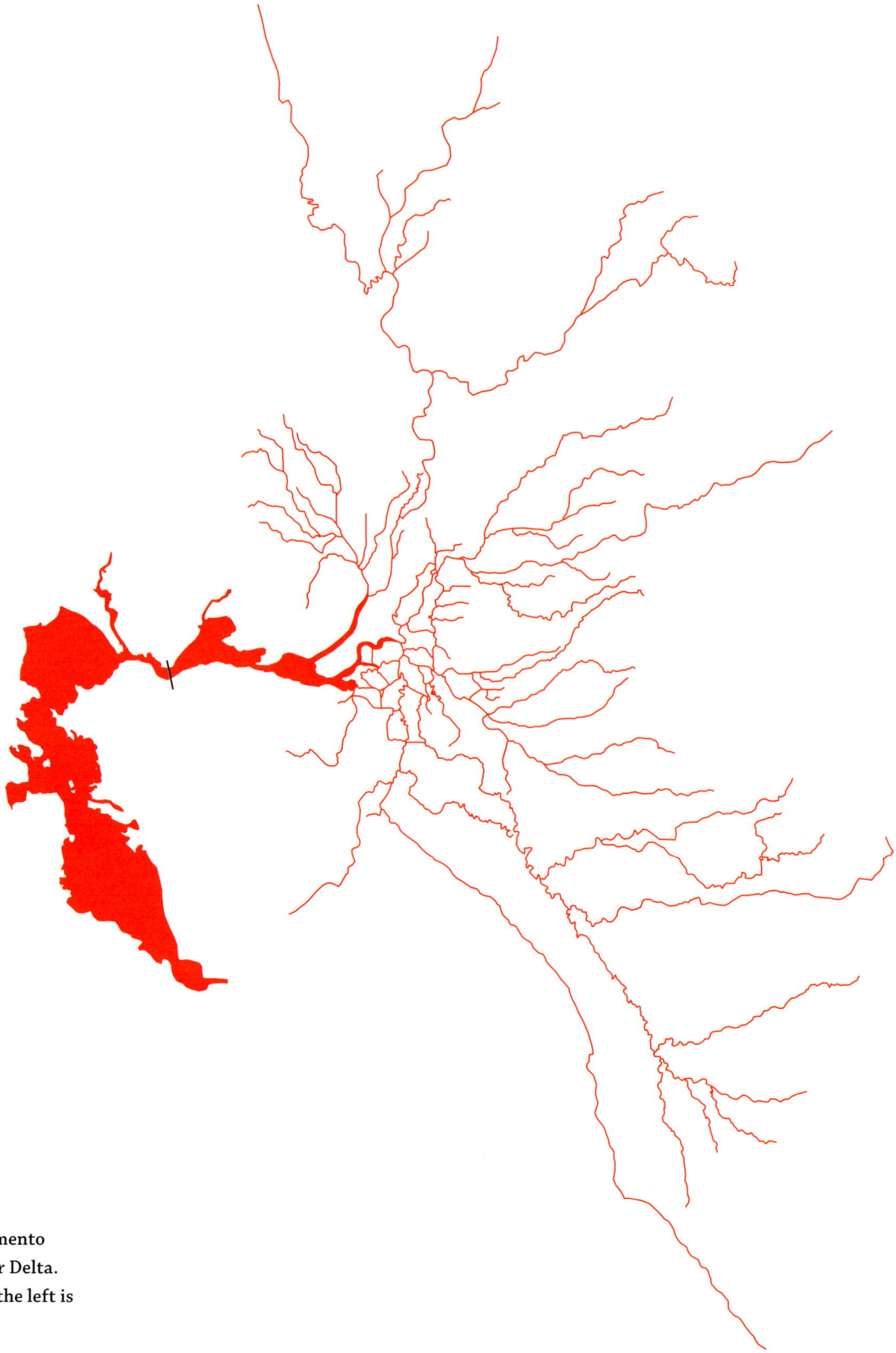

Drawing of the Sacramento and San Joaquin River Delta. The large red area on the left is San Francisco Bay.

bly fertile and potentially productive agricultural land. Sustained farming, however, cannot tolerate seasonal flooding that could carry away entire crops. In the late nineteenth century, the federal and state governments began a subsidized process of drainage and reclamation. The islands of the Delta were surrounded with levees and the protected interiors drained. Unfortunately, the rich peat-like organic soil dries into an extremely friable layer that blows away in the wind and compresses greatly under the weight of cultivating equipment. When extensively drained, these formerly submerged peat soils are exposed to air. Oxygen accelerates decay, and as the tules and peat decompose, the land literally vaporizes and sinks. When wet, peat becomes a sticky unworkable mud that teams of horses cannot plow because they will sink up to their bellies. The familiar Caterpillar, or continuous-tread tractor, was invented in the Delta expressly for these soils. Rusting tractors lie abandoned in fallow fields as reminders of the struggle to till these marshes. Over time, the Delta islands continued to retreat, forming a sunken leveed landscape of raised roads and waterways and depressed bowls of crop fields. As the interiors of the islands sink, their protecting levees become higher and more unstable, increasing the likelihood of rupture. It is an incessant battle between subsidence and levee repair. The productivity of Delta farms makes the continuous effort of dikes and pumping worthwhile. An acre of Delta land produces two to three times the yield of the relatively rich typical Central Valley farmland, and the Delta soil supports two crop rotations a year.

The red drainage drawing of the Central Valley shows the flow from the Sierra Mountains as a converging fan-like pattern of tributaries that flow westward into the organic form of a braided and twisted delta before squeezing through the narrow Carquinez Straits into San Francisco Bay. The drawing clearly implies the sources of most streams flowing into the Delta: the Sierras. The Sierras are a great granite block lifted up with a steeper profile on the eastern face than the west. The western slope declines gradually along its entire five-hundred-mile length into the Central Valley. Streams channel the tremendous water flow from winter rains and spring snowmelts down the western slopes into two rivers: the south-flowing Sacramento and the north-flowing San Joaquin, which together converge at the Delta. Little precipitation falls in the Central Valley, yet these rivers swell dramatically from the very significant snowfall of the high mountains. Spring's warm temperatures bring torrents off the granite domes of the Sierras that inundate the flat Delta and much of the surrounding Central Valley with expansive sheets of water. Constricted by the Carquinez Strait, this water backs up into the sloughs and creeks of the Delta, held back by sinuous levees that act like huge holding reservoirs.

Abandoned International Harvester tractor, Central Valley

Even with the levees, however, numerous disastrous floods destroyed crops and submerged towns, so control dams and reservoirs were continuously constructed during the entire twentieth century on the tributary streams in the Sierras to hold back the spring floods and release measured amounts of water during the long growing seasons. These dams along the Sierras' western flank effectively severed the entire hydrological system of California, cutting in half an ecosystem five hundred miles long. Today, over 1,600 dams control and distribute water into the most extensive and convoluted allocations across the state; some for agricultural irrigation in the Central Valley, some for the growing metropolitan areas along the coast, some south to Los Angeles and San Diego, and some for recreational use and to prevent the incursion of salt water into the productive farmlands of the Delta. A central control facility in Sacramento monitors and releases water from the dams to flow down into the Delta before being pumped into more reservoirs. Some water flows down the Delta Mendota Canal into the Central Valley, the rest goes south in the California Aqueduct. Giant pumps lift the water 1,600 feet over the Tehachapi Mountains into Los Angeles. The Delta still functions as a great holding reservoir, yet its water capacity is artificially held constant to satisfy the year-round demands of urban populations and crop rotations.

The northern Central Valley is semi-arid and its southern reaches arid. From May to October little or no rain falls, and annual precipitation is too little to support most crops. In spite of this, the Central Valley has become one of the world's most productive agricultural regions. Artificial irrigation makes this possible by drawing water from the Delta and distributing it hundred of miles southward. None of California's metropolitan centers have enough water to satisfy or sustain their thirsty populations and continuous development. Water from the Delta four hundred miles north has allowed Los Angeles to grow into a great sprawling metropolis. The two aqueducts flowing from the Delta are only two of California's redistribution systems. Los Angeles also drinks from the distant Colorado River, emptying that river completely. San Francisco and San Jose have their own water systems originating in the Sierras, and the northern Central Valley's extensive rice agriculture uses the Tehama-Colusa Canal. The complexity and extent of these statewide water systems is mind-boggling. Even more convoluted are the legal ramifications of water rights, riparian ownership, and environmental complications. If one of the effects of global warming is the gradual reduction of snow cover on the earth's high mountains, then California's entire premise of using meltwater from the north to supply an arid south will collapse.

Aerial photograph of the canal and levee system in California's Delta

The Delta is a highly exploited landscape at great risk from either too much water from floods or from too little water because of salinity incursions. Either disaster would affect much of the state's agriculture and millions of people. To the detriment of all its natural ecological systems, the main function of the Delta today is as a source for fresh water for much of California, yet the biggest threat to the Delta is saltwater incursion. Fresh water keeps the salt water of the Pacific Ocean from coming through San Francisco Bay into the marshes and channels of the Delta. If too much fresh water is pumped out of the Delta to satisfy the competing demands of agriculture and domestic water use, then the line of salinity moves inland or upstream. If the salt water flows into the water-export facilities, then the agriculture of the southern Central Valley will be affected. Such an unfavorable freshwater gradient would also pollute the drinking water destined for Los Angeles. The tracts and islands of the Delta provide a barrier to saltwater incursion as well as protection from catastrophic flooding.

The manipulation of the natural cycles of flooding of the Delta began in the late nineteenth century as a result of three concurrent and particular circumstances. As the sources of gold in the lower foothills of the Sierras played out, prospectors moved into the higher terrain. To clear earth quickly, miners developed a system of high-pressure hoses to wash away overburden. A creek was dammed at a higher elevation, and impounded water was forced through an enormous hose to a water cannon directed at a hillside. Entire landscapes were pressure-washed downstream into the Sacramento River and the Delta. The resulting silt raised the Delta's water level and exacerbated the seasonal flooding. The massive and destructive flood of 1878 finally led to demands that hydraulic mining practices be stopped to keep the Delta safe. The dams built by mining companies on the creeks and streams, however, often remained in place for flood control and as reservoirs for drinking and irrigation water. Thus began a long torturous process of dam construction. The flooding still continued, so the levees were built higher around the Delta's misnamed islands, as the land sunk into deeper and deeper basins. As the levees grew higher, they became more precarious and failed more often, requiring almost continuous repair. Until the development of the clamshell dredge in the early twentieth century, all earthwork on the levees was done by hand and horses.

Chinese immigrants provided the labor for the drainage of the Delta and construction of the extensive levee system. Over ten thousand Chinese immigrant workers built the Central Pacific through the Sierras and out into Nevada; once the transcontinental railroad was completed in 1867, they were a ready supply of available workers willing to toil for low wages and in the deplorable conditions of levee construction. Quickly railroads extended tracks into the agricultural areas of the Central Valley and some, like the Western Pacific, into the Delta at Terminous. With adequate bulk transportation available, the demand for canned and dried fruit and vegetables grew immediately. More land in the Delta was drained and converted to farms, which required higher and more reliable levees. The Chinese workers who migrated to California in the nineteenth century came from the Pearl River Region of Southern China, a region made famous by author Pearl Buck in her prize-winning novel *The Good Earth*. The Pearl River too has a delta of multiple channels and islands. Over the millennia of China's history, this delta has been drained, diked, and farmed. The Pearl River ecosystem collapsed in the nineteenth century causing untold misery, but also providing impetus for Chinese migration to other parts of the world, including the United States. Thus many Chinese, ironically, who came to the California Delta found its ecology familiar even though they were in a strange and savagely hostile land whose European inhabitants were all too willing to exploit both human and natural resources.

We have seen in earlier chapters American culture's shameless ability to self-promote. The bird's-eye-view maps of New England mill towns extolled the benefits of manufacturing jobs; the early-twentieth-century road map covers promoted the expansion of automobile travel. The bold graphics of California fruit labels on produce crates effervesce with hyperbole: "On the Square Bartlett Pears" or "Oh Yes, We Grow the Best." Like all states along the way of our westward expansion, California advertised its amazing positive attributes. Unlike others, however, California was the furthest extension of our dreams. And it was the repository of the dreams of others from across the Pacific, from China, Japan, and the Philippines. Sparsely settled and little regarded before the discovery of gold, California burst instantly into America's and the world's consciousness in 1849. While the stories of Americans' travels across the continent, around Cape Horn, or through the Isthmus of Panama have been well documented, others came to America from far across the Pacific and Atlantic seeking fortunes. People traveled from Australia, from Asia, and from Europe hoping to find wealth in the foothills of the Sierras. The Chinese description of California as the "Golden Mountain" expressed their longing for riches and opportunities beyond the poverty and restrictions of their native country. What the Chinese actually found in California was far different from their dreams and more sinister than they could imagine. That Chinese immigrants continued to refer to California as the Golden Mountain after several generations attests to their determination and resilience.

As the gold ran out after the Civil War, settlers in California quickly realized that there were other sources of wealth to be mined, principally the golden sun. Crops could be grown year-round in the warm sunshine and fertile soils. If enough irrigation was provided, extensive areas could be farmed. California began to sell sunshine and easy abundance. In the particularly American way of grandiose promotion, the idea of California sprang from its self-conception as America's cornucopia. As California's agriculture grew, so did its myth of copious and inexhaustible bounty. Even the fruit labels advertised this bounty with images of yellow ripe pears or thick green bundles of asparagus. Like so much of California's history, however, these delicious images belie another, more poisonous reality hidden beneath the flagrant embellishment of ripe fruit. In an endeavor as hand-labor intensive as fruit or vegetable production, someone had to plant and then pick and pack the produce. Others had to scrape and shovel the landscape into shapes and surfaces receptive to crops. Someone had to dig the irrigation ditches and form the protective levees that give the Delta region its particular landscape today.

By promising unlimited movement to anyone who can purchase an automobile and by offering equal access to all, highways such as I-5 allow us to bypass our histories. Interstate highway travel erases forgotten fragments of the regions through which they pass and renders our different narratives invisible. We turn now to the experience of those who made the Delta landscape and acquired ownership, not in fee simple, but through their backbreaking and bitter labor.

Bitter Melon

Popular histories of the United States conceal many bitter narratives of immigrant struggles as people journeyed from all parts of the globe seeking opportunities in this richly endowed young nation. Few ethnic groups, however, encountered such hostility and savagery in their adopted land as did the Chinese in California in the late nineteenth and early twentieth centuries. Disenfranchisement of the Chinese was so complete and pervasive in California that outside of large cities like San Francisco, records of their attempts at assimilation lie scattered, hidden in tiny towns to be discovered only through old maps. Living and working in forgotten places beyond West Coast cities, Chinese immigrants once had an important presence in California. They furnished the labor that built the transcontinental railroads and helped propel California's Central Valley into the agricultural cornucopia it is today. Ironically, the largest center of nineteenth- and early-twentieth-century Chinese settlement in America that remains, San Francisco's Chinatown, today exists as an important tourist attraction, an exotic pastiche of markets, stores, and restaurants that totally camouflage a wretched past.

Americans tend to discard unwanted histories and, instead, carry forward into the present only those stories that reinforce the myth of the United States as a place of opportunity. California is the apotheosis of this recurrent myth, a supposedly golden state formed by rugged forty-niners and sturdy European emigrants whose strength and vision nourished America's inevitable expansion from sea to shining sea. The part of the narrative we erase, however, is that these landscapes were, and still are, mostly shaped by invisible laborers from distant and unfamiliar lands. This section, like those in the chapters before, investigates this process of erasure and uncovers the fascinating part that four tiny California Delta towns contributed to America's prosperity. The twisted waterways of the Delta's labyrinthine channels discussed in the previous section hide fragments of complex cultural histories such as rusted tractors and abandoned produce barns.

Fruit-crate labels

Because much of the physical evidence has disappeared, my writings depend on old photographs and historic maps, especially detailed Sanborn Fire Insurance Maps from the 1920s, to reconnect vanished neighborhoods with the remnants of their small towns. Like missing pieces from an unfinished jigsaw puzzle, these documents complete the fragmented physical context within each town. The abbreviations and casual handwritten notes on these maps are biased reminders of past segregation and exploitation. Together with their notations, these maps help unlock clues about former inhabitants—the Chinese immigrants to the Delta who excavated the levees, planted the fruit trees and vegetables, harvested and canned the produce, and fabricated the wooden crates called "shooks" that bore the bright sunny labels of "California's Best."[1]

Like many other fortune seekers from different parts of the world, the Chinese initially came to California in search of gold. The Chinese name for California, and by extension America, *Gum Shan,* translates into "gold mountain." By 1851, there were almost five thousand Chinese in California; by 1890, more than seventy thousand. While at first many young Chinese men came to prospect for gold, others soon followed to labor on the construction of the Central Pacific Railroad. The Central Pacific Railroad started in Sacramento and climbed through the Sierras to ultimately complete, with the Union Pacific, the transcontinental link across the American continent. The heroic stories and struggles of these Chinese workers as they blasted through the granite of formidable mountain ranges are well documented.[2] The success of the Central Pacific's race out onto the Great Plains was mostly due to the organization and fortitude of Chinese laborers.

Successive surges of immigrants to California came from China's southern province of Guangdong, historically one of China's most populous areas. The South China Sea reaches deep into Guangdong's serrated coastline at the Pearl River Delta, a landscape of islands, winding waterways, and drained marshes. The Pearl River Delta also contains extensive earthworks for flood control that allowed productive agriculture over the millennia of Chinese history. Floods, overpopulation, and famines put enormous pressures on the people of this region in the nineteenth century. Unlike the rest of China's population during the Qing Dynasty, the Chinese along the southern coast had traditionally migrated to other countries to relieve the impossible living conditions of their homeland. In the mid- and late nineteenth century, a series of natural and political disasters further exacerbated the intolerable conditions in Guangdong, so some impoverished yet adventurous people booked the expensive and long passage across the Pacific to California. Lured by tales of legendary riches, the first Chinese immigrants headed for the gold fields on the western flanks of the

1. The towns of Isleton, Walnut Grove, and Courtland have a parallel narrative about Japanese immigrants and their horrendous treatment in America, especially the internment camps of the Second World War.

2. See M. R. Coolidge, *Chinese Immigrants;* Hoexter, *From Canton to California;* McDonald, *California Chinese Heritage;* and especially Steiner, *Fusang.*

Abandoned shook barn for the storage of vegetable crates, Central Valley

Sierras. They were met, however, with hostility and discrimination. Most were driven from their legitimately filed mining claims by force or at gunpoint; some were murdered, others fled to the safety of Sacramento or San Francisco. Both these cities quickly developed protective enclaves or "Chinatowns," of which San Francisco's was the most extensive and famous. During the early decades of their immigration to America, the Chinese were fighting for their lives, having to endure concerted campaigns of persecution, lynching, and murder that are shocking even for our history of violent racial hatred. The Chinese in California suffered far worse attacks than any other group that came voluntarily to our shores. Realizing how difficult and dangerous their situation was in this new land, the Chinese quickly searched for other ways of making a living. In 1866, the Central Pacific Railroad began laying its tracks from Sacramento across California's Central Valley toward the granite wall of the Sierras. The Central Pacific Railroad's subsidy from the federal government depended entirely on miles of track laid. The Central Pacific began hiring young Chinese laborers when it realized the Sierras were an impenetrable barrier requiring working conditions unacceptable to anyone else. The railroad even paid passage from China to America in its efforts to recruit young male workers. Known as the credit-ticket system, the railroad paid the steamer fare across the Pacific, while the Chinese worker repaid his debt by laying track. The conditions were brutal, and the wages were lower than those paid to "Americans," yet more than ten thousand Chinese came to blast tunnels and cuts through the dense rock as the tracks climbed higher into the freezing cold and snows of the Sierras. Three years later, when the golden spike was driven in 1869, most of the work of building America's transcontinental railroad in the West had been done by highly motivated, organized, and skilled Chinese labor.

Once the transcontinental railroads were completed, some Chinese worked on rail expansion in central and southern California; others turned to a variety of tasks such as the garment industry, cigar making, and shoe manufacturing. Racial discrimination prohibited them from most established trades, so many Chinese invented their own, such as the Chinese laundry we saw in Clifton, Arizona, in the second section of chapter 6. The ubiquitous Chinese laundries that were found in so many American cities were the result of the Chinese filling a service niche that no one else wanted. Laundry businesses eventually provided many other social, financial, and networking functions for the Chinese community. Most Chinese did not intend to remain in California, but they became trapped. They needed to make enough money for return passage and to purchase land in China, but they were unable to because of low wages resulting from constant discrimination in the American workplace.

A horrific cover from the *Wasp* magazine of Saturday, November 14, 1885, illustrates the depth and fierceness of this bigotry. A many-handed grotesque characterization of a Chinese man sits with its winged fists reaching out to take jobs from obviously white Americans. One clawed hand offers an opium pipe to a reclining figure; other hands block work opportunities or strangle hapless victims. The caption reads, "The Chinese: Many Handed but Soulless." It is a truly awful image made all the more abhorrent by its graphic skill, but one that conveys better than words the intolerance toward the Chinese and also the intense fear they inspired by their industry and distinctive culture.

The *Wasp* was a weekly satire magazine published in San Francisco from 1876 into the 1880s. Its original owners were the Korbel brothers, who immigrated to California from Bohemia. They made their fortune developing beautiful colored labels for redwood cigar boxes. This lithographic technology found its way into the journal's cartoons and onto its covers. After ten years of virulent anti-Chinese propaganda, the brothers sold the magazine to concentrate on their wineries along the Russian River; the wines and champagne still bear their name today: Korbel Champagne Cellars of California.

Ordinances and laws were passed in California that specifically targeted the Chinese. The Foreign Miners License Tax required all nonnative born prospectors to pay the enormous sum of twenty dollars per month just

Chinese laborers drilling in railroad cut, Monterey County, California

for the right to mine. In 1870, San Francisco passed the Sidewalk Ordinance prohibiting Chinese from carrying produce and other supplies in their traditional manner of baskets suspended from a pole across their shoulder. In 1873, the city again passed another ordinance prohibiting the traditional Qing Dynasty hairstyle of a bald forehead with a long braided queue down the back. Chinese immigrants had little legal recourse against this harassment as California's laws prohibited them from testifying in court against white Americans. Then in 1882, the U.S. Congress passed the Chinese Exclusion Act that prevented Chinese from immigrating into the United States under threat of imprisonment and immediate deportation. The Exclusion Act prohibited Chinese from obtaining citizenship and from ownership of land, and it effectively denied any Chinese then in America from bringing over their families. This act was unique in targeting a specific ethnic population. The first of many significant restrictions on immigration into the United States, this act made a mockery of the fact that the Statue of Liberty, with all its symbolism, was being erected at the exact same time as Congress voted the Exclusion Act into law. Against this

"The Chinese: Many Handed But Soulless"; cover from the *Wasp* 15 *(opposite)*

The Wasp
SAN FRANCISCO, SATURDAY, NOVEMBER 14, 1885.
SCHMIDT LABEL & LITHO. CO., SAN FRANCISCO
THE CHINESE: MANY HANDED BUT SOULLESS.

hostility, remarkably, the numbers of Chinese immigrants in California grew constantly, reaching a peak in 1890 and then dramatically declining until China became our ally in the Second World War, and we again opened our borders to them.

After the gold mines closed and the California rail network was completed, many remaining Chinese immigrants found work as agricultural laborers in the Central Valley. They were both skilled farmers and knowledgeable about levee building and irrigation, for the landscapes of marshes and rivers of the Delta were similar to those of their homeland of Guangdong, China. They gravitated to the Delta because few others would accept the arduous, wet work of shoveling the thick tule muck. Before the advent of steam dredges and powerful tractors, all earth moving was by hand or horse. As the Delta wetlands were drained and reclaimed, the demand for hand labor shifted to planting and harvesting crops. Pear trees thrived on the better-drained soils of the levee slopes, while asparagus grew well in the thick peaty fields, although other crops were rotated depending upon demand beyond California. Chinese workers quickly adapted to farm labor, planting, cultivating, and harvesting row crops such as asparagus and caring for fruit trees. Not only were the Chinese willing to do the backbreaking labor of bending over to harvest asparagus, but they were also familiar with the pruning and grafting of fruit trees. Perhaps the best-known cultivar of cherries, the Bing cherry, developed in the Pacific Northwest; it is named after a Chinese immigrant, Ah Bing. Ironically, he returned to China in 1889, and the enforcement of the Chinese Exclusion Act of 1882 prevented him from ever returning to America.

In the days before widespread refrigeration, vegetables and fruits were canned for distribution worldwide. The First World War especially increased demand as America had to feed thousands of soldiers far across the Atlantic Ocean. The Chinese soon became workers in the numerous large canneries built along the Delta's waterways. The Bartlett pear, so prominently grown along Delta levees, is one of the most important fruits for canning, especially with its sugary juices. Asparagus is an ideal crop for preserving as its linear stalks are easily fitted to a can.

Shallow barges transported this increasingly bountiful harvest from the Delta's fields to markets along the many winding waterways. Produce would be piled onto boats directly from the fields and carried to larger facilities served by one of the rail spurs that connected the Delta farmland to Sacramento and Stockton. As illustrated in the first section of this chapter, the docking and storage buildings at these river-to-rail transfer places were long narrow sheds perched along the levees. Floating docks moved up or down with the fluctuating water levels. Hoists carried crates to the

Chinese worker tending an irrigation ditch in an orchard, Los Angeles County, California, 1888

top of the levee to railroad tracks and sidings that paralleled the sheds' long loading platforms. Fruit companies constructed their canning operations at these same locations. The canning factories were surrounded by camps or minimally constructed dormitory-like bunkhouses for migrant workers who provided the seasonally intensive labor required by the cycles of agricultural planting and harvesting. Soon small towns clustered behind the levees to accommodate more permanent retail and commercial services and their white owners. Permanent residents, schools, and other civic institutions followed. This typical settlement sequence of the Delta was responsive to and dependent upon the protection of the levees. The larger docking and canning facilities and tracks sat on the levee, with the town's commercial core and housing on the lowland behind. Flooding was a common and disastrous occurrence for all Delta towns as the great spring snowmelts in the Sierras overwhelmed the levees in the age-old cycle of water flow through the Central Valley. Levee improvement and repair became a constant effort throughout the Delta as the protected agricultural land behind them continually subsided.

A unique building design developed in these communities that offered the opportunity for two levels of entry into the buildings that backed up to the levee: one entry from the top of the levee and another opposite from the street a story height below. Because of the linear mound-like shape of the levees, street and building arrangements also followed a similar linear layout. A cross-section through the town of Locke illustrates this unusual urban composition. On the far left of the drawing, a barge on the Sacramento River approaches the docking and storage facility that hangs off the levee. The wide levee supports tracks and a road. The commercial building on the right side of the levee can be entered over a small bridge into its second story from the levee top or alternatively into its lower ground level from the lower street. Thus a single building could have two commercial fronts: one above for road traffic and one below and behind the levee for pedestrians. Wooden steps between buildings connect from the levee down to the narrow street. The pedestrian street, festooned with flags and lanterns, is lined on both sides with two-story facades that have an open arcade over the sidewalk and a porch or balcony above. The arcade offered protection from the hot Delta summer sun, while the balcony gave a private vantage point from which to observe the activity of the public street below. This two-story arrangement makes for a very dense urban space. Beyond the main structures fronting the street is an alley and then single-story houses facing a second street. Behind the single-family dwellings, community gardens reached out to the surrounding orchards. The entire composition is a wonderful adaption to a manipulated topography. The continuous sinuous mounds of the levees determined all aspects of the Delta's landscape: the sunken agricultural fields below, the alignment of roads, and the placement and cross-section of the towns nestled behind their earthen bulwarks.

The many young men from China who took advantage of the opportunities in agriculture to move into the Delta as field hands were housed in primitive camps near their work. These were often no more than rows of tents with communal kitchen and dining spaces. As the growing seasons determined the planting and harvesting schedule, during slack periods the Chinese workers would retreat back to the Chinese neighborhoods in nearby cities such as Sacramento or San Francisco. There, they would stay in crowded shared rooms waiting for the next chance to earn money, or, as

Ink drawing of a cross-section through the Sacramento River levee and the town of Locke, California *(above)*

The main street of Locke, California *(left)*

it was ironically called, "one day, one dollar" labor.[3] As the Delta harvests prospered, fruit and vegetable companies built canneries at important landing places in the Delta and soon recruited Chinese to labor in the factories. These same large companies constructed warehouses and transient worker housing in orderly complexes near their canneries.

The factories and worker housing have disappeared completely, leaving behind cracked and weed-covered concrete floor slabs as reminders of the large open structures that bracketed every town. At the end of Isleton's main street, blue thistle grows over the abandoned remains of the steps to the office entrance to the Isleton Canning Company. Today, these steps lead nowhere except into an empty lot. Nothing remains of the worker housing. Four examples, however, have been extracted from Sanborn maps and arranged together to illustrate the typical organization of these complexes: three are from the Delta town of Isleton and one from nearby Locke. Even though these compositions all oriented differently depending upon the twists and turns of the Sacramento River, they have been placed similarly on the page with the river to the left. The plans are remarkably alike: the levee constrains the river, while warehouses, roads, and canning

3. Leung, *One Day, One Dollar,* from a poem by the author, iii, and the title of the book.

factories align parallel on top of the levee. The factories had several standardized buildings or areas within a building: a sorting room for cleaning and washing produce, a cooking area, a cooling room, and a canning room. Sometimes there would be a syrup room for the sweet liquid used in canning fruits. Each factory had an associated boiler house because the sterilization of food in the canning process requires high temperatures. Each complex included a box and shook warehouse. A shook is a bundle of ready-made wooden sides, tops and bottoms that are put together to form a crate for transporting cans and produce. The fanciful labels illustrated earlier in this chapter would then be glued to the finished crate.

Grouped behind the large structure of the factory in orderly rows were several different types of housing accommodations: long rectangular dormitories and smaller individual dwellings. The dormitory buildings were single interior spaces with barrack-like sleeping arrangements. The cabins were small (twenty feet by twenty feet) individual dwellings in larger groupings of as many as eighty units. None of these had any interior plumbing or kitchens, for each housing group had separate dining or cafeteria buildings for communal eating and separate communal toilet facilities. Surrounding the transient worker housing on all sides were either cultivated fields or rows of fruit trees. The number of sleeping and living accommodations indicates that the canning factories were sizable endeavors; Isleton's three factories employed over seven hundred people during the busy times of the year. These four examples of worker housing are remarkable for their consistency and for their single-minded organization. No adjustments were made for any other community uses such as retail stores or recreational opportunities. The factories were utilitarian, impersonal, and anonymous. Because many Chinese were illegal immigrants, they could be exploited, and few concessions were made for their well-being.

Small permanent communities near the warehouse, tracks, and canning factories provided the necessary services and civic functions that were omitted from the transient worker clusters. Of course, white owners controlled land ownership; the Chinese were not allowed to purchase property. Chinese merchants, however, were allowed into the United States with their wives and families. These merchants often accumulated enough capital to rent land and establish businesses in these small communities. Stores, restaurants, and boarding houses operated by the Chinese soon flourished to serve the predominantly single-male population working throughout the Delta.

Strung along the western side of the Sacramento River between Sacramento and Stockton, deep within the Delta's winding waterways, are three remarkable towns, Courtland, Walnut Grove, and Isleton. Each had its own

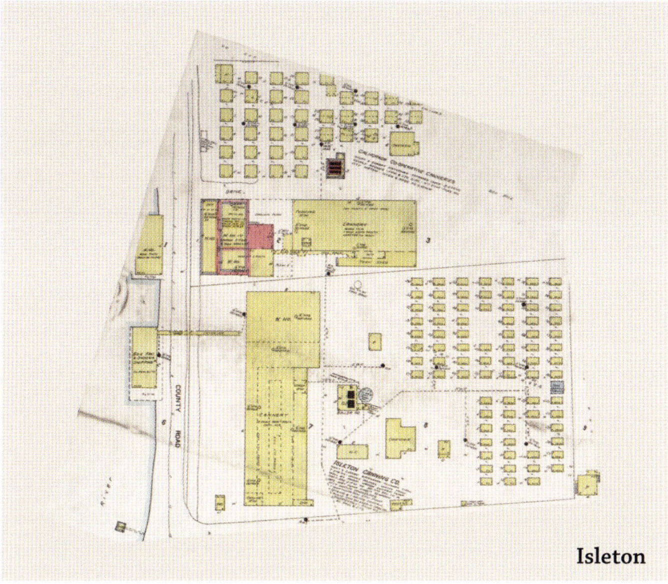

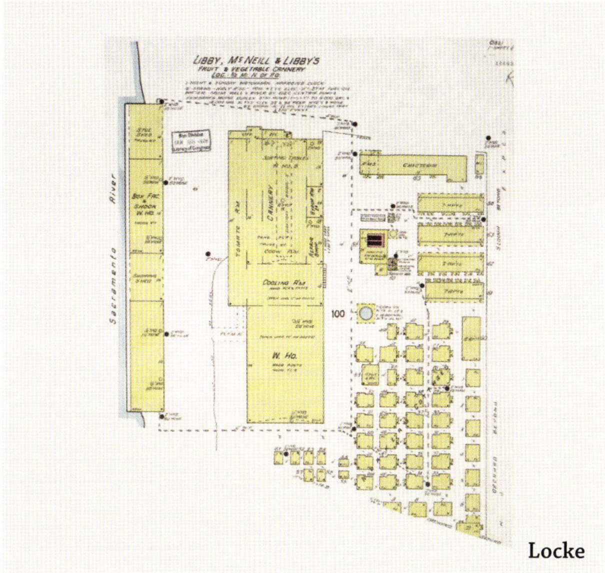

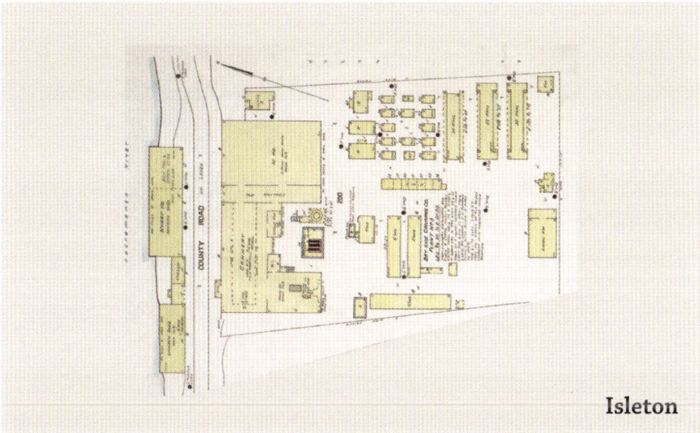

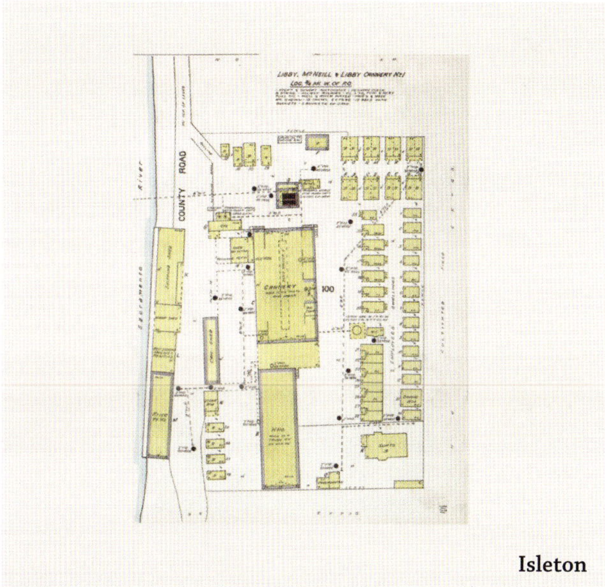

Details of canning factories and worker housing, Isleton and Locke, California, Sanborn maps, 1928 and 1927

miniature Chinatown, and each Chinatown was segregated from the rest of the town into a discreet neighborhood. All three towns sit on sweeping bends of the Sacramento River between two great pieces of modern infrastructure: the Sacramento Deep Water Ship Channel and Interstate 5. The twisting channels of the Delta have limited exit ramps from I-5 except at Terminous, which has isolated and protected these three towns from the usual strip development associated with the interstate traffic a short distance to the east.

Segregation and ghettoization are embedded in the urban form of each town. A figure-ground study of Isleton graphically abstracts the town's plan

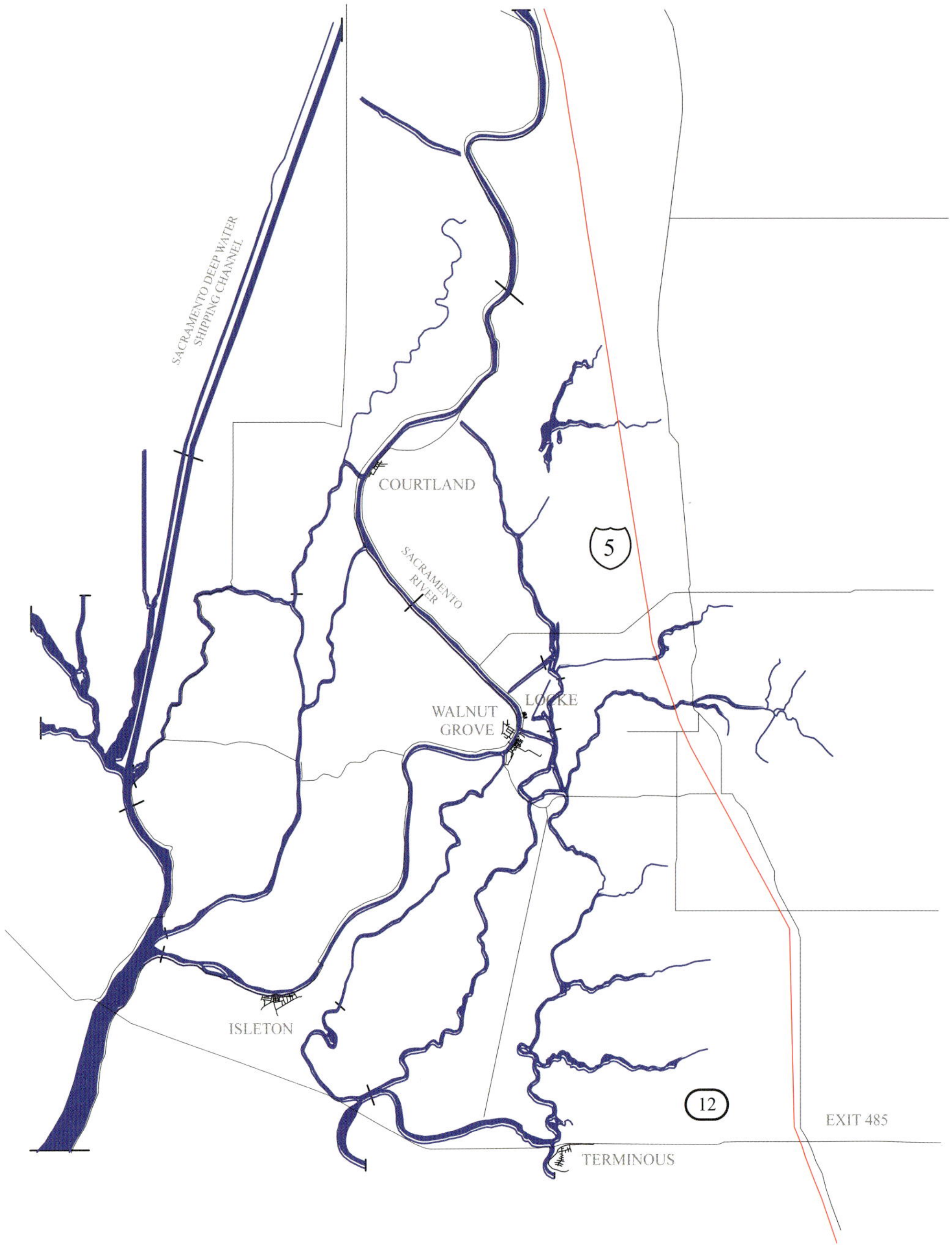

Map of the Delta showing the location of the four towns of Courtland, Walnut Grove, Isleton, and Locke, California

to make this partition into discreet ethnic enclaves dramatically obvious. This figure-ground drawing is interpolated from several spliced Sanborn maps. As the Sanborn map contains much information, the figure-ground study is a reductive drawing. By focusing on two-dimensional spatial relationships, the size and intervals of the black rectangles (the figures), on a neutral or undescribed background (the ground), the drawing helps one see a pattern, or in this case, three different patterns. This black and white representation is a simplified subset of the vastly more complex human relationships that have long ago disappeared. Few Chinese now live in Isleton, and the factories and worker housing have vanished, yet the highly selective figure-ground diagram proves an assertion of segregated districts of urban form. At the bottom or the western end of Isleton are large figures, isolated from each other by areas of white space. These are individual dwellings on spacious lots with expansive yards indicative of independent ownership. This was the white neighborhood with its own separate commercial center. Just above is a very large, long figure, the Isleton Union School, which sits on the edge of a wide play yard. Slightly above is a smaller figure, the Migratory School that served the transient population. Perpendicular to the Migratory School is another long rectangle, the Oriental School for Asians. These three figures of decreasing size form the hinge or demarcation between white landowners and the Asian neighborhoods beyond. An orderly double row of figures stretches further up, lining a main street. The figures are almost all long narrow rectangular shapes with consistent alignment on the street frontage. There is a break in the consistency, however, about midway. This is F Street, perpendicular to Main Street, and demarcates the separation between the Chinese and Japanese.[4] This ethnic division was just as rigid as between the Asians and whites. Beyond the Japanese neighborhood off the figure-ground was the Isleton Canning Company complex with its surrounding transient housing. The figure-ground study clearly expresses the racial segregation found in the spatial organization and hierarchy of buildings and open space. Big houses, big spaces for whites; smaller buildings and denser clusters for non-land-owning Asians; and tiny dwellings for transient workers. The unequal placement and sizes of the schools in the middle emphasizes the gulf between the owners of property and wealth and the rest of the town's inhabitants. With minor adjustments, the same diagram could be made of Courtland and Walnut Grove. In the following paragraphs, a closer reading of the Sanborn maps of all three towns enables the extraction of details of the different ethnic groupings including building uses and occupancies. Unlike the other three towns, Locke is an exception because it was built on a fresh site by the Chinese for themselves and with no other ethnic groups. However, Locke does include a similar urban typology and building occupancies.

The orchards and agricultural fields of the Delta were a long way from the sheltering Chinese community of San Francisco with its recreational and socializing opportunities. Laborers made the daylong or overnight boat journey from the Delta to San Francisco when canning or agricultural work was slack. It was not long, however, before Chinese merchants recognized the business opportunities that large populations of migrant

4. Japanese immigrants began arriving in the Delta soon after the Exclusionary Act of 1882 prohibited Chinese from entering the United States. With the decline of available Chinese field labor, Japanese immigration was encouraged by large agricultural interests.

Figure-ground study of Isleton, California

workers presented, and they began to establish retail stores and boarding houses in the Delta itself. By the early twentieth century, Courtland, Walnut Grove, and Isleton each had its own Chinese community. In 1915, Walnut Grove's Chinatown burned, and several Chinese merchants moved upriver to establish Locke at a site where there was already a Chinese saloon, gaming hall, and boarding house. Locke's streets were laid out quickly, and by 1927, it was built essentially as it looks today. Building uses and occupancies developed similarly in each of the three other communities. To understand these unique places, it is necessary to look more closely at their demographics.

The transient expectations of these young men from the other side of the world needs to be emphasized, because it strongly influenced the kinds

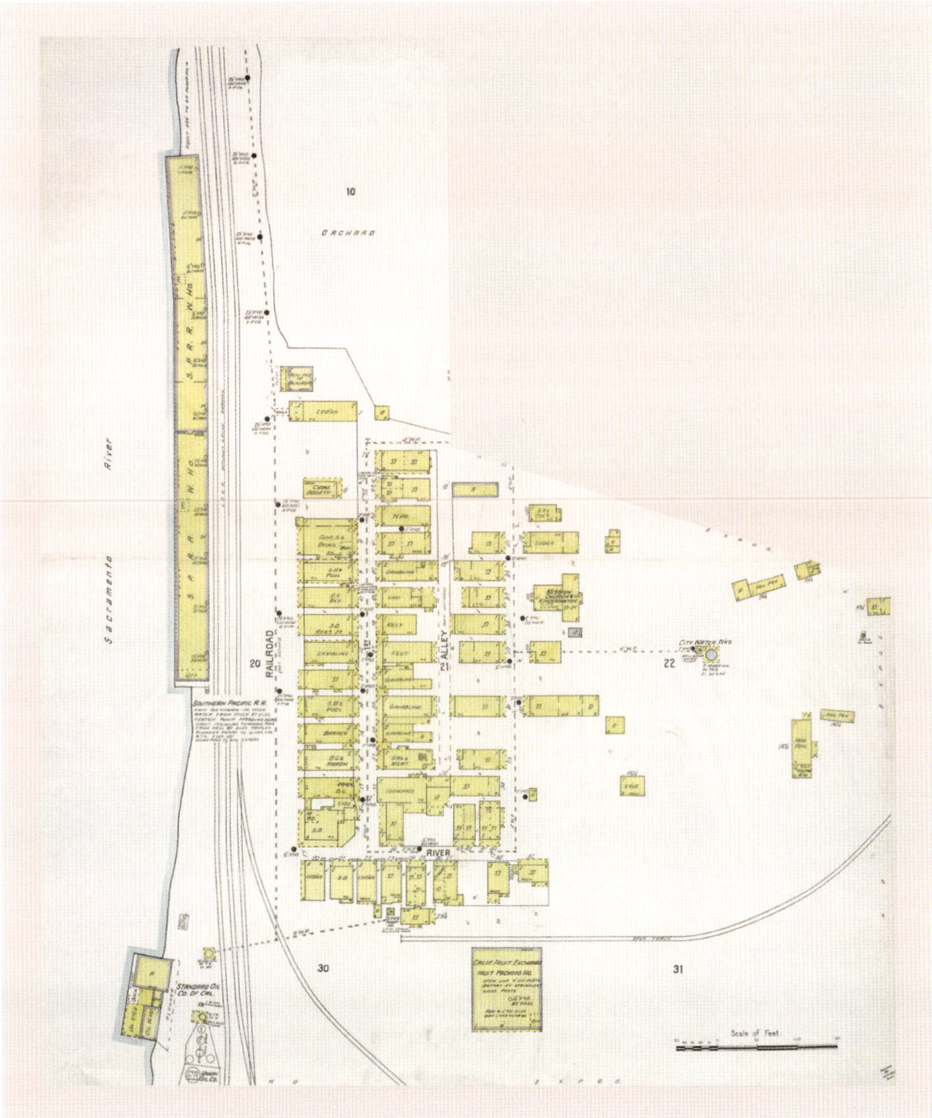

Sanborn map of Locke, California, 1927

of building uses in all Chinatowns, large or small, found in California. Chinese came to America to earn enough to alleviate their often desperate situations back home in China. Some would travel back and forth several times, others would become marooned here; few made enough to return and establish themselves successfully in their homeland. Immigration restrictions excluded them from bringing wives, so most were single, hoping to gain a wife upon their return to China. Immediate relatives of the Chinese already established here were sometimes granted entry into the United States, so there were many cases of falsified documentation of "paper brothers," young men vouched for by established Chinese merchants in San Francisco. Because most planned to stay only a short time, they seldom learned English or American customs and particularly the behavior of the predominately white English-speaking majority. Sadly, this lack of assimilation exacerbated the perception of the Chinese as strange and foreign and facilitated their exclusion from America's legal protections.

The urban plans of Courtland, Walnut Grove, and Locke are very similar. A narrow main street, an alley really, sixteen or eighteen feet wide, is enclosed on both sides by uniformly aligned two-story facades. Each building had a balcony accessible from the second floor that provided a covered arcade over the sidewalk. A space of five or six feet separated each building to prevent the rapid spread of fire. These side elevations were often sheathed in tin sheets for further fireproofing. The Sanborn maps note all this with yellow rectangles for the wood frame construction, a narrow band of gray for tin siding, and dotted lines with a "2X" indicating a second-story balcony. Fire was an obvious concern with such closely spaced, highly combustible wood construction; thus the Sanborn maps indicate numerous water hydrants. Courtland's street has ten hydrants connecting to a water main running the full length of its pedestrian street. Clearly the water tower and pumps could not provide adequate pressure since Courtland burned to the ground in 1930.

What gives these tiny urban compositions such focus is the regularity of height, alignment, and facade construction enclosing such a narrow public space. The rear of the buildings, by contrast, are not aligned; they extend at different lengths toward their lot lines. Locke is an exception as its rear, or front facades, depending on which side one enters, are positioned in a row against the levee slope. Walnut Grove has two parallel main streets each a block long; Courtland's Chinatown was separated by a small Japantown from its main downtown. Its single narrow main street appears to end in agricultural fields, yet its determined clarity of composition makes a marked contrast to the lack of coherence in the rest of Courtland's plan. The main street of Courtland's Chinatown must have been very similar

Tin-siding fireproofing, Isleton, California

to Locke's. Unfortunately, after fire destroyed Courtland's Chinatown, the landowner refused to renew the land leases. Many of the Chinese inhabitants relocated to Walnut Grove or Locke. Today, nothing remains of Courtland's Chinatown.

Details from all four Chinatowns are presented together on facing pages for comparison. Unlike the other three plans, the field surveyor for the Sanborn Company did not note the specific uses of each building in Courtland; there is just a generic note across the entire block "Chinese Stores and Lodgings." Isleton follows the same urban model with a considerably wider main street that stretches for two long blocks. In the early decades of the twentieth century, Japanese replaced Chinese in the second block north of F Street; thus the Sanborn map, drawn in 1928, indicates a Japanese and a Chinese section. Today there are numerous open spaces between buildings because a fire destroyed most structures in the Chinese block. The map indicates many buildings sheathed in tin, and there are five new brick buildings indicated by the color pink and even an ice plant constructed of reinforced concrete—all reactions to the devastating fire two years earlier.

A photograph taken in 1926 shows Isleton's Main Street before the fire and gives an idea of the architecture that existed in all four towns. The building facades line up along a broad sidewalk, each with an overhanging balcony. Each one has a distinctive stepped facade or parapet that hides the gabled roof behind. The sign above the center of the photograph advertises chop suey and noodles, as does the restaurant across the street behind the

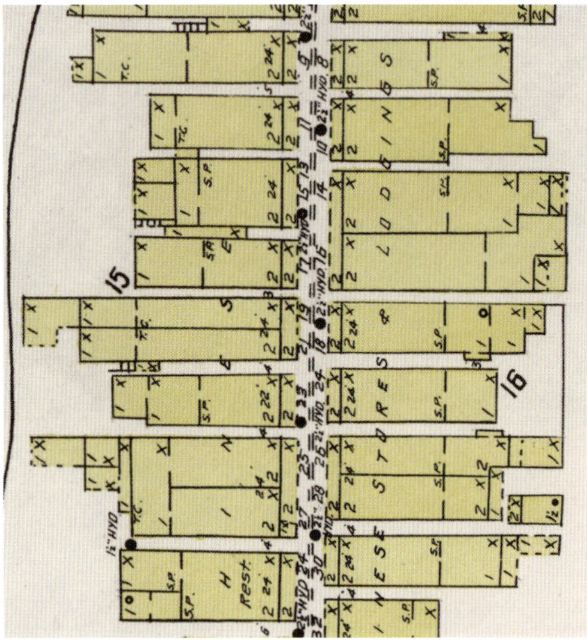

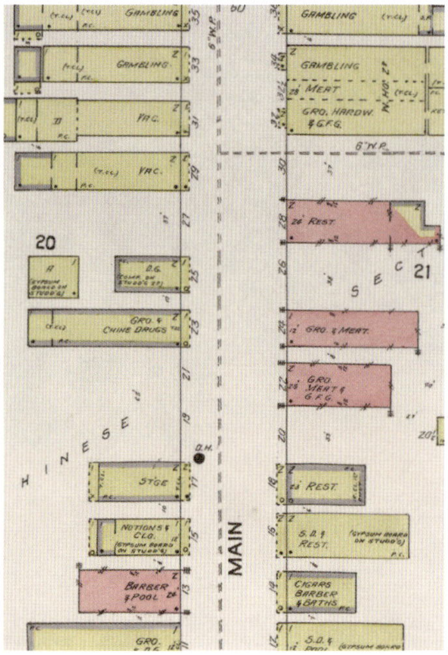

Detail of Chinese section of Courtland, Sanborn map, 1928 ***(above left)***

Detail of Chinese section of Isleton, Sanborn map, 1928 ***(above right)***

touring car. The familiar American-Chinese dish chop suey, cooked meat and vegetables served over rice, was a staple meal in the Taishan District of Guangdong Province, China. Most of the Chinese in California's Delta came from Taishan.

The street in the photograph is wet from rain. There are few people visible except one scurrying along the sidewalk just beyond the car and a group gathered in the distance. The well-maintained touring car probably belonged to clientele of the restaurant. Laundry hangs on the balcony above, protected from the rain and indicating that this floor contained dwellings. It seems unlikely that Chinese locals would have wanted to be identified in a photograph, especially as these were taken with a large format 8 × 10 camera with a tripod and all the attendant gear.[5]

In Locke, Walnut Grove, and Isleton, the use of each building is carefully noted on the Sanborn map, often with an abbreviation. These abbreviations have been the subject of much conjecture, and some are unclear. In these Delta town maps, however, most are decipherable. Certain uses occur frequently: first-floor stores—such as those selling dry goods (D.G.), groceries, hardware, and meat and groceries—barbershops, restaurants, pool halls, and cigars shops. Each Chinatown has a drugstore that would have been stocked with traditional Chinese herbs. The most frequent establishments in all four towns were gambling places.

The Chinese did not consider gambling a vice—unless, of course, it was taken to excess. Gambling was an accepted and popular form of social discourse with centuries-old games such a mahjong and fan-tan played for

5. The photographer for this and several other remarkable photographs of Isleton in the California State Library collection was Harold J. McCurry. According to the California State Library records, the photograph was taken around 1926. For more information on McCurry, see Reed and Unger, *History of Sacramento County, California*, 471.

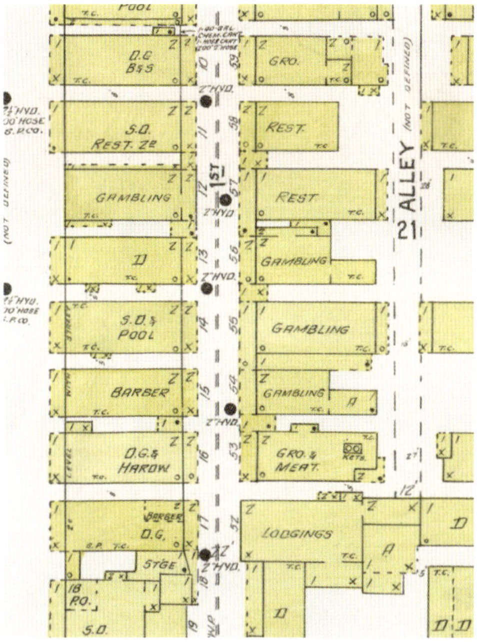

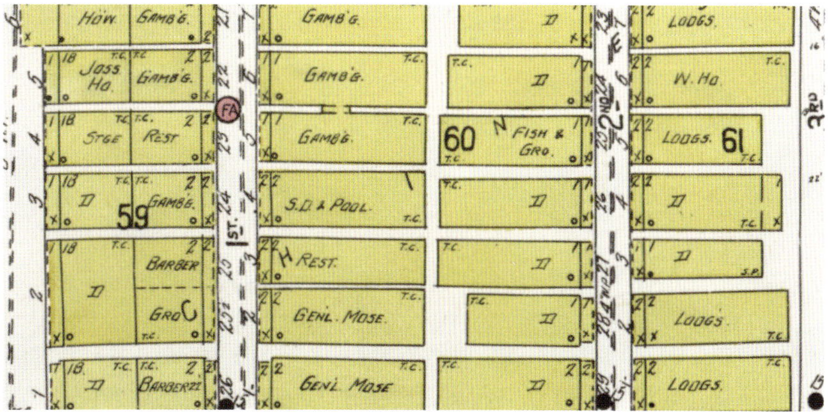

Detail of Chinese section of Locke, Sanborn map, 1927 *(above left)*

Detail of Chinese section of Walnut Grove, Sanborn map, 1927 *(above right)*

recreation and wager. In the Delta Chinatowns, gambling houses were places for transient laborers to congregate, socialize, meet friends, read Chinese-language newspapers, collect mail, and eat communal meals. They functioned somewhat like a union hall where work opportunities were posted and Chinese foremen came to recruit. They were an essential meeting place for workers living in these small towns between jobs out in the fields. Of course, there was excess and all the vices common to a predominately male transient population.

The second floors of these buildings were dwellings, sometimes occupied by the owners of the commercial establishments below, but most often they were rented accommodations for workers between harvests. Laborers would have lived in small crowded spaces shared by several men with hardly more than a bed and storage. Often as in Locke, the streets removed one block from the main space were single-story houses for stable occupants such a merchants, cooks, or barbers. Isleton and Locke had Chinese schools for the children of families among the permanent residents.

Chinese communities in the Delta were accommodations adapted to specific sociological needs. A small group of permanent residents provided the necessary services and goods for a much larger itinerant population. These communities were tiny centers located along the Delta's winding waterways, and their physical forms were pragmatic adjustments to unusual constraints. The buildings on rented property formed a public space that was enclosed, yet open to the community. This space afforded an implied degree of protection from the outside. Any non-Chinese person who ven-

Chinatown, Isleton, 1926

tured into these narrow main streets would have been immediately obvious. As the embodiment of safety and seclusion in a tenuous and hostile outside world, Delta Chinatowns functioned admirably. Their uniqueness and specificity, however, could not survive the rapid loss of their Chinese populations, and so Courtland's Chinatown has disappeared; Walnut Grove still has some buildings; Isleton struggles to record and preserve its Chinese history; and beautiful Locke remains complete with a few businesses and several memorials.

Communities require a past; narrative histories provide continuity for the passing of generations. Familiar institutions such as churches and town halls keep the records of these histories with birth and death certificates and wedding licenses. Voting rolls and church memberships are tangible examples of civic engagement. Perhaps the most enduring record, however, of a community's history is its cemetery. Headstones mark the small permanent resting place of individuals with names and dates of birth and death. Lovingly cared for and beautifully planted, cemeteries provide a community with both permanence and generational context. Often all that remains of a vanished settlement is a small graveyard, enclosed by a rusted cast-iron fence. The inscribed names and lichen-filled dates on slanted slate headstones allow the past to inhabit and hold a inviolate space.

Cemeteries require permanent landownership, as each individual acquires a plot for perpetuity. The Chinese in California could not purchase land; they had no way to anchor themselves or their parents to the earth. Their communities forfeited a continuity with the past and floated free from the landscape. As the Chinese moved away or returned to China, the dwellings, gambling houses, and places of work disappeared. So too did the memories of the thousands of immigrants who once inhabited the landscape of the Delta. Without graveyards, cemeteries, or tombs, there was nothing to impede the total erasure of their communities.

Some Chinese had their bones returned to their homeland to be interred in their native soil. Others simply disappeared into communal or pauper's graves. The town of Locke has set aside a small lot as a memorial to past generations. Marked by two tiny stone lion statues, it contains several markers to the workers and immigrants who shaped California's landscape. Individual square paving stones record the names of ancestors obviously placed there by their children or children's children. In an ideal world, the entire town of Locke should remain intact and unchanged as an apology and a fitting memorial to a unique type of collected urban form that arose out of the concentration of Chinese immigrants in California's Delta.

In a small nondescript town on the very eastern edge of the Delta, just a short way from the continuous traffic of I-5, is the community of French Camp, named after a group of French fur traders. A Chinese cemetery lies beside a wide road leading through subdivisions into the flatness of the Delta; its haunting isolation contrasts with the continuous development of surrounding suburban repetitive housing. Beautifully maintained and obviously cared for as evidenced by the many offerings of fruit and burned incense sticks, the elegant calligraphic inscriptions are mute reminders of the long journeys of hope across the Pacific Ocean that ended here. Or perhaps instead these graves mark the beginnings of another journey, for each marker is new, placed here by subsequent generations whose place in America was secured by the endurance and sacrifice of their parents.

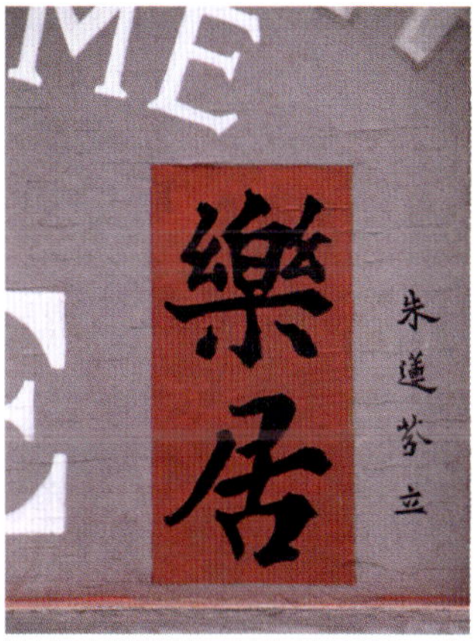

Detail from a paper couplet pasted to a sign on Locke's main street. The large characters say "Happy Dwelling"; the small characters on the lower right state the family's name and the individual's name: Zhu Lianfen. Lian means "lotus," and fen means "fragrance." (Translation by Xi Cao)

CONCLUSION THE GLASS OF TIME

DURING THE TEN YEARS that I researched and wrote this book, I traveled thousands of miles across America and visited over three hundred small towns. As I crisscrossed the highways and obscure back roads in each of these five regions, I became acutely aware of the diversity of America's landscapes, settlements, and people. At first the obvious differences between east–west and north–south hid the more subtle regional shifts, but as I familiarized myself with each of my study areas, the everyday deflections from common expectations became more apparent. Tiny inconsequential exchanges such as ordering a cup of coffee presented nuanced variations. I like coffee for its strong, black bitter taste, but if I ordered a "regular coffee" in a New England diner, I got coffee with cream already mixed in. When I ordered a "black" coffee in Nebraska, I was told: "that's with cream." The cream, not milk, will be on the side, regardless. If I ordered a black coffee in southern Georgia, its taste will be unassertive, requiring at least three "fill-ups" to get enough caffeine. In the south, each cup's pouring always brought questions about my curious accent or intended destination. I love these tiny, seemly insignificant regional distinctions, for they are part of the richness of the United States and reminders of the distances between far-flung places. I could not avoid, however, confronting other, less nostalgic, inescapable histories that define our regionalism, for these too are part of our legacies. These are broad pervasive histories intractably buried in our culture.

This is a book about urban form, and my focus is the physical environment we see, so I did not set out to explore broader social and cultural issues. My travels and observations brought two issues, racism and environmental degradation, to my attention. In retrospect, it was inevitable that I would need to write about these two hidden narratives, for form without content, or towns without histories, make little sense. I did find, however, that these compelling, yet darker, histories pulled me away from my original intent, and that I constantly had to refocus my explorations on the concrete, visible landscape. In the end, I could not escape commenting upon either racism or our destruction of the environment, for they are common across all regions, themes that contain essential truths about America's landscapes, whether we wish to accept them or not. As a student of urban form, my authority for my conclusions derives from direct experience, the streets I have walked in the humid afternoon Georgia heat, or the roads I have driven in the early fall snow, gray and dirty on the stubble of a Nebraska corn field. This is my research, one that integrates my studies of old maps with field observations and long days' drives and empty buildings.

I found a vacant sharecropper's house sitting on the far edge of a plowed field in southern Georgia. It was winter and cold. Two large leafless trees framed the house symmetrically to either side, their gray branches the same color as the unpainted siding of the house. The rusted tin roof had slipped forward to hide the porch in deep shadow, but the faded white railing still caught the afternoon sun. Leaning and broken fence posts trailed off into the encroaching weeds. Shelters for chickens, and perhaps a pig, lay open around the back; their inhabitants escaped long ago. Behind the house a green tangle of new growth marked a further field let fallow and abandoned. I walked across the dirt space to trespass onto the porch. The shoddy construction and small size of the house disquieted me. The walls of exposed wood studs on a layer of poorly matched boards gave little protection from the biting wind. The wide cracks and open knotholes must have been welcoming gaps for summer's insects. The underside of the tin roof was visible in the dank interior. The noise of the rain would have been thunderous. The interior contained two rooms, one for cooking and one for communal sleeping. Old furniture spilled out of the house onto the porch, and a broken and torn screen hung precariously off a smashed window. As I turned back across the open field, I was struck by the way the dilapidated house straddled two narratives: the plowed field in front ready for spring's planting and the abandoned overgrown woods behind, slowly engulfing the house and its surrounding yard. The trees, the house, the vegetation, the fence posts, formed a sharp line along a boundary incised into the exposed rural landscape. The southern Georgia landscape has many of these reminders of a past that lies forgotten along edges of fields and down side streets in courthouse-square towns. Racial injustice has not yet released its grip from the American South. The terrible aftershocks of slavery, the Jim Crow and segregation years, became so deeply embedded in southern culture that it will require the passing of many more generations to fully erase.[1] The fraudulent forms of Western democracy embodied by the beautiful landscapes of courthouse squares across Georgia carry that baleful message still. As the centerpiece of a public space, the apparitional courthouse murmurs a false promise, symbolizing one thing while hiding another.

1. Foner, *Forever Free,* "Epilogue," 225.

Abandoned tenant farmer's house, Pierce County, Georgia

I expected to find these residues of racial strife in the American South, but not necessarily in the narratives of so many other regions across this country. I found that an obverse of the diversity of urban form I celebrate in this book is the unrelenting difficulties of incorporating others into America's dominant white European culture. Rather than the traditional melting pot metaphor with its implications of a seamless blending of our many ethnic and racial strands, another analogy should be used, one of separate ingredients that obstinately remain divided. Locke, California, discussed in the second section of chapter 7, is the perfect example of this isolation. It was established to be separate. While other Delta towns, like Walnut Grove and Isleton, segregated neighborhoods, the inhabitants of Locke withdrew entirely. With its tightly enclosed street so detached from its surroundings and its shuttered porches filtering sunlight onto empty storefronts, Locke slowly fades away, quiet testimony to human tenacity. Locke is not alone as an isolated example in our far-western states, for as we saw with Sonora, Arizona, entire towns retreated behind their own ethnic barriers. New England mill towns segregated into distinct neighborhoods based upon race and religion, each group's territory clearly marked, as in Webster, Massachusetts, by separate monumental churches that function more like protective castles than houses of worship. Even on the Great Plains of Nebraska, settled mainly by homogeneous northern Europeans, these same forces of racial exclusion and compartmentalization exist, only over a whole region rather than within a small town. As I explored the diversity of urban forms across America, I wondered if small towns actually foster integration or if big cities work better because of their greater scale and easy anonymity. Eventually I had to set aside this issue, for as I finish this book, the struggle for America's character continues unabated with the same friction between those who would deny this country's obvious immigrant past and immigrants who want to share our bounty.

America's bounty seemed to have no limits as immigrants arrived in the nineteenth century. The North American continent's incredible wealth of natural resources enabled an unprecedented expansion both in territory and population. Water to power mills in New England, longleaf pine forests from which to build these same mills, the fertile soils of the Great Plains, the minerals of Arizona, and the water, sun, and soil of California's Central Valley—all were there for the taking. The number and quality of our small towns testify to the wealth of this expansion, for these places are not poorly conceived or meagerly executed. The eighty-five courthouses of southern Georgia are all handsome, well-constructed, even extravagant buildings. The great mills of New England were solid, well-detailed structures. Even the buildings along the single empty street of Clifton, Arizona, were made of finely detailed brick and stone. Deserted, with boarded windows and doors, Clifton's buildings are still beautiful.

So many of our small towns grew around the extractive processes of these plentiful resources: mining towns, coal towns, mill towns, and farming communities. They all served the immigrant labor populations necessary to create America's richness. This continuous and unrelenting extraction of resources, however, came with terrible consequences. With a rather depressing consistency, our excesses followed us across a continent as illustrated in this book's five narratives: we polluted and fouled the rivers and streams of New England; we clear-cut the longleaf pine forests of the South; we are depleting the soil and the aquifers of Nebraska; copper mining is an environmental disaster; and the natural hydrological systems of California's Delta are badly compromised by competing demands. Today, America's perception of seemingly inexhaustible natural resources repeatedly couples with our unbounded need to exploit them beyond possible renewal. The deeper histories I have uncovered in my explorations of urban form are all uniformly rapacious and unsustainable. While industrial detritus such as abandoned mines or ruined mills remain as evidence of this past, little endures after agricultural or forest deprecations, except for the towns associated with such extractive occupations. We move on, but our places of inhabitation are more durably anchored to their place and to the past. We founded towns for pragmatic purposes, to be near our work or our transportation networks, yet when the work or other activity disappears, the town remains, a referent without a subject. Those towns that endure beg us to ask why they are where they are.

The most important question, then, to ask about any town is why it is *placed* where it is. What were its founding circumstances? The answer tells everything.

Each of the five main chapters in this book begins directly or by implication with this question. In chronicling the particular region's narrative, I presented some, but not all, of the explanations. Of course, this approach is not unique or new. It employs the traditional role of geographers: to explore the earth, its inhabitants and complexities, and all their interrelationships. Writing as a landscape architect–urbanist, I have become also a geographer of built form. If the reason for a town's placement depends upon a fixed geological feature such as an ore deposit or a waterfall for hydropower, then transportation systems must extend to that town, and town and transportation become fixed specifically to a spot. The simplest example of a town tied to a transportation network is Holbrook, Arizona, discussed in chapter 6. Originally just a construction-staging site on a westward expanding rail track, the town's plan was a straightforward grid parallel to the tracks. The distance necessary to transport and lay wooden ties and iron rails along a survey line determined Holbrook's placement on the high desert. The survey line had to avoid steep grades and deep streams, but Holbrook's position was a spot marked by logistics. The placement of towns such as Moultrie, Georgia, or Edgar, Nebraska, are more complex and depend upon a day's ride for a circuit judge or acres of harvested corn. Even Locke was dependent upon the Sacramento River on the other side of the earthen levee for transportation.

Yet as specific and determined as these placements are, the towns depend upon forces far beyond their narrow topographic or geological confines. Markets for minerals, labor, or transportation costs can make or ruin a town, depending on national or international demands. A corner druggist in Edgar, Nebraska, should care about famine in Southeast Asia. The rise and fall of corn futures and agribusinesses' responses to these far-away demands will determine the future of Edgar, and that of the corner druggist. Towns have an amazingly fragile existence within the larger impersonal financial and political world. Globalism is not new, for the settling of America was probably one of the most global movements in the history of humankind, but it has come into sharper focus as we can now see the dependency of these small towns on forces beyond their narrow quiet streets.

The off-ramp towns discussed in chapter 2 are an anomaly, for they are completely tied to a transportation system and to the volume of travelers on that system. They are also located only at those points where the new network intersects with an older subsumed system of previous highways. Spawned by transience, attached only to interstates, off-ramp towns are unique across America because they are the same in all regions. With no diversity of form and character, they are regional-less, adaptable to anywhere. And yet they are totally dependent upon the price of a single global resource, the cost of oil.

The interstates and their associated off-ramp towns can be used as a standardized template to measure the diversity of urban form. The interstates provide a useful datum, a constant mark on the landscape, a figure that spans the ground of an entire continent, against which one can evaluate both the diversity and persistence, as well as the impermanence, of our small towns. The interstate, built quickly, consistently, and to conform to standards, is a ruler with equal gradations: every sign, every radius, every cross-section, and every interchange the same. One conclusion of this book is that interstates, while instruments of change, are a convenient measure of a great shift in American settlements, away from many small towns to a few spreading metropolitan centers. An interstate in Georgia is exactly the same as one in Nebraska. What are not the same are the landscapes or the towns that are bypassed.

My book is about these different towns and the beautiful examples of urban form that emerge out of this diverse richness. I want to conclude by explaining what I mean by urban form and how I attribute aesthetic value to a small town's physical characteristics. A town's form is made up of many distinctive parts, each one important, but none as important as its combined totality. The first component is the contextual topography: rolling hills of New England, flat open prairies of Nebraska, or the constructed levees of California's Delta. The placement of the town, its buildings, and the layout of its streets must respond to these topographic constraints. Locke's unique, double-level section could only happen because of its placement against the levee's backside. Topography and vegetation go together. The dense hardwoods of New England accent the rolling hills and drape the millponds and flumes with deep shadows. Lack of vegetation gives Clifton's rugged setting even more drama within its rocked-walled canyon. A Great Plains town's incredible density of planted shade trees resulted directly from the need for protection from summer's hot sun and winter's cold blasts. Artificially or naturally, topography and vegetation together provide the first layer of a town's appearance.

A town's initial street layout must conform to topography. In the Great Plains, with little topographic constraints, most town surveyors utilized a simple grid. Ease of measurement on the ground and of lot distribution and sale made grids ubiquitous. This ubiquity, however, does not make these towns dull or monotonous as the coalescence of the commercial center, the shifting of the grid for the railroad, and the apportionment of residential neighborhoods all added differences and specificity that are expressed through architectural accommodations. Clifton, by contrast, has but a single street, parallel to the looming cliffs on one side and the creek wash on the other. A review of street plans in this book reveals as many differences as there are towns: the gentle arc of Webster, the square of Moultrie, the slashed grid of Edgar, the dense, curved main streets of Globe and Clifton, and finally the mall-like singularity of Locke. One could make diagrams of all the towns included in this book for comparisons of their different figures, from the simple line of Clifton to the complex radial patterns of Webster, from the squares of southern courthouses to the county seat of York, Nebraska. These drawings could be grouped into typological categories such as railroad grids or main street towns like Holbrook, Arizona, to further illustrate the richness and variety of two-dimensional plans across America.

As spaces, streets are inseparable from a town's totality and a prime element in its overall form. The graphic figures of the street plans represent the public open spaces of a town. These street spaces are perhaps the most important part of a town's urban form, maybe even more important than the town's architecture. Streets are rooms, with dimensions of width and section, or height, enclosed by buildings and trees. As the great American architect Louis Kahn said, "The street is a room by agreement, a community room, the walls of which belong to the donors, dedicated to the city for common use."[2] Locke's single main street is the perfect example, for it is the town's only real public space. The street is enclosed by two-story arcades and open only at one end; access can be gained as well through hidden steps and alleys. Locke's street is essentially a room that can be entered abruptly or secretively, a very distinctive public space that is the essence of Locke's form.

Public space may be the most important component of urban form, yet we seldom acknowledge our streets as spaces. Instead, we focus on traffic and parking. The discussion of Nebraska railroad towns emphasized the receding space of the tracks defined by the corn silos, but one could just as easily accentuate the wonderful scaled spaces of the tree-lined residential streets that extend perpendicularly on either side of the tracks. Consistent setbacks of houses, each with its welcoming porch, wide green lawns cropped by linked sidewalks, all sheltered by towering shade trees, make Nebraska town streets the envy of everyone wanting to recapture the essence of small town urbanity.

Perhaps one of the most obvious public spaces in any American town is the courthouse square. All the streets of a county seat are laid out to draw attention to the space of the square and then to the object, the courthouse placed within the space. Unlike great cities, towns are generally too small to have more than one important space, beyond a single square, a main commercial street, or the track sidings with their passenger station. All subsidiary streets are usually residential and provide a simple foil to the single tiny urban center. A review of the aerial photograph of Moultrie in chapter 4 shows the importance of the framing of the square by the consistency of all the retail buildings, each positioned similarly around the four sides. Arcaded sidewalks add both shade and additional conformity. Moultrie's plan is a modified grid, so its regularized residential streets help determine the symmetry of the commercial frame, which in turn accentuates the uniqueness of the square's open space with its central object. It is a simple hierarchical composition that works together with all its parts to give Moultrie's urban form its beauty.

Buildings do not necessarily need to be distinguished architecture to define the boundaries of a town's urban core. Consistency of height, setbacks, and materials

2. Kahn, qtd. in Lobell, *Between Silence and Light,* 46.

is more important. We are all familiar with the false facades and tin cornices of midwestern retail storefronts that so effectively enclose the street space. They are like stage sets, promoting the establishment's presence, decorated with dates and founders' names, to increase the public's awareness of the retailer's reputation. Lot sizes in most towns' commercial cores are more valuable and hence narrower than in the residential quarters, so buildings are constructed with shared party walls, pressed together, forming a continuous wall of storefronts. This continuity of facades makes the retail core of even the smallest town distinctive, recognizable, separate, and very urban.

The main street can have other kinds of enclosure, as we saw in Holbrook, Arizona. Holbrook's main street, Route 66, is wide with many motels that are each set back behind an open space for parking. At the street edge each establishment has a huge sign advertising its presence. Looking down this wide boulevard, with the empty desert beyond, one sees a space with fantastic signs aligned in receding rows on either side. Holbrook is an example of one of America's most iconic and unique urban spaces: the commercial strip, a place defined by signs, accessible only by automobile, yet compellingly urban.[3] The signs enclose the street; the buildings' setbacks and heights are consistent; the order of the composition is easily understood; and, lastly, at night, the strip must have glowed with excitement.

A review and comparison of the different town maps in the previous chapters, as well as the photographs of the main streets, gives a sense of the many different ways of forming urban space. Compare, for example, Locke's tight pedestrian street with Holbrook's wide avenue, or look at the Sanborn Fire Insurance Map of Globe's dense Main Street next to Moultrie's expansive square. These comparisons and the many others in this book illustrate the more inclusive definition of space as a major component of urban form.

Architecture can be relatively anonymous yet still enclose urban space. As we have seen, consistency of positioning and height are most important when framing a public square. America's small towns do, however, contain some wonderfully distinctive architectural monuments. Southern Georgia courthouses run the gamut from wood to stone, from neoclassical to Victorian, yet all are of similar scale, and all are placed similarly within their context. Small towns also contain beautiful buildings with substantial architectural merit: corner banks as in Globe, libraries, churches, train stations, schools, all gain importance from the care devoted to their architecture. Even tiny Edgar, Nebraska, has a finely detailed library, sadly now vacant. These important buildings evidence pride of place and use in every town, no matter how remote or insignificant.

Topographic placement, street spaces, building mass, and architectural hierarchy are the most important aspects of urban form. But it is the totality of all four together, their consistency and completeness, that makes for a beautiful example

3. The definitive book on America commercial strips is *Learning from Las Vegas* by Venturi, Brown, and Izenour. Aside from being the seminal book on "pop" architecture, it has beautiful figure-ground studies and other kinds of analytical drawings of urban form.

of urban form. Urban form is like a tiny tapestry dependent upon the interweaving of all strands to be successful. Remove a segment, and the whole becomes unraveled. Take out buildings along a main street for a bank drive-through or a fast-food parking lot, and the urban form unravels. As suggested by Kahn's earlier quote, the agreement of the street is abrogated, and the room of the street loses its enclosure. The "donors' have removed their dedicated contribution to the "common use." A town is a whole composition, and like any two- or three-dimensional composition, it can have different levels of quality. Even if the town is totally vacant like Clifton, its form remains and can be understood on its formal qualities. So many of the towns in this book are partially empty, their form eroded by abandoned lots, yet enough remains, explained further by old maps of their past, to understand their beauty. The beauty of their urbanism can be appreciated as a vernacular art form.

Many cities in America were planned based upon formal design principles. Savannah, Georgia, is a well-known and beautiful example. Washington DC, Detroit, Chicago, and many others were all planned in the grand baroque manner with diagonal streets carrying to distant vistas. There were even some aberrant or strange plans suggested for small towns.[4] The designs of the towns discussed in this book, however, and most, if not all, American small-town plans were based upon simple and common ideas of geometry. Grids, squares, or single linear streets served as plan generators. These are vernacular approaches to design, practical and accessible. When a town's composition, even though simple, remains complete with consistent architecture, it can be considered an art form.

These towns are not just echoes of their past, blank facades hiding hollow interiors inhabited only by owls. They are, or were, real places, full of people's hopes and dreams. We must judge them as art, defined by both form and content, and for their ability to encapsulate those hopes and dreams. Form—be it two-dimensional or three, painting, sculptural, or urban—represents something deeper than just paint on a canvas or bricks and mortar. Towns stand for community, our willingness and need to dwell together. In this sense, towns are truly works of art, complex physical manifestations of an idea, and this idea cannot be separated from its form. The streets, the squares, the buildings embody the histories and aspirations of the inhabitants.

When we return to Hopper's painting of Orleans discussed in the introduction to this book and the suggestion that he painted an empty town to communicate the idea of alienation, then we understand that Edgar, Nebraska, also communicates the same alienation, a similar shift in our expectations of ourselves that took place during the late twentieth century. Edgar, like all towns in this book, is disappearing. On any given day but a single person walks its sidewalks, peering into empty storefronts. One or two pickup trucks park in front of anonymous buildings whose identifying signs have long been removed. Edgar, Moultrie,

4. Reps, *Making of Urban America,* 475. Reps calls these "mutant plans."

Locke, Holbrook—all America's small towns are adrift in an alien world, lost among faraway forces that rush forward into a different future, a future that does not include any of them.

This book began by documenting the inexorable homogenization of America's cultural landscapes during the second half of the twentieth century. From all the myriad and complex reasons for this emerging uniformity, my writings concentrate on the most salient and obvious, the expansion of automobile travel and its quintessential expression through the interstate highway system. The transformations caused by the interstate highway system in the decades following the Second World War are clearly visible across our distinctively different landscapes. These great highways stretch in all directions and reach across a continent, dramatically shortening travel times through easy access and consistent, safe engineering, while also dramatically changing our settlement patterns.

The building of the interstate highways has had enormous consequences for America's towns and cities: some anticipated and promoted, others unintended and disastrous. This book's thesis posited that one of these consequences has been a decided shift in our settlements from thousands of diverse small towns to far fewer, monotonously similar developments spawned by the same limited access that makes highways so secure for high-speed travel. My early chapters chronicled the origins and relentless growth of these places, coining the descriptive moniker "off-ramp towns." Subsequent chapters explored five specific examples of small-town heterogeneity and the influence of a nearby interstate on each. These explorations uncovered an amazing diversity among towns: diversity of form, of responses to geography, of ethnic origins, and of ways of creating wealth. Having written this book, I discovered that the depth and breadth of this diversity exceeded even my enthusiastic imagination. Nineteenth- and early-twentieth-century America's most remarkable contribution to the history of urbanism has to be its wonderful collection of thousands of uniquely different small towns.

The extensive geographical diversity of the American continent partly explains such a wide variance of town types. The settlement of America over a short time span of two hundred years by different peoples from the far corners of the earth also accounts for the wealth of responses to this geographical variety. These two circumstances, wide geographical and population differences, were unique to the founding of America.

Underlying my thesis is the strong conviction that in human culture, as in all ecological systems, diversity of forms and responses to constraints and opportunities is of great importance. In each regional example chosen for this book, I explained several facets of a town's physical form conditioned by its unique circumstances. All five examples illustrate extraordinary differences, yet a random sampling of towns from any region in this country would offer the same diversity. All across America, however, the populations of these small towns are contracting, boarding up storefronts, and vacating downtowns. Each town's economic and social vitality slowly shifts away to other commercial places that attach to our highway interchanges and extrude into strip malls. Like thousands of tiny grains in an hourglass, these unrecorded towns are slipping away, taking with them something of irretrievable value. We must resonate with their diminution, for we constantly support their re-creation as theme parks or historic restorations such as Main Street USA, Disney World, or Colonial Williamsburg. We seem unwilling or unable, however, to reverse their inevitable decline in all but a fortunate few examples. Contrary to my original intentions, I have written about an unfolding tragedy, continental in scope, not about the success of the vast highway network, but of the loss of a rich cultural heritage, celebrated in my five examples, replicated a thousandfold across America, each town equally unique, equally beautiful, and equally condemned to vanish through the narrow neck in the glass of time.

A NOTE ON RESEARCH, WRITING, AND RESOURCES

This brief essay follows the format to which I adhered during my research and writing of *Easy On, Easy Off.* I began my extensive travel and research with field notes, drawings, and models, so I first explain my use of these tools for discovery. Then, as I did when writing the book, I review sources on the U.S. Interstate Highway System followed by a discussion of books about urban form and the composition of spaces in cities. The essay then shifts to increasingly more regional and topical literature. These regional discussions correspond to the outline of the five examples of *Easy On, Easy Off,* from east to west. I include a discussion about the interpretation of maps as an important bibliographic technique used throughout *Easy On, Easy Off.* I conclude this essay with a short recapitulation of the influence of my architectural training on a scholarship of integration.

Travel, field research, and direct observations gave me many insights about each of the five specific regions in my book and were a cornerstone of my methodology. As I planned my first field trip to an area, I would make a notebook with three documents of each town I anticipated visiting: a U.S. Geological Survey map, an aerial photograph, and a composite Sanborn map. In the field, I extensively covered these maps with observations, drawings, and notes. Using these notes, I would begin my selection process. Usually I started with thirty or forty towns to visit. After several weeks of driving a wide area, I would winnow those down to five or six towns for a return trip at a later time. My initial criterion for including a town was its integrity of urban form. Did it have all its parts? Were its streets still fully enclosed with no missing "teeth" or buildings? Georgia was an exception, as I eventually visited all eighty-five courthouse-square towns below the fall line before selecting Moultrie. I would mark up a Delorme Atlas & Gazetteer for both context and as a record of where I had been. It was during these visits that I collected photographs. Obviously all this field research necessitated a lot of travel, driving, staying at anonymous motels, and eating in forlorn diners. During these trips I became acquainted with off-ramp towns.

Having selected towns for further study, I would schedule a second or often third trip to spend time in local libraries, historical societies, and walking the streets of towns armed with Sanborn maps for detailed comparisons. Sanborn maps were a great prompt for discussions with merchants, librarians, and others. No one can resist a map that shows their own property, especially from a hundred years earlier.

As an architect, I find that valuable research is accomplished by drawing and making models. My field studies are documented in my notebooks. In fact, my travels throughout my life have been recorded in standard 8½" by 11" notebooks. When visiting a town, I walk its main streets or square and make a drawing of its plan. The process of making the drawing, more than the drawing itself, enables me to both remember the spaces and to understand the complexity of a town's urban form.I constructed small wooden models of many towns that abstract components of their form and clarify the town's structure. These little *modelli, maquettes,* or *bozzetti* help clarify the essential urban characteristics of a place. Usually a town has a single salient idea waiting to be discovered, and the making of a model brings this idea to the surface. The discovery of the diagonal space of the tracks in Edgar and other railroad towns of Nebraska came about as

Study model of Edgar, Nebraska; wood and acrylic paint on canvas, 14 × 14 in.

Study model of Locke, California; wood and acrylic paint on canvas, 14 × 14 in.

the small model with the blue grain silos took shape on my desk. Several models of Locke, California, allowed me to conceptualize the parallel linear connection of its main street space to the long raised levee and the widening river beyond. I made the cross-sectional drawing of Locke in chapter 7 to summarize these connections.

Both drawing and model making are important research tools for me that lead to discoveries of relationships and help clarify concepts. Together, they continually reinforce the study of maps, field trips, and the reading of written sources. My research methodology owes a great deal to my training and practice as an architect and consequently reverses the normal order of a literature review followed by field verification. Like an architect about to begin a design, I first visit a site and, through observation, drawing, and mapping, search out hidden relationships and connections. I try to understand the movement of the sun, the flow of water across the earth's surface, and the origin of materials such as vegetation or man-made bricks and stones. This gathering process lets ideas emerge, for I never have a clear concept of what is important in a region until I have finished my explorations.

I would visit state historical societies to examine statewide historic maps and old photographs. The Rhode Island Historical Society, for example, let me spend three days studying their collection of D. G. Beers & Company maps of late-nineteenth-century settlements. The Georgia State Archives have an especially well-organized and comprehensive collection of maps from the beginning of the colony in the eighteenth century to the present. Because of its great agricultural history, Nebraska's Extension Services have a wealth of maps and satellite images of corn production, railroad development, and county cadastral grids. One such nineteenth-century map of survey sections gained me access to a corn collective's grain elevators, where I spent two days learning about trains, corn harvesting, corn storage, and grain futures.

During the ten years of writing *Easy On, Easy Off,* I visited the map collection of the Library of Congress numerous times. I would usually prepare for my visit by scouring the Library's web pages for relevant maps. I cannot emphasize enough the wonderful resources of this website, its accessibility, and its ease of navigation. As I knew the exact maps I wanted to see at the map room, the staff would provide me with table space and the original maps. I would sit with a magnifying glass for hours "reading" the maps, searching every notation, every tiny hachure for information. I would become eagerly lost in the sorrowful labyrinth of the past. The Library of Congress's collection of over 700,000 original Sanborn maps is full of extraordinary amounts of information. Much of the information in *Easy On, Easy Off* comes from either field research and observation or from the reading of old maps. And while I have included an extensive bibliography of the literature I have explored, my time and efforts these past ten years have been spent with maps and travel. One has only to compare a Sanborn map of Superior, Arizona, in 1920 with a visit to the actual town today to gain a true perspective on the town's tragic demise.

Sanborn maps are drawn at the scale of one inch equals fifty feet on 22 × 24–inch sheets. Sometimes a sheet contains an insert or smaller map at a scale of one inch equals a hundred feet. These sheets only show partial areas of a town. In contrast, *Easy On, Easy Off* constructs composite Sanborns of Moultrie, York, Globe, and Clifton. As twelve to fourteen Sanborn sheets make up the entire downtown of a town such as Globe, I would cut and paste sheets together to form a whole. The sheets were never intended to be fitted together along all their edges; thus this process took a certain amount of creativity and digital adaption.

Most books on the Interstate Highways System pay homage to the grand engineering feat of its construction. Others probe deeply into the political and economic history behind its final alignment. Two books stand out for their critical assessment of the impact of the Federal Highways on America's cities. A. Q. Mowbray's *Road to Ruin* and Helen Leavitt's *Superhighway—Superhoax* both examine the destructive consequences of limited-access highways constructed through historic city centers.

Perhaps the most important book about the interstate highway system is the innocuously titled *General Location of National System of Interstate Highways, Including All Additional Routes at Urban Areas Designated in September, 1955,* issued by the U.S. Bureau of Public Roads. Known as the *Yellow Book* because of its cover, this hundred-page document contains no text, only maps. Its modest and simple diagrams outline the entire interstate system both as a whole and city by city. Apocryphally, in the early 1950s, the Bureau of Public Roads put a copy on each U.S. congressman's or congresswoman's desk, yet no one paid attention to the plan's potentially devastating impact on America's cities.

Professors John A. Jakle and Keith A. Sculle have made the study of highway services the subject of their trilogy: *The Gas Station in America; Fast Food: Roadside Restaurants in the Automobile Age;* and, with Jefferson S. Rogers, *The Motel in America*. These three books cover the history of the major components of highway development through the twentieth century. The economic and marketing aspect of familiar franchises is especially well covered.

An aesthetic of urban form in small towns as posited in *Easy On, Easy Off* is such an elusive concept that few books or writers address it. Of course, most everyone has his or her favorite picturesque small town, but we usually admire these fortunate examples for their nostalgic qualities associated with either tourism or connections to one's own past. Outside the United States, I have three especially favorite towns because they encapsulate everything that I study and write about: Evoramonte, Portugal, because of its setting; Sante Fe de Antioquia, Colombia, because of the fresh food stalls around its plaza; and the most pristine and complete example, Pienza, Italy, because it has a delightful hotel in a convent. Within the United State, my favorite towns are included in my first book, *East 40 Degrees,* and this, my second book, *Easy On, Easy Off,* although I am always searching for that next town that will be the most representative and a complete work of art. These reasons, while universal, are not the foundations for an aesthetic theory. To find this theory, one needs instead to turn back to the 1950s and 1960s and the rediscovery of city cores and the reaction against urban renewal by architectural theorists such as Aldo Rossi in his brilliant book *The Architecture of the City.* Even though it was written thirty years ago, Rossi's emphasis on the importance of the public realm and his concerned critique of the destruction of cities still resonates today. Successful urban form for Rossi has two components: a background fabric of residential neighborhoods that give context to the episodes of grand spaces or monumental buildings. This contextual relationship is now well understood in historic city cores and is applicable, as well, to even the smallest towns. The courthouse-square town of Moultrie, Georgia, discussed in chapter 4 is the best example, for the entire town provides the context for the dramatic setting of the courthouse. The destruction of this fabric or background texture is one of the greatest threats to any town's aesthetic completeness.

Edmund Bacon's classic book *Design of Cities* should be read for his clear discussion of the awareness of space as an urban experience. Using beautiful illustrations and drawings, Bacon writes passionately about urban space, "The basic ingredient of architectural design consists of two elements, mass and space."[1] While both Rossi's and Bacon's books are about large cities, their discussions and ideas about urbanism, urban form, and the beauty of urban space can be easily translated to an aesthetic of urban form in small towns. The principles of the formation of space and the components of form in cities and towns are similar, only at different scales.

Alan Jacobs's wonderful book *Great Streets* is still the best book about the role of streets in forming our cities' public spaces. The book's drawings of street sections and diagrams including figure-ground studies are invaluable for an understanding of civic space. *Easy On, Easy Off* shares Jacobs's emphasis on civic streets and squares. Although Jacobs, like Rossi and Bacon, writes primarily about cities, his discussions and drawings are easily interpolated to the small scale and dimensions of towns. The main street of tiny Locke, California, for example, hardly qualifies as a major boulevard, yet the intimate scale of its two-storied street contrasts dramatically with the parallel spaces of the raised levees along the Sacramento River. Other small towns such as Webster, Massachusetts, and Globe, Arizona, have equally pedestrian-scaled street spaces that form the most important component of their downtowns. The derelict main buildings of Clifton, Arizona, still function as consistent urban elevations; their deeply recessed stone bases capped by thick brick pilasters and finely detailed window and cornice bands enclose the street along both sides.

Two excellent books by Spiro Kostof are good general primers for anyone with an interest in the history of urban form. *The City Assembled: The Elements of Urban Form through History* and *The City Shaped: Urban Patterns and Meaning through History* deal mostly with great cities around the world, yet his writings are applicable to any scale of urban form, as he reminds us that "urban form is never innocent of social context."[2]

Rossi, Bacon, Jacobs, and Kostof present a strong argument for both the aesthetics and beauty of urban form. It is telling when such arguments must be made at all, for it should be so obvious that our cities are wonderful works of art. If our well-known and beloved cities suffer from neglect and abandonment, then reversing the destruction of our small towns seems even more difficult. Growing suburbanism across the United States and around the world at the expense of other forms of smaller, rural settlements is not necessarily a worthy goal of development. We should encourage many kinds of settlements. An inclusive urbanism that feeds and nourishes the human spirit at many scales should be our aspiration. I do not believe any of these four authors would have disagreed in spite of their emphasis on great cities.

1. Bacon, *Design of Cities*, 15.
2. Kostof, *City Assembled*, 8.

The concept of emergence is introduced in *Easy On, Easy Off* with a quote from *The Immense Journey* by Loren Eiseley. Professor Eiseley was an anthropologist at the University of Pennsylvania. I first heard him speak in a class taught by the influential landscape architect Ian McHarg in the early 1960s. In fact, a lecture given by Loren Eiseley in 1961 is referenced in McHarg's seminal book, *Design with Nature.* Loren Eiseley was a profound thinker with a beautiful writing style; all of his books, not just *The Immense Journey,* should be read. Emergence as a way of explaining the world has become popular once again among a generation of scholars and scientists especially in the fields of evolution and computer science. The idea that towns have emergent qualities across a region is my own discovery. Two studies in *Easy On, Easy Off* deserve to be carried further: the spacing and urban form of courthouse-square towns of Georgia and farm communities of Nebraska.

J. B. Jackson, a prolific author on the American landscape, wrote several greatly admired books: *Discovering the Vernacular Landscape; The Necessity for Ruins and Other Topics;* and *A Sense of Place, a Sense of Time. Easy On, Easy Off,* like most books on America's cultural landscapes, owes its emphasis on field observation to the writings of J. B. Jackson. Jackson's works and all these aforementioned books give a general theoretical context to *Easy On, Easy Off;* all contributed to the broad themes of the beauty of urbanism and the elegance of emerging settlement patterns whose close relationship to geography influenced their form.

One seminal book does address aspects of America's settlements on a continental basis. John W. Reps's remarkable and extensive *The Making of Urban America* still remains the definitive work on urban growth in the United States. Reps surveys the development of cities from the colonial period to the early twentieth century. Unlike Rossi or Bacon, both of whom were architects, Reps is a historian of planning. As suggested by his book's subtitle, *A History of City Planning in the United States,* he writes mainly about the development of plans and not about urban spaces. He touches occasionally upon an aesthetic of plans but mostly concentrates on an exhaustive historical exploration of city planning. His categories of regions fascinatingly follow the ethnic origins of America's settlements. European—by which he means primarily English, Spanish, and French—planning dominated the early years of colonial cities. He then shifts to typologies such as baroque, gridiron, or railroad towns.

Reps's focus on the diversity of American settlements bolsters one of the main theses of *Easy On, Easy Off*: America's variety of peoples from around the globe contributed to its variety of urban forms, and from these many differences comes the rich diversity of this country's small towns. *The Making of Urban America* has a wonderful essay, "Notes on Cartographic Research Methods." The passage of fifty years since the publication of *The Making of Urban America* has not diminished its relevance.

John Reps has written many other books on specific regions of the United States. His *Tidewater Towns: City Planning in Colonial Virginia and Maryland* addresses the major cities of Annapolis, Williamsburg, Richmond, and Baltimore, as well as several small communities. He writes extensively about the placement of towns—why they are situated in specific topographic settings. Well illustrated with maps and drawings, *Tidewater Towns* is a comprehensive study of early American planning. Another book by Reps, *The Forgotten Frontier: Urban Planning in the American West before 1890,* deals with both the specifics of western prairie towns and the grander discussion of the settlement of the West. By "West," Reps includes Texas and the Great Plains and areas to the Pacific Ocean. This small book still remains one of the best studies of the influence of the westward spread of railroads on towns of the Great Plains. It makes a good companion to *Easy On, Easy Off*'s chapter on Nebraska towns. Unlike Reps, however, I argue that railroad gridiron towns are not inherently dull, but rather contain one of America's iconic spaces where the rail tracks transect a town's streets.

Bill Hubbard Jr.'s recently published *American Boundaries: The Nation, the States, the Rectangular Survey* is a most important and readable addition to the literature of America's development. Hubbard writes about the history of the cadastral survey of the entire continent. The book is much more than just a history of surveys, for the study of the acquisition and division of states is, as well, a detailed history of the United States. One would be well advised to read Hubbard's book together with the map of "The United States and territories, showing the extent of public surveys, 1867," prepared under the direction of Jos. S. Wilson that is discussed in chapter 5 of *Easy On, Easy Off.* Hubbard's book and Wilson's map together present the logic behind America's westward expansion; their correlation offers a perfect exercise in cartographic discovery.

I discovered Wilson's map inadvertently on a visit to the Library of Congress map collection. It was displayed on a wall as part of a continuously changing exhibition of maps. Twenty-eight by fifty-four inches, Wilson's map is exquisitely drawn by the draftsman Joseph Gorlinski. It summarizes an important moment in America's history and has yet to be published.

This Remarkable Continent: An Atlas of United States and Canadian Society and Cultures, edited by John Rooney, Wilbur Zelinsky, and Dean R. Louder, contains extensive discussions of the cultural differences across the North American continent. Much information on regionalism is presented graphically through diagrams, charts, or tables. It holds a wealth of data that emphasize the diversity of America and Canada. As a comprehensive statistical companion to *Easy On, East Off,* it makes fascinating reading.

The research for *Easy On, Easy Off* presented another difficulty that is perhaps endemic to any broad comparative study of issues that spans the entire United States. Research libraries, depositories of archival materials, and maps are all organized by state. There are fifty states, fifty state archives, fifty state historical societies, all separate and unconnected. These discrete state entities reflect the federalized way we view America that conditions how we collect and organize historical resources. While *Easy On, Easy Off* is divided into five regional sections, each section does explore an area within a specific state, with the exception of the chapter on New England mill towns. Because of the small dimensions of the study area at the juncture of Massachusetts, Connecticut, and Rhode Island, by necessity this section on mills and watersheds covers three states. The segregation of our country into information that is available mainly state-by-state does raise some interesting questions about our regional boundaries and regionalism generally. The towns of Nebraska, Georgia, and New England could all be considered examples of three different regional typologies, yet both the center and the outer boundaries of each region are difficult to determine. Are they ecological units or cultural units? For example, Nebraska is part of the Great Plains; southern Georgia is a small segment of the wire grass ecology; and New England is bounded by the Piedmont coastal plain. The settlements of each of these areas are cultural constructs that spread across a broad region that is not defined by state boundaries. *Easy On, Easy Off* only touches upon this fascinating possible study, yet there seem to be no authors who have written about the disparate urban typologies characteristic of America's distinctive regionalism.

The many state repositories are, however, each wonderfully organized and supportive of their collections. In fact, I found these state libraries and archives remarkable, not only for their wealth of information but also for their staffs' helpful willingness to share. Because of this state-specific organization, there are excellent studies of towns within individual states. An exceptionally beautiful book, *The Plazas of New Mexico* edited by Chris Wilson and Stefanos Polyzoides, gives a thorough explanation of the histories of plaza towns in New Mexico and their Hispanic origins through copious photographs and drawings. Figure-grounds, plaza sections, and urban plans throughout the book permit a close reading of the spaces of these small towns. *The Plazas of New Mexico* has a very detailed appendix on comparative figure-grounds and what they tell us. As a study in urban history and a unique typology of urban form, *The Plazas of New Mexico* provides an important recent addition to the literature on small towns.

A valuable companion to Wilson and Polyzoides's book is Elizabeth Barlow Rogers's *Learning Las Vegas: Portrait of a Northern New Mexico Place.* Las Vegas, New Mexico, is one of the plaza towns discussed in *The Plazas of New Mexico.* Rogers's poignant in-depth study and haunting photographs of the residents of Las Vegas is a fitting reminder of Kostof's admonition that urban form can never be studied separately from its inhabitants.

Another detailed study of the social history of domestic life in small towns is Alison Hoagland's *Mine Towns: Buildings for Workers in Michigan's Copper Country.*

Hoagland focuses on copper mining towns in the Keweenaw Peninsula of Michigan. Unlike in other books about social history, Hoagland uses the built form of the towns, their houses and communal structures, rather than only written documents, to interpolate the conflicts between workers and management.

Atlante del Veneto, edited by Franco Posocco, is an atlas of uniquely drawn urban plans and the most unbelievably detailed aerial photographs of small towns in Italy's Piedmont. The book's format is simple: full-page plans, each drawn with a standard graphic template, and, on the opposite page, an aerial photograph of a smaller portion of the town's plan. The text is in Italian, but the plans and photographs capture such a wealth of information about urban form that the book should be studied as a primer on urban spaces. These are some of the most beautiful small towns in the world. As examples of urban form, they have no equal. *Atlante del Veneto* elegantly captures the beauty of these places. A close reading of its illustrations will convince students of settlements that there is indeed an aesthetic of urban form of astounding variety and value.

Several books are of interest for their applicability to histories of each of the five regions discussed in *Easy On, Easy Off.* These books are not definitive studies of towns or settlements but rather offer insights into unique aspects of our culture that ultimately influenced towns and even cities. I could easily expand this list to include most of my bibliography, but I choose a few examples to illustrate the decidedly peripatetic paths of my research. The lack of titles specifically about towns and town development necessitated such wide-ranging searches.

In 1885, the United States Census Office produced a remarkable document that surveyed water power across the entire country: *Statistics of Power and Machinery Employed in Manufactures: Reports of the Water Power of the United States.* This dense volume makes fascinating reading about mills, rivers, and the extensive industrial complexity of the United States just after the Civil War. It was the best and most comprehensive primary source for *Easy On, Easy Off*'s discussions of mills in Massachusetts, Connecticut, and Rhode Island. Because most nineteenth-century water-powered industries were located in New England, the 1885 volume concentrates on this region. Filled with charts and tables, it also has detailed and readable summaries. The first book in Louis C. Hunter's excellent three-volume *A History of Industrial Power in the United States, 1780–1930* draws heavily from the 1885 Census Office report but also covers the nineteenth-century change from water power to steam. *The Run of the Mill: A Pictorial Narrative of the Expansion, Dominion, Decline and Enduring Impact of the New England Textile Industry* by Steve Dunwell contains beautiful photographs along with clear explanations of the economic forces that caused the demise of New England mills. Dunwell has continued his career as an exceptional photographer of New England cultural landscapes. His professional website (stevedunwell.com) contains very beautiful and evocative photographs of old New England mills and the people who worked in them.

To understand the influence and importance of Georgia's local political structures on national events—especially the struggle for civil rights—Robert A. Caro's magisterial *Master of the Senate: The Years of Lyndon Johnson* makes for compelling reading.

Robert B. Outland's accessible book *Tapping the Pines: The Naval Stores Industry in the American South* gives a history of the naval stores industry in the South and the causes for the demise of the longleaf pine forests. This book and Lawrence S. Early's *Looking for Longleaf: The Fall and Rise of an American Forest* helped solve the mystery of the consistent late-nineteenth-century construction dates of all Georgia's courthouses erected below the fall line as discussed in chapter 4.

Walter Prescott Webb's classic *The Great Plains* is essential reading for anyone interested in the history of this extensive ecosystem that covers a third of our continent. While the book was written over eighty years ago, Webb presciently foretells a future of water and land degradation that today threatens America's agriculture future. Published more recently, Paul A. Johnsgard's *The Nature of Nebraska: Ecology and Biodiversity* describes the incredible biodiversity of the Great Plains. Reading his chapter 5, "Borne on the Wind," inspired me to construct the map of hydrological patterns in my chapter 5. His book has an extensive and accessible bibliography. The weeks I spent driving the section line roads of Nebraska caused me to reflect on Johnsgard's writings and the erasure of Nebraska's ecosystem. Coupled with my experience driving across Georgia's decimated longleaf pine forests, these reflections completely biased my conclusions in *Easy On, Easy Off* about the connection between settlement growth and environmental depletion. My studies and readings about California's Central Valley water problems reinforced my bleak environmental outlook that lies beneath the surface in *Easy On, Easy Off.*

Several individual state governments have produced historical atlases about their particular state. Georgia and Massachusetts both have comprehensively gathered information on all aspects of their individual state's development. The beautifully illustrated *Historical Atlas of California* by Derek Hayes contains an outstanding collection of historical maps arranged chronologically. More than just a compilation of data, Hayes's book is a primer on using maps to decipher the past. David J. Wishart's the *Encyclopedia of the Great Plains* is an exception to the state-by-state treatment of information. This amazingly comprehensive book covers all aspects of the ecological area defined as the Great Plains. Although such a region's boundaries are open to interpretation, Wishart covers the changing history of America's largest and most complex ecosystems.

An awareness of a region's geology is essential to understanding both its history and its settlements. Anyone wishing to gather geological information about a region should begin with Antony Orme's *The Physical Geography of North*

America. This book starts with an overall history of North America's geology, climatic zones, and hydrological and weathering processes. Each geological region of the United States is given a separate chapter in "Regional Environments." A different expert deals with each region and adds exhaustive bibliographic notes. I often followed these bibliographic notes to more detailed discussions of regional particularities. Most state archives have geological maps at the state or county scale that provide more corroboration of the broader discussions in Orme's book. For example, Orme's encyclopedic book explained the fractured landscape zone between the uplifted Colorado Plateau and the desert below that I first noticed on my drive along Route 60 in Arizona. I would also strongly recommend that anyone exploring the geology of North America purchase a readily available plastic three-dimension relief map of the region of interest. These beautifully colored maps made by Hubbard Scientific are the best source for information about our earth's surface. I often write with such a map propped up on my desk for reference.

Little has been written about towns such as Holbrook, Arizona, but there is a plethora of literature about the history of Route 66. Because of the fascination for American pop culture, many books detail the strip of Route 66 that remains as Holbrook's main street. Michael Wallis's *Route 66: The Mother Road* has especially comprehensive illustrations and maps.

Because copper mining generates so many hazardous byproducts, a certain amount of secrecy surrounds the industry. *Copper for America: The United States Copper Industry from Colonial Times to the 1990s* by Charles K. Hyde provides a comprehensive history of the copper industry from colonial times to the 1990s. For a more contradictory and environmentally conscious narrative, Bill Carter's *Boom, Bust, Boom: A Story about Copper, the Metal That Runs the World* tells the story of copper mining's irrevocable damage to the earth.

Bitter melon is the translation of a common Chinese expression that means to suffer the harsh conditions of one's fate. The phrase aptly sums up the Chinese experience in nineteenth-century California. The particular melon *Momordica charantia* is a type of squash or gourd native to Asia used to give bitterness to cooking. In their book *Bitter Melon: Inside America's Last Rural Chinese Town* about Locke, California, Jeff Gillenkirk and James Motlow use oral histories and photographs to capture the poignant life stories of the last Chinese inhabitants of this beautiful small town.

Two books explain California's unimaginably complex water problems. The California Natural History Guide *Introduction to Water in California* by David Carle is the clearest study of this unsolvable ecological disaster. Using diagrams and many illustrations, Carle explains all the intricacies of the differing stakeholders across California. A wonderfully conceived and illustrated book, *Delta Primer: A Field Guide to the California Delta* by Jane Wolff covers the same material as David

Carle but with beautiful and original graphics, many drawn by Wolff. *Delta Primer* is an exquisite book that serves as an example of writing and scholarship for all interested in the environment.

I used vintage gasoline company highway maps for their valuable information about road networks before the construction of the interstates. With the old maps as a base, I have drawn the interstate right-of-ways over the underlying local roads and included these composite maps in each section of the book. These colorful maps help visualize which intersecting local roads would become the armature for off-ramp developments and also illustrate the disruption the interstates caused to all the roads they severed. While these maps are available on eBay for a few dollars, the Road Map Collectors Association maintains a website (roadmaps.org) with catalogs of maps by oil company, state, and year. The RMCA also hosts annual map fairs where members browse thousands of maps for trade or sale.

Several times over the ten years of writing *Easy On, Easy Off* I made false starts. I discarded entire regions of Nebraska and Arizona when my field explorations and writings were not substantiated by the literature. I made the mistake of concentrating on Georgia's towns above the fall line, only to discover the longleaf forest never existed that far north. I dropped my studies of mining towns in California's Sierras the moment I entered into Locke's little street. Only when a hypothesis emerged from my observations did I turn to readings to better understand the history, geology, or politics of a place. This approach is more clearly like that of design rather than traditional scholarship. In his brilliant study *Building Community* about design education, Ernest Boyer suggests the imperatives behind an integration of knowledge that connects related disciplines such as architecture, landscape architecture, and urban design with other areas of study such as the liberal arts. Design is about the discovery of knowledge and the interconnectedness of the world. It is the "ability to synthesize social, environmental, technical and aesthetic considerations into a cohesive and unified entity and includes an understanding of process and product."[3] I believe that like writing, "design should be about making knowledge, not just consuming it."[4]

3. Boyer and Mitgang, *Building Community,* 73.

4. As quoted from Alan Plattus, associate dean of Yale University, School of Architecture. Boyer and Mitgang, *Building Community,* 73.

BIBLIOGRAPHY

Agee, James. *Selected Journalism.* Edited by Paul Ashdown. Knoxville: University of Tennessee Press, 1985.

Alabama Highway Research. *HPR Report No. 23: 1966 Photographic Comparison of Land Use Areas Adjacent to Interchange Limits of the Interstate System.* Montgomery: State of Alabama Highway Department, 1966.

———. *HPR Report No. 30: 1967 Photographic Comparison of Land Use Areas Adjacent to Interchange Limits of the Interstate System.* Montgomery: State of Alabama Highway Department, 1967.

———. *HPR Report No 46: 1969 Photographic Comparison of Land Use Areas Adjacent to Interchange Limits of the Interstate System.* Montgomery: State of Alabama Highway Department, 1969.

Andrist, Ralph K. *The Long Death: The Last Days of the Plains Indian.* New York: Macmillan, 1964.

Appleyard, Donald, Kevin Lynch, and John R. Myer. *The View from the Road.* Cambridge, MA: MIT Press, 1964.

Association County Commissioners of Georgia. *Foundations of Government: The Georgia Counties.* Edited by Kay R. Morgareidge. Atlanta: Association County Commissioners of Georgia, Hill R. Healan, Publisher, 1976.

Bacon, Edmund. *Design of Cities.* New York: Viking Press, 1967.

Bailey, Lynn R. *Bisbee: Queen of the Copper Camps.* Tucson, AZ: Westernlore Press, 2002.

Baltensperger, Bradley H. *Nebraska: A Geography.* Boulder, CO: Westview Press, 1985.

Bartels, Michael M., and James J. Reisdorff. *Ghost Railroads of Nebraska—A Pictorial.* David City, NE: South Platte Press, 2002.

Bartram, William. *Bartram Travels: Travels through North & South Carolina, East & West Florida, the Cherokee county, the extensive territories of the Muscogulges, or Creek confederacy, and the country of the Chactaws.* Philadelphia: James & Johnson, 1791.

———. *Travels and Other Writings.* Ed. Thomas P. Slaughter. New York: Library of America, 1996.

Bel Geddes, Norman. *Magic Motorways.* New York: American Book-Stratford Press, 1940.

Bellerose, Robert R. *Images of America: Woonsocket.* Charleston, SC: Arcadia, 1997.

Bender, Thomas. *Toward an Urban Vision: Ideas and Institutions in Nineteenth-Century America.* Louisville: University of Kentucky Press, 1975.

Blake, Peter. *God's Own Junkyard: The Planned Deterioration of America's Landscape.* New York: Holt, Rinehart and Winston, 1964.

Boyer, Ernest L., and Lee D. Mitgang. *Building Community: A New Future for Architectural Education and Practice.* Princeton, NJ: Carnegie Foundation for the Advancement of Teaching, 1996.

Brands, H. W. *The Age of Gold: The California Gold Rush and the New American Dream.* New York: Doubleday, 2002.

Bryant, Pat. *Georgia Counties: Their Changing Boundaries.* 2nd ed., revised by Ingrid Shields. Atlanta: State Printing Office, 1983.

Buisseret, David, ed. *From Sea Charts to Satellite Images: Interpreting North American History through Maps.* Chicago: University of Chicago Press, 1990.

Burton, Anthony. *The Rise and Fall of King Cotton.* London: British Broadcasting Corporation, 1984.

Cadle, Farris W. *Georgia Land Surveying History and Law.* Athens: University of Georgia Press, 1991.

Canty, J. Michael, and Michael N. Greeley, eds. *History of Mining in Arizona*. 3 vols. Tucson, AZ: Mining Foundation of the Southwest, 1999.

Capra, Fritjof. *The Hidden Connections: Integrating the Biological, Cognitive, and Social Dimensions of Life into a Science of Sustainability.* New York: Doubleday, 2002.

Carle, David. *Introduction to Water in California.* California Natural History Guides no. 76. Berkeley: University of California Press, 2004.

———. *Water and the California Dream: Choices for the New Millennium.* San Francisco: Sierra Club Books, 2000.

Caro, Robert A. *Master of the Senate: The Years of Lyndon Johnson.* New York: Alfred A. Knopf, 2002.

Carter, Bill. *Boom, Bust, Boom: A Story about Copper, the Metal That Runs the World.* New York: Scribner, 2112.

Caughey, John, and Norris Hundley Jr. *California: History of a Remarkable State.* Englewood Cliffs, NJ: Prentice-Hall, 1982.

Chalfant, William Y. *Cheyennes and Horse Soldiers.* Norman: University of Oklahoma Press, 1989.

Chapman, S. D. *The Cotton Industry in the Industrial Revolution.* London: Macmillan, 1972.

Chen, Yong. *Chinese San Francisco, 1850–1943: A Trans-Pacific Community.* Stanford: Stanford University Press, 2000.

Chronic, Halka. *Roadside Geology of Arizona.* Missoula, MT: Mountain Press, 1983.

Cleland, Robert Glass, and Osgood Hardy. *March of Industry.* Los Angeles: Powell, 1929.

Cohen, Paul E. *Mapping the West: America's Westward Movement, 1524–1890.* New York: Rizzoli, 2002.

Conzen, Michael P., ed. *The Making of the American Landscape.* New York: Routledge, 1994.

Cook, Sherburne F. *The Conflict between the California Indian and White Civilization.* Berkeley: University of California Press, 1976.

Coolidge, John. *Mill and Mansion: A Study of Architecture and Society in Lowell, Massachusetts, 1820–1865.* New York: Columbia University Press, 1942.

Coolidge, Mary Roberts. *Chinese Immigration.* Taipei: Ch'eng-Wen, 1968.

Corbett, Christopher. *The Poker Bride: The First Chinese in the Wild West.* New York: Atlantic Monthly Press, 2010.

Cronon, William. *Nature's Metropolis: Chicago and the Great West.* New York: W. W. Norton, 1991.

Crouch, Dora, Daniel J. Garr, and Axel I. Mundigo. *Spanish City Planning in North America.* Cambridge, MA: MIT Press, 1982.

Curran, H. Allen, Drew M. Young II, Philip S. Justus, and John B. Garver Jr. *Atlas of Landforms.* 3rd ed. New York: John Wiley, 1984.

Danson, Edwin. *Drawing the Line: How Mason and Dixon Surveyed the Most Famous Border in America.* New York: John Wiley, 2001.

Darwin, Charles. *The Origin of Species.* Oxford: Oxford University Press, 1996.

Dasmann, Raymond F. *The Destruction of California.* New York: Macmillan, 1965.

Dellinger, Matt. *Interstate 69: The Unfinished History of the Last Great American Highway.* New York: Scribner, 2010.

Dick, Everett. *The Lure of the Land: A Social History of the Public Lands from the Articles of Confederation to the New Deal.* Lincoln: University of Nebraska Press, 1970.

———. *The Sod-House Frontier: Everyday Life in Kansas, Nebraska and Dakota, 1854–1890.* Lincoln, NE: Johnsen, 1954.

Doering, David J. *Last Train to Wymore: The Story of a Prairie Local.* David City, NE: South Platte Press, 2008.

Dunwell, Steve. *The Run of the Mill: A Pictorial Narrative of the Expansion, Dominion, Decline and Enduring Impact of the New England Textile Industry.* Boston: David R. Godine, 1978.

Early, Lawrence S. *Looking for Longleaf: The Fall and Rise of an American Forest.* Chapel Hill: University of North Carolina Press, 2004.

Easterling, Keller. *Organization Space: Landscapes, Highways, and Houses in America.* Cambridge, MA: MIT, 1999.

Egan, Timothy. *The Worst Hard Time.* New York: Houghton Mifflin, 2006.

Ehrenberg, Ralph E., ed. *Pattern and Process: Research in Historical Geography.* Washington, DC: Howard University Press, 1975.

Eiseley, Loren C. *The Immense Journey.* New York: Random House, 1957.

Fenneman, Nevin M. *Physiography of the Eastern United States*. New York: McGraw-Hill, 1938.

Fitzpatrick, Lilian. *Nebraska Place-Names*. Lincoln: University of Nebraska Press, 1960.

Fire Insurance Maps in the Library of Congress. Washington, DC: Library of Congress, 1981.

Foner, Eric. *Forever Free: The Story of Emancipation and Reconstruction*. New York: Alfred A. Knopf, 2005.

Frazier, Ian. *Great Plains*. New York: Penguin, 1989.

Georgia Writers' Project. *Georgia: A Guide to Its Towns and Countryside*. American Guide series. Athens: University of Georgia Press, 1946.

Gerstle, Cary. *Working-Class Americanism: The Politics of Labor in a Textile City, 1914–1960*. Cambridge: Cambridge University Press, 1989.

Gillenkirk, Jeff, and James Motlow. *Bitter Melon: Inside America's Last Rural Chinese Town*. 3rd ed. Berkeley, CA: Heyday Books, 1997.

Girouard, Mark. *Cities & People: A Social and Architectural History*. New Haven, CT: Yale University Press, 1985.

———. *The English Town: A History of Urban Life*. New Haven, CT: Yale University Press, 1990.

Goff, John H. *Placenames of Georgia: Essays of John H. Goff*. Edited by Francis Lee Utley and Marion R. Hemperley. Athens: University of Georgia Press, 1975.

Gohlke, Frank. *Measure of Emptiness: Grain Elevators in the American Landscape*. Baltimore: Johns Hopkins University Press, 1992.

Green, Hardy. *The Company Town: The Industrial Edens and Satanic Mills That Shaped the American Economy*. New York: Basic Books, 2010.

Greer, Scott. *The Emerging City: Myth and Reality*. New Brunswick, NJ: Transaction, 1999. First published 1962 by Free Press.

Haak, Wilbur A., and Lynn F. Haak. *Globe*. Images of America series. Charleston, SC: Arcadia, 2008.

Hall, Captain Basil. *Travels in North America in the Years 1827 and 1828*. Edinburgh: Cadell, 1829.

Halprin, Lawrence. *Freeways*. New York: Reinhold, 1966.

Hansen, Gladys C., ed. *The Chinese in California: A Brief Bibliographic History*. Annotated by William F. Heintz. Portland, OR: Richard Abel, 1970.

Harden, Deborah R. *California Geology*. Upper Saddle River, NJ: Prentice-Hall, 1998.

Harris, J. William. *The Making of the American South: A Short History, 1500–1877*. Oxford: Blackwell, 2006.

Harper, Roland M. "Development of Agriculture in Lower Georgia from 1850 to 1880." *Georgia Historical Quarterly* 6, no. 2 (June 1922): 97–121.

———. "Development of Agriculture in Lower Georgia from 1890 to 1920 with a Summary of the Whole State from 1850 to 1920." *Georgia Historical Quarterly* 6, no. 4 (December 1922): 323–54.

Hart, John. *San Francisco Bay: Portrait of an Estuary.* Berkeley: University of California Press, 2003.

Hayes, Derek. *Historical Atlas of California.* Berkeley: University of California Press, 2007.

Heat-Moon, William Least. *Blue Highways: A Journey into America.* Boston: Houghton Mifflin, 1991.

Hepburn, Mary A. *County Government in Georgia.* Athens: Institute of Government, University of Georgia, 1976.

Hills, Richard L. *Power in the Industrial Revolution.* New York: Augustus M. Kelly, 1970.

Hinkley, Jim. *Backroads of Arizona: Your Guide to Arizona's Most Scenic Backroad Adventures.* Minneapolis: Voyageur Press, 2006.

Hitchcock, Henry-Russell, Jr. *Rhode Island Architecture.* Providence: Rhode Island Museum Press, 1939.

Hoagland, Alison K. *Mine Towns: Buildings for Workers in Michigan's Copper Country.* Minneapolis: University of Minnesota Press, 2010.

Hoexter, Corinne K. *From Canton to California: The Epic of Chinese Immigration.* New York: Four Winds Press, 1976.

Hubbard, Bill, Jr. *American Boundaries: The Nation, the States, the Rectangular Survey.* Chicago: University of Chicago Press, 2009.

Hudson, John C. *Plains Country Towns.* Minneapolis: University of Minnesota Press, 1985.

Hughes, Melvin Clyde. *County Government in Georgia.* Athens: University of Georgia Press, 1944.

Hunter, Louis C. *A History of Industrial Power in the United States, 1780–1930.* Vol. 1: *Waterpower in the Century of the Steam Engine.* Charlottesville: University Press of Virginia, 1979.

Hyde, Charles K. *Copper for America: The United States Copper Industry from Colonial Times to the 1990s.* Tucson: University of Arizona Press, 1998.

Isenberg, Alison. *Downtown America: A History of the Place and the People Who Made It.* Chicago: University of Chicago Press, 2004.

Jackson, John Brinckerhoff. *Discovering the Vernacular Landscape.* New Haven, CT: Yale University Press, 1984.

———. *The Necessity for Ruins and Other Topics.* Amherst: University of Massachusetts Press, 1980.

———. *A Sense of Place, a Sense of Time.* New Haven, CT: Yale University Press, 1994.

Jacobs, Alan B. *Great Streets.* Cambridge, MA: MIT Press, 1993.

Jakle, John A., and Keith A. Sculle. *The Gas Station in America.* Baltimore: Johns Hopkins University Press, 1994.

———. *Fast Food: Roadside Restaurants in the Automobile Age.* Baltimore: Johns Hopkins University Press, 1999.

Jakle, John A., Keith A. Sculle, and Jefferson S. Rogers. *The Motel in America.* Baltimore:

Johns Hopkins University Press, 1996.

Jeffery, Blake R., Tanis J. Salant, and Alan L. Boroshok. *County Government Structure: A State by State Report.* Washington, DC: National Association of Counties, 1989.

Jellicoe, G. A. *Motopia: A Study in the Evolution of Urban Landscape.* London: Studio Books, 1961.

Johnsgard, Paul A. *The Nature of Nebraska: Ecology and Biodiversity.* Lincoln: University of Nebraska Press, 2001.

Johnson, Hildegard Binder. *Order upon the Land: The Rectangular Land Survey and the Upper Mississippi Country.* New York: Oxford University Press, 1976.

Johnson, Stephen, Gerald Haslam, and Robert Dawson. *The Great Central Valley: California's Heartland.* Berkeley: University of California Press, 1993.

Kammen, Michael. *Mystic Chords of Memory: The Transformation of Tradition in American Culture.* New York: Knopf, 1991.

Kaszynski, William. *The American Highway: The History and Culture of Roads in the United States.* Jefferson, NC: McFarland, 2000.

Kistler, Richard C. *Burlington Route: The Wymore Story.* David City, NE: South Platte Press, 2001.

Kostof, Spiro. *The City Assembled: The Elements of Urban Form through History.* Boston: Bulfinch Press, 1992.

———. *The City Shaped: Urban Patterns and Meanings through History.* Boston: Bulfinch Press, 1991.

Krell, Dorothy, ed. *The California Missions: A Pictorial History.* Menlo Park, CA: Sunset Books, 1979.

Leach, William. *Land of Desire: Merchants, Power, and the Rise of a New American Culture.* New York: Vintage Books, 1994.

Leavitt, Helen. *Superhighway—Superhoax.* Garden City, NY: Doubleday, 1970.

Lemann, Nicholas. *Redemption: The Last Battle of the Civil War.* New York: Farrar, Straus and Giroux, 2006.

Leung, Peter C. Y. *One Day, One Dollar: The Chinese Farming Experience in the Sacramento River Delta, California.* Taipei: Liberal Arts Press, 1994.

Levy, Jacques. *Cesar Chavez: Autobiography of La Causa.* New York: Norton, 1975.

Lewis, Oscar. *Sutter's Fort: Gateway to the Gold Fields.* Englewood Cliffs, NJ: Prentice-Hall, 1966.

Lewis, Tom. *Divided Highways: Building the Interstate Highways, Transforming American Life.* New York: Penguin Books, 1999.

Li, Lillian M., Alison J. Dray-Novey, and Haili Kong. *Beijing: From Imperial Capital to Olympic City.* New York: Palgrave Macmillan, 2007.

Liebs, Chester H. *Main Street to Miracle Mile: American Roadside Architecture.* Baltimore: Johns Hopkins University Press, 1995.

Lindgren, Waldemar. *The Copper Deposits of the Clifton-Morenci District, Arizona.* Washington, DC: Government Printing Office, 1905.

Linklater, Andro. *Measuring America: How the United States Was Shaped by the Greatest Land Sale in History.* New York: Plume, 2003.

Lobell, John. *Between Silence and Light: Spirit in the Architecture of Louis I. Kahn.* Boston: Shambhala, 1985.

Luebke, Frederick C. *Nebraska: An Illustrated History.* Lincoln: University of Nebraska Press, 1995.

Macaulay, David. *Mill.* New York: Houghton Mifflin, 1983.

Mahar, Lisa. *American Signs: Form and Meaning on Route 66.* New York: Monacelli Press, 2002.

Maher, Harmon D., Jr., with George F. Engelman and Robert D. Shuster. *Roadside Geology of Nebraska.* Missoula, MT: Mountain Press, 2003.

Mann, Ralph. *After the Gold Rush: Society in Grass Valley and Nevada City, California, 1849–1870.* Stanford: Stanford University Press, 1982.

Manning, Richard. *Grasslands: The History, Biology, Politics, and Promise of the American Prairie.* New York: Penguin, 1995.

Mattes, Merrill J. *The Great Platte River Road: The Covered Wagon Mainline via Fort Kearny to Fort Laramie.* Lincoln: University of Nebraska Press, 1969.

McDonald, Thomas A. *California's Chinese Heritage: A Legacy of Places.* Stockton, California: Heritage West Books, 2000.

McHarg, Ian L. *Design with Nature.* New York: Natural History Press, 1969.

McNichols, Dan. *The Roads That Built America: The Incredible Story of the U.S. Interstate System.* New York: Sterling, 2006.

McPhee, John. *Assembling California.* New York: Farrar, Straus and Giroux, 1993.

McWhiney, Grady. *Cracker Culture: Celtic Ways in the Old South.* Tuscaloosa: University of Alabama Press, 1988.

Meinig, D. W., ed. *The Interpretation of Ordinary Landscapes: Geographical Essays.* Oxford: Oxford University Press, 1979.

Moon, Henry. *The Interstate Highway System.* Washington, DC: Association of American Geographers, 1994.

Morisawa, Marie. *Rivers: Form and Process.* London: Longman, 1985.

———. *Streams: Their Dynamics and Morphology.* New York: McGraw-Hill, 1968.

Morris, A. E. J. *History of Urban Form: Before the Industrial Revolutions.* 3rd ed. New York: Prentice-Hall, 1994.

Moulton, Candy. *Roadside History of Nebraska.* Missoula, MT: Mountain Press, 1997.

Mowbray, A. Q. *Road to Ruin.* Philadelphia: J. B. Lippincott, 1969.

Nabhan, Gary Paul, and Caroline Wilson. *Canyons of Color: Utah's Slick Rock Wildlands.* New York: HarperCollins, 1995.

National Association of Counties. *County Government Structure: A State by State Report.* Washington, DC: National Association of Counties, 1989.

National Park Service. *Lowell: The Story of an Industrial City.* Handbook no. 140. Washington, DC: National Park Service, 1992.

Nations, Dale, and Edmund Stump. *Geology of Arizona.* 2nd ed. Dubuque, IA: Kendall/Hunt, 1996.

The Next EXIT: Your Guide to Gas, Food, Lodging, Medical Services, and Retail Stores at Every Interstate Highway Exit! Garden City, UT: Next EXIT, 2001.

Nicoll, Bruce H., and Gilbert M. Savery, eds. *Nebraska: A Pictorial History.* Bicentennial ed. Lincoln: University of Nebraska Press, 1975.

Olmsted, Frederick Law. *The Cotton Kingdom. A Traveller's Observations on Cotton and Slavery in the American Slave States, 1853–1861.* New York: Da Capo Press, 1996.

Olson, James C., and Ronald C. Naugle. *History of Nebraska.* 3rd ed. Lincoln: University of Nebraska Press, 1997.

Orme, Antony R., ed. *The Physical Geography of North America.* Oxford: Oxford University Press, 2002.

Orser, Charles E., Jr. *The Material Basis of the Postbellum Tenant Plantation: Historical Archaeology in the South Carolina Piedmont.* Athens: University of Georgia Press, 1988.

Ottoson, Howard W., ed. *Land Use Policy and Problems in the United States.* Lincoln: University of Nebraska Press, 1963.

Outland, Robert B., III. *Tapping the Pines: The Naval Stores Industry in the American South.* Baton Rouge: Louisiana State University Press, 2004.

Overton, Richard C. *Burlington Route: A History of the Burlington Lines.* New York: Knopf, 1965.

Palmer, Tim. *Stanislaus: The Struggle for a River.* Berkeley: University of California Press, 1982.

Pattison, William D. *Beginnings of the American Rectangular Land Survey System, 1784–1800.* Chicago: University of Chicago Press, 1964.

Posocco, Franco, ed. *Atlante del Veneto: La Forma degli insediamenti urbani di antica origine nella rappresentazione fotografica e cartografica.* Venice: Marsillo, 1991.

Prude, Jonathan. *The Coming of the Industrial Order: Town and Factory Life in Rural Massachusetts, 1810–1860.* Amherst: University of Massachusetts Press, 1983.

Rae, John B., *The American Automobile: A Brief History.* Chicago: University of Chicago Press, 1965.

Reed, G. Walter, and William Ladd Willis. *History of Sacramento County, California: With Biographical Sketches of the Leading Men and Women of the County.* Los Angeles: Historic Record, 1923.

Reps, John W. *Cities of the American West: A History of Frontier Urban Planning.* Princeton, NJ: Princeton University Press, 1979.

———. *Cities of the Mississippi: Nineteenth-Century Images of Urban Development.* Columbia: University of Missouri Press, 1994.

———. *The Forgotten Frontier: Urban Planning in the American West before 1890.* Columbia: University of Missouri Press, 1981.

———. *The Making of Urban America: A History of City Planning in the United States.* Princeton, NJ: Princeton University Press, 1965.

———. *Tidewater Towns: City Planning in Colonial Virginia and Maryland.* Charlottesville: University Press of Virginia, 1972.

Reynolds, Douglas M., and Marjory Myers, eds. *Working in the Blackstone River Valley: Exploring the Heritage of Industrialization.* Woonsocket, RI: Sheahan Printing, 1990.

Reynolds, Terry S. *Stronger Than a Hundred Men: A History of the Vertical Water Wheel.* Baltimore: Johns Hopkins University Press, 1983.

Richards, Leonard L. *The California Gold Rush and the Coming of the Civil War.* New York: Random House, 2007.

Rivard, Paul E. *A New Order of Things: How the Textile Industry Transformed New England.* Hanover, NH: University Press of New England, 2002.

Robinson, W. W. *Land in California: The Story of Mission Lands, Ranchos, Squatters, Mining Claims, Railroad Grants, Land Scrip, Homesteads.* Berkeley: University of California Press, 1948.

Rogers, Elizabeth Barlow. *Learning Las Vegas: Portrait of a Northern New Mexico Place.* Santa Fe: Museum of New Mexico Press, with the Foundation for Landscape Studies, 2013.

Rooney, John, Wilbur Zelinsky, and Dean R. Louder, eds. *This Remarkable Continent: An Atlas of United States and Canadian Society and Cultures.* College Station: Texas A&M Press, 1982.

Rose, Mark H. *Interstate: Express Highway Politics, 1939–1989.* Knoxville: University of Tennessee Press, 1990.

Rosenblum, Jonathan D. *Copper Crucible: How the Arizona Miners' Strike of 1983 Recast Labor-Management Relations in America.* Ithaca, NY: Cornell University Press, 1998.

Rossi, Aldo. *The Architecture of the City.* Cambridge, MA: MIT Press, 1982.

Rupp, Richard A., and Peter R. Townsend. *The Mills at Remington's Run: A Chronological History of the Arkwright Manufacturing Company, 1809–1999.* Greenwich, RI: Meridian Printing, 1999.

Sanders, Brad. *Guide to William Bartram's Travels: Following the Trail of America's First Great Naturalist.* Athens, GA: Fevertree Press, 2002.

Sears, Joan Niles. *The First One Hundred Years of Town Planning in Georgia.* Atlanta: Cherokee, 1979.

Shannon, Fred A. *The Farmer's Last Frontier: Agriculture, 1860–1897.* Vol. 5: *The Economic History of the United States.* New York: Holt, Rinehart and Winston, 1961.

Sheldon, Addison E. *Land Systems and Land Policies in Nebraska.* Lincoln: Nebraska State Historical Society, 1936.

Sheridan, Thomas. *Arizona: A History.* Tucson: University of Arizona Press, 1995.

Sides, Hampton. *Blood and Thunder: An Epic of the American West.* New York: Random House, 2006.

Starr, Kevin. *California: A History.* New York: Modern Library, 2005.

———. *Coast of Dreams: California on the Edge, 1990–2003.* New York: Alfred A. Knopf, 2004.

———. *Endangered Dreams: The Great Depression in California.* New York: Oxford University Press, 1996.

St. Clair, David J. *The Motorization of American Cities.* New York: Praeger, 1986.

Stein, Walter J. *California and the Dust Bowl Migration.* Westport, CT: Greenwood Press, 1973.

Steinberg, Theodore. *Nature Incorporated: Industrialization and the Water of New England.* Cambridge: Cambridge University Press, 1991.

Steiner, Stan. *Fusang: The Chinese Who Built America.* New York: Harper & Row, 1979.

Stewart, Lowell O. *Public Land Surveys: History, Instructions, Methods.* Minneapolis: Meyers Printing, 1976.

Stewart, Mart A. *"What Nature Suffers to Groe": Life, Labor, and Landscape on the Georgia Coast, 1680–1920.* Athens: University of Georgia Press, 1996.

Strasser, Susan. *Satisfaction Guaranteed: The Making of the American Mass Market.* New York: Pantheon Books, 1989.

Sullivan, Buddy, in association with the Georgia Historical Society. *Georgia: A State History.* Charleston, SC: Arcadia, 2003.

Tedlow, Richard S. *New and Improved: The Story of Mass Marketing in America.* New York: Basic Books, 1990.

Thrower, Norman J. W. *Original Survey and Land Subdivision: A Comparative Study of the Form and Effect of Contrasting Cadastral Surveys.* Chicago: Rand McNally, 1966.

Trimble, Marshall. *Arizona: A Cavalcade of History.* Tucson, AZ: Rio Nuevo, 2003.

———. *Roadside History of Arizona.* Missoula, MT: Mountain Press, 1986.

Tucker, Barbara M. *Samuel Slater and the Origins of the American Textile Industry, 1790–1860.* Ithaca, NY: Cornell University Press, 1984.

Tunnard, Christopher, and Boris Puskarev. *Man-Made America: Chaos or Control.* New Haven, CT: Yale University Press, 1963.

U.S. Bureau of Public Roads. *General Location of National System of Interstate Highways Including All Additional Routes at Urban Areas Designated in September, 1955.* Washington, DC: U.S. Government Printing Office, 1955.

U.S. Department of the Interior, Census Office. *Reports of the Water-power of the United States.* Washington, DC: Government Printing Office, 1885.

Usner, Don J. *Sabino's Map: Life in Chimayo's Old Plaza.* Santa Fe: Museum of New Mexico Press, 1995.

Vance, James E., Jr. *The Continuing City: Urban Morphology in Western Civilization.* Baltimore: Johns Hopkins University Press, 1990.

———. *The North American Railroad: Its Origin, Evolution and Geography.* Baltimore: Johns Hopkins University Press, 1995.

Vance, Rupert Bayless. *How the Other Half Is Housed: A Pictorial Record of Subminimum Farm Housing in the South.* Southern Policy Papers no. 4. Chapel Hill: University of North Carolina Press, 1936.

Vanderhill, Burke G., and Frank A. Unger. "Georgia's Crenelated County Boundaries." *West Georgia College Studies in the Social Sciences* 16 (1977): 59–72.

Varney, Phillip. *Arizona Ghost Towns and Mining Camps.* Phoenix: Arizona Department of Transportation, 2000.

Venturi, Robert, Denise Scott Brown, and Steven Izenour. *Learning from Las Vegas: The Forgotten Symbolism of Architectural Form.* Cambridge, MA: MIT Press, 1972.

Walker, Henry P., and Don Bufkin. *Historical Atlas of Arizona.* 2nd ed. Norman: University of Oklahoma Press, 1986.

Walker, Laurence C. *The Southern Forest: A Chronicle.* Austin: University of Texas Press, 1991.

Walker, Laurence C., and Brian P. Oswald. *The Southern Forest: Geography, Ecology, and Silviculture.* Boca Raton, FL: CRC Press, 2000.

Wallace, Anthony F. C. *Rockdale: The Growth of an American Village in the Early Industrial Revolution.* New York: Alfred A. Knopf, 1978.

Wallis, Michael, *Route 66: The Mother Road.* New York: St. Martin's Press, 2001.

Ware, Caroline F. *The Early New England Cotton Manufacture: A Study in Industrial Beginnings.* New York: Houghton Mifflin, 1931.

Webb, Walter Prescott. *The Great Plains.* Boston: Ginn, 1959.

Weeks, J. Devereux. *Inventory of General Home Rule & Revenue Powers of Georgia Counties.* Athens: Carl Vinson Institute of Government, University of Georgia, 1984.

Weeks, J. Devereux, and Paul T. Hardy, eds. *Handbook for Georgia County Commissioners.* 3rd ed. Athens: Carl Vinson Institute of Government, University of Georgia, 1993.

Wetherington, Mark V. *The New South Comes to Wire Grass Georgia, 1860.* Knoxville: University of Tennessee Press, 1994.

White, C. Albert. *A History of the Rectangular Survey System.* Washington, DC: U.S. Government Printing Office, n.d.

Williams, James H., and Douglas Murfield, eds. *Agricultural Atlas of Nebraska.* Lincoln: University of Nebraska Press, 1977.

Williams, John Hoyt. *A Great and Shining Road: The Epic Story of the Transcontinental Railroad.* New York: Times Books, 1988.

Wilson, Chris, and Stefanos Polyzoides, eds. *The Plazas of New Mexico.* San Antonio: Trinity University Press, 2011.

Wilson, Eldred D. *Guidebook 1—Highways of Arizona: U.S. Highway 666.* Arizona Bureau of Mines, bulletin 174. Tucson: University of Arizona Press, 1965.

Wishart, David J., ed. *Encyclopedia of the Great Plains.* Lincoln: University of Nebraska Press, 2004.

Wolff, Jane. *Delta Primer: A Field Guide to the California Delta.* San Francisco: William Stout, 2003.

Wollenberg, Charles, ed. *Ethnic Conflict in California History.* Los Angeles: Tinnon-Brown, 1970.

Yorke, Douglas A., John Margolis, and Eric Baker. *Hitting the Road: The Art of the American Road Map.* San Francisco: Chronicle Books, 1996.

Zevin, Robert Brooke. *The Growth of Manufacturing in Early Nineteenth Century New England.* New York: Arno Press, 1975.

Zimiles, Martha, and Murray Zimiles. *Early American Mills.* New York: Clarkson N. Potter, 1973.

ILLUSTRATION CREDITS

Illustrations not otherwise credited are by the author or from his collection. Photographers/artists/cartographers and drawing/photograph/map numbers are noted parenthetically where identified.

Auburn University Library Map Collection, Auburn, Alabama: page 95

California Department of Conservation, California Geological Survey, Sacramento, California: page 236

California Department of Water Resources, Sacramento, California: page 242

California History Room, California State Library, Sacramento, California: pages 232, 250, 253, 266

Connecticut Historical Society, Hartford, Connecticut: page 65 (John Warner Barber [1798-1885], artist)

Fine Arts Museum of San Francisco, gift of Jerrold and June Kingsley, 1991.32: page xvi

Forest History Society, Durham, North Carolina: page 96 (FHS 3411)

Georgia Archives, Morrow, Georgia: page 101 (RG 3-3-24; Archibald McIntyre, District Surveyor, certified 10 September 1820; Carlton Wellborn, Surveyor General, 1825–1827; District Plats of Survey, Survey Records, Surveyor General); page 107 (top) (Vanishing Georgia Collection [ctm280], Keystone View Company); page 115 (RG 3-3-24; certified 30 October 1819 by Charles McKinnon; Thomas Mitchell, Surveyor General; District Plats of Survey, Survey Records, Surveyor General); page 116 (RG 3-9-66; Amanda Barnett, Topographer; County Maps, Surveyor General); page 118 (RG 3-8-65; Young & Delleker, Sc., in unidentified atlas [21]; Historic Maps, Surveyor General); page 119 (RG 3-8-65; J. H. Young in unidentified atlas [20]; Historic Maps, Surveyor General); page 132 (Vanishing Georgia Collection, Office of Secretary of State)

Gila County Historical Museum, Globe, Arizona: page 213 (bottom)

Library of Congress, Washington, DC: page 27 (Edward Penfield, 1866-1925, artist); page 34 (bottom) (Marion Post Wolcott, photographer); page 38; page 39 (Arthur Rothstein, photographer); page 49 (top) (O. H. Bailey & Co.); pages 59, 61, 62, 75, 82, 85; page 86 (drawn and published by Messrs. O. H. Bailey & J. C. Hazen; C. H. Vogt, lith.; printed by J. Knauber & Co.); page 107 (bottom) (Jack Delano, photographer); pages 130, 146-47, 150; page 159 (G. W. & C. B. Colton & Co.); pages 161, 175, 188, 189, 209, 211, 213 (top), 218, 222, 257, 261,, 264, 265

Michael McKee: page 13

Nebraska State Historical Society, Lincoln, Nebraska: page 176 (RG2367.PH4-16)

Rhode Island Historical Society: page 63 (Rhi X3 4681; S. B. Cushing, artist); page 68 (Rhi X5 329; Newell Nelson, artist); page 69 (Rhi X5 323; from D. G. Beers & Co., Atlas of Rhode Island); page 72 (RHi X5 325; from D. G. Beers & Co., Atlas of Rhode Island)

Sky-Shots: page 126

Matt Stanton: pages 14, 25, 40, 42, 46, 47, 55, 73, 76, 79, 91, 92 (top), 92 (bottom), 97, 104, 110, 120, 124, 137, 140, 149, 151, 153, 155, 165, 166, 168, 178, 179, 184, 201, 231 (top), 231 (bottom), 233, 238, 258, 260

United States Geological Survey, Department of the Interior: pages 54, 154, 195, 200; pages 214, 221 (USGS Historical File, Topographic Division); page 229 (Kathleen Edwards and R. M. Batson)

Bancroft Library, University of California, Berkeley: page 251

Wadsworth Atheneum Museum of Art, Hartford, Connecticut, the Ella Gallup Sumner and Mary Catlin Sumner Collection Fund: page 58

INDEX

Italicized page numbers refer to illustrations.